Anonymous

Old London

Papers read at the London congress, July, 1866

Anonymous

Old London
Papers read at the London congress, July, 1866

ISBN/EAN: 9783337233211

Printed in Europe, USA, Canada, Australia, Japan

Cover: Foto ©Suzi / pixelio.de

More available books at **www.hansebooks.com**

ARCHÆOLOGICAL INSTITUTE
OF GREAT BRITAIN AND IRELAND.

OLD LONDON.

PAPERS READ AT THE LONDON CONGRESS,
JULY, 1866.

LONDON:
JOHN MURRAY, ALBEMARLE STREET.
1867.

LONDON:
BRADBURY, EVANS, AND CO., PRINTERS, WHITEFRIARS.

CONTENTS.

	PAGE
PRELIMINARY ADDRESS. By A. J. B. BERESFORD-HOPE, M.P.	v
ARCHÆOLOGY IN ITS RELIGIOUS ASPECT. By DEAN STANLEY	1
SOME PARTICULARS CONCERNING THE MILITARY ARCHITECTURE OF THE TOWER OF LONDON. By G. T. CLARK	13
THE CHAPTER-HOUSE OF WESTMINSTER. By GEORGE GILBERT SCOTT, R.A.	141
ON THE SCULPTURE IN WESTMINSTER ABBEY. By PROFESSOR WESTMACOTT, R.A., F.R.S.	159
WESTMINSTER HALL. By EDWARD FOSS, F.S.A. . . .	219
PUBLIC RECORD OFFICE. By JOSEPH BURTT	241
LONDON AND HER ELECTION OF STEPHEN. By REV. J. R. GREEN	261
ROYAL PICTURE GALLERIES. By GEORGE SCHARF, F.S.A. .	281

PRELIMINARY ADDRESS.

MR. BERESFORD HOPE, in taking the chair of the Architectural Section, began by vindicating for London—which was too commonly regarded as a mere modern town of trade and politics—the possession of vast stores of antiquarian treasures, which amply justified the Archæological Institute for holding its congress there. He then called attention to the importance which was currently attributed to London, in its corporate identity, in the imaginative and patriotic literature of the sixteenth and seventeenth centuries as the central idealization of that which made English citizenship precious. The shock of the Reformation had disturbed the currents of thought which otherwise might have set in from a more recent period, and led to the general glorification of Plantagenet history; so that poetry, pedantry and caution combined to exhume a much earlier symbolism, in reaching of which no treacherous ground had to be trodden. The personified "Britannia," though she began to appear early in the seventeenth century, was not fully accepted till "La Belle Stuart" sat for her effigy on our pence in the time of Charles II., while she attained her greatest glory when Thomson ordered her to rule the waves. But at an earlier and fresher period, commencing from the Elizabethan outburst of literature, the old Trojan story of Geoffrey of Monmouth, with its ingenious metamorphosis of the Trinobantes into Troynovant, was laid hold of by the poets as their centre of patriotic personification. For example, Spenser told his readers that—

> "Noble Britons spronge of Trojans bolde,
> And Troynovant was built of old Troye's ashes colde;"

while Drayton, in his "Polyolbion," recurs, over and over again, to the enticing theme in the course of his stately though it may be somewhat involved flow of verse. The same impulse of constructing the myth of a Trojan origin led the imaginative French chroniclers of the renaissance, to dream of Paris, the son of Priam, somehow rescued from Achilles' sword, having been the founder of the chief city of the Isle of France. But for all this, during the contemporaneous epoch of French literature, no similar glorification of the capital of France could be found. The cause of this difference was partly political—in the earlier and more complete consolidation of the kingdom of England—but it was also partly physical, in the commercial importance possessed by London, with its unequalled river and port, while Paris was, after all, only a great *residenz*. No doubt in the third place the "Paris" invention was rather recent and scholastic, while the Brutian épopée was already ancient at the invention of printing; but, per contra, this fact proved that the circumstances of England were more opportune for the development of the feeling of embodied pride in the capital than those of France. Expressive, therefore, as the Elizabethan poetry was of the growing consciousness on the part of Englishmen of the commercial and constitutional future of the country, it was natural that the recognized *eponymus* of the realm should be rather found in the city planted on the great and still unsullied outlet of its trade, than in a region which, to the townsmen of these days, comprised not only the fertile fields of the south and midland, but the wastes of Dartmoor, the Peak, Yorkshire, and Northumberland. It was also natural that with London to be glorified the poetic elements of its glorification should be sought in the Trojan legend, so flattering in an uncritical age to national vanity. They need go no further than the sixteenth and seventeenth "Songs" of Drayton, to learn how thoroughly identified were the ideas of London and of the Thames, for in them they might see how

"Then Westminster the next great Tames doth entertaine;
That counts her Palace large, and her most sumptuous Fane:
The Land's Tribunall seate that challengeth for hers,
The crowning of our Kings, their famous sepulchers.
Then goes he on by that more beautious Strand,
Expressing both the wealth and bravery of the land.
(So many sumptuous Bowres, within so little space,
The All-beholding Sun scarce sees in all his race.)
And on by *London* leads, which like a Crescent lies,
Whose windowes seem to mock the Star-befreckled skies;
Besides her rising spyres, so thick themselves that show,
As doe the bristling reeds, within his Banks that growe,
There sees his crouded wharves and people-pestred shores,
His Bosome over-spread, with shoales of labouring ores;
With that most costly Bridge, that doth him most renowne,
By which he cleerely puts all other Rivers downe."

But in the meanwhile he was wandering from his subject, which was rather that of inviting the examination of the buildings of old London one by one, than the realization of the city as a social whole. In spite of the many writers, Stow, Howell, Newcome, Entick, Pennant, Maitland, Brayley, &c., who had successively tried their hands upon the topography and antiquities of the capital, no really complete history of London and Westminster, in an archæological sense, yet existed. He would consider that this Congress would have more than amply done its work, if it could only lay the foundations of such a production. Of course it could not do so directly. The volume which it would produce would be but at best a series of detached essays and monographs. Still the stone might be set rolling for such a complete and exhaustive history as would be worthy of the age, of the writers, and of the subject—he meant, as he hardly need say, a history which should include the municipal, the historical, the legal, the social, the biographical, the picturesque, and the genealogical, as well as the architectural records of our mighty Troynovant—the work, it must be, of many labouring hands, although acting under one controlling mind.

There was one incident which he especially commended to the editor of such a history, whenever he might be found, viz., the analysis of the way in which the present "town" had been gradually kneaded together out of — or had overrun, to adopt another metaphor—the different villages and estates in the neighbourhood. The cause of this abnormal lateral extension might, he believed, be found, in the difference of the tenures by which house property was held in London to that which existed in continental cities. In these, from of old, each house was, generally speaking, a separate freehold, and was therefore piled up as high as its owner found it possible to do. In London the system of every Englishman contenting himself with "his own castle," in the form of a hired house, had grown up from the development of the system of leases, into a kind of partnership, most legitimate in its commercial advantages, between the ground landlord and the speculating builder. The natural result has been, that a competition of estate-holders has of old been created, each of them finding it to be his immediate interest to cover over his whole area with houses before some rival landowner should press into the field with some more distant estate. Thus has come into existence the mighty area cropped with low inadequate houses which composes that London, of which the veritable High Street from Notting Hill to Stratford-le-Bow is a continuous though curved line of houses, or of town-made park, some ten miles long.

With regard to the architectural department of topography, the need of a really intelligent and learned examination, such as London had not yet received, was particularly crying. To be convinced of this, they had but to consider the number of buildings of antiquarian interest which had been swept away during the course of the present century, of which he proceeded to give a long and lamentable list, including both mediæval remains, and many very curious structures of the sixteenth and seventeenth centuries, almshouses, etc. To take but a few as examples: at the commencement of the nineteenth century, remains of the conventual premises of St. Helen's, Bishopsgate, were still preserved, and considerable portions existed of the domestic buildings of the Savoy Palace, all of which had now been swept away; the construction of St. Katharine's Docks had involved the obliteration of the Collegiate Church and adjunct buildings of St. Katharine's—as lately as 1822, the beautiful Corporation Chapel attached to Guildhall was still standing; all knew how much of Westminster Palace and of St. Stephen's Chapel, which have now perished, was revealed after the great fire of 1834; while the restoration of the choir of St. Mary Overie (or St. Saviour's, Southwark,) was followed by the total and wanton demolition of its nave, and the construction instead of the most barbarous abortion that ever pretended to be Gothic. Old London Bridge too, a most picturesque though inconvenient fragment of the Middle Ages, was still standing when William IV. ascended the throne.

He did not say that many of these demolitions were not called for by the course of modern improvement, or from the unhealthfulness of their position, or their ruinous condition; but he did say that others were wanton and barbarous, and that previously to the buildings having been pulled down, care ought to have been taken to have had them accurately planned, drawn, and described.

Those that overthrew them ought at least to have

made sure that they should leave their memorial behind them—an obligation of which, except in the case of the Palace of Westminster, they seemed totally oblivious. Now, as it was almost unnecessary to observe, that we possess that great instrument of photography, of which our fathers were ignorant, any neglect on this head would, to a tenfold greater degree, become inexcusable.

With these observations, he declared the section opened.

HISTORY OF OLD LONDON.

I.
ARCHÆOLOGY IN ITS RELIGIOUS ASPECT.

A DISCOURSE, DELIVERED IN WESTMINSTER ABBEY, BY ARTHUR PENRHYN STANLEY, D.D., DEAN OF WESTMINSTER, JULY 22ND, 1866.

"See what manner of stones and what buildings are here!"— *Mark* xiii. 1.

So spoke the antiquarian architectural spirit of the first century in the midst of the most venerable and the most magnificent city of the East, even of the whole then known world. It reached back to an antiquity in the presence of which the city of the Seven Hills was a mere infant. The centre of its Temple was a relic of the Stone age of mankind— the rocky threshing-floor, with its shaggy cave, in which Araunah, the last king of the primeval race of the land, had taken refuge. Its walls, though thrice destroyed and thrice restored, contained fragments of each succeeding epoch. In Solomon's cloister, if nowhere else, were to be seen the remains of the first architecture of the Jewish nation. Its towers and fortresses were raised on the foundations laid perhaps by Melchisedek, certainly by David. It had shown the effort of the passion for architectural restoration which characterised that age. The same impulse throughout the civilised world, which had caused Augustus Cæsar to change Rome from a city of brick into a city of marble, had penetrated to Judea. For the last forty and six years the restorations of Herod and his family had been conducted with a splendour which almost outshone that of Solomon. Corinthian porticoes, gilded gates, carved portals, made the old Temple of Zorobabel and Ezra shine like a mountain of snow fretted with gold. And to enjoy this sight, a new taste had been awakened in the age, which rendered it keenly alive to the glories both of the past and the present. When the disciples broke out with their admiring exclamation, "See what manner of stones and what buildings are here," they, the unlettered peasants of Galilee, expressed by an unconscious impulse the instinct of the nation. They, as they measured with their hands those stones, which we can still see, twenty, thirty feet long,—they, as they looked up towards those lofty towers which have long since perished, were but saying in their brief, simple fashion what the more highly cultivated intellects of their countrymen were expressing in well-turned periods and elaborate treatises. There were, doubtless, not a few among the doctors of the law who had pored over the ancient records of the nation: there was one youth who might have stood by, as the Apostles wound their way down the Temple hill, Josephus,—warrior, statesman, and writer, all in one. He must already have begun to lay up the stores of that *Archæologia* of the Jewish people, which, in imitation of the Greek work of the Halicarnassian Dionysius bearing the same name, on the early history of the Roman people, was to be his special contribution to the literature of his country. He must then have been taking those measurements and making those observations which, with all their shortcomings, yet render his account of the Jewish city and Temple the best antiquarian and architectural description that the ancient world contains.

And now, is not this the feeling which has called together so large a portion of my present congregation and which has occupied so many of us during the past week? We have met together, day by day, to "see what manner of stones and what buildings are here" in this ancient edifice, and in this great metropolis and its neighbourhood. We account it an honour and a duty to trace the records of the successive ages of our country from the rude fragment of primitive rock, from the deep dyke, from the Roman rampart, onwards through the various forms of grace and beauty by which Christian architecture has been developed through Norman vault and Mediæval arch and Byzantine dome to our own time. Our lot, too, has fallen in an age when the passion for adorning and building is as ardent as it was in the age of Herod and Augustus—when the delight in antiquity and the charm of the past is more keenly felt than it has perhaps ever been since the world began; when the spirit and the beauty of ancient buildings and ancient history is more fully appreciated than it was even by the builders and the actors themselves.

Now is this feeling right or wrong? What are its dangers and what its advantages? What is there in it of the earth earthy? and what, of the heavenly and immortal? In itself, no one can doubt that the interest expressed by the earlier disciples in the text is perfectly innocent. It arose evidently from the first feeling of a genuine childlike heart. It was the same feeling as that with which the Psalmist spoke almost the same words—" Walk about Zion, go round about her, tell the towers thereof, mark well her bulwarks;" or, still more pathetically, " Thy servants take pleasure in her stones, and favour the dust thereof." And although it is true that the immediate answer of our Lord on this occasion was one of dark and terrible import, "Seest thou these stones? there shall not be left one stone upon another, that shall not be thrown down," yet those very buildings which, in one point of view, called forth the stern malediction, from a more general point of view called forth His loving admiration. He was wont to walk to and fro in the porch or cloister, which was called after the name of Solomon, and was filled with the relics of olden times. When, on the Mount of Olives, the unsympathetic bystanders would have repressed the shouts of the children who proclaimed His coming, He appealed from the hard heart of the present to the dead stones of the past. He reminded them that, " if they should hold their peace, these stones," the old historic stones of that sacred hill, which had seen the farewells of David and the teachings of the Prophets, would immediately cry out, with a voice of their own, louder than the acclamations of the multitudes; and when He advanced a few steps further, and the sight of that splendid and venerable city flashed upon him, the tears of affectionate sympathy rushed into His eyes. "He wept over the city," and breathed the hope that even then, at that last moment, she might have known the things that belonged to her peace, and risen to a position worthy of her ancient glory and present splendour. How then are we, who are always saying, "See what manner of stones and what buildings are here," to avoid the censure and gain the blessing of Him who knows what is in man? What is the true religious aspect of Archæology?

I. First of all we must profit to the full by that warning voice which checked for the moment the enthusiasm of the antiquarian disciple. The admiration for stones and buildings, however innocent, and good, and useful, is not religion. The regard for antiquity, the love of the past, if pushed to excess, may become the ruin of religion. It might have been supposed, from the language of some of those who revived these archæological studies thirty years ago, that Gothic architecture was one of the cardinal virtues. It might be supposed, from the manner in which antiquity is sometimes extolled, that it is the one test of truth and excellence of all sorts. Against this our Lord's warning is decisive. Of the most sacred stones and buildings that this earth has ever borne, He pronounced, not without exultation, that not one of those stones should be left upon another. One of the most venerable relics that has ever been handed down to the guardianship of succeeding ages, the brazen serpent that Moses made in the wilderness—the symbol in coming times of the future Redeemer—was ruthlessly destroyed by the most pious of the Jewish kings. Solomon and Herod, the most munificent of builders, were not the best of the Jewish kings; they were amongst the worst.

In one word, Christianity is not antiquarianism, and antiquarianism is not Christianity. There are times, and places, and circumstances, when antiquity must give way to truth, the beauty of form to the beauty of holiness, and the delights of poetic and historic recollections to the stern necessities of fact and duty. It was well to be reminded, even at Jerusalem, that there was something more enduring than the stones of the Temple. It is well, even here, to be reminded of that often-predicted prospect which future generations may view from the broken arches of our stateliest bridges, over the ruin of our noblest churches.

II. But having been thus forewarned, we are forearmed. If the text in the first instance suggests the one correction which is needed, it also suggests, by its relation to those other passages which I have quoted, the true lesson to be derived from antiquarian research. Let me describe briefly the important benefits which it may confer on the world even in a religious point of view.

1. It awakens that love of the past, which is so necessary a counterpoise to the excitement of the present and the future. "I have considered," says the Psalmist in one of the most philosophic and exalted strains of

the Psalter, "I have considered the days of old, the years of ancient times." He had considered them as a refuge from the turmoil and distress of the times in which he lived. They were to him, and they may be to us, as a cool shade, a calm haven, a sweet repose. The study of them links the child to the man—"the days of nations each to each by natural piety." And yet more, it opens to us a new world; it enlarges our acquaintance; it makes us feel that we do not stand alone on the earth, but that we are what we are, under God, because of the deeds and thoughts of those who have lived before us, and to whom we thus owe a debt which we have constantly to repay to our posterity. And when we consider how, beyond all former example, this insight into the past is increased in our own age, we ought to be thankful for the merciful provision of God which, by creating this new gift within us, compensates to us, as it were, for the continually receding distance of ancient times. Through this increased insight, whole epochs and races of mankind have been manifested to us, as they never have been manifested since they were actually beheld upon earth. Not only Greeks and Romans, but Egyptians and Assyrians, are familiar to the nineteenth century, as they have not been to any age since the fall of Nineveh, and the overthrow of the Pharaohs. And much more: as we reach our own country, king, and prelate, and statesman, with all their individual peculiarities physical and mental, rise before us through the magic touch of scientific and antiquarian research. "This only is the witchcraft we have used;" and through it we see those venerable figures "ascending as gods from the earth." They are ours almost for the first time—ours not merely as dead phantoms, but in their living flesh and blood, "all the kings of the nations, every one in his own house." What a grasp of the ages that are dead and gone has God in His mercy given us by these new powers! But what a pledge also of the power that may yet be developed within us, as our race advances—as our mortality puts on immortality!

2. And this leads me to the importance of these studies in unfolding those rarest of God's gifts to man—a love of truth and a love of justice, the will and the power to see things as they really are, and in their just proportion to each other. If some antiquarians have been childishly enslaved to the forms of other days, it is certain that the more profound investigators have been distinguished by their boldness in asserting the principles of justice, freedom, and progress. Such were the two who lie within these walls—Camden and Spelman. Such were and are some of their most distinguished successors.

To trace the successive stages through which taste, and custom, and belief have passed—to know the contempt which each age has lavished on that immediately preceding—to track to their homely origin the forms of buildings or of ritual which have since been, in the eyes of the less instructed, invested with an exclusive sacredness—this, which is the special duty and delight of the modern antiquarian, is also the best check to exaggerated and partial veneration. To appreciate the truly grand and the truly beautiful in art or in sentiment—to condense within the same view the beginning and end of great institutions and edifices—has an effect not narrowing or depressing, but widening and elevating in a high degree. A reverent admiration for religious art is far more reasonable, far less superstitious, than an undiscriminating iconoclasm, whether Byzantine or Puritan. A conscientious search for truth and for truth only, such as the revival of archæology in our times specially encourages, is the very duty which we most need to have impressed upon us in all things. How many is the fable which the honest explorer of past ages has banished from the earth! how many is the illusion which he has cleared away!—how many the false judgments of characters and events which have been rectified by the discovery of a lost letter, or an ancient coin, or a forgotten manuscript! Truly in this sense, according to the great philosophic poet,—

"The world's whole history is its judgment day."

The antiquarian hardly knows how much he may do to retrieve the errors and injustice of the past. Those who are dead and gone may be indebted, they will never know how much, to the faithful, careful labours of the self-denying painstaking antiquarian.

3. The more thoroughly ancient forms are understood, the more eagerly ancient buildings are restored and beautified, so much the better is the framework prepared for the reception of new thoughts and new ideas. It has been sometimes said that the great

periods of building and of admiration for the past have been the precursors of the fall of the religions or the nations which they represented. The burst of splendid architecture of which I spoke, under the Herods, immediately preceded, it is said, the fall of Judaism. The like display under the Antonines preceded the fall of Paganism. The like display at the beginning of the sixteenth century preceded the fall of the Church of the Middle Ages.

There is truth in this—the same truth at which I have already glanced. There is a tendency in an expiring system to develop itself in outward form when its inward spirit has died away. But this is not the whole truth—and the higher truth is something quite different, namely, that these magnificent displays of art, these profound investigations of the past, in the Herodian, the Antonine, and the Tudor era, formed part of the new throes of the human mind and heart, which accompanied the birth of the new and better religion which in each case succeeded. Those vast Herodian and Augustan buildings suggested to the Apostles half the imagery by which they expressed the most sublime and spiritual truths. The chief " corner-stone " —the " stones joined and compacted together"—" the pillars that never should be moved "—the whole idea of " edification," that most expressive word, the architecture, so to speak, of the Christian soul—all these were drawn straight from the superb edifices which everywhere rose before St. Paul's eyes. And so in the last great efflorescence of mediæval architecture, Religion, instead of dying out with that effort, awoke to a new life throughout Europe; and the very increase of knowledge and devotion, thus engendered, has been the means of enabling us in our age to understand better than ever before, all that there is of great and noble in the buildings and the events of those earlier times.

Therefore it is with no doubting heart that we may still say with the disciples, "See what manner of stones and what buildings are here!" if only we take care to "see" them truly—to "see" them without exaggeration, without distortion—to "see" through them into the spirit behind and within them. To try to bring back the present to the past, or to revive the past exactly as it was—this would be to fight against God, this would be to invoke the ruin which would not leave one stone standing on another. But to learn what the past was—to put new meanings into old words—to make the forms of the past a framework for the spirit of the present and the future—this is to work with the will of God, and for the good of man. "Stand upon the old paths," so let us take Lord Bacon's paraphrase of the words of Jeremiah, "Stand upon the old paths, and then look about us and discover what is the straight and right way, and so to walk in it." That is the true combination. The desire and the power to gather up the fragments that remain to us from former times—to appreciate, understand, admire them—this, as I have said, has been God's peculiar gift to the nineteenth century. But the use of this power for the purpose of enshrining and promoting new truths—for strengthening the stakes and enlarging the cords of human society—for bringing us nearer to God and nearer to one another—this is the gift which, it may be, is reserved in full for the century which is yet to come. To help forward this blessed end, belongs not to students and antiquarians only, but to all of us. O may God grant that the glory of the Third Temple may as much excel the glory of the Second, as the Second exceeded the glory of the First. Cast not away the old—cherish it, understand it, value it to the utmost; but "see" what it means, see what it embraces, see what it indicates, see what manner of stone it is, see "what manner" of building it is—and then, as in the case of sacred and ancient words, so also in the case of sacred and ancient buildings, they will become, as Luther said, not dead stones, but "living creatures with hands and feet," living stones, which will cry out with a thousand voices; stones which will be full of sermons—dry bones which, when the Son of Man prophesies over them, will stand upon their feet, an exceeding great army—ancient everlasting gates which shall turn on their rusty hinges, and lift up their hoary heads, that the Lord of Hosts may come in—a heavenly city which hath foundations, deeper than any earthly foundations, whose builder and maker is God.

II.

SOME PARTICULARS CONCERNING

THE MILITARY ARCHITECTURE OF THE TOWER OF LONDON.

BY G. T. CLARK.

ALTHOUGH Britain presents numerous examples of military works, and her Welsh and Scottish borders are very thickly set with the castles of the Lords Marchers and local gentry, the circumstances of the country have not been favourable to the production of military buildings of the first class. Our insular position has enabled us to dispense altogether with grand frontier fortresses; and our great nobles, although they often held their own against the Crown, and even encroached upon its legitimate powers, drew their resources from estates more or less scattered in position, and seldom possessed whole provinces, or ruled over a territory sufficiently compact and extensive to justify the construction of a great castle-palace like those of France, for the defence of the lordship and the residence of the baron. The keeps of Arques, Etampes, Provins, and Vez; the towers of Coucy and Beaucaire; the walls of Avignon; and the fortresses of Château-Gailliard, Carcassonne, Villeneuve-les-Avignon, and Pierrefonds, the details of which are familiar to the readers of the exhaustive work of M.

Viollet le Duc, are due to a period when France was divided into provinces, the rulers of which were scarcely subordinate to its Crown, and were either actual monarchs elsewhere, or held much of the state privilege and power of independent sovereigns.

It happens, however, that in that particular class of fortress of which the quadrangular Norman keep is the type, we have less to fear comparison, seeing that castles of this description are confined, or very nearly so, to our own country and to Normandy. Whereas, on the continent of Europe, in Italy, Spain, France, and Germany, the earlier castles appear to have sprung directly from Roman, or debased Roman patterns, in Normandy a simpler and more original type prevailed, unlike what is seen in other parts of France, and which there is some reason to regard as the invention of the Normans themselves. These buildings, so remarkable for their simple quadrangular form and the immense solidity of their masonry, were erected in Normandy during the eleventh century, and are well known by such examples as Arques near Dieppe, Falaise, and Caen.

By the Normans this class of fortress was introduced into England. It is quite unlike the Roman castles which preceded it, and to which, as at Portchester and Lincoln, it was sometimes superadded; and had, of course, still less in common with the Celtic and Saxon works of earth and timber of which we have so many traces. No doubt the same circumstances that sometimes governed the pre-Norman natives in their choice of a military position—the neighbourhood of a river, a detached rock, a marshy frontier, or an adjacent highway—governed also the Normans; and if it indeed be the fact that the "motte," or mound so common in Norman castles, both in England and in Normandy, is usually of earlier date, they must very frequently indeed have availed themselves of the earthworks of already existing strong places.

Until recently the mound was looked upon not only as Norman, but as an integral and almost typical feature in a Norman castle. It is, however, evident that heavy Norman walls, such as those remaining at Cardiff and Arundel, and known to have crowned many another earthwork, could only have been safely constructed upon ground consolidated by a considerable lapse of time. Military mounds also are found quite unconnected with Norman or later castles; and on the other hand, some of the finest examples of Norman fortresses have no mound: and this is remarkably the case in the subject of the present memoir, not only one of the earliest and most important of the works of the Conqueror, but placed where a mound of large size would have been peculiarly useful. The mound may be, and probably is, in some, perhaps in many cases, of Norman construction, but it is the quadrangular keep, rather than the mound, which is the grand characteristic of by far the greater number of Norman fortresses.

The pre-eminence of the Tower of London, even in a purely military and architectural point of view, does not, however, depend alone upon its keep. It is, in its present state, a fine and very complete example of the concentric fortress, not indeed the execution of one period, but nevertheless presenting much harmony of design.

An unaltered Norman castle is very rare, if indeed such exists at all. It is, however, certain that the keep had an enceinte defence and ditch, the latter sometimes part of an earlier earthwork; and in the base court thus formed were stabling and barracks, and other subordinate accommodations. These buildings were at first often of timber, and the enceinte a stout palisade, the object having been to protect the workmen and the garrison during the construction of the stone keep. Both at Dover and Windsor the enceinte wall, part of which is of late Norman date, stands upon the scarp of the ditch of an earlier earthwork, the solid chalk of which, as at Arques, is traversed by subterranean galleries. Where, as at Cardiff and the Tower, the enceinte wall is of great strength, and of the twelfth century, it is probable that the palisade was retained longer than usual, and the wall now seen the first constructed. No regular Norman wall would so soon have required reconstruction.

Where the Norman enceinte was of light construction or insufficient area, it was frequently removed and in the larger works replaced by a double and concentric ring of defences. These additions, usually due to the reigns of Henry III. and Edward I., show that military engineering had made great progress, and that less dependence was placed upon passive strength, and more upon a skilful distribution of material.

Having regard to the state of the military art at that period, and to the cross and long bows, catapults, rams, scorpions, and moveable turrets that formed the weapons of attack, it would be difficult to improve upon these concentric works, either in general design or in detail of construction, or to show greater skill in flanking defences than appears at Corfe, Caerphilly, Conway, or Beaumaris, or in many other of the castles built by Henry and his son. This science, so successfully grafted upon the pure Norman works, was no doubt in some considerable measure derived from the East, where Cœur de Lion seems to have acquired the skill displayed in the construction of Chateau-Gailliard, and which, in the opinion of M. Le Duc, places him at the head of the military engineers of his day.

When, having crossed the Thames, the Conqueror marched in person to complete the investment of London, he found that ancient city resting upon the left bank of its river, protected on its landward side by a strong wall, with mural towers and an exterior ditch.

The enclosure, of about 370 acres, was in general figure a semicircle ; the river forming the chord. The defences, commencing on the Thames at Blackfriars, upon the east bank of the Flete, swept in an irregular curve northward and eastward, by Ludgate, Aldersgate, Cripplegate, and the line of London Wall to where, trending eastward and southward, they took the line of Houndsditch, and appear to have abutted upon the Thames a little east of or below Billingsgate.

Upon the west the Flete formed a respectable natural defence, and upon the east the line took the crest of the high ground just where it begins to subside into the low lands long occupied by St. Katherine's Hospital, and now, more suitably, by the docks of that name. Towards the north the defence must have been wholly artificial, and is reputed to have been by a ditch which, in the later reign of King John, was deepened and made 204 feet broad, but which must have been a sufficient defence even at the time of the Conqueror. Ludgate, like the later Newgate, was placed in a re-entering angle of the wall, so that the road approaching it from the west ran for a short distance parallel to, and commanded by the ramparts.

London, therefore,—

"A læva muris, dextris in flumine tuta,"

resembled in plan and mode of entrance those large half-round Celtic earthworks sometimes found upon the banks of a water-course; nor does there appear to have been attached to or within it anything of the character of a prætorium or citadel.

It is related that before the Conqueror entered London he directed a fortress to be built which should command the city. This of course was a temporary camp, and it was probably while he was at Westminster, or in the camp at Barking, that he studied the ground and selected as the site of his future citadel a point upon the eastern flank of the city defences, displacing for that purpose, we are told, a part of the Roman wall, including the two towers next to the Thames.

William was crowned in 1066, and it was from Barking, immediately after the ceremony, that he directed the actual commencement of the works, which were no doubt a deep ditch and strong palisade only; for the keep, probably the earliest work in masonry, appears not to have been begun till twelve or fourteen years later. It is said to stand upon the site of the second Roman bulwark; but looking to the well-known line of the city defences, it seems more probable that so massive a structure was placed on undisturbed ground, a little to the east and outside of both wall and ditch. Roman remains have been found within the precinct.

The new castle thus more than supplied the place of the removed works, for it could not only protect, but overawe the city, and, if necessary, cut off its trade and supplies by water.

Such was the origin of this grand old fortress, the chief and central part of which gives mass and character to the group, and has from its earliest times caused the whole to pass under the name of "The Tower."

The new fortress was supported by two other considerable works within the city, Baynard's Castle upon the Thames' strand, built about the same time by Baynard, the Castellan and standard-bearer of the city, and Montfitchet's Castle, near it, built by a knight of that name. Later kings had "Tower Royal," in Vintry Ward, where Stephen lodged, and to which the mother of Richard II. fled from the Tower in Wat Tyler's rebellion. Edward II. also built a strong place near Blackfriars.

The Tower, though all save the keep is later, and most of it considerably later than the eleventh century, probably supplements the original design. The area enclosed and the strength of the walls and gates are in keeping with the dimensions and impregnable character of the keep ; and the circumscribing ditch, though unusually broad and deep, was by no means too secure a defence against a turbulent and notoriously brave body of citizens.

The Tower, in its present form, is a fine example of a concentric castle, of mixed composition, but general harmony of design, and covering, with its circumscribing ditch, above twelve acres of ground.

Nearly in the centre, but now detached and alone, stands the keep, the oldest and most stable part of the fortress. Around it is the inner ward, in plan generally four-sided, but with a salient on the north front, and contained within a wall strengthened by a gate-house and twelve mural towers.

Encircling this is the outer ward, following the same general plan, and contained within a wall rising from and forming the scarp of the ditch. Upon it are bold drum bastions, at the angles of the north front; and the south, or Thames front, is protected by five mural towers, of which one covers the land and one the water-gate, and two others are connected with posterns.

The ditch, which completely girdles the fortress, is divided from the river by a narrow strip of land used as a wharf, but also ingeniously contrived to cut off the water of the ditch from the tidal stream.

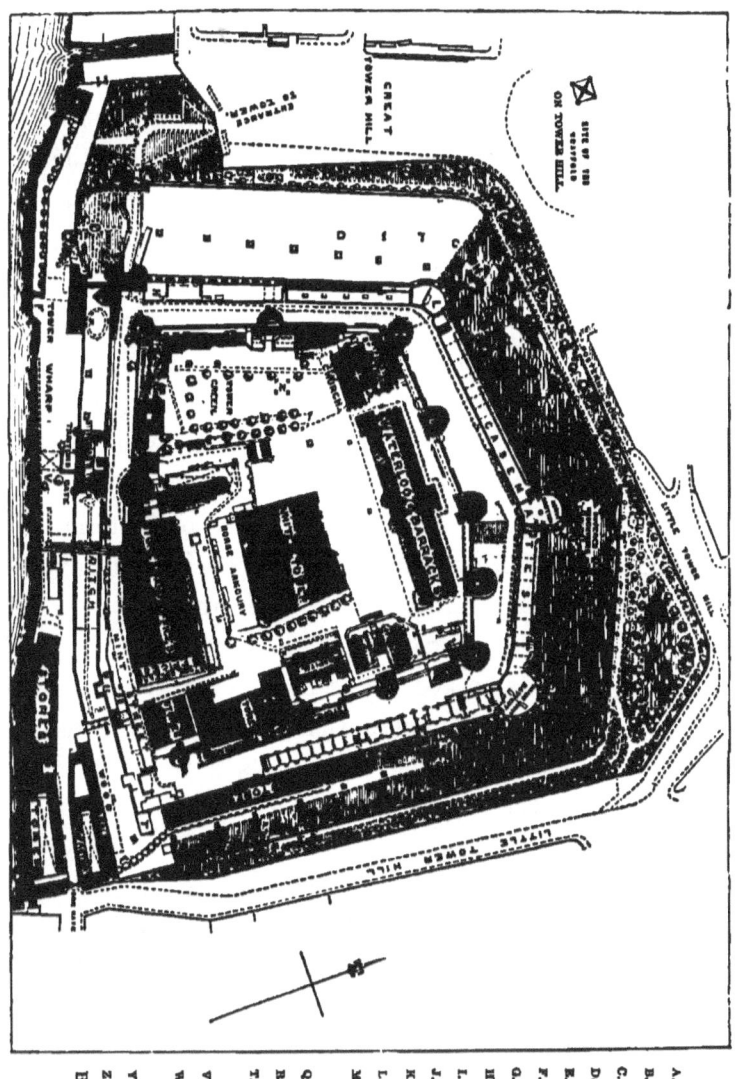

PLAN OF THE TOWER OF LONDON IN 1866.

(From Lord De Ros's Memorials of the Tower.)

REFERENCES.

A. Tower Stairs and Petty Wales.
B. Wharfinger's Quarters.
C. Middle Tower.
D. Byward Tower.
E. Byward Postern.
F. Queen's Stairs.
G. Bell Tower.
H. Police Quarters.
J. Beauchamp Tower.
K. Devereux Tower.
L. Legge's Mount.
M. Flint, N, Bowyer, O, Brick, and P, Martin's Tower.
Q. Jewel House.
R. Constable s, and s, Salt Tower.
T. Galleyman's, and U, Cradle Tower.
V. Traitors' Gate.
W. Wakefield, and X, Bloody Tower.
Y. Main Guard.
Z. Scaffold.
Between R and S, is Broad Arrow Tower; and between T and U, Well Tower.

The space outside the ditch, forming the esplanade of the fortress, is known as Tower Hill. It was once divided by the city wall, which extended from the north to the edge of the ditch, having a postern at the junction, which still gives name to a row of houses, and to the east of which is Little Tower Hill. The ground covered by the Tower rises from the river, so that parts of the inner ward are forty feet above the water, and the ground north of and outside the ditch is eight to ten feet higher. This disadvantage was neutralised by the breadth of the ditch, while the descent towards the south, or entrance side, was of material advantage in repelling an attack. The object being to command the river and fill the ditch, the keep was placed as high as was consistent with these points.

It has been remarked by Sir F. Palgrave, that William, in settling the jurisdiction of his new fortress respected, as far as possible, the limits of the city of London. Only the smaller half of the enclosure was within the line of the old wall; and while the Tower liberties, if St. Katherine's be included within them, extend some distance eastward, or into the county of Middlesex, on the west frontier the authority of the Constable ranges but a little way beyond the counterscarp of the ditch. The area of the liberties proper is about twenty-six acres, of which the western portion stands in Tower Ward and All-Hallows Barking parish, and the eastern portion in the county of Middlesex.

DETAILED DESCRIPTION.

The WHITE, or CÆSAR'S TOWER, is the keep of the

fortress. It stands a little to the south-east of the centre of the inner ward, upon ground which, on the north is 40 ft., and on the south 15 ft. above the ordnance mean water-mark, so that the basement is at the ground level on one side, and above it on the other. It is quadrangular, 107 ft. north and south, by 118 ft. east and west. Its two western angles are square. That on the north-east is capped by a round stair-turret, 22 ft. diameter, about one-third engaged, and having 3 ft. more projection upon the north than upon the east face. The south wall terminates eastward in a bold half-round bow of 42 ft. diameter, projecting on the east wall. This marks the apse of the chapel, and is the great peculiarity of this tower.

The keep rises 90 ft. from the floor to the crest of the present battlement. It is composed of three floors, or four stages. The walls are reinforced by the usual pilaster strips; on the east face two, on the north three, on the west and south, four each. The round turret has four pilasters, two being at its junction with the walls, and the bow four. They vary from 3 ft. to 6 ft. broad, and all are of 18 in. projection. They lessen by two sets-off, at 50 ft. and 75 ft. from the ground, and die away 8 ft. below the battlement. Also upon the flank of each front containing the two square angles is a strip 12 ft. broad, two to each angle, but so placed as not quite to cover it, so that three salient angles appear at each of the two corners. These four pilasters rise from the plinth unbroken to 16 ft. above the battlement, forming square turrets. A third turret, also square, is placed on the roof, where, but for the bow, would be the south-east angle. Thus the keep is crowned by three square turrets and one round one.

The loops of the basement are seen to open just below those, now windows, of the second stage. The openings of the third stage, probably single-light windows of moderate size, but now enlarged, appear, one between each pair of pilasters, and each below a large plain round-headed and slightly-recessed relieving arch, springing from a strip of wall left as a sort of pier against each pilaster. The base of this arcade is a set-off in the wall stopped by the pilasters.

The lights of the fourth or upper stage may be of about their original size. On the south wall, between the two western pilasters, the windows, of 2 ft. opening, are in pairs, having a plain baluster in common, and each pair being within a shallow, round-headed recess, so that the eight windows form a short arcade. One pair are probably the only windows in the keep that present quite their original appearance; for the baluster, long since removed, was found bricked-up in the adjacent wall, and is now in its proper place. It was from one of these windows that Bishop Flambard let himself down.

The exterior has been defaced by pointing with flint chips and mortar, and the substitution of Portland for the old ashlar dressings, but the windows, though enlarged into casements, represent the old openings; and enough of the aspect of the original building may be inferred, to justify the restorations judiciously commenced by Mr. Salvin.

The stair-case, 11 ft. diameter, contained within the circular or north-east turret, rises from the floor to the summit, and communicates with every floor, and with the leads.

The *Basement* is below ground on the north, at the ground level on the south front. The walls are from 12 ft. to 15 ft. thick, and the internal area about 91 ft. by 73 ft. This is crossed by a wall 10 ft. thick, which rises to the summit, and divides the building into a larger western and smaller eastern portion. The latter is again subdivided into a larger northern and smaller southern part, by another wall, also carried through, so that every floor is divided into three chambers. The larger chambers are all ceiled with timber; all the smaller are vaulted. The basement was reached only from above by the great wellstair. The west chamber is 91 ft. by 35 ft.; the eastern 67 ft. by 28 ft.; and the vault, the sub-crypt of the chapel, known in Tower phrase as "Little Ease," is 15 ft. by 47 ft., the east end being semi-circular. A door leads from the east into the west chamber, and from the former into Little Ease. Bold recesses in the walls ascend to a line of loops, giving air, but very little light.

In modern times a shaft has been sunk 10 ft. in the south-west angle of this floor, and a tunnel cut through its twenty-four feet of foundation towards the river quay, and another door on the other side of the angle has been cut at the ground level. The two larger chambers have been vaulted in modern brick, and are filled with iron bedsteads. Little Ease has been lined with deal, as a powder magazine, and passages cut through its east and west ends.

The *Second Stage* much resembles the basement. The walls are about 13 ft. thick, the cross-wall 8 ft. In the latter are three openings 6 ft. wide and 15 ft. high, round-headed and quite plain, between a doorway at the north end, 4 ft. 6 in. wide and 12 ft. high, and one at the south end, 4 ft. wide and 9 ft. high. These five openings communicate between the eastern and western chambers. The western room, 92 ft. by 37 ft., has in its west wall five plain, round-headed recesses, once converging into loops, but now enlarged into windows. In the south wall is a similar recess, and in the north wall two. Between one of these and the west angle is a small mural passage, 2 ft. 10 in. wide, and bent at right angles. This is vaulted, quadripartite, with plain hips, very rough, but good. Under its exterior loop was the garderobe shaft.

The eastern room, 68 ft. by 30 ft., has in its east wall three recesses for loops. In its north wall is a recess, now cut into a door, and communicating with the outside by a double flight of modern stone steps. There is also an original door of 3 ft. opening, leading by a short mural passage, 5 ft. wide, to the well-stair, which supplies each stage. In the south wall a door leads into the crypt of the chapel, called Raleigh's prison, 13 ft. 6 in. broad by 39 ft. long, having an apsidal east end, and 17 ft. high to the crown of its very plain vault. In the north wall of the crypt, near the apse, a passage 2 ft. broad leads into a vaulted cell, 8 ft. by 10 ft., formed in the wall, and quite dark. In the south wall three round-headed recesses, 6 ft. broad and 13 ft. high, terminated in loops, as did one at the east end, now converted into an entrance. This crypt is now "Queen Elizabeth's armoury," so called from a figure of the queen on horseback, which occupies the western recess.

The two larger rooms on this stage are 15 ft. high, and recently their respective open ceilings were supported by eighteen and twelve large posts in double rows. These no doubt were inserted when the rooms were given up to stores and records. Recently, they have been removed, and the beams stiffened with iron, to carry the weight of small-arms here stored up. Possibly there was originally a single line of posts, as 30 ft. and 37 ft. are large spans for single untrussed beams.

Ascending by the well-stair from this stage, a Tudor door is seen cut in the shell of the staircase, and leading into the adjacent armourer's shops. A similar door, below this, has been cut at the ground level.

The *Third Stage*, or second floor, has also three chambers: the western, 95 ft. by 40 ft.; the eastern, 64 ft. by 32 ft.; both 15 ft. high, and until recently propped by posts. The cross chamber is the chapel, which occupies this and the upper stage, to the roof. The exterior walls are here 10 ft. to 11 ft., and the party-wall 6 ft. thick. In the latter are five openings, as below, all apparently doorways. The rebates show that the doors of the four to the south opened into the east chamber, and the north door the other way. In the north wall, close to this door, are two mural gardcrobes, resembling that already described, one serving the west, and one the east room.

Within the north-west and south-west angles of this stage commence well-stairs, 9 ft. diameter, which rise to the roof. They do not open, as usual, direct into the room; but, by short passages, into the jamb of

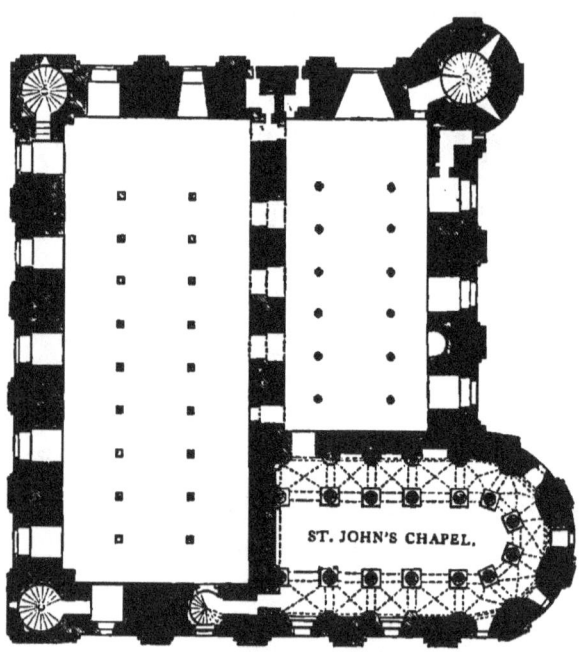

The Keep —Third Stage.

the nearest loop recess. The east chamber is entered from the main stair, in a similar way, by a passage 3 ft. wide, in the north wall. In the south wall of this room is only a small door opening into the north aisle of the chapel. In its east wall are three loop recesses, and from the jamb of one a gardcrobe opens, resembling those described. In this wall also is the plain round-headed opening of a fire-place, with an inclined back and vertical flue, the outlet of which has not been followed. It resembles somewhat a fireplace in Colchester Keep. This room is called the "Banqueting Chamber."

Besides its regular recesses for loops, 7 ft. wide and 14 ft. high, of which there are five on the west side, two on the north, and one on

Fire-place in Keep.

the south, the west room has in its south wall a round-headed opening, which is the summit and landing of a well-stair, which commences, about 15 ft. above the ground level, by an external door, and thence leads to the third stage. From its head there is also a mural passage leading into the west end of the south aisle of the chapel. This was no doubt the private way from the palace to the chapel and state-rooms of the Keep. It was at the foot of this stair, in the wall, that were found the bones supposed to be those of the children of Edward IV., and now in Westminster Abbey.

The *Fourth*, or upper *stage*, is the "state floor." Its tripartite arrangement resembles those below, and the two larger chambers have open ceilings 21 ft. high, until recently supported by posts, as below. The outer walls range from 10 ft. to 11 ft. thick, the party-wall is 6 ft., and the short cross wall which shuts off the triforium of the chapel is 4 ft. The western, or great council-chamber, is 95 ft. by 40 ft.; the eastern, 65 ft. by 32 ft. Between them are three plain openings 7 ft. wide and 14 ft. high, and flanking these, two

St. John's Chapel, South Aisle (from Lord de Ros's Memorials).

doorways of smaller dimensions. It may be remarked that the square of the two western turrets is preserved in the council chamber. The angles project about

MILITARY ARCHITECTURE OF THE TOWER. 31

7 in. into the room. The opposite are hollow angles as usual. The exterior wall of these two chambers is threaded by a vaulted mural gallery, 13 ft. high and 3 ft. to 3 ft. 6 in. wide. One end of it opens into the west end of the south aisle of the chapel triforium, and the other end into its north aisle near the chevet.

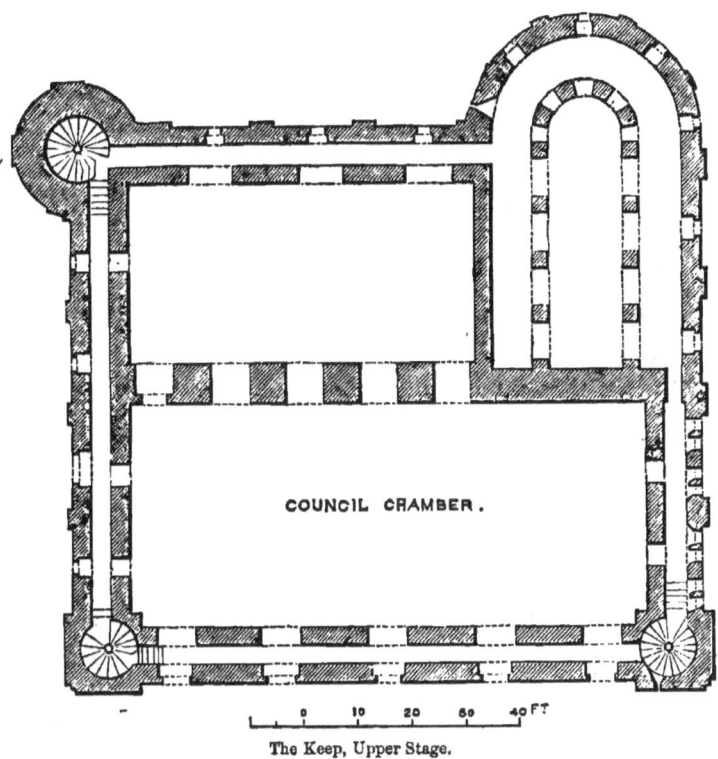

The Keep, Upper Stage.

It communicates with the main stair in the north-east turret, and with those in the two western turrets. It pierces the jambs of each of the window recesses, of which there are in the west room five in the west wall, two in the north, and two in the south wall; and in the east room three in the east wall, and one in the north. Where the gallery traverses the window recesses, the vault is raised a step. In this gallery, in the south wall of the state-room, are the coupled windows already described as escaped from by Flambard. This was the royal council-chamber, at least as

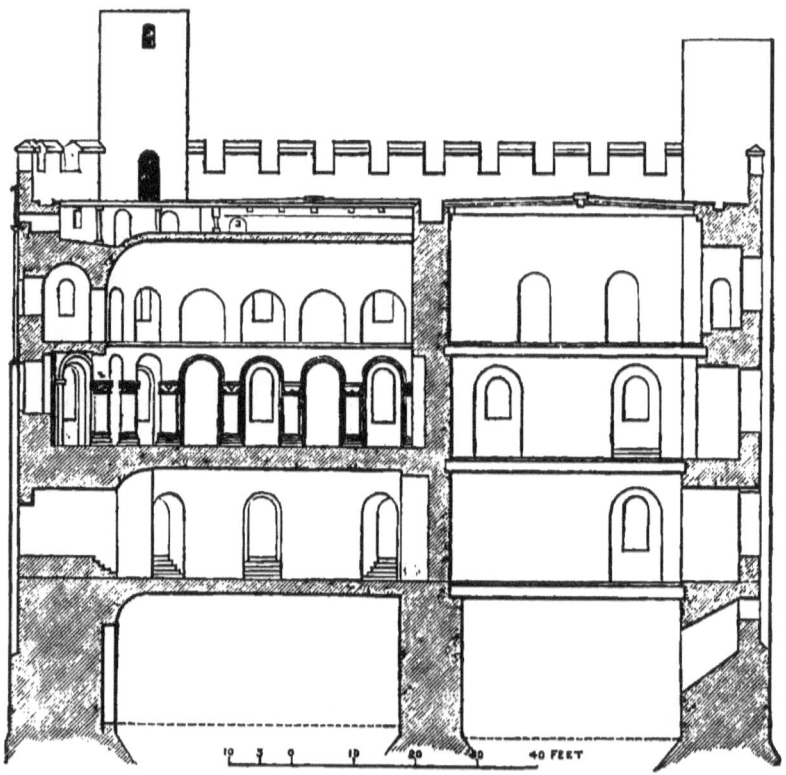

The Keep, Vertical Section, East and West.

late as the reign of Richard III. Here Charles of Orleans, and probably John of France, were confined. And hence Edward Lord Hastings, the celebrated Chamberlain, was taken from the council-board to execution.

The vertical section of the Keep, upon a line east and west, looking south, and here given, shows on the ground floor "Little-Ease," and the lower store-room; on the first floor, the chapel crypt, and the upper store-room. On the second floor is the chapel nave and aisle, and the lower armoury; on the third floor, the chapel triforium and space above the vault, and the upper armoury or council-chamber.

The *Chapel*, dedicated to St. John the Evangelist, is a rare, if not a singular example of such an apartment, so large and so complete, in the original and interior arrangements of a Norman keep. It is in plan a rectangle, 40 ft. by 31 ft., terminating eastward in a semicircular apse of its full breadth; its extreme length, therefore, with this addition, being 55 ft. 6 in.

It is divided into a nave and aisles, the latter being continued as a chevet round the east end of the former.

The nave, 14 ft. 6 in. broad, and 40 ft. long, has an eastern apse, giving 7 ft. 3 in. additional for the altar. It is divided from the aisles by four columns, and a western respond or half-column, on each side; and by four columns which contain the apse. The whole support thirteen arches. The columns are cylinders of 2 ft. 6 in. diameter, and 6 ft. 6 in. high, with plain torus bases resting upon a square stone of two stages, giving, with the base, an additional 20 inches. The capitals vary in pattern, some being plain cushion, others a combination of four cushions, giving a scalloped or invected outline in the elevation, others again are chamfered at the angles, and others finished with a stiff rude volute of an Ionic aspect.

The capitals of the eight eastern columns are unfinished, having a block in the form of a Tau, or cross-potent, upon each face, evidently intended to be carved into the usual central flower of a Corinthian capital; and the astragal is set round with a row of stiff upright feathers, like a plume. Each capital has a plain abacus, with varieties of the half-round, ogee, and hollow mouldings, excepting the western responds, of which the faces of the abaci are cut into the star-pattern found in early Norman work. Beneath is a light cable bead. These capitals vary from 34 in. to 40 in. square, and are 22 in. high, so that from the floor to the top of each is 10 ft. Each capital is a single block, and each abacus a single slab.

The thirteen arches springing from these capitals in the nave, are 7 ft., and in the apse, 2 ft. 9 in. diameter. The five apsidal arches are stilted, the rest semicircular, the crowns of all being level. The whole are perfectly plain openings in a 22 in. wall, without chamfer or rib.

Twenty inches above these crowns is a plain chamfered string-course, and upon this the arcade of the triforium, each arch being exactly above, and of the same diameter with, that below. These arches spring from piers 30 in. square, and 4 ft. 3 in. high, without either base or cap. As the apsidal arches are not stilted, the piers are taller, so that the crowns still range.

The nave roof is a barrel vault, commencing imperceptibly at the crown level of the triforial arches, and ending eastwards in a semi-dome. The height to the crowns of the nave arches is 13 ft. 6 in., to those of the triforium 23 ft. 9 in., and to the crown of the vault 32 ft. The vault abuts against the west wall, in which is a plain round-headed recess, 18 in. deep, 12 ft. diameter, and 13 ft. 6 in. high.

The aisle is 6 ft. 6 in. broad. Opposite to each nave column is a flat pilaster, advanced three steps from the wall surface, and having a plain chamfered abacus, or string-cap, and from each springs a broad flat rib. The aisle is thus divided into thirteen bays, four on each side, and five in the chevet, the sides of these latter being convergent. Each bay is hip-vaulted, the vaults being groined, and entirely in rubble work. The aisle is 13 ft. 6 in. high. The wall of each bay is recessed, and the recesses form an arcade. In the southern recesses are four windows, of which two open between, and two upon the exterior pilaster strips. Four of the five apsidal bays also have windows, one being to the east. There are two doors: one in the north aisle, opening into the eastern room on the third stage of the Keep, and one in the west wall of the south aisle, leading by a short mural gallery to the well-stair in the south wall, and into the great or western chamber of the Keep.

The triforium is 7 ft. 6 in. diameter. It is a mere plain gallery, without pilasters, string-course, or moulding of any kind, 8 ft. high to the spring of its side barrel-vault, which gives 3 ft. 9 in. more.

In its south wall are three windows, one opening in the face of an outer pilaster; and in the apse are five. In the north wall, and at the west end of the south limb, are the openings of the mural gallery which surrounds the Keep at this, the council-chamber level; the chapel, as has been stated, rising through the two upper stories to the roof. The walls of the aisle are 4 ft. thick; of the west and east ends, 5 ft. Of the triforium, the north, south, and east walls are 4 ft., and the west wall 5 ft. 6 in. thick.

This, the earliest and simplest, as well as most complete Norman chapel in Britain, must have witnessed the devotions of the Conqueror, and his immediate descendants; the church, when afterwards built, having evidently been intended rather for the garrison at large than for the Sovereign. The upper gallery, communicating with the state-rooms, was, no doubt, as was often the case in domestic chapels, intended for the principal persons, the household occupying the floor below. Always architecturally plain, the walls were probably painted and hung with tapestry, and the eastern windows contained stained glass, placed there, with other ornaments, by the piety of Henry III.

Henry also, in 1261, on the death of his sister-in-law, Saunchia, Countess of Cornwall, wife of his brother Richard, charged upon the Exchequer, in favour of the adjacent Hospital of St. Katherine, fifty shillings per annum for the support of a chaplain, here to pray for her soul; he having already, 1240-1, provided a similar endowment for the sustenance of a regular priest there, with vesture, and chalice, and everything necessary for his office. The obit payment probably fell into arrear ; for, in 1290 (18 Edw. I.), the Brethren and Sisters of St. Katherine petition for the fifty shillings given by Henry III. for the spiritual benefit of Saunchia. This chapel was dismantled by an Order of Council, 22nd August, 1550, directing, in both church and chapel, all such crosses, images, and plate of gold as remain, to be melted down. The chapel thus desecrated was for years, perhaps centuries, employed as a repository for records. Very recently these have been removed, the walls restored to their primitive simplicity, and the whole paved with tiles of a plain and suitable character. It is due to the interference of the present lieutenant-governor that this chapel is not at present a tailor's warehouse.

Above the fourth stage of the Keep is the flat leaded roof, affording an area between the parapet wall, of 100 ft. east and west, by 113 ft. north and south. The turrets rise about 16 ft. above the platform, upon which they open by doors, the north-west, south-west, and north-east crowning well-stairs. The fourth, or south-east turret, is built over the chapel wall, and contains a chamber, entered from the leads. The large circular, or north-east turret, of 16 ft. interior diameter, and of two floors, was used as an observatory by Flamsteed, before the construction of the present building at Greenwich. Its upper floor seems to have been entered by an exterior stair, on the south side, for the support of which the parapet, as may be seen, has an exterior projection. These turrets have been cased, but the old Norman masonry may still be detected.

There is a sort of "entre-sol" between the chapel-vault and the roof, which, over the aisles, is about 7 ft. high, and capable of being turned to account. Some of the old drawings show loopholes pierced in the south wall, and there are traces in the south-west turret of a doorway, which seems, from its level, to have led into this vacant space.

The place and manner of the original entrance to the Keep are unknown. The local, probably traditional opinion is, that it was on the north side, at the second stage, or first floor level, near the east end of the wall, where there is at present an entrance by stone steps, 12 ft. above the ground. No doubt this opening is so far original, that if not a door it was a loop, the interior arch of the recess remaining. But a close examination of the exterior shows that the present door has been cut through masonry not intended to cover a large opening, for the joints are horizontal, and there is no relieving arch. In the next, or middle opening, where also a modern door has been cut, through which stores are lifted into the armouries, there are traces of an arch above, intended to cover an opening of unusual size, and here, therefore, was probably the principal door. Why it should have been placed on the north, and most exposed side, it is difficult to say. There are no traces of the applied fore-building or barbican common in later Norman keeps, as Rochester, or Scarborough, covering the entrance.

The southern door and well-stair are certainly

original; but this, of small size, and opening into the third stage only, could scarcely have been more than a postern from the palace communicating directly with the chapel and the state apartments of the Keep.

It is remarkable that this Keep, intended as the refuge of royalty, and the citadel of the metropolitan fortress, should contain but one fire-place, no well, no garderobe on the second, three on the third stage, only four altogether, and none of those other mural chambers so common in later Norman keeps of far inferior pretensions. Neither is there any trace of the usual Norman chevron, or zigzag ornament.

Although much injured and obscured by injudicious repairs, parts of the original surface may be detected. The base, quoins, and pilaster strips were evidently of ashlar, very open jointed. The rest of the wall was of rubble, rudely coursed, but with a great preponderance of mortar, much resembling the earliest work at Malling Abbey and St. Leonard's Tower. The arches throughout are semicircular, and quite plain. The vaulting, though sometimes groined, is never ribbed. It may also be remarked, that there is no subterranean chamber in the Keep, or anywhere throughout the fortress.

The arrangements within are very peculiar, and show a prevision against surprise, carried, if not to excess, yet to a degree fatal to the convenience of the royal personages and great officers of state, for whose deliberations and occasional residence the building was designed.

The main door, supposing it to be as indicated, opened upon a very gloomy first floor, from which a turnpike stair led downwards to the basement, and upwards to the second floor. To this the way from the stair was along a bent and narrow mural passage, and from the inner room by two staircases to the upper story and battlements. Having attained the upper story, the entrance to the state rooms was again only by mural galleries, admitting but one person abreast.

For purely military purposes all this was advantageous. Supposing a score of resolute men to garrison the Keep, they could hold the main door and postern against an army; or supposing them, by surprise, to have lost the lower stories, they could still defend the passage to the second floor without fear of being outflanked; while above there was easy access from the state floor to the battlements, whence the enemy could be assailed to most advantage. There remained indeed to the besiegers the last and most terrible resource of firing the place, and, once within the walls, this would be easy and irresistible. Not even this immensely solid masonry would have resisted the conflagration which a torch flung upon the wooden floors of the building would be sure to kindle.

For purposes of state the great altitude of the council-chamber, its excessive coldness, the difficulty of access, the inconvenience of the frequent posts, probably necessary for the support of its roof, and finally, the entire absence of privacy in a room so large and with so many lateral openings, must have been serious drawbacks. No doubt the rooms were bratticed off into smaller chambers, and hung with tapestry, but even then the absence of fire-places, so common in Norman buildings, must have been felt, and the nature of the floors, ceilings, and partitions, must have rendered the employment of stoves and bratticed chimneys very dangerous.

Neither is it easy to understand the intention of the arches in the party wall. Where, as at Rochester, these openings were of large span, the chambers admitted, on occasions of state, of being thrown into one. Here, however, though inconveniently large for doorways, they were far too small to make the rooms common. They could scarcely be intended to economise material, else the wall might have been safely much reduced in thickness, without piercing it completely through; and below they have no rebates or recesses for doors, or wooden partitions. On the third floor, where the doors are rebated, it is clear that they opened opposite ways, so that one, if not both the chambers, was subdivided. The rebates, however, may not be original.

The absence of all ornament, the very sparing use of ashlar, and the general roughness of the work, especially of the lower floor of this Keep, lead to the conclusion that it was executed in haste, and with an insufficient command of good material. The vaulting especially is very coarse, and impressions remaining upon, and the occasional fragments of oak imbedded in, the mortar, show that the centering was composed of small rough oak slabs, not even cut to lengths, but overlapping, and that occasionally the form of the arch was preserved by the intervention of a rough coat of mortar. This used to be apparent even in the vaults of the chapel, and may still be seen in the mural galleries and staircases.

Against the east wall of the Keep, a large rectangular building, now an armourer's shop, was constructed, it is said, by Edward III.; since when, it has been raised a story, and otherwise so completely altered, that nothing can be made out of its original details. The lower walls are thick, and its south-east angle seems to have been rounded off, perhaps as a turret. It encloses a narrow court, whence a part of the east face of the Keep may be inspected. It is evidently an addition, and had nothing to do with any raised or covered entrance to the Keep. The way through it into "Little Ease" is modern, and vaulted in brick.

The INNER WARD is enclosed within a curtain-wall, having four sides, twelve mural towers, and a gatehouse. The base or longest side faces the river. The east and west sides incline inwards, so that the north face is narrower than the base. This face is broken by an obtuse angle, having a central salient.

The level of much of this enclosure is 15 to 20 feet above that of the outer ward. Possibly part of the clay from the ditch, excavated by Longchamp, was here piled up. By reason of this difference, the lower part of this ward wall is a revetment, retaining the ground along the west and north, and part of the south and east fronts. The inequality is seen at the

MILITARY ARCHITECTURE OF THE TOWER.   43

gate-house, the passage through which rises one foot in ten to the middle of the ward ; and, at St. Martin's staircase, at the north-east corner. Where the palace stood, from Wakefield to Salt tower, the levels are nearly equal. This ward is much encumbered with buildings, some of the age of Henry VIII., some later, while others have been lately removed. No doubt this ward was always thus occupied, as the Tower was a depôt for all sorts of military stores, and a residence for petty officers of the Court and garrison. In 1213, King John ordered to be salted and hung up "bacones nostros qui sunt apud Turrim ;" and, in 1224, he drew upon the Tower for thirty dolia of wine ; so that pig-styes and wine-stores formed a part of its contents. Lead, and the more expensive building-materials, were also kept here.

The *Church* of St. Peter ad Vincula, mentioned in the reign of John, and rebuilt in the late Perpendicular period, still occupies the north-west quarter of the ward. In the south-east quarter stood the *Royal Palace*, destroyed, at various times, by James, Cromwell, or after the Restoration. The keep in Norman castles was intended rather for the occasional than the regular residence of the lord, whose ordinary lodgings were more conveniently placed in the inner ward. This was so at Rochester, in 1281, at Bamborough, Carlisle, Porchester, and elsewhere. Here the palace stood between the Keep and the ward wall, and, besides, had walls of its own ; one crossing from Wakefield tower to the Keep, where were drum-towers and a gateway known as Cold Harbour, and another called the Wardrobe gallery, crossing from Broad Arrow tower to the Keep, and having upon it Wardrobe tower, also circular, with a circular turret. The Queen's gallery extended from Salt to Lanthorn tower, on the line of the curtain, and the great hall was connected with Wakefield tower. The whole space was occupied by small courts and gardens, lodgings, and offices; and the buildings in the reign of Henry III. seem to have encroached upon the outer ward, where were two posterns for the service of the palace. These buildings, after the manner of royal houses, were always under repair; and seem to have absorbed much of the money expended on the Tower. The mainguard-house stands on the site of Cold Harbour, and the ordnance office on that of the Queen's gallery and great hall. Norman masonry is said to have been discovered in the foundations of the latter office. In the earlier surveys, the palace quarter is called the "Inner Ward." Cold Harbour was probably very lofty; for, in 1572, complaint was made that Sir Owen Hopton, the lieutenant, allowed his prisoners to meet and walk on the "leads of Cold Harbour;" and, on the 29th December, the Earl of Southampton staid leaping upon the tower, his wife being on the opposite side of the ditch.

Of the twelve mural towers of this ward one caps each of the five angles. Two were intermediate on the south face, as two still are upon the east, and two upon the north, one on each side of the salient. The west, or shortest face, has one large intermediate tower. The gate-house, called the Bloody tower, stands considerably west of the centre of the south front, and opposite to Traitor's gate. It is contiguous to Wakefield tower, which flanks it on the east, and probably determined its position and that of Traitor's gate.

Commencing with *Wakefield*, and passing westwards, the towers are, *Bloody, Bell, Beauchamp, Devereux, Flint, Bowyer, Brick, St. Martin's*, or *Jewel, Constable's, Broad-Arrow, Salt*, and *Lanthorn* tower, now destroyed.

Wakefield tower deserves very close attention, its lower story being next to the keep in antiquity. It is also known as the Record tower; records having been

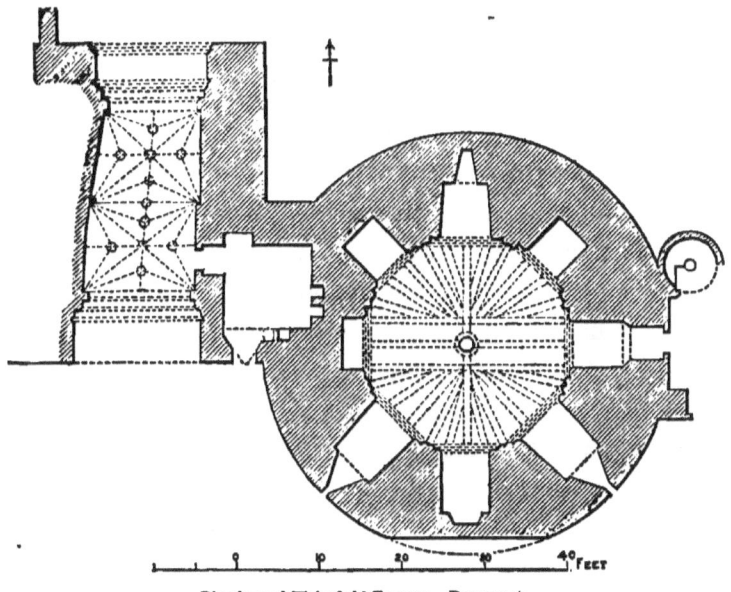

Bloody and Wakefield Towers.—Basement.

kept there from an early period until a short time ago. In the survey of Elizabeth it is called the Hall tower from its proximity to the royal hall, destroyed during the Commonwealth.

It is in plan a cylinder of 50 ft. diameter, and is about 50 ft. high. Its projection from the line of the south curtain is about 22 ft. Whether it was originally intended to cap an angle, is uncertain. No doubt the curtains from Lanthorn tower on the east and Cold Harbour on the north abutted upon it on two faces, and were coeval with it; but it is unknown whether the third curtain from the west, now replaced by the Gatehouse, was of the same date; and, in fact, whether the original design included the present inner ward.

This tower has two, and had three stages. The basement, the floor of which is upon the ground-level, contains an octagon chamber, 23 ft. from face to face, with walls 13 ft. 6 in. thick. In each face is a recess, 6 ft. broad, having a semicircular head, the edge of which has a double chamfer with an angular recess between. The northern and the three southern recesses are 8 ft. deep, and have a flat end also 6 ft. across, so that there is no splay. In the end is an opening, round-headed, and about 4 ft. across, which contracts rapidly to a loop-hole. The north-east and north-west recesses are 7 ft. and 6 ft. deep, and are blank, without loops. The west recess is only 2 ft. 6 in. deep, and was probably closed when the Bloody tower was built. The eastern recess is the present entrance, but the curtain must have abutted on this side, so that it is not improbable that the original entrance was in the north-eastern recess. The chamber is, however, so dark, and the recesses so obscured and encumbered by stores and brick walls, that it is difficult to examine them minutely.

The chamber is 10 ft. high. It has a flat timber covering, which if not original is very old, and may well represent the original. Probably it dates from the rebuilding of the upper story, in the reign of Henry III. In the centre of the chamber, upon a plain stone cheese-like base, is set up an oak post, 18 in. square, with the angles taken off. Upon this rest two beams, 11 in. square, at right angles, crossing the chamber east and west and north and south. Parallel to the former, 2 ft. from it on each side, are two other similar beams also crossing the chamber. There are, therefore, left outside these beams, and divided by the north and south beam, four quadrants, and these are filled up each with five beams, also 11 in. square, which radiate fan-like towards the walls, where all seem to have rested upon a stone ledge or wall plate. The radiating beams are morticed into the main beams. These timbers have rotted at the wall ends, and to support them, and the load of records above them, two octagonal frames have been placed beneath, one close to the wall, and one half-way between the walls and the central post, and these are supported each by eight props, so that the interior of the chamber is disfigured by a regular forest of seventeen posts.

The ordnance office abuts upon this tower on the east, and takes the place of the old curtain. In the present entrance, and applied to the exterior and north-east side of the tower, is a later well-stair, 6 ft. 6 in. diameter, which ascends to the first floor and the battlements.

This upper or first floor, also an octagon chamber, is of 30 ft. diameter, and has a recess in seven of its eight faces. Of these three to the south, and that to the north-west, terminate in modern enlargements of the old windows, as does that to the west, of which the opening is skewed, to avoid the Bloody tower. In the

Palace Entrance.   Wakefield Tower.   Oratory.

north face is a fireplace, probably representing an original one. The north-east recess is closed at 4 ft. deep, and that to the east is occupied by two openings; one, the present door, evidently not original; close north of which, beneath a drop arch, is the original entrance from the palace, 5 ft. 5 in. broad, and at 2 ft. 6 in. deep reduced to 4 ft. broad, where it forms a lofty doorway, now closed. These recesses have each a drop arch, supported by a plain chamfered rib.

The south-east recess has been fitted up as an oratory, and its sides are produced inwards by two walls, buttressed in tabernacle work at their west ends, and connected above by a plain bold drop arch, rather light, and flatter than the rest. This no doubt is the chapel mentioned in 1238. It is possible that the recess to the north-east was the royal door, and that the narrow eastern opening led to the stair and to the rampart of the curtain.

The south recess also differs from the rest, in having within it a second rib, of 3 ft. opening, as though above a doorway, and the opening is twisted to bring it opposite to the door of St. Thomas's tower, between which openings, 18 ft. apart, there was evidently either a cross wall or a light bridge, giving a short cut from the palace to the ramparts of the water-gate.

The intention was to vault this chamber, and in each angle is a semi-octagon pier, with a rude base, and without a cap. The total height of the ceiling, now flat, is 25 ft., so that the vault was to have had a high pitch with eight cells. It is clear that this never was executed.

A line of blocked-up arches in the outer wall shows that an upper story was contemplated, and probably constructed, since in St. Thomas's tower is a second or upper door, evidently intended for a second bridge, or passage along a cross rampart, above that already mentioned.

The arch-rings within, and the whole of the basement story without, of this tower, are of finely-jointed ashlar, and it appears from the decay of some of the stones, and from other indications, that the joints were not mere face-work, but were equally fine through the whole depth of each outer stone, a degree of precision unknown now, and rare at any age. The upper story is of uncoursed rubble. It has been pointed and stuck over with chips of flint, but the acute relieving arches over the windows are seen, both of the first and second floor. The parapet is of brick, and encrusts an older wall of stone.

The basement of Wakefield tower is probably late Norman, perhaps of the reign of Stephen, or Henry II., although this is no doubt early for masonry so finely jointed. The superstructure is early in the reign of Henry III., perhaps 1220—30, as in 1238 mention is made of the chapel in the new tower next the hall, and towards the Thames. The records of the realm were lodged in the New Temple as late as 20 Edw. I., but 33 Edw. I. they were in the Tower, no doubt the keep, whence "extra magnam turrim," to make room for King John of France, they were removed, 1360, probably to this tower. In August of that year the clerk of the works was to repair the roof, doors, and windows of the house provided for the records, and this is repeated next year for the tower in which are the Chancery rolls.

The *Bloody tower* is the gatehouse of the inner

ward. It stands in the south front, west of the centre, opposite to the earlier Traitor's gate, and it abuts against the also earlier Wakefield tower. The exterior face ranges with the curtain. Its position was no doubt determined by that of Traitor's gate, and by the advantages offered by the flanking defence of Wakefield tower on the outside and Cold Harbour wall on the inside.

It is rectangular or nearly so in plan, 25 ft. broad and 38 ft. deep, and pierced by a vaulted passage, the axis of which has a twist to the east. It is of three stages, and 47 ft. high from the outer gate cill to the parapet, which is modern, and of brick.

The portal, 15 ft. wide, opens under a low-browed drop arch, 8 ft. high at the spring, and 14 ft. at the crown; 3 ft. 6 in. within the entrance is a 6 in. portcullis groove, working through the vault in a chase 2 ft. 6 in. broad, so as to admit a heavy wooden frame. Then follows a double chamfered gateway, reducing the passage to 11 ft. 8 in. Next is the body of the gatehouse, 21 ft. long and vaulted, having a pair of gates at each end, and on the right a porter's lodge. The inner pair of gates are succeeded by another chamfered gateway of 11 ft. opening, and this by a second portcullis, with a chase only 1 ft. 4 in. broad, followed by the inner portal of 15 ft. opening. The passage rises about one foot in ten, and this rise, giving a great advantage to the defenders, is continued to opposite the White tower, where it ends in a short flight of steps.

The vaulted space occupying the central part of the

passage is about 22 ft. long by 13 ft. broad, and is divided into two not quite equal bays. The vault springs from four corner, and two intermediate corbels, representing lions' heads, each supporting an octangular bracket.

Each bay is divided by four main hip ribs into four cells, and along the axis of each cell is a ridge rib, longitudinal and transverse. These cells are subdivided each by a secondary rib, springing also from the six corbels, and, with the ridge rib, dividing each cell into four compartments. Thus, besides the two wall half-ribs, from each intermediate corbel spring seven ribs, and from each angle corbel three ribs.

There are no regular bosses, but at each point of intersection the ribs abut upon an open circle, the centre of which is occupied by a lion's face, dropped in from above. There are, therefore, three main and eight smaller circles, besides six half-circles at the junction of the ridge and wall-ribs. The ribs and circles, though of one pattern, are of two sizes. All have been clumsily cobbled with Roman cement.

The porter's lodge, on the east side of the entrance, is a vaulted chamber 10 ft. square, with a window of two lights, no doubt replacing a loop towards the south or front. A door, now closed, on its north side, seems to have led in the wall to the upper floors. About 4 ft. of this lodge is excavated in the thickness of the wall of Wakefield tower.

The entrance-way, on passing the gate-house, lies between a retaining wall on the left, or west, and the main guard, which supersedes Cold Harbour wall, on the right. A modern staircase, no doubt representing an old one, ascends in the substance of the west wall, and opens on the parade before the Constable's house, and here also is a door entering the first-floor of the gate-house.

This is a Decorated, or Early Perpendicular door, leading into a chamber 28 ft. by 18 ft., having a large double light window in the west wall by the door, and in the east wall a loop towards Cold Harbour, and a passage which, through a Caernarvon-headed door, leads into a small vaulted and ribbed garderobe on the left, and onward into what is no doubt the well-stair from below, now closed; and which seems to have ascended to the roof.

This, which was the portcullis chamber, has also windows at either end over the portals, and across its south end a low four-centred arch, in which are fastened two sheaves carrying the portcullis, which rises through a chase in the floor, and is lifted by a rude long wooden windlass worked by three sets of capstan bars.

The northern portcullis was lighter, and perhaps never actually inserted. The only trace of its working arrangements is a part of a flat-topped recess, from which it might have been suspended.

An upper floor, reached by a well-stair cut in the wall between this and the Wakefield tower, contains a room 25 ft. long by 18 ft. broad, at the south end of which is walled off a passage 26 ft. long by 4 ft. broad, at the west end of which a door, now walled up, opened upon the ramparts, showing that this curious passage made a part of the rampart walk, which accounts for a door and loop which opens upon it from the gatehouse upper floor. The well-stair is continued to the leads of the tower, 10 ft. above the curtain.

The doors, window, and portcullis arch in the first floor, all have a deep bold quarter-circle hollow, replacing the angle, instead of the usual chamfer.

This gatehouse is generally attributed to Edward III., who may have constructed it in the later part of his reign; or it may be the work of Richard II. The vaulting and portcullis-arch appear of later date than the walls, but the whole is probably of the transition period between Decorated and Perpendicular.

In the survey of Henry VIII. this is called the Garden tower, being close to the constable's garden, now the parade. In the survey of 1597, it is called by its present name; and popular prejudice, rather than Tower tradition, has attributed that name to the murder of the sons of Edward IV., idly said to have been perpetrated here.

As Garden tower, this building was a well-known Tudor prison. From hence to Bell tower, 150 ft., the original *curtain* remains, of its full height of about 40 ft., and its base thickness about 10 ft. It is, however, so defaced outside, and inside so encrusted with houses of the Tudor period, that but little of its detail can be seen. It is pretty clear that there is no range of loop-holes in its substance. A cell, recently a stable, is really a Tudor brick vault built against it.

Near to Bell tower is an original mural chamber, probably a garderobe, lighted by a recess and loop. This recess shows the original wall, about 7 ft. thick; and an interior addition of 3 ft. more. The original recess has an acute, and the addition a drop arch. The one may be Early English, and the other of Decorated date. Above this the full thickness of the wall is seen in the great modern window, cut through it, in the Constable's lodging.

Bell Tower is so called from the alarm bell once suspended from its summit. The bell now discharges the less exciting duty of summoning the garrison to

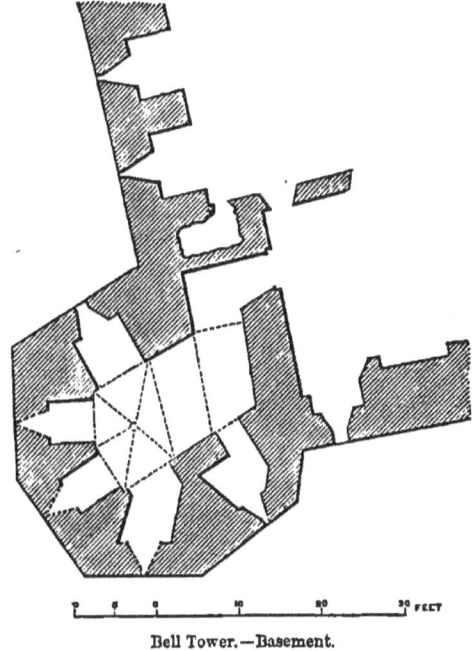

Bell Tower.—Basement.

St. Peter's church, and the bell turret has been replaced by a "gazebo." The tower caps the south-west angle of the ward, and stands 40 ft. within the Byward gate, which it commands. It is in plan an irregular octagon, about 35 ft. mean diameter, and 60 ft. high, from the level of the outer ward. Five and a-half of its sides project beyond the curtains. Above, the angles are rudely rounded off, and the upper 20 ft. is cylindrical, and may be an early addition. The two southern faces have a chamfered plinth, 6 ft. high. The walls have been stuck over with chips of flint, and the parapet is a brick addition; but it is evident that the basement was originally of fine jointed ashlar, almost equal to Wakefield. Five cruciform loops mark the line of the interior basement, about 14 ft. above the exterior ground.

The lower 10 ft. of this tower is solid, and above this are two stages. The basement, now a cellar and boot-hole, is of irregular plan, and may be called a rectangle with inclined ends. The walls are from 9 ft. to 13 ft. thick, and contain four pointed arched recesses with loops, and a mural chamber, also looped. The entrance passage from the gorge is bent at right angles.

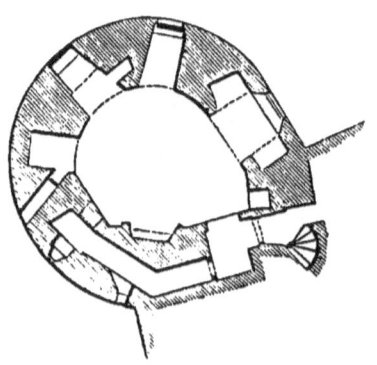
Bell Tower.—First-floor.

This chamber is vaulted and ribbed, its outer end terminating in a rude pentagon, traversed by five hip-ribs, of plain rectangular section, and meeting by a high-pitched arch, in a central boss. This boss and the capitals whence spring three of the ribs, are of Early English character. The shafts are wanting.

The upper chamber is rudely circular, and about 18 ft. across. The walls are 8 ft. thick. From the well-stair, which commences at this level, a short passage opens into a rectangular lobby, also vaulted, 4 ft. by 5 ft. 6 in., from which a door leads into the chamber, and another into a small flag-roofed mural gallery, which threads the south wall for 22 feet, and has two loops, one raking the south curtain, the other lighting a garderobe, which seems to have another opening direct into the tower.

The main chamber was lighted by four loops, of which two have been converted into windows, and two stopped up. These recesses are of irregular breadth, with high drop arches, the crowns 10 ft. 3 in. from the ground, with traces of a broad moulding above each. The north loop rakes the west curtain, and has cupboards right and left under flat drop arches for archer's tools. Another has a lateral squint towards the south, and another, with a hole in its arch, widened by the rubbing of the old bell-rope, has evidently been used as a doorway. No doubt it opened upon the gatehouse, now removed, which crossed the outer ward at this point, close north of the Byward gate. This chamber is rudely domed in with overhanging courses of tile stone and flat rubble, like an ancient dovecote. No doubt a proper vault was intended. To the spring of the dome is 14 ft., to its crown 22 ft.

It was in this chamber that, in 1830, was discovered an inscription commemorating the imprisonment here,

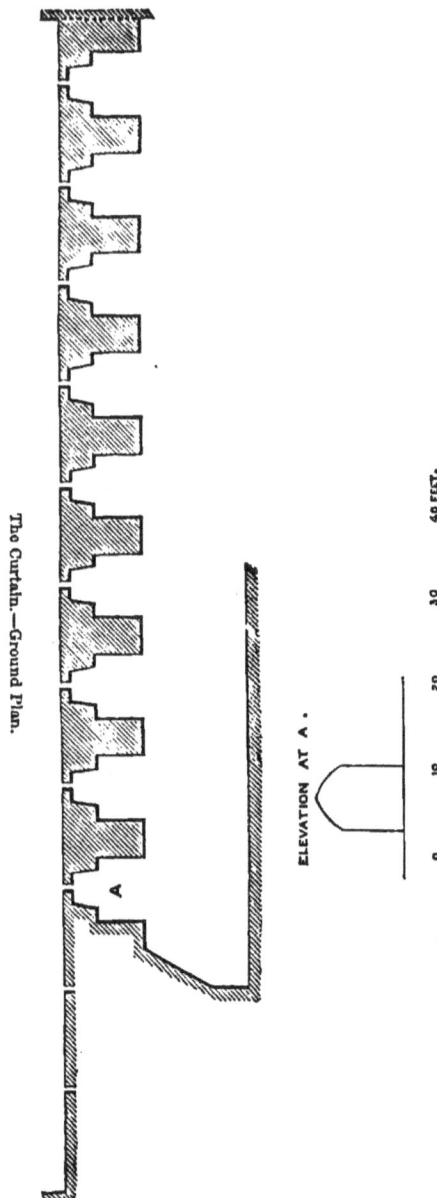

The Curtain.—Ground Plan.

20th June, 1565, of Lady Mary Douglas, Countess of Lennox, for the marriage of her son, Lord Darnley, to the Queen of Scots.

The well-stair ascends from this floor to the battlements; and at its foot a narrow door, set in a square recess, opens upon the rampart wall of the west curtain, leading to the Beauchamp tower. The Bell tower has been the subject of an interesting paper by the Rev. Thomas Hugo, read in Suffolk Street, in 1858. It may safely be attributed to the reign of John, or even of Richard I., that is, to the last twenty years of the twelfth century.

The *Curtain*, from

Bell to Beauchamp tower, 138 ft. in length, 37 ft. high above the outer, and 18 ft. above the inner ward, and 10 ft. thick, is very perfect, but still much encrusted by dwelling-houses. The exterior of this wall shows eleven loops about 12 ft. from the ground, 12 ft. apart, and these are found within to represent eleven recesses of 7 ft. 4 in. opening, with drop arches of 3 ft. 4 in. rise, so that the curtain was pierced by an arcade intended for the defence of its base against the outer ward, but which would have been fatal to the security of the heavy superstructure, had the most ordinary battering engine been brought to bear upon it. The recess next to Beauchamp tower seems to have been walled up when that tower was built. At the base of the parapet was a string-course, now much mutilated. The rampart walk remains open, but a part of it lies between the roofs of houses. The loops are of one pattern, of about four inches opening, and cruciform. The three upper ends are square; the lower expands into a round oillet.

This mural arcade is very singular. Such of the recesses as are accessible are found to be lined with brick, and can scarcely, in their present form, be earlier than the reigns of Edward IV. or Richard III., if so early. In fact they much resemble the work of Henry VIII. Still it is difficult to suppose that the openings themselves are later than the wall, which they so seriously weaken. They evidently exist beyond the Beauchamp to the Devereux tower, as the loops are visible, although the back of the wall is so shut in with dwelling-houses and the vaults of the church, as to be inaccessible. Nothing like them has been detected between the Bell and Bloody tower, or in the fragments of the original curtain on the east side, about the Broad Arrow tower. In the short low cross curtains connected with Salt tower, something like these recesses may be seen, and apparently of early date.

The *Beauchamp*, or Cobham tower, stands towards the centre of the west wall, into which it has been inserted, either as an addition, or more probably in place of an earlier tower. Its plan is a semi-circle of 36 ft. exterior diameter, and 18 ft. projection beyond the curtain. The exterior wall is 8 ft., and the gorge wall 4 ft. thick, and ranging with the inner face of the curtain.

This tower is of three stages, not vaulted, the middle being at the rampart level. A well-stair, 9 ft. diameter, in the curtain, close south of the tower, opens from the inner ward, and communicates with each floor, the curtain ramparts, and the battlements of the tower. The stair is looped towards the field, and its passage has a small window towards the inner ward.

The middle chamber is that possessing most interest, from the number and quality of the memorials cut upon its walls by its distinguished prisoners. Its plan is rectangular, with a western bow of three sides of an octagon. In the gorge wall is a large modern restored window, and in the bow two loops and one central window, no doubt once a loop towards the field. One face is occupied by a fire-place, perhaps of modern date. Though used as a prison, it was evidently constructed for defence only, as a *place d'armes* upon the rampart. Hence the rampart walk is continued right through it, and from the passage opens a small mural chamber, 6 ft. by 8 ft., with a loop to the field, and near it a small mural garderobe, 5 ft. by 4 ft. The staircase on the south, and these chambers on the north, occupy the two square turrets which flank the Beauchamp tower.

Beauchamp tower is in the Decorated style, and the work of the fourteenth century, probably of Edward III. It is evidently later than the contiguous curtain into which it has been inserted. Its name of Beauchamp is probably derived from Thomas Earl of Warwick, who was imprisoned here towards the end of the fourteenth century, and it has also been called "Cobham," from the well-known prisoner of that name, who was lodged here in consequence of Wyatt's conspiracy. It is built of uncoursed rubble, much resembling St. Thomas's and Salt tower, and very different from the basements of Wakefield, Bell, and Martin towers. The rubble is broken into vertical compartments by lines of ashlar, of single stones, set like coign stones, though on a plain surface.

The *curtain* from Beauchamp to Devereux tower is 148 ft. in length, and about 30 ft. high outside, the rampart being level, and the ground rising. It is original, and about 10 ft. thick, except where it expands to 14 ft. on joining the Beauchamp tower. The cells in its base are indicated by their exterior loops. Near to Devereux tower this curtain has been altered and renewed, and a raised platform, covering the church vaults, and a brick chamber, annexed to the tower, have been built against it.

Devereux Tower caps the north-west angle of the ward. In plan it is about three-quarters of an irregular circle, 35 ft. across at the gorge, and of about

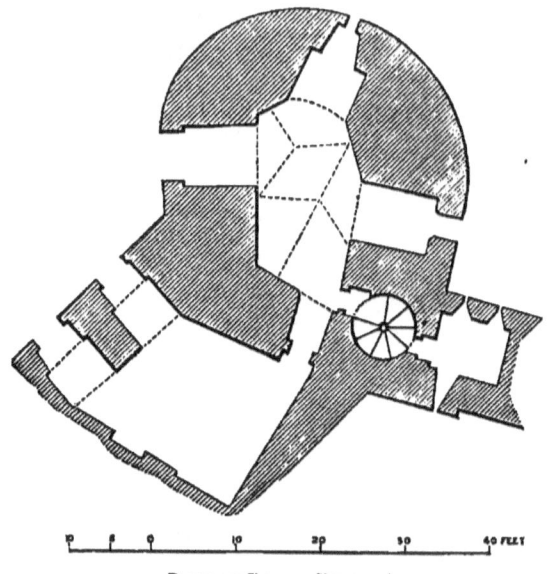

Devereux Tower.—Basement.

30 ft. projection. It is of two stages; the lower 10 ft. or 12 ft. being solid. A well-stair at its junction with the north curtain leads downwards from the church platform to the basement, and to a vaulted garderobe, 7 ft. 10 in. by 6 ft. 7 in. with two exterior loops, and one towards the inner ward. This is in the curtain.

The basement is of an irregular figure, a sort of polygon of four very unequal sides, with a curved outer end. It is vaulted, and its outward portion has three, and its inward four hip-ribs, plain, chamfered, and 13 in. broad, springing from the wall without pier or corbel, and meeting irregularly in mitred joints at the crown. The wall is about 12 ft. thick, and in two of the sides and the curved end are three round-headed recesses of 7 ft. 6 in. opening, intended for loops, but now fitted with windows. The ring-stones of these recesses appear original, and much resemble those in Wakefield tower.

The entrance-door from the stairs has a slightly drop arch, and near it another similar but larger door, set in a deep recess, opens into a vault about 22 ft. by 16 ft., looped outwards. This vault is a Tudor casemate of brick, but half of it is in the old curtain, and probably old, though lined. As the door is certainly old, this may have been an original mural chamber, or it may have opened on the "terre-plein" before the church vaults were built. The vaulting of the tower is chalk, the ribs and coigns of harder material. Possibly the walls and recesses of this tower are Late Norman, of the age of the Wakefield, and the ribs and vaulting Early English, or later additions, or, which is more probable, the whole is of one date, Richard I., or John. It is a very curious structure. Bayley says that courses of tiles were seen in the masonry like those found in the adjacent city wall, of the fragments of which it may certainly have been constructed. If the whitewash were removed, and the exposed masonry examined, we should probably learn whether the base of the tower be a part of the ancient enceinte of the fortress, the work of Henry II. or his son.

The survey of 1597 shows two circular turrets at its junction with its curtains, and calls it "Robyn the Devyll's Tower," or, later, "Develin Tower." Its present appellation is derived from Robert, Earl of Essex, confined here in 1601. The superstructure is modern.

Flint Tower was taken down in the last century, and rebuilt of brick, and was again rebuilt in stone, a few years ago. In its present form it is a rectangle, 40 ft. square, having a slight interior and bold exterior projection, and its outer face is rounded. The survey of 1597 shows the interior projection and the usual flanking turrets, but the whole of the present tower appears new, and even the exterior base is either new or has been cased. In the curtain, close west, is a modern staircase in the wall.

The *Curtain* from Devereux to Flint tower, 90 ft., though capped with a modern parapet, and casemated within, seems in substance to be old; as does the *Curtain*, also 90 ft., from Flint to Bowyer tower.

Bowyer Tower caps the salient of 160 degrees which breaks the north front of this ward. It is in plan a half-round, flat-sided, of 45 ft. diameter, 28 ft. projection from the exterior of the curtain, and ranging with its interior face, here thickened by the addition of modern casemates. It had in 1597 one circular turret at its junction with its east curtain. The basement is original, and only altered by the substitution of windows for loops. In plan it is rectangular, with a bow of three faces, in each a recess for a loop, the walls being 10 ft. thick. There is also a blank recess in the west wall. The entrance door is in the south side, and close east of it, is a smaller door, communicating with a chamber in the east wall. Above the entrance-door is a trace of a large closed-up arch in the wall. The arches are all drop-pointed. The chamber is vaulted, and from its angles, without piers or corbels, spring four plain, heavy, chamfered hip-ribs, which meet, without boss or ornament, in the crown. They are of the pattern of those in Devereux tower, and no doubt of rather Early Decorated date, and probably of the reign of Edward III.

The upper floor is wholly new, as is the whole casing of the exterior.

Bowyer tower was, from an early date, the residence and probably workshop of the royal maker of bows. In 1223 Grillot was making "balistas corneas;" and, for his encouragement, he had, in 1224, a robe for his wife. Soon afterwards the Archbishop of York had orders to send up Roger Balistarius, with all his implements, to the Tower, paying his expenses. Bayley gives a good perspective drawing of the interior.

From Bowyer to Brick tower, 62 ft., the *Curtain* is lined with modern casemates, but seems in substance original, though capped with a new parapet, and cased at its exterior base.

Brick Tower, in 1532 Burbidge tower, was, in 1597, shown as a half-round, with a circular turret upon its eastern flank, in the base of which was a mural chamber, and no doubt a staircase. It appears to have been recently rebuilt from the foundation, and is now a horse-shoe tower, of 44 ft. diameter, and 42 ft. at the gorge, applied to very ignoble purposes. Its projection from the curtain is 36 ft.

The *Curtain* from hence to Martin's tower, 65 ft., seems to have been rebuilt. It is casemated, and, close to the latter tower, is pierced for a staircase of twenty-seven steps, which ascends from the outer to the inner ward, and shows the point of greatest difference of level between them.

[St.] *Martin*, or Jewel, formerly Brick tower, is the residence of the keeper of the jewels. It caps the north-east angle of the ward, and is in plan an irregular circle 40 ft. diameter. Its base for 12 ft. or 14 ft., seen in the outer ward, is solid; but, unlike the other towers, is mere rough foundation work, evidently intended to be covered up. Possibly Brass mount, a bastion of the outer ward, just in front of this tower, was a small mound or cavalier, and extended backwards to the tower. But, however this may have been, the outer ward, at the base of this tower, was certainly 10 ft. to 12 ft. higher than it now is.

Above the foundation, the wall of the tower, some way up the basement floor, is of fine close-jointed ashlar, like that of Bell tower. Still higher, the wall is rubble, with vertical lines of ashlar, as described in Beauchamp tower.

The interior of this tower is so disfigured with lath and plaster partitions, and linings of wood, and so cut up into small domestic apartments, that little or nothing can be made of its original details, which probably remain but slightly altered. The basement floor, until recently the Jewel-house, and now a kitchen, is circular, or nearly so, in plan, with three loops opening beneath pointed arch recesses. This floor has plain chamfered ribs. The entrance was at the gorge; and on the right, or south, is a well-stair; and on the left traces of a mural chamber. These no doubt occupied the two circular turrets shown appended to this tower in the view of 1597. The first floor is evidently original, though still more obscured than that below. This tower is probably of the reign of Henry III.

The jewels seem to have been moved here soon after 1641, from the south side of the White tower, then used as a powder-magazine, which it was feared might be endangered by the adjacent chimneys. The present Jewel-house is a modern brick building, 48 ft. by 28 ft., built close south of this tower, and in the line of the curtain, which seems to have been pulled down to make place for it.

The Crown jewels, regalia, and the public treasures, were originally lodged in the New Temple. King John, however, employed the Tower as a treasury; and sent 4000 marks thither in 1212. The Bishop of Winchester was his treasurer there in 1215. In 1218, when De Fawkenberg was treasurer, money was kept both here and at the Temple. 37 Hen. III., (1252-3), the Royal jewels and treasure were kept at both places. But, in that year, the regalia were sent, sealed up, to the tower; and, from this reign, the Treasury was here. Thus, (14 Edw. III.), certain jewels are described as "En la Blaunche Tour deinz la tour de Londres." And, (18 Edw. III.), are mentioned: "Claves interioris cameræ juxta aulam nigram in Turre Lond^s. ubi jocalia Regis privata reponuntur." And, (30 Edw. III.), we hear of the "Tresorie deinz la haute Toure de Londres." Long afterwards there were, perhaps, two strong places; for, (20 Jas. I.), occurs: "His Majesty's secret Jewell house in the Tower."—[Kal. of the Exch. iii., 197, 208, 225, 424]. And such entries are numerous.

It was in 1673, while the regalia were in Martin tower, that the attempt of the notorious Colonel Blood was made upon them.

Constable's Tower stands 102 ft. south of Martin's tower. It seems to have resembled Broad Arrow tower in pattern and dimensions; but it has, to all appearance, been recently rebuilt from the foundations. It is now a half-round tower of 32 ft. diameter, rising a story above the curtain, which seems also to have been rebuilt. It bore its present name under Henry VIII., and was a prison at least as early as 1641.—[Harl. MS., 1326].

From hence to Broad Arrow tower, the *Curtain*, 102 ft. in length, seems, for the most part, to be old; but it is completely locked in, on both faces, by houses.

Broad Arrow Tower, though obscured by modern buildings, does not seem to have been much altered. In general arrangement it resembles Beauchamp tower, but has only two stages, and is much smaller, being 26 ft. diameter, with a projection on the curtain of 13 ft. Its inner face is flush with the curtain. On each flank is a small square turret. That on the north contains a steep narrow stair, not a well, entered below by a Caernarvon doorway. That on the south contains a small chamber, probably a garderobe. The ground floor is entered from the gorge, and is a rude, half round chamber with three loops under drop-pointed arches.

The upper chamber seems to have had four outward faces, and a loop in each; and another in the gorge wall. The mural chamber, 6 ft. by 4 ft., has a lancet vault and door, and a loop commanding its curtain southward. A passage from the rampart traverses this upper floor, making it a *place d'armes*. The stair is continued to the battlements. In 1532, this was "The tower at the east end of the wardrobe," and as late as the reign of Elizabeth, the wardrobe gallery abutted on this tower, extending from it towards the Keep.

The *Curtain* from Broad Arrow to Salt tower, 156 ft., is so completely locked in by high buildings on each face, that its rampart walk serves as a gutter between the two lines of roof. It is evidently

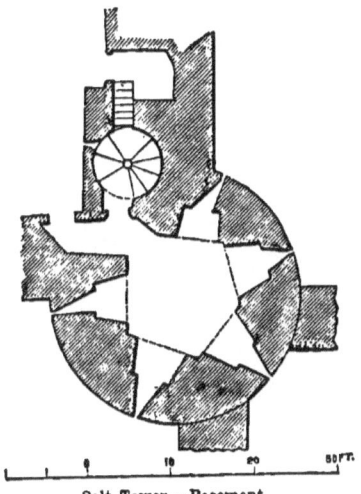

Salt Tower.—Basement.

original, about 30 ft. high, and 12 ft. thick at the base. It does not appear to contain any cells like those in the west curtain.

Salt Tower, in 1532 Julius Cæsar's tower, caps the south-east angle of the ward. It is circular in plan, 30 ft. in diameter, and 62 ft. high. It is constructed of uncoursed rubble, with vertical lines of ashlar, resembling coigns, as in Beauchamp tower.

The ground floor, entered from the inner ward between the two curtains, is an irregular pentagon with five loops beneath drop-arched recesses. The door opens into a short passage at the north end of the west wall under a segmental arch, against which abuts a similar but half-arch in the north wall, under which a small door with a drop-arch leads into the ascending well-stair. The arch rings are all of good ashlar, but the room is not vaulted.

The well-stair, which lies between the tower and its north curtain, at a height of about 10 ft. leads by a narrow branch to a niche or recess in the curtain, having a drop-arch reinforced by a plain chamfered rib. This recess is open in the rear, and has a loop raking the outside of the tower and the cross wall of the outer ward.

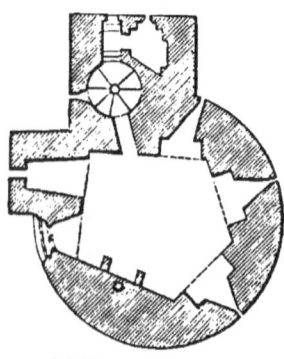

Salt Tower.—First floor.

The stair goes on to the first and second floor and leads. The first floor, also a pentagon, has on the south face a good but plain Early Decorated stone chimney hood, with scroll moulding and plain corbels. In the two eastern faces are loops. In the west is a large two-light window, a modern restoration, and close to it a lancet opening, no doubt once a door leading to the south curtain. The staircase door enters on the north side, and close to it is a loop pointing north along the face of the curtain. From this floor a passage leads along the curtain towards the Broad Arrow tower; from it opens a small garderobe.

There is a third stage, and above it the battlements.

Salt tower was the meeting point of four curtains. The east and south walls of the inner ward, of equal height and thickness, and two walls of smaller dimensions, of which one ran east, and traversed the east member of the outer ward, and one ran south to Well tower, and traversed the south member. Each of these had a gateway, opening into the space between them, and leading to the Iron gate postern. Of the five loops on the ground floor of Salt tower, two opened north-eastward upon the outer ward, two south-westward upon that ward towards Cradle tower, and one south-eastwards towards Galleyman tower and the postern.

Salt tower has undergone recent and complete restoration. Its original features, however, seem to have been preserved.

A section of the *Curtain* between Salt and Lanthorn tower seen against the wall of the former, shows it to have been 10 ft. thick and about 20 ft. high, but the rest of it was probably removed before 1532 to make way for the queen's gallery. This curtain terminated in the Lanthorn tower.

The *Lanthorn Tower* has been long since pulled

down, and its place is now occupied by the modern Ordnance office. It formed a part of the palace, and contained the king's bedchamber and private closet. It was circular, and probably originally of the age, size, and fashion of Wakefield tower. As in 1532 it was called the New tower, it may have been rebuilt in that or the preceding century. It was injured by fire in 1788 and pulled down, with a contiguous gateway which traversed the outer ward at this point.

Lanthorn tower is stated in the survey of 1532 to have been 106 ft. distant from Wakefield tower. The actual distance occupied by Lanthorn tower and its curtains, that is from Salt to Wakefield tower, was 343 ft.

The OUTER WARD is a strip of from 20 ft. to 110 ft. in breadth, which completely surrounds the inner ward, and is itself contained within the ditch, of which its wall forms the scarp. This wall, though generally, is not strictly, parallel to the inner curtain. Like it, its east and west faces are straight, and the north face has a salient angle near its centre. The river front is also bent, though slightly.

On the south side this ward varies in breadth from 20 ft. to 80 ft.; on the east from 60 ft. to 90 ft.; on the west from 60 ft. to 70 ft.; and on the north, the salient of which is rather bolder than that behind it, and a little nearer to the east end, the breadth ranges from 90 ft. to 110 ft. The lengths of the faces upon the ditch in the same order are, 750 ft., 580 ft., 460 ft., and 620 ft., being a girth of 800 yards.

The wall has been so altered and strengthened by

modern casemates, and so encrusted by buildings, that it is difficult to arrive at its original dimensions. The height varies from 15 ft. to 20 ft. inside, and is about 12 ft. more to the bottom of the present ditch. The usual thickness is about 6 ft. On the river front the wall was only 10 ft. high, and apparently only of moderate thickness.

The north-east and north-west angles are capped by drum bastions, parts of circles of about 80 ft. diameter. They are called Brass Mount and Legge's Mount, probably from cavaliers once upon them. *Legge's Mount* has the lesser projection, and seems to be solid. The lower part of its exterior wall looks as old as the adjacent curtains, but the upper part is new, and contains a casemate pierced for six guns. *Brass Mount*, that towards Little Tower Hill, is pierced by a well-stair from above and a cross gallery below. This leads from a door in the gorge to the middle of a circular gallery, vaulted in brick, which envelops the bastion and has numerous loops for musketry, and others altered to suit small cannon. This gallery is probably an addition of the Tudor period, excavated within the old retaining walls. The salient between these two mounts has recently been capped by the *North Bastion*, an additional and perfectly new work, being two-thirds of a circle of about 60 ft. diameter, with flattened sides, and containing three tiers of casemates, each pierced for five guns.

The only regular towers of the outer ward are upon the south front, where the ditch is narrow and the palace buildings were most exposed. These are five,

Develin, Well, Cradle, St. Thomas's, and *Byward Tower.*

Develin Tower, in 4 Richard II. "Galighmaies Tower," when no cart or dray was to come before it into St. Katherine's unless the brethren pay a fine to the constable, was, in 1549, Galleyman, and in 1641 Iron-gate tower. It is now a powder magazine, and is of course lined with wood, without windows, and not to be entered with a light. These conditions are not favourable to the study of its interior. It is a long rectangular tower, 18 ft. by 32 ft., and built wholly in the ditch, one end being applied to the face of the curtain, so that it projects like a buttress from the south end of the east curtain, while its south side is a prolongation of the river front. The exterior has been partially cased, but it is evidently old, and in substance as originally built. Its basement is solid, but about 10 ft. above the ditch is a line of loops on the north and south, or two longer faces. There has been an upper story, the walls of which remain, but seem later than the lower. At this level, in the east face, is the outline of a door, which, if a postern, opened 20 ft. above the ditch. The view of 1597 shows a double wall, probably an embattled dam serving as a bridge, extending from this tower across the ditch, and crowned on the counterscarp by a small work, called the "Iron Gate." If this drawing be correct, the roadway was through the basement chamber, and the upper floor led to the rampart of the wall. This gate led into the precinct of St. Katherine's. The tower is probably the work of

MILITARY ARCHITECTURE OF THE TOWER.

Henry III., and connected with an original dam for keeping up the water of the ditch. Forty feet west of Develin is Well tower.

Well Tower, also rectangular, forms a part of the curtain, and has a projection into the ditch 10 ft. by 16 ft. wide. Its basement, below the present level of the inner ward, and scarcely above the water level of the ditch, contains a chamber, 14 ft. by 10 ft., vaulted at a high pitch in two unequal bays, the north the larger, parted by a transverse rib. Each bay is vaulted in four cells, with four hip-ribs meeting in a plain mitred joint. There is a half or wall rib in the gable of each cell. The ribs are 7½ in. broad by 6¾ in. deep, with a plain chamfer, and spring from four corner and two intermediate circular bell corbels, the tops of which are 3 ft. 4 in. from the floor. The height of the chamber is 11 ft. 6 in. There are four

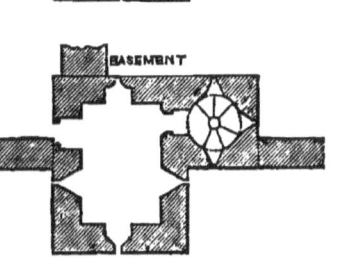

loops, one pointing northwards into the ward, and the rest opening towards the ditch. All are under drop-arches. In the west side is a door of 3 ft. opening in a drop-arched recess, which may have led into a mural cell in the curtain, or have been an entrance from the ward. On the east side a rectangular appendage, entered by a square-headed door, contains a well-stair of 6 ft. 3 in. diameter, looped upon the inner face of the curtain and the ditch. This stair leads to an upper room on the rampart level, not vaulted, 15 ft. by 10 ft., looped to the field and upon the face of the west curtain. In its north wall an original door, 2 ft. 3 in. wide, opens on the rampart. The second floor is modern. Well tower is a good example of the Early English style.

Well tower stands due south of Salt tower, and a short curtain, with a gateway, connected them. Part of it remains, 12 ft. high and 6 ft. thick, pierced with loops at the ground level, and embattled against an attack on the east. This rampart was reached from Well tower, and did not communicate with Salt tower. A similar cross curtain connected Salt tower with the outer ward wall westward. This also was looped, had a central gate, and was embattled for defence from a south attack. These two curtains thus enclosed the approach to the Iron-gate postern, and prevented either part of the outer ward from being entered by

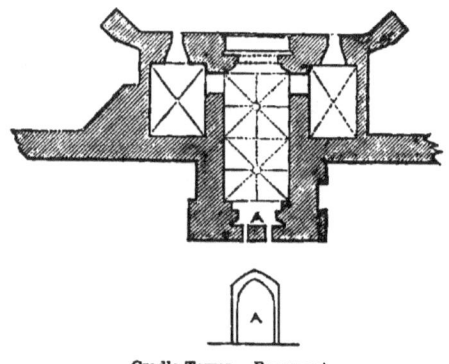

Cradle Tower.—Basement.

surprise. These arrangements are evidently as early

as the time of Henry III., and are shown in the view of 1597.

Cradle Tower comes next west, at 118 ft. distant. It stands on the outer wall, and projects 9 ft. into the ditch, with a breadth of 16 ft. It is a gatehouse, and though of small dimension, very complete in its design, and of excellent construction. It stood nearly in front of the bye-gate of the royal quarter, and allowed a direct passage from thence to the quay.

It is in plan T-shaped, the portal running through the main limb, which projects into the ditch, and the lateral wings, each containing a lodge, forming a gorge or main front of 26 ft. width, and flanked by two diagonal buttresses, which cap the angles and project into the ward. Between these is the doorway, and on either side of it a small lancet window, cinquefoil-headed. One of these windows is quite unaltered.

Cradle Tower.—Window.

The doorway is 7 ft. 2 in. broad, with a drop arch and light chamfer moulding. Two feet in is a portcullis groove, succeeded by a doorway of 5 ft. opening, of which the valves move inwards. The wall is 4 ft. 7 in. thick.

The passage is a chamber of two squares 7 ft. broad, and 12 ft. 6 in. high. It is vaulted in two equal bays, parted by a transverse rib. Each bay has four hip-ribs, and a straight rib takes the crown line of each vaulting cell, so that eight ribs meet in the centre of each bay, the point of junction being a hollow circle. There is besides a wall-rib in each gable. The rib parting the two bays, and the longitudinal rib, have a plain mitred junction. The rib and circle-mouldings are the same. They are light and bold, 5 in. broad and 7 in. deep. The base of the rib has a hollow chamfer, and its apex is an ogee. The ribs spring from four corner and two intermediate corbels, the tops of which are 7 ft. from the ground. These are octagonal and embattled. The bracket below is much defaced.

The doorway in the south end, of 4 ft. 6 in. opening, had gates opening inwards, and outside them is a second portcullis groove, now, with the exterior of the gate, walled up.

The lodges open from the central passage close to the ward entrance, by doors, 2 ft. 10 in. wide, one of which has the remains of the cusps of a cinquefoil in the head. They are 12 ft. broad by 8 ft. 9 in. long and 12 ft. high, having the small windows already noticed towards the ward. They are hip-vaulted in chalk, with four cells, having four ribs 7 in. broad by 7 in. deep, springing from corbels, now knocked off, but the tops of which were 7 ft. above the floor. There are no wall ribs. The portal arches of the main passage are drop in recesses, of which one is so low as to be nearly, and the other is quite segmental. The vault-arches are equilateral, or nearly so.

On either side of the part of this tower that projects into the ditch, on the outside, is a recess, on the west face 4 ft. 6 in., and on the east face 3 ft. broad, and

1 ft. 4 in. deep. Possibly these were the shoots of garderobes from the upper floor and battlements, now removed. On the west side, at the old water level, are indications of an arched drain, now covered up.

In the curtain, close west of this tower, are traces of a well-stair, which probably led from the west lodge to the roof.

The superstructure of Cradle tower is said to have formed a part of the palace quarter, and the view of 1597 shows it as a water-gate, with a square turret on its west flank, where was the supposed staircase. It shows also, west of this, a considerable tower extending across the ward, here very narrow, to the Lanthorn tower, and which no doubt contained the Lanthorn gate.

The details of this tower are rather Decorated than Early English ; and if, as is historically probable, it be the work of Henry III., it must be late in his reign, and was perhaps completed by his son. Owing to the cumbrous character of the sluices and gates of St. Thomas's tower, state prisoners were sometimes admitted by this gate, then fitted with a draw-bridge.

St. Thomas's Tower, better known from its ancient function as Traitors' gate, is the water-gate of the Tower, and also contained and commanded the communication between the Thames and the main ditch. It is, in fact, a barbican, and a very singular one, placed astride upon the ditch, here 40 ft. broad, and perforated by a passage leading from the river. It stands considerably west of the south front, being in advance of the Bloody tower 30 ft., the breadth, at this point, of the outer ward.

The quay, in front of this tower, is traversed by a channel, 28 ft. broad and 13 ft. 6 in. deep, partly arched over and newly lined with granite, which opens from the Thames, through an archway 21 ft.

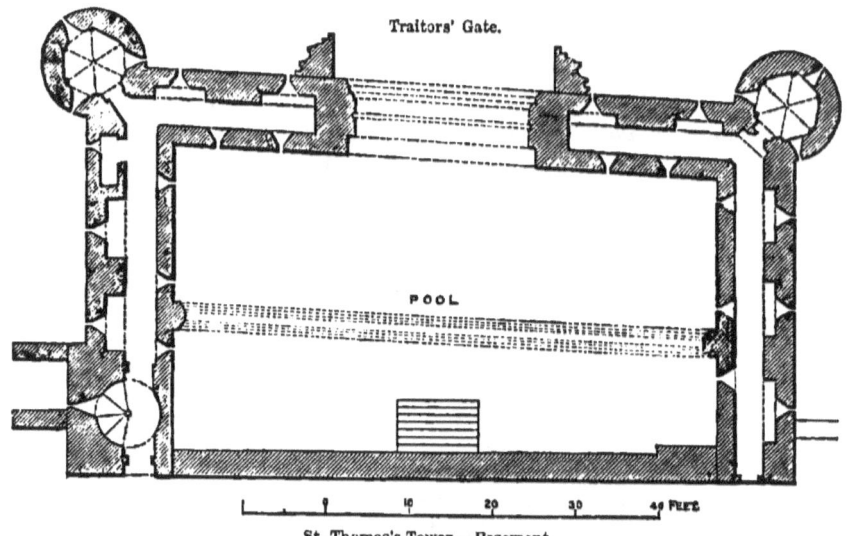

St. Thomas's Tower.—Basement.

broad, into a rectangular basin or pool, 66 ft. by 40 ft., and 18 ft. deep, lined and paved with stone, and containing, when the gates are opened, about 8 ft. of water at high water. A flight of steps from the water, on the inner or north side of this basin, landed the prisoner within 30 ft. of the gateway of the inner ward.

The tower proper is placed above the outer 18 ft. of this basin, but its side walls are prolonged backwards, so that both the front and sides of the basin are protected. The south wall, 9 ft. thick, is pierced below by a low-browed water portal, already mentioned, beneath a drop arch, ribbed and chamfered. Between the ribs is

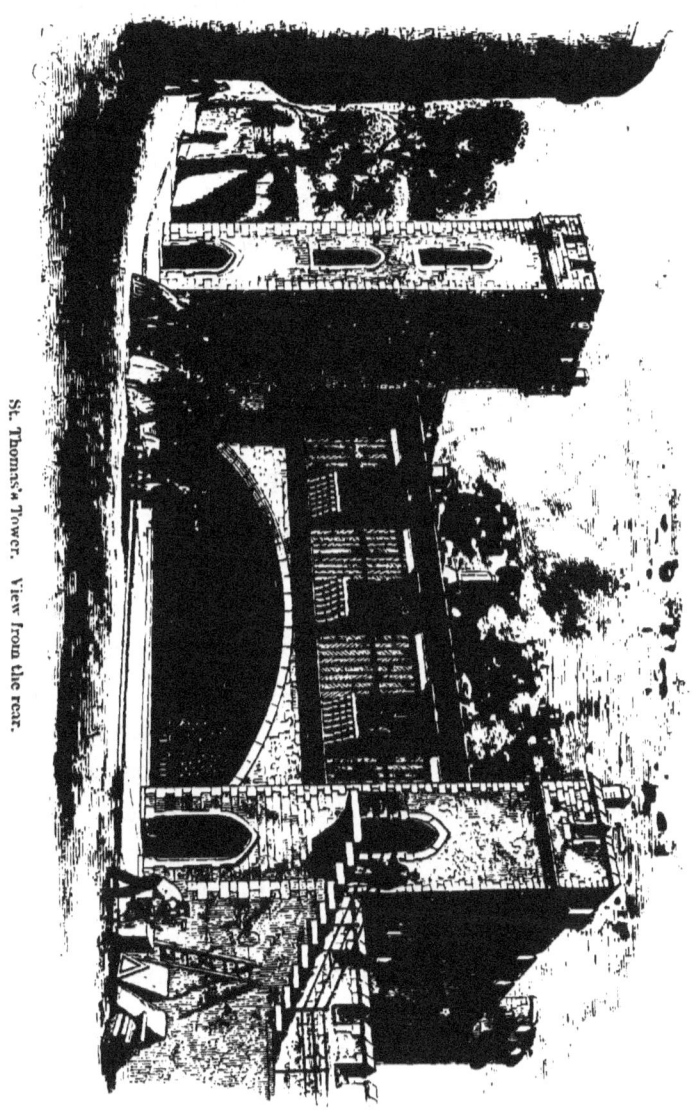

St. Thomas's Tower. View from the rear.

a groove, 6 in. broad, for an iron sluice or portcullis.

worked in the building above; and in the jambs are two holes, 6 in. diameter, lined with iron, for the passage of a chain. Within this, on the inner face of the portal, were folding gates opening inwards.

Seventeen feet within this outer wall the basin is crossed by an arch, supporting a light wall of brick and timber, which was the rear wall of the tower. This arch is a very remarkable piece of construction. It springs from two half-octagonal piers, and is segmental, of 61 ft. span and 15½ ft. rise. The voussoirs form two ribs, and the inner one is composed of 75 stones, united by a simple joggle or rebate.

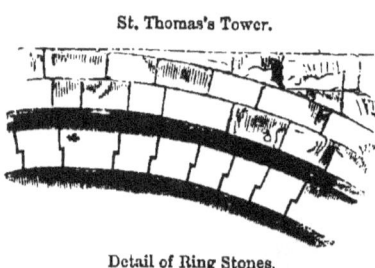

St. Thomas's Tower.

Detail of Ring Stones.

The rectangular tower, which thus rises from the walls of the outer half of the basin, is 86 ft. east and west by 18 ft. north and south, and capped at its two Thames-ward angles by light cylindrical turrets, three-quarters engaged, and rising above the parapet of the tower. The side walls, prolonged backwards an additional 30 ft., terminate in two square turrets, which occupy the northern angles, and also rise above the battlements.

Two doors in the north faces of these turrets, on the ground level, open into a mural gallery in each wall, looped on one face towards the ditch and on the other towards the basin. These galleries communicate with the southern turrets, and are continued within the south wall, having each two loops towards the Thames and two towards the basin. They do not meet, being stopped by the jambs of the sluice-gate. They were also used to receive the slack of the chain when drawn up.

The floor of the tower, which is above the level of these galleries, contained the machinery for lifting the sluice, which must have been heavy. The walls of this floor are also pierced with loops, and contain two garderobes. In the river-front are two Early-Decorated windows, of two lights each. The two upper chambers in the south turrets open into this floor, which is reached by a winding stair in the north-east turret, and by an exterior stone stair in the north-west turret.

The four chambers in the two cylindrical turrets are of excellent design and delicate workmanship, as may be seen from the plate in the "Vetusta Monumenta." They are in plan octagons, having slender columns, with high bases and bell caps, all cylindrical, and slightly engaged, in each angle, from each of which springs a light chamfered rib, meeting in a plain joint at the centre. There

St. Thomas's Tower.—Piscina.

are thus eight cells, each with a lancet-gable, supported by two half-ribs. Three of the faces have windows or loops, and another is occupied by the door. In the lower rooms the loops have chamfered recesses beneath drop arches. In the upper, the loops are larger, but still square-headed, and their recesses have an arch-rib with a hollow chamfer. The south-east upper chamber was an oratory. The window-sills on each side the east windows are Purbeck slabs, hollowed into bowls—on the south for a piscina, on the north for holy water. Both slabs projected, and have been broken off when the walls were wainscoted.

There is a second floor, reached by a well-stair in the square turrets, which ascend further to the roof, but it contains nothing of interest. The well-stair in the north-east turret leads to a door that opens on the north face, 20 ft. from the ground, and which opened outwards, and was barred on the outside. The meaning of this is only explicable on the supposition that a bridge, or perhaps an embattled cross-wall, connected this door with the corresponding opening in Wakefield tower, 18 ft. distant. By this means a person leaving St. Thomas's tower, and barring the door behind him, would reach Wakefield tower, and therefore the palace, and cut off pursuit. In the second floor of St. Thomas's tower is another door, above and similar to the first, which in like manner communicated with the top floor of Wakefield tower; so that either there were two draw-bridges, or a wall pierced by a mural gallery at 20 ft. high, and with a rampart-walk at its summit.

St. Thomas's tower was, until lately, occupied by a water-engine, to the great injury of its walls. The upper rooms were cut up into lodgings by means of wainscot and lath-and-plaster. All has lately been cleared out, and the tower restored in good taste.

St. Thomas's tower is attributed, and no doubt justly,

to Henry III. ; but although the octagon chambers have an Early-English aspect, the grand arch, the staircase-doors, and the windows towards the river are decidedly Decorated, though probably early in that style. If, therefore, this tower be of one date, it must be very late in the reign of Henry, but more probably it was completed and the grand arch turned in that of his son. The material is a ragstone laid in uncoursed rubble masonry, like Beauchamp and Salt towers, with ashlar dressings. The pool below was extensively repaired by Henry VIII. There is some reason to suppose that this was the tower that fell twice while being built.

The curtain along this front is original, though capped and patched in modern times. It seems to have been about 20 ft. high above the water, and from 12 to 14 on the inner side. In parts it was 12 ft. thick; but the addition of brick casemates in Tudor times, to enable the ramparts to carry cannon, prevents an accurate examination. It is no doubt the work of Henry III. From St. Thomas's to Byward tower is 160 ft.

BYWARD tower is the great gate-house of the outer ward, and is placed upon the scarp of the west ditch, at its junction with the south ditch. It is in plan rectangular, 50 ft. broad by 24 ft. deep, and its two outward angles are capped by drum towers, 23 ft. diameter, one quarter engaged, which rise out of the moat. Between them is a curtain of 14 ft., pierced by the main entrance. The towers, below the roadway, are solid; above it they are of three stages, and 49 ft.

high to the crest of the parapet, which, with most of the casing, is modern.

The portal opens from the bridge by a low drop arch, 12 ft. broad and 12 ft. high, reduced by two deep chamfers to 10 ft. opening, followed by a broad jamb, in which are loop openings from the lodges. This is succeeded by a 6-in. portcullis groove, with a chase of 16 in. in the vault, to allow of the passage of a heavy wooden grate. Then follows a heavy rib, pierced with three round holes, which slightly converge, and are thought by Mr. Parker to have been for the pouring

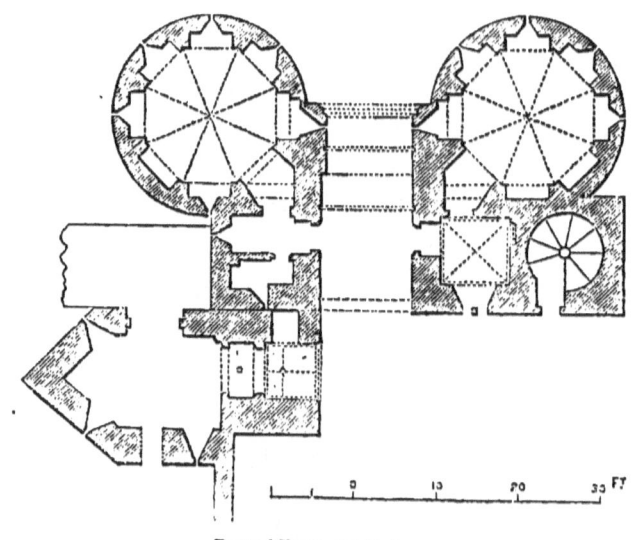

Byward Tower and Postern.

down of water, supposing the gates to be assailed with fire; and behind is a rebate with hinges for the valves of a door, opening inwards. The middle portion of the portal, which begins here, has a flat timber roof, 18 ft. high. In it is a second portcullis groove, and the doors of the warders' lodges. Finally is the inner archway, without jambs, but with a bold triple rib forming the arch.

The south lodge door enters a lobby, 8 ft. by 4 ft., vaulted in chalk, with a southern loop raking the postern. A pointed door on the left or east opens into a garderobe, with a loop to the east, now closed. Opposite, a short passage, also vaulted, and with a cross rib, leads into the south or warders' lodge.

This is an octagon, 15 ft. 9 in. from face to face. In each angle is a slender octagonal pier, engaged on a face and two half-faces, with a sort of bell cap and stilted base, both octagonal. From each pier spring a main rib and two half-ribs. The former meet in the centre in a plain joint; the latter form lancet arches at the gable of each cell. All are narrow and plainly chamfered. Of the eight vaulting cells the ridge lines are horizontal, and have no ribs. The ribs and piers are of freestone, the vaults of chalk. From the floor to the pier caps is 6 ft. 11 in. The total height is 17 ft.

In each of the faces is a recess. That on the north-east is the entrance. The south-east is occupied by a fireplace, no doubt representing an original one. The other six are looped.

The north lodge is entered through a lobby 7 ft. 9 in. square and 15 ft. high, vaulted in four cells, with four slender chamfered hip-ribs, springing from four octangular corbels, one at each angle. There is no boss. Each cell has a profile half-rib in its gable.

In the east side is a long two-light window beneath a segmental recess, which seems original. This window, and the proportions and general elegance of this chamber, point to its possible use as an oratory. Those who entered the Tower might well need to be met by spiritual support on the threshold.

In its north wall is a small lancet doorway, leading to a well-stair, but probably always closed. A west door leads through a short passage into the lodge, now a Police Barrack. This lodge resembles closely that on

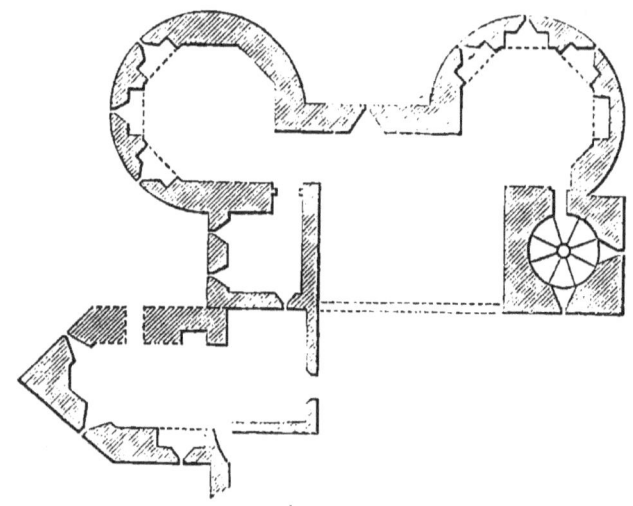

Byward Tower.—First-floor.

the south side, save that the east recess is closed up, and the fireplace, the brackets of which are original, occupies the north-east face. The upper part of this chamber, towards the ditch, has been pierced, probably for musquetry, so as to command the approach from Tower Street. In the north-east angle of this gatehouse is a well-stair, entered by a separate door from the east and outer side.

The first-floor contains two large octagonal chambers

MILITARY ARCHITECTURE OF THE TOWER.

in the towers. The staircase opens into one of these in the north-east angle, and a chamber 8 ft. square occupies the south-east angle. The rear wall between these two turrets is wanting, so that this gate-house, with its portcullis chamber, was intended to be open in the rear, or was closed, as now, by a lath-and-plaster brattice. There was a small window to the west, over the entrance gate, looking on the bridge.

The arrangements of the second-floor are still more simple. The staircase remains, and the two octagon chambers, but the small south-east chamber is wanting. The rear is open.

At the battlement level the staircase and its turret cease. There is now nothing above the parapet.

In the rear of and attached to the south-east part of this gatehouse is a low tower, of later date, intended to cover a postern bridge, traversing the south ditch, and dropping on the quay. The tower is rectangular in plan, 14 ft. broad and 29 ft. long, besides an acute salient of 12 ft. more, which projects into the south ditch, and prevents it from being raked.

It is pierced north and south by a portal 6 ft. 9 in. broad, which commences by a square cell, vaulted, with a cross and longitudinal rib, chamfered, and pierced at the intersection by an octagonal cavity. Two door jambs then reduce the opening by a foot, and between them, in the vault is a hole 6 in. diameter, apparently intended for a chain, which passed out over the rib of the further door, and worked, still within the tower, a light bridge, the recess for which is seen outside the door. The chamber here widens by 3 ft., to allow space for those defending the east wall. When this bridge was down, a way was opened to a door in the west wall, outside which is a platform, whence a second bridge dropped southwards across the ditch. The upper story of this postern tower was one large chamber for working the inner bridge. A door leads from it upon the rampart walk of the east curtain. Above this were the battlements of the postern, two stages below that of the contiguous tower. In the Tudor reigns these buildings have been encumbered with additions in brick, timber, and plaster, which still remain, and much obscure the original details. This postern tower is Perpendicular, perhaps the work of Richard II.

Besides the bulwarks and towers just described, the inner ward was strengthened against surprise by several cross walls and gates, breaking it up into independent sections. One of these gates crossed from Bell to Byward tower, and another, it is said, crossed north of Beauchamp tower. There were walls with gates across the ward, on either side of Traitors' gate, so that prisoners could be brought in by water and led across into the Bloody tower gate, without any chance of rescue in the outer ward, and indeed without being seen. Another gateway of a stronger description, and with towers, extended from Lanthorn to near Cradle tower; and another also, already mentioned, opened in the small curtain between Salt and Well tower. There was at least one more gateway in the short curtain east from Salt tower. The ward, between all these gates, must have been intended to be open; but, at least since the Tudor reigns, it has been encumbered with private houses. Here the operations of the Mint were carried on with much inconvenience; and the north and west limbs of the ward still bear the name of Mint Street, and the east limb, of Irish Mint Street.

The curtain or scarp wall of this ward was, no doubt, the work of Henry III., and much of the wall is still original. In the west wall, near Byward, below a modern battery of two guns, are six loops, probably old, but lighting modern casemates, and beneath each an air-hole. Also, on the north front, close west of the new bastion in the wall, is a Pointed arched door, long closed up, but probably an original water-gate. West of this also is an original loop, no doubt marking the place of a mural chamber not now accessible.

The modern additions to this curtain consist in a line of casemates, storehouses, canteens, magazines, and workshops, built against and concealing its inner face, and giving a rampart or platform of 30 ft. width. This is completed along the west and north and about half of the east face. All is well built—likely to last for ever—and quite destructive of the character of the place.

This exterior wall has been built with great care on a broad and deep foundation, since it shows no sign of settlement, though built in what, until recently, was a deep and muddy ditch. At one part indeed, close south of Brass Mount, it has been strengthened by three very clumsy buttresses of 12 ft. in breadth and 22 ft. projection. One covers the internal angle of the

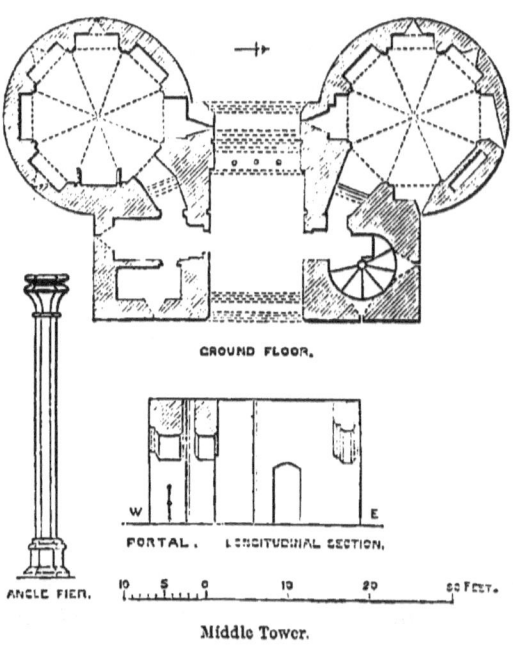

Middle Tower.

bastion; the next is about 40 ft. distant; and the third, at about the same space, is in fact a rectangular mural tower, resembling Galleyman, and contains a small chamber having two loops on each of its three free faces. Its parapet is new, and pierced for two guns.

MIDDLE tower is the outwork of Byward tower, and a barbican covering the landward entrance to the fortress. It stands on the counterscarp of the ditch, at the outer end of the bridge, and was originally enveloped by a special ditch of its own, a loop from the main ditch of the place, filled up in the eighteenth century. In design and execution it resembles closely Byward tower, though rather smaller, its breadth being 40 ft., and its height 30 ft. from the roadway. It is evidently of the date of Byward, and like it was open at the rear. It also has been cased with Portland stone. Its portal has a double portcullis, gateway, vertical holes, side loops and lodges, and its

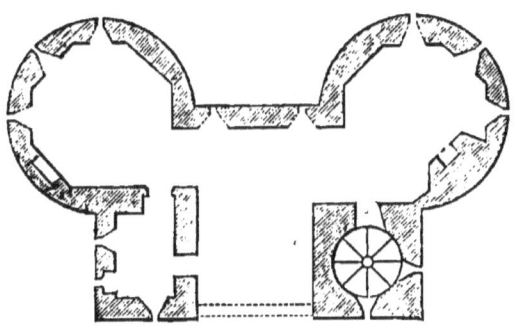

Middle Tower.—First-floor.

central part is ceiled with timber. In neither tower is there any trace of a drawbridge. The lodges are tolerably perfect; the stair in the north-east angle is in use, and takes the place of the Byward oratory; and in the south-east turret is a lobby and a garderobe, and above these a chamber 7 ft. by 8 ft. 6 in., and again on the leads another chamber 7 ft. 4 in. by 10 ft. 10 in.

Between the two gate-houses the ditch is traversed by a *stone bridge*, 130 ft. long, and at the narrowest

20 ft. wide. As the towers are not precisely opposite, the line of the bridge is broken by a slight zigzag. In the centre appears to have been an opening of 20 ft., now a stone arch, once the place of a drawbridge, as shown in old drawings.

The QUAY does not appear to have had any permanent parapet wall, which indeed would have interfered with its uses. It was sufficiently commanded by the defences of the outer ward. It was probably the work of Henry III., in the twelfth of whose reign it is first mentioned, and called "Kaia Regis;" and John de Crumbwell, Custos 8—9 Edward III., had then an order for 300 alder poles from Windsor forest for repairing it. The quay is in length about 1130 ft., that being the full frontage of the Tower.

The Ditch.—This, by far the most formidable of the defences of the Tower, varies in breadth from 100 ft. on the east to 110 ft. on the north, and 120 ft. on the west or City side. Along the south or river front it is only 40 ft. broad, probably because on that side it was covered by the wharf, the narrow limits of which did not permit any great force of assailants to be drawn up upon it; besides which the tower covering Traitors' gate, and the two small postern bridges which it was convenient to have towards the wharf and river, did not allow any great breadth of ditch.

The ditch was not only broad, but of great depth, so that when filled to the level of high water it was scarcely to be passed, and indeed when the water was low, the mud which accumulated there, and which made it of late years an unhealthy nuisance, must have been quite as formidable as a defence. Nevertheless, care was taken to cleanse it, and the "Liber Albus" informs us that, in the reign of Edward III., the penalty for bathing in the Tower foss, or in the Thames near the Tower, was death! (vol. i. p. xlix.) Its exterior circuit is computed at 3156 ft.

Also, from the great height of the ground to the west and north, the counterscarp is so very high as to be in itself a considerable obstacle to crossing the ditch, although no doubt this was in other respects advantageous to besiegers. Besides the main bridge, the ditch was crossed by St. Thomas's tower and the dam between Galleyman and Iron gate, all of which served to hold up the water. There were also the posterns of Iron gate, Byward, and Cradle tower.

No doubt the Conqueror's ditch, even when deepened by Longchamp, was fed by the Thames; and the water rose and fell with the tide. The intervention of the wharf, and the St. Thomas's sluice-gate, were devised to make the water in the ditch independent of the tide, and thus add materially to the strength of the defences. The ditch was drained and its bottom raised and levelled by the Duke of Wellington during his constabulate. There are seen in the modern brick revetment of the counterscarp a number of walled-up arches, resembling sewer-mouths, which appear to have been intended to facilitate the mining the glacis in the event of a siege.

The outwork in advance of Middle tower, though its ditch is filled up, and its other buildings removed, is still indicated by a line of stockades, which contain the ticket-office and a small engine-house. Here stood the Lion tower, and the Royal Menagerie ; and this whole *tête-du-pont* was further protected by a smaller tower and drawbridge of its own, shown in some of the early drawings.

Lions were a part of the royal state, and lodged in the Tower bulwark, in the reign of Henry I. The Emperor Frederick, in 1235, sent Henry II. three leopards ; and, in 1252, Henry III. received a white bear from Norway, for whose sustenance, with his keeper, the sheriffs of London provided four-pence daily, with a muzzle and iron chain, to keep him when " extra aquam," and a stout cord to hold him when a-fishing in the Thames. In 1254, Louis of France sent the King an elephant. He was brought from Sandwich to the Tower, where the sheriffs were to build him a strong and suitable house, 40 ft. by 20 ft., and to support him and his keeper. Edward I. and Edward II. kept lions here. At a time when the allowance for an esquire was one penny per day, a lion had a quarter of mutton and three-halfpence for the keeper; and, afterwards, sixpence was the lion's allowance ; the same for a leopard, and three-halfpence for the keeper. 16 Edw. III., there were a lion and lioness, a leopard, and two cat-lions. In 1543, the Duke of Najara saw here four large and fierce lions, and two leopards. The menagerie was finally closed about 1830. Its establishment on this particular spot was probably due to Henry III.

The whole outward space was, in 1597, called the Bulwark, and sometimes the Spur-yard.

HISTORY.*

Having decided to build an "Arx Palatina," and having some years' experience of the value of the proposed site as a temporary camp, the Conqueror at length determined to erect a regular castle, and entrusted the work to Gundulf, a monk of Bec, who in 1077, soon after his arrival in England, was consecrated Bishop of Rochester.

Gundulf brought with him from Normandy some reputation as an architect, which vocation he pursued in this country. Rochester keep, that strong but graceful tower, placed so judiciously above the ancient passage of the Medway, and long attributed to the bishop, is now known to be of later date; and the only existing buildings, besides the White tower, which can safely be attributed to him are the Record tower, parts of the old crypt of Rochester cathedral, and perhaps a small part of its west front; the lower stage of the west front, and some of the adjacent walls of his own abbey of Malling, founded in 1090, and dedicated in 1103; the very perfect and unaltered shell of his keep, there known as St. Leonard's; possibly the broad massive tower of the adjacent church, and it may be the Norman portions of that of Dartford. These remains

* The writer of the present paper has to express his obligations to Bayley's "History of the Tower," a laborious and valuable work, the descriptive parts of which are far more elaborate and far more correct than was usual forty-five years ago. He has also to acknowledge the courtesy of Lord de Ros, the present Lieutenant of the Tower, for ready and unreserved permission to visit every part of the fortress under the care and with the valuable assistance of Mr. Hughes, the principal warder.

however, the White tower, and the testimony of many generations, may be regarded as sufficient for the confirmation of his fame.

A direct evidence for the employment of Gundulf upon the White tower, is afforded by the "Textus Roffensis," written about 1143, or within eighty years of the Conquest, and printed by Hearne. This record also preserves the fact that Gundulf while so employed lodged at the house of Ædmer Anhœnde, a burgess of London. No doubt he was a friend of the bishop, as he was a donor to his church at Rochester, and directed his body and that of his wife to be there buried, and to have an annual obit.*

It is generally supposed that Gundulf's first attention was given to his cathedral, and that he did not commence the Tower until 1078, up to which time the ground was occupied by certain temporary defences. This must have been the case at Dover, which is spoken of as a castle long before the Norman walls could have been ready, but where the earthworks were already considerable and strong, and no doubt crested by a stockade.

Gundulf reached the age of eighty-four, and lived till 1108, that is, through the reigns of the Conqueror and Rufus, and to the ninth of Henry I.; it is, therefore, certain that he lived to see the Keep completed,

* "Hæc est conventio inter Gundulfum episcopum et Eadmerum Anhœnde Burgensem Londoniæ."

"Dum idem Gundulfus, ex præcepto regis Willielmi Magni, præ esset operi magnæ turris Londoniæ, et hospitatus fuisset apud ipsum Ædmerum quadam vice ipso cœpit episcopum rogare etc."— Textus Roff. Ed. Hearne, p. 212.

perhaps by Rufus; and he most probably made some progress in the walls of the enceinte, and the buildings of the palace, and perhaps of the Wakefield tower.

The fortress designed by the Conqueror no doubt included very much of the space within the present walls. Less would scarcely suffice to contain a citadel, a palace, and an arsenal; and the liberties were evidently of no greater area than was necessary.

The west boundary line runs but a few yards outside the counterscarp of the ditch, and includes only what may be called a narrow glacis, and nothing of the open space or esplanade usually reserved around a fortress. It is, however, probable that no permanent exterior defences were executed by the Conqueror. Probably those first commenced were the curtains from the Wakefield to the present Broad Arrow tower, and the cross walls of the Wardrobe gallery and Coldharbour, which, with the keep, included the space set apart for the palace. This was for many centuries known as the inner ward; and the Wardrobe and Lanthorn towers and those of the Coldharbour gatehouse, all now destroyed, are represented in the reign of Elizabeth as cylindrical, and resembling in design the Wakefield tower, which is Late Norman. It is, therefore, probable that the old inner or palace ward was first completed.

The rest of the enceinte, forming what is now known as the inner ward, could not, however, have been much later. According to the "Anglo-Saxon Chronicle," Gervase, and Le Livere, Rufus was, in 1097, building about the Tower a wall of sufficient magnitude, with the new Hall at Westminster, to be the cause of heavy taxation, and the subject of general discontent, augmented, no doubt, by the impregnable character of his work. The existing curtain of the inner ward, being from 9 ft. to 12 ft. thick, from 39 ft. to 40 ft. high, and of sound but rude masonry, cannot be later than John, by which reign the wall of Rufus could not have fallen into decay. It is far more probable, and quite consistent with the dimensions and character of the work, that this was the actual wall commenced by Rufus, and upon which he was employed in 1097.

Bell tower indeed, which seems to bond into the curtain, and the base of which presents masonry very like that of Wakefield, is octagonal, and its vaulting can scarcely be earlier than John; but Devereux tower, which is cylindrical outside, and has round-headed recesses in its polygonal basement chamber, may be as old as Wakefield, and therefore, in substance, the work of Rufus. The vaulting is later, but both may have been, as was Wakefield, taken down to the first floor at a later period, to which the vaulting may belong. Beauchamp, Bowyer, and all the other towers on this wall, are evidently later insertions; but the wall itself, where it remains, as on the west and part of the east and south fronts, is of a very early character, and not unlike the wall of John at Corfe and the earlier one attributed to Robert Consal at Cardiff.

Most of the chroniclers record a violent storm that swept over London towards the close of the eleventh century. Le Livere dates it Friday, 27th October, and Malmesbury, 28th November, 1091, and says it unroofed St. Mary-le-Bow, and destroyed 600 houses, as houses then were. Stowe adds that the White tower was damaged "by tempest and winde sore shaken," and that it was repaired by Rufus and Henry I.; but he gives no authority for this statement, which the extreme solidity of the building renders very improbable. The outworks however, both wall and towers, if in course of construction, with scaffolding up, might very well have suffered severely.

The Tower, therefore, of the close of the reign of Rufus, and of those of Henry I. and Stephen, was probably composed of the White tower with a palace ward upon its south-east side, and a wall, probably that we now see, and certainly along its general course, including what is now known as the inner ward. No doubt there was a ditch, but probably not a very formidable one.

Ralph Flambard, Bishop of Durham, and the faithful and rapacious minister of Rufus,—"pacitator Ranulphus, vir pessimus,"—by his severe exactions greatly promoted the works of the Tower. Singularly enough he is the first person known to have been imprisoned there. Henry, on his accession, and by the advice of his council, 15th August, 1100, shut up Flambard in the Tower. Palgrave says he was lodged in the uppermost or council-chamber of the White tower, under the custody of Walter de Magnaville, the hereditary constable. Probably his imprisonment was only intended to satisfy the popular cry, for two shillings, at that time a considerable sum, was allowed for his daily sustenance. He employed it, as is said, in feasting his keepers; and having received a rope in a flagon, took advantage of their drunken state to let himself down from the window of the south gallery, on the night of 4th February, 1101, taking his pastoral staff with him. The rope proved too short for the descent of 65 ft., and he was injured by a fall, but he escaped in safety to Normandy, and, as is well known, lived to recover his see of Durham, where he completed the Cathedral, added a moat to the Palatine Castle, founded Norham on the Tweed, built Framwellgate bridge, and endowed the hospital of Kepyer. Palgrave cites no authority for the escape of Flambard from the gallery; but these windows are the only ones not seen from the interior chamber, and of which the central column afforded a convenient place to which to make fast the rope. The Tower was probably from the first a state prison, for in 1106 the Earl of Mortaigne, taken with Henry Duke of Normandy by Henry I., was, says Ædmer, shut up there. The remaining Pipe Roll of the 21 Henry I. records "17l. 0s. 6d. In operatione Turris Lond."

In the time of Stephen the Tower was regarded as impregnable. Geoffrey, grandson of Geoffrey de Magnaville, the companion of the Conqueror, and the third hereditary constable, was created Earl of Essex by the king, who in 1140 kept his solitary Whitsun in the Tower. "Eodem anno, 1140, in Pentecoste resedit Rex Londiniæ in Turri, tantum modo Episcopo Sagiensi presente: cæteri vel fastidierunt, vel timuerunt venire." [R. de Hoveden]. The new earl proved false, and shifted his allegiance to the empress, who, by charter in 1141, confirmed him in his earldom and the constableship.

When the power of Maud declined, the citizens, to whom Geoffrey was as odious as his fortress, laid siege to it. Their efforts were so unsuccessful that on one occasion the earl made a raid as far as Fulham, and captured the bishop.

In 1143 the earl trusted himself in the royal presence at St. Albans, depending on the king's word. The temptation to obtain the Tower was too great,— "magis ex necessitate quam honestate,"—he was detained, and the Tower was his ransom. Stephen held it until 1153, close upon the conclusion of his reign, when, by the Treaty of Winchester, he gave it up to Richard de Lacy the Justiciary, who was to hold it until Stephen's death, when it was to pass to Henry, which accordingly was done in 1154. It is clear, therefore, that at that time the fortifications of the Tower were both complete and strong; and this, in the absence of a wet ditch, which it will be shown did not then exist, could scarcely be the case with walls of inferior strength to those now seen.

Henry II. is said to have placed Becket in command of the Tower, the government of which had ceased to be hereditary. But there is no proof of this, or that Becket repaired it; though at a later period, indeed, one of his demands, as archbishop, was the custody of Rochester Castle and the Tower. By this reign "London's lasting shame" had attained its gloomy reputation, and Fitz-Stephen describes the "Arx Palatina" as "great and strong, with encircling walls rising from a deep foundation, and built with mortar tempered with the blood of beasts."

. The Pipe Rolls of this reign contain frequent entries of large sums issued for the repair of the king's houses in the Tower, his chapel, and his gaol. In 2 Hen. II, 6s. 1d. was paid for carrying the king's breastplates to the Tower; but the regular series of accounts does not begin until the 13 Hen. II., and ends with the 34th. The entries for Westminster and the Tower are also much mixed up together, though sometimes distinct. Thus in 13 Hen. II. the king's houses in the two places and the queen's chamber cost 64l., and, in 19 Hen. II., 60l. was paid for the repairs of the Tower and of the houses in it. In the preceding year the king's houses in the bailey of the Tower cost 21l. In 20 Hen II., Alnod the engineer had 6l. 13s. 4d. for works at the Tower, and afterwards 100s. Similar payments continually occur, sometimes for lead for the repairs of the chapel, sometimes for carriage of timber and planks, sometimes for the kitchen, the gateways of the gaol, the repairs of the houses, and sometimes for the Tower itself.

The necessity for each expenditure is often certified to by the view of two officers, Edward Blund and William Magnus; the works were executed by the engineer Alnod; and the brief, authorising payment, was signed either by the king himself, or by Richard de Lucy or Ranulph de Glanville, no doubt as justiciars. The sums paid varied from 1s. 4d. to 64l., and the total for the thirteen years of which the rolls remain, is 215*l*. 15*s*. and 50 marks.

When in February, 1190, Cœur de Lion departed from Normandy to the East, he placed the Tower in charge of William Longchamp, Bishop of Ely and Chancellor, sharing the power of chief justiciary with Pudsey, Bishop of Durham, to which the Pope added the office of legate. These combined honours seem to have turned Longchamp's head. Always of intense activity of character, he spurned all colleagues in his power. His first act on reaching England seems to have been to provide for his personal security by girdling the Tower with a wall and deep ditch, which he proposed to fill from the Thames. In this, however, he failed, after spending a large sum of money.*

The wall was probably that of the outer ward, which would be necessary to retain the banks of the ditch, and the commencement of that which still remains. The failure could scarcely be in the admission of the Thames, which required only a certain depth of excavation, but was rather in the retaining it full at low tide, so as to make it really a wet ditch. This important object was attained in a later reign, by a new and ingenious arrangement. In his excavations Longchamp encroached upon land belonging to Trinity Church, East Smithfield, and took a mill from St. Katherine's Hospital. These trespasses were

* A.D. 1190. "Sub his diebus W^s Eliensis Ep^s, Angliæ Justiciarius et Apostolicæ sedis legatus, fecit Turrim Londinensem fossato profundissimo circumcingi, sperans se posse Tamisiæ fluenta in urbem ducere. Sed post multos de fisco sumptus se laborare inutilita comprobavit."—M. Paris Ed., 1646, p. 161.

much complained of, and seem to have been the same on account of which a compensating rent-charge was afterwards paid by Edward I. There is still a small burial-ground on the east glacis of the Tower, which is said to be a part of the land then taken. There was also an earlier trespass on Church lands by the constables, for Geoffrey, Earl of Essex, took by force from Trinity Priory, in East Smithfield, land near the Tower to make a vineyard, which was not restored to that church until towards 1137.

Longchamp, whose patent directed the lieges to obey him, even as the king himself, commenced by imprisoning Bishop Pudsey, his rival justiciar. His unpopularity was fostered by Prince John, who headed a party against him, and took occasion of his ill treatment of the Archbishop of York to summon Longchamp to appear before a council at Loddon, by Reading. Longchamp refused compliance, but retired before John's superior force to London, where he entered the Tower with all his train, pressed by the citizens, who took part against him and blockaded the fortress by land and water. John, with many barons and bishops, reached London on the 8th of October, 1191, and held a council in the Chapter-House, in St. Paul's churchyard, on the 9th, summoning the people by the sound of the bell. Here the Archbishop of Rouen and William Mareschal produced Richard's declaration from Messina, limiting the independent powers of the justiciar, whom the meeting then deposed by acclamation. Four earls and as many bishops conveyed this sentence to Longchamp, who fell senseless upon the floor. On the following

morning, at an early hour, John assembled an immense host in East Smithfield, a great green plain near the Tower, and summoned the justiciar to a parley. He surrendered upon terms at once, far too soon for his credit, and marched out with his followers and household stuff to Bermondsey, whence with much difficulty and through various dangers he reached Normandy.*
The Archbishop of Rouen then took charge of the Tower; but the chancellor, as is well known, retained or resumed his office, and on November 21, 1194, the well-known William Fitz-Osbert impleaded his brother Richard in the Curia Regis (Rot. Cur. Regis. xi., xvii.) for having said, "In recompense for the money taken from me by the chancellor within the Tower of London, I would lay out forty marks to purchase a chain in which to hang both king and chancellor."

Various entries in the Pipe Rolls of Richard show that the usual repairs of the Tower, and especially of the royal apartments therein, still went on. Unfortunately, although the sums are given, the detail of their outlay is very generally omitted.

The entries extend from the first to the tenth of the reign, and relate to nine years, during which about

"Itaque spe frustratus, in arcem se regiam cum suis omnibus recessit; quorum tantus erat numerus, ut in stricti loci angustiis sua illis esset nocivior multitudo, quam hostium foris frementium multitudo. Æstuebat turris interius comprehensiore multitudinis inclusæ, cito evomitura quos prodendo magis quam tuendos susceperat. Denique post unam noctem egressus ad Johannem et obsessores cæteros. Ille paulo ante rhinoceros sed jam homo, humili alloquio abeundi facultatem impetravit inclusis."—W. Heming: p. 530.

610*l.* was spent on the Tower and its houses. The recipient was sometimes Wm. Puincell, the constable, at others, Jordan de Turri, Richard le Duc, John Fitz-Erlecum, and others. Sometimes under the king's brief, sometimes the chancellor's. In one year, lime cost 46*l.* 9*s.* 6*d.* In the first of the king, 50 marcs were spent upon the "Royal Chapel in the Tower." The ditches are mentioned 5 Rich. I.

Longchamp's reign was so short that it is difficult to understand how he managed to execute as much as he undoubtedly did. The rolls of the early years of Rich. I. do not indeed show above one or two hundred pounds of outlay, but the chancellor had the command of other funds; and one cause of his excessive unpopularity with the citizens was the avidity with which he took upon himself to tax them.

Prince John, when he succeeded to the throne in 1199, was not inattentive to the wants of the Tower. In his two first years, Elias the engineer was employed upon the king's houses and works, and similar entries appear in the fifth, tenth, sixteenth, and seventeenth years. In the sixteenth the sum was considerable,— 117*l.* 15*s.* 8*d.*; and in the seventeenth the charge, 12*l.*, is for building the mud or "clay wall between the Tower [precinct] and city," which wall is often referred to in later surveys. On the whole, the Pipe Rolls of the reign are scanty as regards the Tower, but they are in some degree replaced by entries upon the Mise, Close, and Patent Rolls, which show that it was kept up as a royal residence, and that the king occasionally staid there.

In 1209 and 1210, 9s. 4d. were given in alms to one hundred poor there; and, in the latter year, Osmund, a knight bound for Poictou, received a gift of ten marks, and, to buy a horse, a hundred shillings from the king. This was given in the "Church of St. Peter at the Tower of London;" and is the earliest known mention of that building. Here also, on Sunday, the morrow of St. Philip and Jacob, Steffan, the messenger of the emperor, received half a marc on his return to his lord, and other payments were made here.

In 1212, the Archdeacon of Durham and Philip de Ulecote are ordered to send in all haste to London thirty carratas (cart-loads) of lead for covering the Tower; and, in 1213, among orders for repairs for the castles of Rochester, Canterbury, and Guildford, is mention of carriage of timber and "busca" (logs), for the works of the Castle of Dover and the Tower of London. It was about this time that the city ditch was deepened, and widened to a breadth of 200 ft. In 1215, Henry de Nevill was to supply ten oaks for the works at the Tower, five from within Havering Park, and five from outside it.

It was also in 1215 that the barons seized upon London, and that the Tower was given over to be held by the Archbishop of Canterbury, until Assumption Day, as a pledge for the king's performance of certain engagements. The rights of either party to the Tower were suspended, and the king was not to reinforce the garrison. The great charter was signed 15th June. The barons, however, continued virtually in possession until the arrival of the Dauphin, to whom it was given up in 1216, and by him held until he left the kingdom.

Mr. Hardy, in his valuable "Itinerary of King John," shows that he executed instruments at the Tower upon seventy-two days during his reign of seventeen years and a half. In 1204, he was there 28—30th January, 27—30th May, 2—3rd November. In 1205, 28th April and 13—16th August. In 1207, 2nd July. In 1208, 21st January, 10th, 19th—21st February. In 1209, 9th October. In 1210, 2nd, 3rd, 5th, 6th, 19th February, 2nd May, and 27th October. In 1211, 1—3rd, and 18th April. In 1212, 18—20th May; 2—4th June; and 20—22nd September. In 1213, 16th and 17th April; and 21—23rd, 26—29th December. In 1214, 2—5th, 12th, 13th January; and 29—31st October. In 1215, 1—6th, and 14—18th March; and 19th April.

As Henry III. has usually been regarded as the builder of much of the Tower as it now stands, and did undoubtedly execute considerable works there, it will be convenient here to examine into the probable condition of the fortress at the time of his accession.

It has been shown, from structural evidence, that the Wakefield tower, and probably the shell of Devereux tower, and perhaps of Bell tower, are at least as old as the reign of John; and that there is great reason to regard the original Wardrobe and Lanthorn tower and its curtains, and the Coldharbour wall and Gate towers, and the contained palace, all now destroyed, as of the age of Wakefield tower. Also, as St. Peter's church existed in the reign of John, and was "apud Turrim," or within the walls, these, between the Bell and Devereux towers, where they pass close to the church, were also then existing. We should thus have the wall of enceinte of the present Inner ward, from Lanthorn tower to Wakefield, Bell, and Devereux towers, as the extent of the fortress on the south and west fronts. The north curtain, now mostly destroyed, seems to have been of the same date as is the east curtain, though probably some of the towers upon these, the Bowyer, Jewel, Constable's, Broad Arrow, and Salt, are of later reigns.

Then there was the ditch deepened and widened by Longchamp, with a wall on the line of that of the present outer ward. The quay and the river front, from Iron gate to Byward, with St. Thomas's tower, were not then constructed, nor was the Bloody or Gatehouse tower. Probably the inner ward wall abutted direct upon the river shore.

Henry III. began his reign in 1216, and the attention of his prudent guardian, the "rector regis et regni," seems at once to have been turned to the Tower. In 1217, the sheriff of Essex and Herts is to pay to Nicholas Rowland 10$l.$ for repairs of the king's houses in the Tower; to which is added, in the next year, 8$l.$ 9$s.$ 11$d.$, and 19$l.$ 9$s.$ 11$d.$, also to the same Nicholas. About the same time (2 Hen. III.) 6$s.$ 1$d.$ is paid for the transporting the king's breastplates (loricas) to the Tower; 3 Hen. III., 9$l.$ 13$s.$ 1$d.$ is paid for repairs of the king's hall, and the broken wall of the chamber; and the houses within the ballium of the Tower are to be repaired upon the view and testimony of certain lawful men; and (5 Hen. III.), at a cost of 17s., four tables "ad mensam," for the use of the king, are to be placed in the Tower. The year before this (4 Hen. III.), the Pleas of the Crown, in the city of London, were heard before the justices in the Tower.

In 1221, Peter, Bishop of Winchester, was to have 11l. 10s. for the repairs of the king's house, executed when the Tower was in his hands; and Richard de Munfitchet was to supply Stephen de Segrave, the constable, with timber of the best quality, from Havering, for planks for the completion of the "jarellum" about the Tower.

The king was there in person in these years, for his expenses for five days there, in 1219, were 19l. 1s. 7¼d.; and next year 100 marcs were paid towards his expenses there during Lent, and 200 marcs repaid to Pandulph the legate, then Bishop of Norwich, advanced on the same account. In that year, also, the king had at the Tower a supply of 10 lampreys, part of a debt due from the city of Gloucester to his lamprey-loving father.

1221 was a busy year at the Tower. Many military implements and stores, and seven cartloads of prisoners, were brought in by Alex. de Sabrichtsworth, from Biham, the surrendered castle of Wm. de Fortibus, at a cost of 5s. 10d. Henry was there 28th February and 5th March. The next year also included several accounts connected with the siege of Biham. The works were also continued. Stephen de Segrave had 30 marcs for the repairs of the ballium wall; and Peter de St. Edward, with Andrew Buckerell, the chamberlain, 70 marcs of the amerciament levied on the London vintners, for works at the Tower. 8th Dec., 1221, Nicholas Mazon, who made the well, had 5 marcs. Timber and materials were sent in by the sheriffs of Essex and Bucks.

In 1222, 8s. 1d. was paid for the repairs of the wardrobe in the king's chamber at the Tower, and for making a chimney in the same, and 10s. for a robe for Robert le Champenies, clerk of the works. Chimneys, in those days, were not always flues within the wall, but shafts of wood, or other temporary material, placed against it.

7th Henry III., 1222-3. The Close Roll credits Richard Benger and Thomas Lamberde with 10l. 12s. 1d., which they paid by the king's precept to Peter of Poictou and his companions, keepers of the works of the "New Turrelle," or turret, of the Tower of London, for the work of the said turret. Mr. Hugo applies this entry to the Bell tower; it may, with equal or more probability, be applied to the superstructure of the Wakefield tower.

Pandulph the legate appears to have been custos in 1223, and in that capacity entertained at the Tower John de Brienne, titular King of Jerusalem, and the Grand master of the Hospital, then in England to promote a crusade. In this year the king acknowledged the receipt of "unum austurcum" [a goshawk] at the Tower. John de Monmouth and the vendors of "cableicium," or underwood, in Dean Forest, out of the king's gift thereof to the Priory of Llantony, are to find 40 chevrons for the repairs of the Tower; and the sheriffs of London are to restore the "palum coram postico," or "prop before the postern" of the Tower, and the prop outside of the Tower. 26th May, 1224, the king's crown was lodged in the Tower by the treasurer.

The Pipe Roll of the 9th Henry III., 1224-5, contains various entries relating to the Tower:—34s. 1d. was paid for "pro husciis de cute et de feltrio (housings of hide and of felt or compressed wool, or gambeson), ad balistas Regis etc. cooperiandas," for housing the king's balistæ which are in the Tower; and for iron and steel (ascero) delivered to the constable for the works there, 2 marcs. Also for charcoal (carbo), for the king's smiths' work there, 8s. 6d.; and to Thos. de Blunvill, 50 marcs for the king's works; and for charcoal for making the king's "quarells" (crossbow bolts), etc., by "Thomas Faber" (the smith), in the Tower, 8s. 7d.; and for mending the king's houses in the Tower, 29s. 7¼d.

In the 10th year, besides the sum of 42s. and 3s. 11d., for charcoal for works, Thos. de Blunvill received the value of 12l. 3s. in six caretatis, or cartloads, of lead, "ad novam turrellam turris Lond: cooperiendam," and four loads, value 8l. 0s. 19d., for the same purpose; so that the lead on the roof of the new turret cost at least 20l. 4s. 7d. At this time Blunvill had 40l. per annum as custos.

In the two next years, 1226-8, 96s. 11d. was paid for charcoal, Thos. Faber being the master workman; and Henry Fitz-Alchi had 100 marcs for the Tower works. For the three following years the rolls are silent. In 1232, Hubert de Burgh had a fee of 50l. per annum as constable; and in 16th Henry III., 113s. 10d. was paid for iron, steel, and charcoal, purchased and delivered to Roger de Smith, in the Tower, for making quarells and other work.

In 1233, the Tower became the enforced residence of Isabel, the king's sister, until her marriage with the Emperor Frederick, in 1235; and 28th April, 1236, Henry adopted the unusual course of adjourning a council of his magnates to the Tower. The assembly, as was to be expected, was but thinly attended, and in consequence was further adjourned to Westminster.

On 2nd March, 1238, 22nd Henry III., the Liberate Roll contains an entry, which is repeated as follows in the corresponding Pipe Roll :—" Et in cameris Regis in turri Lond: reparandis et chimenee Camere Regine perficiendis et uno spiro de bordis bono et decenti faciendo inter cameram et capellam nove turrelle eiusdem turris prope aulam Regis versus tamisiam xvili. iijs. viijd. per breve, etc." "And for repairing the King's chamber in the Tower of London, and completing the chimney in the Queen's chamber, and for making a good and fitting spur (partition) of boards between the chamber and chapel of the new turret of the same Tower, near the King's Hall, towards the Thames, 16l. 3s. 8d., by brief, &c." This is one of the few notices of repairs the precise place of which can be identified. The new turret is undoubtedly the first floor of the Wakefield tower, known to have been near the King's Hall and towards the Thames, and of which the chapel, or oratory, still remains.

In the same 1238, 23rd November, the Liberate Roll shows the king to have ordered the constable to cause the walls of the queen's chamber, "which is within our chamber at the Tower, to be whitewashed and pointed," and within the pointings to be painted with flowers; "and to cause the drain of the privy chamber to be made in the fashion of a hollow column, as our beloved servant John of Ely shall more fully declare to thee."

In the 24 Henry III. is a charge of 30*l*. 16*s*. 4*d*. for purchasing and conveying to the Tower, "una navata," or shipload, of marble, and four shiploads of Purbeck marble, for the works of the Tower. It is only in the cills of the two windows of the sacrarium of St. Thomas's tower that Purbeck stone has been discovered in position; but much of this material remains upon the rampart walks and in other places in the fortress, whither, no doubt, much of it was imported in this reign, and especially at this time, for the works then in progress, which in 1239 were considerable. A good deal of Kentish rag was used, and both Ryegate and Caen stone for ashlar. Often the material for building was brought a great distance. Henry II. and Edward III. used Egremont stone for Windsor. Matt. Paris describes the treasury as well filled, which unusual condition, and the looming troubles of the realm, probably disposed Henry to add to the security of his stronghold. The new works were unpopular in the city, the citizens fearing, and not without reason, that they would be employed in some way to their detriment. On this subject they addressed a remonstrance to the king, who assured them that the works were not intended to be employed to their injury. " I only," said he, " imitate my brother, reputed a wiser man than I, in rebuilding my castles."

It seems that a fine gateway and a wall were completed, but fell suddenly on St. George's night (23rd April), 1240, but were immediately rebuilt by the king. A year later, in 1241, the same structures, or as much of them as had been rebuilt, again fell down, and this time the citizens found a supernatural reason for the event. On the night of the second fall, says Matt. Paris, a certain grave and reverend priest saw a robed archbishop, cross in hand, who gazed sternly upon the walls with which the king was then girdling the tower, and striking them sharply, asked, " Why build ye these?" on which the newly built work fell as though shattered by an earthquake. The priest, too alarmed to accost the prelate, addressed himself to the shade of an attendant clerk, " Who, then, is the archbishop?" "St. Thomas the Martyr," was the answer, " by birth a citizen, who resents these works, undertaken in scorn and to the prejudice of the citizens, and destroys them beyond the power of restoration." On which the priest remarked, " What outlay and labour of the hands he has destroyed!" " Had it been," said the clerk, " simply that the starving and needy artificers thence promised themselves food, it had been tolerable, but seeing that the works were undertaken, not for the defence of the realm, but to the hurt of the citizens, even had not St. Thomas destroyed them, they had been swept away utterly by St. Edmund [archbishop] Confessor and his successors."

That night the priest told his tale, and next morning the walls about the Tower, built at a charge of about 12,000 marcs, were seen upon the ground, to the surprise but by no means to the grief of the citizens, to whom they had been as a thorn in the eye. Notwithstanding the prediction of St. Thomas, the works were at once resumed, and this time with complete success.

No doubt the wall and gateway were St. Thomas's water-gate and the adjacent curtain along the south face of the fortress, and upon the bank of the river, where the wet ground and the treacherous character of the London clay, exposed more or less in the old city ditch and that of Longchamp, would render the archbishop's task an easy one. The story may be taken to show that in 1239-40 Henry was engaged in extensive works about the Tower, including the outer ward wall and tower, the quay and the present ditch; and the present works show that they were of sufficient importance to be replaced, at whatever cost, when destroyed by an accident. Probably the architect learnt experience by the event, for it was remarkable that no serious mark of settlement from defective foundation has been observed either in the work of the outer ward or in any other part of the fortress, and this is more singular because part of the masonry must have traversed the line of the old city ditch. This stability is probably due to the great breadth of the foundations, and to the fact that the fortress contains no underground chambers, the towers below the ground level, and sometimes far above it, being solid.

The resumption of the works on the wall and west gateway did not lead to the neglect of the royal residence within. 24th Feb. 1240, 24 Henry III., the king, according to the Liberate Roll, thus addressed the custos of the works:—" We command you to cause the chamber of the queen, in the aforesaid tower, to be wainscotted without delay, and to be thoroughly whitened internally, and newly painted with roses; and to cause to be made a wall [partition] in the fashion of wainscot between the chamber and the wardrobe of the same, and let it be entirely covered externally with tile; and also cause one great chamber in the same tower to be entirely whitewashed and newly painted, and all the windows of the same chamber to be made anew with new wood and bolts and hinges, and to be painted with our arms, and barred with iron where needful. Moreover, repair and mend all the glass windows in the chapel of St. John the Baptist within the said tower, where necessary; and repair all the windows in the great chamber towards the Thames with new wood, with new bolts and hinges, and bar them well with iron; and in the corner of the same chamber make a great round turret towards the Thames, so that the drain of the last chamber may descend into the Thames; and make a new cowl on the top of the kitchen of the great tower."

The Liberate Roll of the same year, January 1240, orders "a mantel" to be painted in the Tower, with a personification of Winter with a sad visage and miserable contortions of the body.

And on the 10th of December following [25 Hen. III.] the keeper is further ordered "To repair the granary within the same tower, etc., and to cause all the leaden gutters of the great tower, through which rain water should fall from the summit of the same tower, to be carried down to the ground; so that the wall of the said tower, *which has been newly whitewashed*, may be in no wise injured by the dropping of rain water, nor be easily weakened. And make on the same tower on the south-side, at the top, deep alures of good and strong timber, entirely and well covered with lead, through which people may look even unto the foot of the said tower, and ascend, and better defend it, if need should be. And also whitewash the whole chapel of St. John the Evangelist in the same tower, and make in the same chapel three glass windows, one, to wit, on the north part, with a certain small figure of Mary holding her child; the other, on the south side, with the [subject of the] Trinity, and the third on the same south side, with St. John the Apostle and Evangelist; and paint the cross and beam beyond the altars of the same chapel, and with good colours. And cause to be made and painted two fair images, where they may be best and most decently made in the same chapel, one of St. Edward holding a ring and giving it to St. John the Evangelist. And whitewash all the old wall around our aforesaid tower."

From these orders we learn that the chapel in the White tower was whitewashed, glazed, had three painted windows, and a painted beam and rood behind the altar, besides painted figures, no doubt in fresco, on the wall, of St. Edward and St. John the Evangelist. The great chamber towards the Thames, being enumerated in conjunction with the chapel, might be supposed to be the state-room in the White tower; but "the great round turret towards the Thames, with the contained drain," could not apply to the White tower, nor indeed to any of the existing towers on the Thames front. It may have been the Lanthorn tower.

The White tower is spoken of as newly whitewashed. This was no doubt intended to make good any irregularities in the masonry, for 28 Henry III., the tower at Corfe was ordered to be pargetted with mortar where necessary, and the whole exterior to be whitewashed. It is not quite clear what were the alures, so minutely specified, on the top of the south front of the White tower; probably a bretasche or hoarding, since no other work would enable the defenders to see the foot of the wall. It might have been supposed that at so great a height no extra defence from missiles would have been necessary, and supposing the inner ward to be taken, it would be from the higher ground on the north, rather than on the south side, that the effect of archery or warlike engines would be the greatest.

In this same 25 Hen. III. Peter Bacun and Richard de Fresingfeld and their fellows, keepers of the Tower works, had 36*l.*; also 24*l.* 40*d.* was paid for twenty breastplates and twenty halbergeons, purchased for the defence of the Tower, and delivered to the constable. So important were the works at this time that an order was made that "before closing the Exchequer the barons were to audit the accounts of the custos of the works of the king's Tower of London." In the 26 Hen. III. the chaplain ministering in the Tower chapel had 50*s.* per annum.

Among the regulations in use about this time were several relating to the legal position of the Tower, recorded in the Liber Albus. Thus, when the Exchequer was closed, the mayor was to be presented at the Tower, and the pleas of the city with the crown were sometimes held there, and when this was the case the city barons were to place their own "janitors" outside the Tower gate, and the king's janitor was to be on the inside. They further had an "ostiarius" outside the door of the hall where the pleas were held, to introduce the barons, and the king had an ostiarius inside. The hall was no doubt the building now superseded by the office of Ordnance, and the entrance to which is thought to have been by the now modernised doorway close east of the Wakefield tower.

The next entry discovered is upon the Liberate Roll, 29 Hen. III., 3rd December, 1244, by which the constable of the Tower is ordered to deliver to Edward Fitz-Otho as much lead as shall be necessary to execute certain specified works at Westminster. It was in this year that Griffith ap Llewelyn, in attempting to escape by a rope from his prison in the Tower, fell and broke his neck. Griffith was corpulent, and the White tower whence he let himself down was lofty. His rope was composed of bed linen and the like, and broke. 30th April, the king publicly declares this unfortunate accident, and attributes the neglect to the attendants, whose duty it was to take charge of the prisoner.

31 Hen. III., 1246-7, the constable had sixty marcs for constructing "quandam turrellam," a certain turret; and next year forty marcs more were paid for making a certain turret, a privy chamber, and other works. 33 Hen. III., fourteen cartloads of lead were purchased for 32*l.* 9*s.* 10*d.*, and delivered to Peter Blund, the constable.

In the 34 Hen. III. the Pipe Roll shows Edward of Westminster and the constable to have had sixty marcs for Tower works, and the keepers thirty marcs for repairing and covering the king's houses and for lead for the works. Next year, 1250-1, ten marcs went for repairing and covering walls and turrets, and 4*l.* 8*s.* 6*d.* for two loads of lead for the same operation upon the king's houses.

37 Hen. III., Adam de Lamburn, master of the Tower works, had 10*l.*, and the keepers, also for works, 30*l.*, and Adam again 12*l.*, and next year the keepers for works fifty marcs more. 39 Hen. III., 1254-5, 22*l.* 20*d.* was paid for a house for the king's elephant, 40 ft. long by 20 ft. wide. This was a present from the

King of France, and is said by Matt. Paris to have been the first elephant seen north of the Alps. There was also paid for repairs of houses and turrets, 59*l.* 6*s.* 2*d.* Next year 52*l.* 11*s.* 3*d.* was paid for works begun by the sheriff of the year preceding, and for Tower shortcomings 37*l.* 2*s.* 9*d.*; and 41 Hen. III., 90*l.* 14*s.* 9*d.* for stones for completing the already commenced Tower quay, and for the Great Wardrobe and other deficiencies.

42 Hen. III., 1257-8, two sums of 101*s.* 8*d.* and 4*l.* 12*s.* 6*d.* were paid for lead gutters and other repairs; and 43 Hen. III., 36*l.* 3*s.* 8*d.* for repairs of the king's houses, and for making a new stable and repairing an old one, and gutters, and a "claustura," or partition, for the same tower, 17*l.* 15*s.* 7*d.*

This was the year, 1258, in which, under the Provisions of Oxford, the barons seized the Tower and placed in it Hugh le Bigod as custos. There was in this year a brief,—"In emendacionem planchicii* turris Lond : et turrella ejusdem turris versus aquam cooperienda, etc." Henry soon afterwards, by the permission of the Pope, broke faith with his subjects, and regained the Tower, where he was resident in February, 1261, and ordered 40*s.* to Theodore de Castell for iron for the King's Tower works, taken from him.

The circumstances of the country forced the king into active measures for the conservation of the fortress. He spent Christmas, 1260, there with his queen, and employed the money at his command in com-

* "Plancherium" is an upper chamber, probably what is meant here.

pleting the defences. Probably it was about this time that the water-gate was ready, and the tidal ditch converted into a wet moat. Matt. Paris mentions the efforts now made to strengthen the place, and how the king at this time invited the citizens to swear fidelity to him, and to take service in his army then mustering outside the city. He also again named the Tower as the place of meeting for a Parliament to be holden 21st February, 1261, 45 Henry III.

The councillors did not respond to the summons. The king kept Easter in the fortress, whither the bailiffs of Gloucester were directed, 18th March, to send up daily as many lampreys as they could take; and, 17th April, the bailiffs of Waltham were to supply 60s. worth of good fine bread and loaves of four for a penny, and to send them to the royal pantler at the Tower for the usual dole on Easter eve. Similar perquisitions were addressed to the bailiffs of Barking and Dartford, to those of Kingston and Watford, to the extent of 40s., and to the mayor and sheriffs of London to 20l. In all 33l. worth of bread was to be distributed. There were also orders for 164 tunics on the part of the king and queen, to be delivered to the royal almoner, and 21 tunics on the part of the royal children; all to be distributed to the poor according to custom. Henry remained at the Tower till about the 20th April.

Prince Edward returned to England in that year, but did not act with his father, whose advisers he distrusted. The king, however, seems to have held the Tower, and kept Christmas of 1261 within its walls.

Thence, leaving John Mansell in charge, he went to Dover, and so by Rochester to Winchester for Whitson. There, however, the barons prepared to seize him, and he retired to the Tower, where he remained till October. Christmas of 1262 he again spent at the Tower.

After some time passed beyond sea, and a Christmas at Canterbury, Henry failed to meet his enemies at Worcester, and returned, 47th Henry III., to the Tower, where, with his queen, Prince Edward, and the King of the Romans, he consulted with the mayor and aldermen of London on the subject of de Montfort, and soon afterwards, with that nobleman himself. One result was the placing Hugh le Despenser in charge of the Tower. It was in this year that the queen, leaving the Tower by water to join the prince at Windsor, was hooted at and pelted by the populace on the bridge, and forced to put back. In the same year John Sperling, at a cost of 7l., erected a "palicium," or palisade, between the Tower and the city wall; and two years later he had altogether 25l. 10s. 3d. for covering-in the king's houses, repairing the king's garderobe, etc.

Henry was again at the Tower in 1265, after the battle of Evesham; and in 1268 the fortress, then commanded by Hugh Fitz-Otho, and containing the Papal legate, Ottobon, was besieged by Gilbert, Earl of Gloucester. The Jews, who with their families had been harboured in the Tower, contributed personally to its defence. Gloucester threw up earthworks and attempted a blockade; but in May and June, Henry, approaching by Windsor and Stratford, encamped there for two months, and, throwing in a reinforcement, brought out the legate by the south postern towards the river, and established him with the army at Stratford, forcing Gloucester to sue for peace.*

The hall of the Tower and other houses cost 20*l.* in repairs in 1268-9, and in other repairs 12*l.* in the next year; but nothing is recorded concerning the following and two closing years of the long reign of Henry III.

With the death of Henry and the earlier years of his son the history of the Tower, as a specimen of military architecture, may be said to decline, and its history as a state prison, if not to begin, to preponderate. Edward at once continued and completed the works commenced by his father, and probably was thus employed for ten or twelve years. In 1274, 2nd Edward, the treasurer was to pay 200 marcs towards the work of the ditch, then nearly made, about the bulwark. This was the loop ditch surrounding the barbican, planned by Henry III., but no doubt then first excavated. Besides this, in 1287, the main ditch seems to have been under enlargement, and its encroachment upon St. Katherine's land was valued in 1302 at 73*s.* per annum. The clay taken out was sold by the constable to the tylers working in East Smithfield. In 1289 it yielded 20*s.*, but had averaged

* " Per posticum quod de Turri plagam meridionalem respicit et fluvio contignatur, legatum potenter eduxit, et ejus loco defensores idoneos intromisit, eductoque legato occupatores urbis non immerito deridebat, et procedens usque Stratford ad tria millaria prope London sine quolibet obice castra fixit."—Chron. T. Wykes.

7*l*.—about 100*l*. in our day. Bayley tells that 600 Jews were at one time imprisoned here by Edward, 1281-2, as clippers of the coin. On 8th Oct., 1303, the king, then at Kinloss, ordered the Abbot of Westminster and his 80 monks to be imprisoned in the Tower, on a charge of stealing 100,000*l*. of the royal treasure. The following mandate, of three years' later date, shows the form in which prisoners were committed. It relates to a Scottish gentleman of rank. "Mons: P: de Graham et vadletz, soient envecz, par bon conduyt, a Londres, et livrez au Conestable de la Tour illucques: et q'il les face garder en fers, en bon et sur lieu, denz meisme la Tour, si sauuement, et si surement, come le Conestable voudra respondre de eux, corps pour corps; et q'il lor face trouver lor sustenance meanement."

In 1307 occurs a curious sanitary order. "Whereas Margaret, Queen of England, is about to dwell awhile in the Tower, the mayor and sheriffs, to prevent infection of the air, 'per accensionem rogorum,' are to prohibit and punish any one 'burning pyres' or doing anything by which the air can be corrupted." Dated, Carlisle, 28 June.

Edward II. was more dependent upon the Tower for personal safety than as a prison. His eldest daughter, hence called "Jane de la Tour," was here born. In 1312 he put the Tower in a state of defence against his barons; and, in 1324, shut here the two Lords, Roger Mortimer of Wigmore and his namesake of Chirk. Their escape is described in the "Opus Chronicorum." They were shut up "in eminentiori et aretiori loco Turris," which should mean the White tower. They drugged the drink of their keepers, and in a stormy night escaped by breaking the wall, and thus reached the annexed palace kitchen, from the top of which, by a rope-ladder and aided from within the walls, they reached the Thames and thus fled the country.

Two years later, Mortimer of Wigmore returned with the queen, and took arms against Edward, who put the Tower in order, sending thither 100 coats of mail [Pell Rolls, 158], and there, 20th June, he received the city authorities. On the 2nd October he fled, leaving his son, John of Eltham, in the Tower, and Stapleton, Bishop of Exeter, in charge of the city. The citizens, as is well known, rose and beheaded the bishop, and next day, falling in with John de Weston, the constable, they extorted from him the keys, and entered the fortress. They seem, however, only to have freed the prisoners, turned out the officials, and appointed their own men, under the nominal authority of Prince John.

The first years of Edward III.'s reign were spent, perforce, in the Tower, until he put down Mortimer and assumed the government. Probably the Beauchamp and Salt towers, and perhaps the Bowyer, were his work. In the 9th of his reign, by commission, dated Berwick, 16th Oct., 1336, he ordered a survey of the defects of the Tower to be made, and a jury to be empanelled to declare what repairs were needed. This return was made without delay, and is printed by Bayley. It mentions the gate towards St. Katherine's, the steps and passages upon the wall, a chamber over the Water gate ; "Corande's" tower and "le Moneye" tower ; the chapel of the Tower ; the king and queen's chapel ; two turrets over the old gate, one called "La Plummerye ;" and the quay opposite the Thames, with the little postern at one end and "Petywales"at the other. Beauchamp, Bowyer, and most of the other towers are not named,—probably because some were not then built, and others, the work of his grandfather, did not need repair. "Le Blanche tour" seems not to be the Keep, called then "Alta turris." The other parts named are numerous, but evidently belonged to the palace ward, now destroyed. The result of the return was, that the Tower, next year, was put in order and garrisoned. The Close Roll (10th Edward III.) mentions that, in 1337, the Sheriffs of London were to pay 40*l*. out of the farm of the city, to be spent on "the great Tower," then in great need of repair ; and the Sheriff of Kent was to bring oak from Havering for the works. The sheriffs of Surrey and Sussex also had to provide 20*l*. for the same service.

The Tower was Edward's chief arsenal. Thither, 1337-8, the sheriffs of London were to send "5 millia ferri et 200 bordas de Estland (East country planks), ac centum quarter carbonum maritimorum" (seacoal), for making anchors for the "Christopher" and "Cogge Edward," and for certain works on the Tower. [Abb. Rot. Orig. II. p. 116.] Edward was at this time much engaged in preparing for foreign wars, and it was to the Tower that he returned suddenly from Tournay, towards midnight, 30th November, 1340, and punished the constable for negligence. Also between 1340 and 1342 he was much at the Tower, and one of his daughters was born here. The records also show that the Mint had a considerable share of the royal attention.

Mr. Hunter has shown [Arch. xxxii. 380] that, as early as 1347, bills were paid for the manufacture, probably two or three years earlier, of "pulvis pro ingeniis;" and in 1346, "ad opus ipsius Regis pro gunnis suis," 9 cwt. 12 lb. of saltpetre, and 886 lb. of quick sulphur, were had; so that gunpowder was then no doubt manufactured in the Tower.

About the same time the Tower received the first of a series of illustrious foreign prisoners of war. John, King of Scots, taken at Neville's Cross, was brought here in January, 1347, and remained here eleven years; so late as 1357-8, 2*l*. 12*s*. 9*d*. being paid for medicines supplied to him. Later, in the same year with John, came Charles of Blois, nephew to Philip of France; and still later John de Vienne, governor of Calais, and the twelve brave burgesses of that town. Finally, in 1350, here was lodged John, King of France, and the nobles taken with him, and in the same place of safety, the 47,171*l*. 1*s*. 4*d*., the first instalment of his ransom.

In 24 Edw. III., 1350-1, John de Alkeshull had commission to take, throughout the kingdom, "petram, buscam, carbones, maeremium, plumbum, vitrum, ferrum et tegulam;" that is, stone, logs, coal, timber, lead, glass, iron and shingle, and all things needful for the king's works at Westminster, Windsor, and the

Tower. How these materials were divided is not known. Windsor probably received the chief share of them.

In 1354 the king proposed to alter the constitution of the chapel of St. Peter ad Vincula at the Tower, and incorporate it as a college with a dean and three canons, instead of a rector and chaplains. This, however, does not seem then to have been effected, as both Richard II. and Henry IV. nominated a rector to the "Free Chapel of St. Peter." The actual incorporation did not come to pass until the last year of the reign of Edward IV. It was in 1354 proposed that the standards of weight and measure should be kept at the Tower; and this year the king ordered the city ditch to be cleansed, and prevented from overflowing into the Tower ditch. In Stowe's time the filth was taken off by a sewer from the city ditch.

Appointments of armourers, bowyers, engineers of the war-slings, &c., show that the store of weapons of war continued to be considerable. In 33 Edw. III. all the bows, strings, arrows, "hancipes (two-handed winches) pro balistis tendendis,"[*] in the custody of W. Rotherel, in the Tower, were to be packed in chests, quivers, butts, pipes and barrels, and sent to Sandwich to cross the water with the king. In 1360-2 various sums were spent in repairs of the king's record-house in the Tower containing the Chancery Rolls; probably the Wakefield tower.

[*] A balista was an engine for throwing darts as a catapult threw stones and heavy substances. Both were worked by windlasses or winches.

Richard II. fulfilled the usual custom of lodging a short time in the Tower before his coronation, that he might proceed in state to that ceremony through the city. Here also he took refuge during Wat Tyler's rebellion, after which Arnold Brocas was paid 3*l*. 6*s*. 8*d*. for repairing the door broken open by the common rebels within the Tower. In 1380-1 a code of regulations was drawn up for the better government of the place. In 1385-6 cannon were sent hence to Porchester. In 1387 Richard came here to escape his uncle the Duke of Gloucester, and at Christmas in that year he was blockaded by the rebel lords, to whom he gave audience within the fortress.

Two years later, in 1389, it was from the Tower that the king went to hold a great feast and tournament in London; and here, in 1396, his new queen, Isabel of France, was lodged before her coronation. Here, finally, Richard signed his abdication in favour of Henry of Lancaster. No work at the Tower can positively be attributed to this reign, or the succeeding one of Henry IV.

It appears from the Issue Roll and the Pell records of the 1 Hen. V., that breakfast was provided at the Tower at a cost of 2*l*. 16*s*. 8*d*., for Thomas Earl of Arundel, Henry le Scrop, LORD DE ROOS, and the mayor of London, commissioners for trying traitors. This was William, seventh baron, ancestor of the present lieutenant-governor, whose ancestors on the male side—the Fitzgeralds—also frequently partook of the hospitality of the Tower, though in the less agreeable capacity of prisoners.

Henry V. revived the old glories of the prison by sending hither Charles Duke of Orleans, taken at Agincourt. An illumination of the period, given by Lord de Ros, shows the duke to have been lodged in the state rooms in the White tower, and shows also the four windows of the Great Hall, which adjoined Wakefield tower on the east.

The strong monarchs employed the Tower as a prison, the weak ones as a fortress; and, under Henry VI., it appears in this latter capacity. In 1460, Lord Scales, the king's governor, was besieged by the Earl of Salisbury, Lord Cobham, and Sir John Wenlock. The city men attacked the west front; Wenlock, from St. Katherine's; and Cobham, with the artillery, from the Southwark shore, firing across the river. When the south ditch was cleared out and levelled in 1842-3, several round shot of iron, and about thirty of Kentish rag-stone, from $4\frac{1}{2}$ to 10 in. and in one case 17 in. diameter, were found, which are supposed to have fallen there on this occasion.

Edward IV. is reputed to have built a bulwark outside the west gate by the Lion tower. In the 11th of his reign payments were made for arms and ammunition for the defence, and for work upon the fortifications of the Tower. The workmen were brought from Calais. In the same year money was allowed for the expenses of Henry VI., then prisoner in the Tower. Richard III., during his brief reign, pressed masons and bricklayers to complete certain repairs at the Tower.

Probably the walls and towers were allowed to decay by Henry VII.; for Henry VIII., in 1532, ordered a survey to be made with a view to a general repair, which was executed shortly afterwards. The repairs were very considerable, and the masonry was executed in Caen stone backed with brick, and, unfortunately, very much of the Tower seems to have been so faced or cased, and otherwise very seriously altered. The survey is very minute, and throws light on much that is now destroyed. Mention is made of "Burbedge tower," on the wall between Bowyer and Brick towers, evidently the present Brick tower, the then "Brick" being the present Martin tower. "St. Martin's" tower was then the outer gate, now "Middle" tower. The present Salt tower was then Julius Cæsar's tower, and the older Lanthorn tower was called New tower. Wakefield is called "the tower where the king's records lie," and "Bloody" was then Garden tower. "Byward" was "the Wardyng gate." Two timber bridges, evidently drawbridges, were to be renewed at the west entrance. The keep was then, as now, the White tower, distinguished by its four turrets.

Byward tower had a narrow escape in 1548. A Frenchman who lodged in "the round bulwark called the Warden gate, between the west gate and the postern, or drawbridge," blew up the bulwark, and himself, with gunpowder. It was rebuilt. There was also in this reign of Edward VI. a drawbridge between Iron and Traitors' gate, evidently Cradle tower. This was used for the reception of great prisoners, the strong iron gate (St. Thomas's) being almost out of use.

The buildings of the palace probably had fallen into

decay in the reign of Elizabeth, by whom, or by James, the Great Hall was removed. Other buildings followed. Many were destroyed by Cromwell, and many by James II., to make room for a new Ordnance office, and the remains of the Lanthorn tower were taken down late in the last century. The White tower underwent a final disfigurement at the hands of Sir C. Wren in 1663, who Italianised its openings, cased a part of its exterior, and rebuilt two of its turrets. Sir Christopher's work may be traced throughout the fortress by the Portland stone introduced by him, just as the work of Henry VIII. is indicated by the use of brickwork and rough-cast, and the practice of closing the joints of the masonry with chips and spawls of flint. The ditch was cleansed in 1663, and the quay refaced.

The Tower, at the commencement of the present century, was an extraordinary jumble of ancient and later buildings, the towers and walls being almost completely encrusted by the small official dwellings by which the area was closely occupied. A great fire in 1841 removed the unsightly armoury of James II. and William III. on the north of the inner ward, but the authorities at the time were not ripe for a fire. The armoury was replaced by a painfully durable Tudor barrack, and the repairs and additions were made with little reference to the character of the fortress. More recently the general improvement in public taste has made its way even into the Tower. Mr. Salvin has been appointed its architect, and Lord de Ros its lieutenant.

Thus much of the Tower as an ancient and very curious military structure, which, throughout the additions, alterations, and subtractions of eight centuries, still preserves the character of an early fortress, and very much of original and peculiar work. It may be that, in some respects, the Tower cannot be compared with others of the great feudal castles of England. It does not, like Dover and Bambro', stand on the edge of a lofty cliff, commanding an equal expanse of land and water. It has not the solitary grandeur of Corfe, nor its old associations with the Anglo-Saxon times. It does not, like Conway, Carnarvon, Beaumaris, and Harlech, bear the impress of one mind in its design, of one hand in its execution: neither can it boast the rich surroundings of Ludlow, Warwick, or Kenilworth, nor the proud pre-eminence of Windsor, the present residence of the Sovereign, the seat of the oldest and most illustrious order of Christian chivalry, the cynosure of four fair counties, rising amidst a rich mantle of forest verdure diversified with the silver windings of the Thames, and the venerable walls and courts of Eton.

The Tower of London can put forth none of these various claims to our attention, but it is not the less the most interesting fortress in Britain. It is the work of the great Norman conqueror of England, founded by the Founder of her monarchy. It is the citadel of the metropolis of Britain, and was long the most secure residence of her greatest race of kings. Here they deposited the treasure of the empire and the jewels and regalia of their crown. Here they secured the persons of their prisoners, and minted and stored up their coin. Here the courts of law and of exchequer were not unfrequently held; here the most valuable records were preserved; and here were fabricated and preserved long-bow and cross-bow, sword lance and pike, armour of proof, balistæ scorpions and catapults, then the artillery and munitions of feudal war. Here, too, as these older machines were laid aside, was first manufactured that "subtle grain," that "pulvis ad faciendum le crak," and these "gonnys and bombards of war," which were to revolutionise the military art, until they themselves should be superseded by later inventions, of which the ancient keep is still the grand storehouse and armoury of the country.

But the Tower has memories surpassing even its associations with the military glories of the state. It has been the prison and the scaffold of not a few of the best and bravest of English blood. Percy and Mortimer, Hastings and Clinton, Neville, and Beauchamp, Arundel, Devereux, Stafford and Howard,—those "old stocks who so long withstood the waves and weathers of time,"—have here found a grave. Here the great house of Plantagenet flourished and was cut down. Here England's Elizabeth learned the uses of adversity, and here Raleigh solaced his confinement with the composition of that History which has made his name great in letters as in naval enterprise.

Here too, captive within these walls, and through these gates led to death, were More and Fisher, martyrs for the ancient, and Anne Askew for the purer faith; Lady Jane Grey, the most innocent and accomplished of victims; Strafford and Laud, firm for the old tyranny; Sir John Elliot, who died broken-hearted in the prison for the new liberty.

No other fortress, no bastile in France, no bargello in Italy, no prison-castle in Spain or Germany, is so deeply associated with the history of its nation, or with the progress of civil and religious liberty.

III.

THE CHAPTER-HOUSE OF WESTMINSTER.

By GEORGE GILBERT SCOTT, R.A.

THE works of King Henry III. at Westminster Abbey hold a very marked position among the productions of English Architecture of the thirteenth century, both on account of their intrinsic excellence, and as being among the earliest of the more developed examples of the second of the two great classes into which the architecture of that century divides itself— that which is characterised by the fully developed tracery window, as distinguished from the detached or grouped lancets of the beginning of the century, and from what Professor Willis has called the "plate tracery" windows, which both accompanied and immediately succeeded them.

The plate tracery, though, as a matter of fact as well as of theory, the transitional link between the lancet and the tracery systems, can hardly be said to have originated at the period of that transition, but seems rather to have been adopted at that time from amongst older forms, and developed as peculiarly fitted to aid in the striving after greater size and unity in the windows than had previously existed.

The principle of placing two or more openings

under a comprising arch, and piercing the enclosed tympanum, was of early date, and among our own buildings we are familiar with it in the triforiums of our Norman as well as early pointed churches, while in domestic architecture it was of common occurrence. At a later period, however, it became more general and more systematic, till it needed only the piercing of the spaces between the openings in the window-heads to convert them into actual tracery.

This final change seems to have been adopted in France somewhat earlier than in England; or, at least, to have found earlier favour there than here. Our old buildings are not sufficiently accurately dated to enable us to say at what precise time it became prevalent, though we certainly find buildings in which it does *not* appear reaching down (as in the case of Bishop Northwold's work at Ely) as late as 1255; while, in Salisbury Cathedral (dating from 1220 to 1258), it only appears here and there, and apparently in the later parts. In the Chapel of Nine Altars at Durham, where it appears in the end windows, it has been proved to be a later insertion. The eastern portions of Lincoln Cathedral, in which it is magnificently developed, are but indefinitely dated as having been carried out between 1256 and 1282, and the chapter-house and cloisters at Salisbury, as well as many other works in this style, are ill-defined as to their precise age.

The work of Henry III. at Westminster would also be but loosely dated, were it not for some remnants of the old accounts which have been recently discovered. Till then we knew little more than that they were commenced in 1245 and brought to a close in 1269.

The chapter-house singles itself out from among these beautiful works as a structure perfect in itself, of a purely English type as to its plan and outline, and as carrying out the principle of window tracery in a fuller and grander degree than any part of the church; and it is a happy accident which has enabled us to determine its date with absolute precision. We had, it is true, an approximation to it in the statement of Matthew Paris, who, under the date of 1250, says, "*Ædificavit Dominus Rex Capitulum incomparabile*," but this might have referred to the laying of the first stone, while the works might have lingered, and the architecture changed from the first intention; but, happily, in a fragment of the old accounts, discovered by my friend Mr. Burtt, bearing date 1253, we have, among other works relating to the chapter-house, an entry for *canvas* to fill in the windows, followed by purchases of glass for them; so that we know that these noble tracery windows were completed at that date; that is to say, within eight years from the commencement of the rebuilding of the church; and thus we may fairly assume that, when in 1245 this work was undertaken, its design and character had been fully determined; and as this date agrees with that of the *Sainte Chapelle* of Paris, the windows of which are of similar character, it would appear that at that time our English Architecture was running a pretty parallel course with that of France.

The chapter-houses of English monastic and capitular establishments were either circular, polygonal, or rectangular, very much, as it would seem, at the option of the builders. The majority were, no doubt, of an oblong form, as those at Canterbury, Gloucester, Exeter, Chester, Bristol, and nearly all of our ruined abbeys, as at Fountains, Furness, &c., and sometimes they were apsidal at the east end, as at Durham and Reading.

The round and polygonal type might have been suggested by the churches and baptisteries of the same form,* and it was so well suited to the purposes of a chapter-house, that one does not wonder at its frequent adoption—though it would appear to have been, on the whole, more favoured by secular canons than by monks. The earliest specimen, so far as I recollect, in England, that at Worcester—which is somewhat early Norman—would, however, suggest that it began with the monks; and our own example, at Westminster, shows that they had by no means discontinued it. Those, however, at Lincoln, Salisbury, Lichfield, York, Southwell, Wells, Hereford, and Howden—all on the same type—belonged to secular establishments.† Nor can I find any regular rule as to

---

* Mr. Clutton suggests that they may have been taken from the *Bema* or apse of the early churches, in which the bishop and clergy sat, somewhat as they afterwards did in chapter-houses.

† Mr. Clutton, whose excellent lecture on Chapter-houses I have referred to since writing the present paper, is of opinion that the rule was definite that the regulars should have rectangular chapter-houses, and the seculars those of the round or polygonal form. He accounts for the round one at Worcester by that church having been

their position; for, though for the most part the chapter-houses of monasteries were entered from the eastern walk of the cloister, the same is the case at Lincoln, Salisbury, Hereford, and Exeter, though the establishments were secular. The irregular approaches, however, from the church itself, as at York, Lichfield, Southwell, Wells, Howden, &c., are, so far as I have noticed, peculiar to secular churches.

What was the form of the Westminster Chapter-house previously to its reconstruction by Henry III., we have no means of ascertaining, so far at least as I am aware. The notice of it in the poetical life of Edward the Confessor which was written during the time of Henry III., only says:—

"Clostre i fait chapitre a frund
Vers Orient vouse e rund"—

which would appear dubious as to whether intended to express that its east end was round (as at Reading), or that it was itself round (as at Worcester), and stood to the east of the cloister; but it seems more naturally to express the latter.

I have sometimes fancied that the walls of the crypt, which are of vast thickness, might be those of

at one time secular, and for the rectangular chapter-house at Exeter by the cathedral having originally belonged to a monastery. The polygonal form of that at Westminster, he has more difficulty in accounting for; but suggests that its uses or dignity as belonging to a royal establishment, might have been peculiar. His rule, that the chapter-houses of secular cathedrals were all of the round or polygonal type, may possibly have held good in England, but certainly not elsewhere. In Wales, for instance, all the four cathedrals were secular, but none of them had polygonal chapter-houses.

L

the early chapter-house; but I can find nothing to confirm this surmise; for, not only does no external surface now visible indicate an early date, but the central line of the chapter-house, when produced westward, crosses the buildings of Edward the Confessor at a point which seems wholly to disagree with the arrangement of its bays, which would hardly have been the case with two structures of the same period.

The chapter-house, like that at Wells, is raised on a substructure, or crypt. It is approached from the cloister by an outer and an inner vestibule; the former of very limited height, owing to its passing under the dormitory; the latter lofty, and containing the flight of steps by which the raised level of the chapter-house is reached.

The outer vestibule is divided into two walks, by small columns of Purbeck marble, and is entered at either end by two low and segmentally-arched openings formed of Purbeck marble, in which no doors were ever hung. The arch in the cloister, which rises above the two outer entrances, is magnificently decorated, its mouldings being filled with foliage and figures, and the surface of the wall being diapered with foliated scroll work, surrounding a niche, which contained a figure of the Blessed Virgin,* on either

---

* This fact we learn from Abbot Ware's book of the Customs of the Abbey, written in the thirteenth century. This volume has always been said to have been destroyed at the fire in the Cotton Library in 1731, but its parched and shrivelled leaves have been preserved in the British Museum, and have recently undergone a restoring process by means of which the whole has become legible. The present Dean has had a copy made which is deposited in the

side of which were angels. The whole, though deplorably decayed, still shows evidences of having been richly coloured and gilt.

One walk of this outer vestibule was, till a few years back, walled off, and a portion of its vaulting had been destroyed to make way for a staircase to the library, which had been formed out of a part of the ancient dormitory. I discovered some time since the position of the original stairs to the dormitory, and, by restoring them, was enabled to remove the obstructions of the vestibule and to restore the lost portion of its vaulting.

The bosses in the vaulting of this vestibule are peculiarly beautiful. One of them is remarkably well preserved, and quite a gem of foliated carving. The paving of the walk which had been so long closed still shows the effects of the monks' feet as they entered in double file.

The inner vestibule is divided into two very unequal bays. Those on the south side are occupied by windows—one of them a single lancet, now blocked up by the enlargement of a buttress, and the other a large window of three lights, with a kind of plate tracery between their heads.

The northern side is also pierced with two windows, but these do not look into the open air, but throw a borrowed light upon the altar of St. Faith in the old revestry, which lay between the vestibules and the

---

Abbey Library. The contents are most curious and interesting, and, were I treating of the *uses* of the chapter-house, would supply me with very full information.

transept of the church.* The west wall of this inner vestibule, over its double entrance, is decorated with window-like tracery, in the openings of which were statues on brackets; but at its eastern end was its chief glory—the magnificent double portal leading into the chapter-house itself. The jambs and arch of this noble entrance are profusely enriched with carved work of the most exquisite description. The shafts, and their richly-carved capitals, are of Purbeck marble, and the mouldings enriched with the most beautiful foliage, interspersed with figures delightfully carved, and treated as sharply and delicately as if wrought in silver.

The doorway was divided in the centre by a column of Purbeck marble, and its head occupied by a large circle, but what this circle contained is unfortunately unknown. Over the arch of the doorway, within the chapter-house, are two fine niches, which contain full-length figures of the Archangel Gabriel and the Blessed Virgin. In the spandrils are angels censing, the intervening surfaces being filled with diaper work. The figure of the Blessed Virgin I had the happiness to discover some years back, before the wainscoting and presses were removed;—that of the Archangel had long since been removed into one of the windows of the vestibule. They are very excellent specimens of the sculpture of this period.

* For the dedication of this altar we are indebted to Abbot Ware's book of *Consuetudines*. The figure painted over the altar had long been said to suit no other than St. Faith, but we had no record of such an altar. In Ware's volume, however, we find the altar of St. Faith committed to the care of the *Revestiarius*.

The chapter-house is an octagon, the diagonals of which measure sixty feet; or, in other words, it is an octagon inscribed in a circle of that diameter. In this dimension it closely agrees with several others of our ancient chapter-houses. In height it exceeds most of them. If its diagonal be viewed as the base of an equilateral triangle, its height would agree with that of the same triangle; or, to take another view, the arches from the central pillar to the angles of the octagon are in height from the floor equal to a double triangle or a perfect vesica piscis of the width of the half diagonal.

The central pillar is of Purbeck marble, consisting of a column surrounded by eight detached shafts. It is of great height and extreme lightness, and its capital beautifully carved. The groining, which shot up from it, has unhappily been lost, excepting only a few courses at the springing; but I have discovered its moulded ribs built up into one of the windows. Each side is occupied by a spacious window, filling nearly the whole width between the corner shafts. These windows are generally of four lights; the mullions are of Purbeck marble, and the heads filled with vast circles and quatrefoils. One of these, which abuts against the angle of the church, is not pierced, but its design and details are the same as the others. Were it not for this, which is far more perfect in its preservation than the actual windows, their design might not readily have been discovered in all its details. The window over the doorway is shorter than the others, and was divided into five lights: its tracery is unfortunately gone.

Nothing can be nobler than this series of vast windows, were they not obstructed and mutilated as we now see them. The spaces beneath the windows are arcaded, with five arches in each. These arches are of a trefoil form, and richly moulded, the spaces over them being filled with diapering of varied patterns. The five arches which occupy the eastern wall are much richer, and more deeply set, than the others. They formed the seats of the five great dignitaries of the Abbey, viz., the abbot (in the centre), the prior or provost, the sub-prior, the third prior, and the fourth prior.*

The capitals of the columns bearing the canopies of these seats are charmingly carved in Purbeck marble.

The seats all round are of stone, in two ranges, with a sort of foot-pace beneath them, or it may be one seat and two foot-paces. It is the backs of this arcading which contain the paintings so justly celebrated. The finest of these, by far, occupy the backs of the eastern stalls—three only now remain, with a small portion of a fourth—and they are in a sadly decayed and mutilated condition. The central arch contains a figure of Our Lord, as if exhibiting His wounds; the side-arches contain large figures of angels surrounded by others of smaller size. They are treated

* This list is taken from Abbot Ware's *Consuetudines*: given not with reference to the chapter-house, but while enumerating the order of the stalls of the choir with their occupants.

with great skill, in a style not much later than that of Giotto. On the feathers of the wings are written the names of virtues.

These paintings are carefully described by Sir Charles Eastlake, in his book on the history of oil painting.

The other sides have paintings of a later period, and very inferior merit, for the most part illustrating the Apocalypse, though containing other scenes from the life of St. John. Beneath these, and also on the fronts of the seats, are remnants of the representations of animals, like those in the old bestiaries, with their names inscribed in English. The floor is paved with magnificent encaustic tiles, which have happily been preserved by a wood floor which covers them, and are among the finest which have come down to us.

The interior, as a whole, is less rich in its details than that of the sister chapter-house at Salisbury, which was probably erected in some degree in imitation of this, a few years later. It is, however, more lofty, and nobler in its character.

The excellent lecture of Mr. Clutton, which I have referred to since first writing this paper, contains an interesting comparison between the two sister works, which I must be excused for transcribing *in extenso* :—

"The peculiarities, then, of Salisbury in reference to those of Westminster, and in which they agree, are these : they are both the largest of existing chapter-houses, being each about 60 ft. in diameter. Like its fellow, Westminster is wonderfully, almost painfully, slight in its construction, but it is *unlike*, in being built.

in a very superior manner, and, be it observed, by the regular clergy, who always built stronger and better than did the secular. This fact is almost universal. The large voids caused by the size of the windows, the very small abutments at the angles of the buildings, in width as well as in projection, are peculiar to both: Westminster, however, has had flying buttresses, one or two of which remain and appear to be of subsequent putting up, although, architecturally, they are of corresponding date with the building.

"The windows in both examples very nearly assimilate. They are composed of four openings, the tracery filling the heads being divided, and again subdivided into two orders. The larger are filled with a circle containing an octofoil; the two smaller with quatrefoils; that at Salisbury within a circle, at Westminster worked out of the principal mouldings. The same profusion in the use of Purbeck marble is also apparent. The central shafts, the columns at the angles supporting the vaulting, and decorating the windows, are of that material, and are for the most part of the same form and arrangement. At Westminster, however, the columns at the angles supporting the vaulting are single ones: at Salisbury they are composed of three. Again, at Westminster these columns and those to the windows have no intervening bands of mouldings, as are to be seen in Salisbury, features which, in their case, greatly improve the appearance of the latter building. I think, from the remains of the groining at Westminster, that that at Salisbury exactly resembles it. These, then, are the chief peculiarities in which it may be seen both correspond. The high-pitched roof at Westminster was removed in 1714; this is a recorded fact, and confirms the opinion set forth in my report, that no chapter-house of a polygonal shape was ever entirely finished without the addition of this very characteristic feature.

"The distinctive features of these two buildings consist, first, in the arcades round the interior walls. At Salisbury each bay is divided into seven stalls: at Westminster the same space into five only. The arches of the former are very delicately and richly moulded; the shafts of Purbeck marble, which sustain them, are compound, with capitals of stone, of very beautiful Early English foliage. The space between the top of the arches and the Purbeck string-mouldings beneath the sills of the windows is enriched with the sculptures, which, from their great beauty, have become so justly celebrated. At Westminster the stalls are very boldly moulded in the form of a circular trefoil-headed arch; the Purbeck marble shafts supporting them are single columns, and the space above the arches filled in with a very beautiful diaper. In both examples the eastern arcades are recessed and elevated one step above the surrounding ones, as possessing greater dignity for the bishop or abbot. Westminster, it must be remembered, was a mitred abbacy; consequently its abbot ranked with bishops. The colour with which both these arcades were decorated was also dissimilar. My restoration of that at Salisbury must necessarily be, to some extent, arbitrary; enough, however, remains, as I have already mentioned in my Report, to warrant a restoration of the moulded parts. It is, therefore, in the representation of the yellow drapery that an authority is required. Perhaps the very obscure lines of folds, still apparent upon the walls, may be thought insufficient to warrant its introduction : if so, I confess to be fairly at a loss what to substitute. There is a most beautiful authority for this drapery, in the example *here* of that which formerly decorated the arcades of the chapel of S. Stephen at Westminster. Nothing can be more exquisite than the original must have been, and the idea, too, that of figures of angels introduced for supporters of the drapery. In the restorations of the Ste. Chapelle at Paris, drapery, conventionalised, of a chocolate colour and powdered with a diaper, has been introduced as a back-ground to the arcades around the walls of the interior ; with what authority I know not, but certainly with admirable effect. The chocolate colour throws up the gilded columns of the arcades to perfection. The yellow colour introduced for the proposed restoration at Salisbury will harmonise best with the grey and silvery tints of the Purbeck marble. At Westminster, colour may be traceable in the mouldings of the arcades, but it is very obscure, and little light can now be obtained for an examination of what remains. This same difficulty, I am sorry to say, also applies to the series of exquisite frescoes on the back-ground of the eastern arcades : the centre one contains a group of the Crucifixion, but almost invisible ; in the two compartments on either side the heads only remain of a series of subjects. These heads are each surrounded by a nimbus of gold, with a raised and architectural pattern upon it, very beautiful. Sir Charles Eastlake has taken notice of these frescoes in his work 'On the Materials for a History of Oil Painting.'

"The sculptured remains at Westminster are not numerous, but very perfect and of a high order of art. The beautiful group of the Annunciation, above the door of entrance within the chapter-house, is very little known; indeed, it was only discovered a few years ago by my friend, Mr. Scott, the architect. It consists of two figures, rather larger than life, of the Angel S. Gabriel and the Blessed Virgin. They stand in niches, one on either side of the doorway, the spandrils of which are panelled and filled with the figures of angels bearing thuribles. Although I have shown the niches over the doorway at Salisbury as charged with paintings, I am inclined to think they were formerly filled with figures, as in the case at Westminster. The positions of the niches exactly correspond: it is in number and size alone that they vary. The peculiarities of the doors of the entrance into the two apartments are as follows: Westminster is a larger one, much higher and of bolder design than that at Salisbury. Both are double doors: that is, they have a centre shaft. At Westminster, as throughout, it is a simple one: at Salisbury it is compound. The quatrefoil, filling the head of the door, in the former has been pierced, in the latter it is solid; a succession of figures, enclosed by foliaged niches, surrounds the arches of both on the outer side of the doorways. Foliage of the ordinary Early English character more or less ornament the caps of the shafts and other parts, in both examples. The recess over the outer side of the doorway at Salisbury in all probability once contained a sculptured representation of the Crucifixion. In the quatrefoil on the inside I have introduced a figure of our Lord in the act of benediction. The stone seats and steps surrounding these chapter-houses do not appear to have varied from the usual arrangement."

Externally, the whole surface has perished in such a manner as to render it doubtful at first sight whether any approach can be made to its correct restoration. There are, however, in one or two places, remnants of the basemoulds and string course; and there are, in one concealed nook, relics of the external window tracery and arch, which are sufficient to prove that the external and internal details of the windows were alike; so that, after all, it is only the cornice and parapet, with the terminations of the buttresses, which are left to conjecture.

The flying buttresses show some evidences of having been a later addition.

On the question, whether the roof was of a high pitch, as those at York and Lincoln, or low, like those at Salisbury and Wells, I find no evidence, but I am disposed to give preference to the *high* roof.

In restoring the interior, it is my intention, first, to indurate the whole of the ancient surfaces by the injection which I have long made use of in the church. Every ancient part will be carefully preserved, and no addition made, excepting where the old portions have been lost by mutilation or other causes. I fear that the south-eastern pier must be partially rebuilt, as it has been pushed tremendously out of the perpendicular by the thrust of the groining.

The groining was taken down many years back owing to its dangerous condition. It will, of course, be replaced, using as much as possible of the old stone ribs which I have already mentioned as having found.

The interior has, within the present year, been freed from the incumbrances which had for so long a period obscured its beauty; and, mutilated and decayed as it is, its forms have come out *most nobly*.

The crypt beneath it has a central pillar and groining in some degree like those of the superstructure, but extremely low and plain. There is in the eastern bay evident proof of its having been used as a chapel, such as the piscina, locker, and marks of a screen. The walls are of the enormous thickness of 17 feet. Why they were so built it seems impossible to guess. I had thought, as I have before named, that they might be founded as a nucleus for the walls of the Confessor's chapter-house, but I do not find anything to substantiate this idea with any certainty. The outer five feet or so in the thickness of these walls seems as if distinct from the inner mass; but even this seems to vanish on closer examination, so that this theory must be viewed as very doubtful.

It is delightful to think that this noble relic, after having been obscured for three centuries by presses, galleries, and all kinds of obstructions, should be about to be again restored to its ancient beauty, and I earnestly trust that I may be able faithfully and successfully to execute this important trust.

There is probably no remnant remaining of the ancient stained glass. We had thought that such was the case with the original glass of the Abbey itself; but within the last few weeks we have had the happiness to discover two large pieces of it walled up behind one of the monuments. It is very fine grisaille, and will furnish an excellent guide for that in the Chapter-house windows, should we fail of finding any remnants of that which actually belonged to them.

The Dean has collected and is about, I believe, to publish many most interesting facts relating to the history of the Chapter-house, the uses to which it has been devoted, and the scenes which have taken place within its walls. The foregoing sketch is limited to the drier subject of its architecture, and I must apologise for its matter-of-fact character, trusting that when the restored building is seen it will not fail to excite all the interest and admiration which the noble character of the structure demands.

IV.

ON THE SCULPTURE IN WESTMINSTER ABBEY.

BY PROFESSOR WESTMACOTT, R.A., F.R.S.

ADDRESS DELIVERED IN HENRY VII. CHAPEL, JULY 19, 1866.

IN reviewing the sculpture in Westminster Abbey, our remarks will, first, be directed to that particular phase of the art, the Gothic, which is found in connexion with the older style of architecture of which the building is so fine an example. Though this sacred edifice has, for many generations, been made the resting-place and the receptacle of the monuments of some of the most remarkable historical personages who have illustrated the annals of England, and thereby has claims to the attention of all who take pride in reflecting on the greatness and glory of our country, yet the interest of the visitor is chiefly drawn to those remains which can be associated with the earlier foundation. Our examination will extend beyond this, and the sculpture of the later periods will be considered with relation to the state of the art at their respective dates; but it is to the Gothic sculpture that attention will be directed in the first instance; and it will be right to show how this is to be judged and estimated.

By the kindness of the Dean the section assembled to hear this discourse is allowed to meet in this beautiful chapel. There could be no more noble theatre for the purpose than such a monument of the skill and taste of our ancestors; while it also affords some of the most admirable examples for illustrating the subject, in the numerous statues that so profusely decorate the different parts of the architecture.

It may be observed that, usually, Mediæval sculpture has been discussed, almost exclusively, by architects, antiquaries and church historians, and so far has only been considered from single points of view: in relation to its connexion with Gothic architecture, or for the illustration it affords of ecclesiastical subjects, as in Scripture and legendary scenes and stories, or for its iconography. On this occasion it will be judged as sculpture; simply as art, and as to the position it is entitled to hold in this respect.

The earliest attempts in sculpture only a few centuries old, cannot, of course, be placed in the same interesting category with the extremely archaic monuments of Assyria, Egypt, Greece, Etruria, Asia Minor, and other ancient nations, dating, it may be said, thousands of years since. Neither can such works be allowed to take rank as monuments of fine art in illustrating the history of sculpture (proper); seeing that they throw no light whatever, practically, on the progress of imitative art, nor æsthetically, as a means of expressing beautiful ideas or sentiment by beautiful forms. Gothic sculpture never, at any time, achieved a development that placed it in the same high position that had been attained by the great schools of the art; for, though it had fallen into neglect and disuse, it must be remembered that sculpture had been brought to the highest state of perfection at least sixteen or seventeen hundred years before the so-called Gothic school had any existence.

Assuming the essential conditions of fine and good sculpture to be refined expression, the highest perfection of form and of physical beauty in all its parts, truth to nature in her boundless variety, and what is understood as *style* in treatment, with fine and careful execution—and putting aside, for the present, any question of the Poetry of Art, both in subject and treatment, as it is seen embodied in the best Greek sculpture—it must be admitted, even by its warmest admirers, that Gothic or Mediæval sculpture must always occupy in these respects a very inferior position. Any interest it possesses must, then, be sought for in qualities quite distinct from that which attaches in the first place, to works of remote antiquity, or, in, the next, that is accorded to the excellence of the art exhibited; for, in fact, it has neither of these recommendations.

The sculpture of the true Gothic period of architecture in this country, dating, that is, from the thirteenth century, and lasting till the middle of the sixteenth century of our era, is remarkable for a character exclusively its own. Generally speaking it exhibits—like all the attempts at art by inexperienced workmen—extreme rudeness in execution, a disregard of all rules of art, false proportion, incorrect anatomy and, for the most part, utter insensibility to beauty of form.

That Gothic sculpture must be judged as a peculiar and exceptional phase of art *sui generis,* and not by the standard of progress and development ordinarily applied by critics, as in the case of Greek sculpture, is seen in the curious fact of its maintaining, like Egyptian and other prescriptive sculpture, its own marked and characteristic idiosyncracy, as *Gothic.* So truly is this the case, that in all modern imitations of Gothic architecture, where this art is employed, this peculiarity is always more or less attempted, as a *sine quâ non* of character; though the general progress of art and the advanced knowledge of the properties which constitute excellence must make it plain to those who adopt such peculiarities that art so exercised, not being truthful as an expression of the present age, is unsound and unreal. This remark does not apply to the mere form of Gothic sculpture, whether in drapery or in the figure; for this, it will be seen in the course of our survey, was much modified, according to the comparative skill or increased practice of the workmen employed, as is especially observable at Wells, Lincoln, Salisbury, Exeter, and in other English ecclesiastical buildings. It refers rather, or entirely, to the distinctive *manner* of the treatment. Here, with much that merits high praise, in its *forms*, it is still constantly in antagonism to sound art principles, and exhibits an utter defiance of those rules of fitness and propriety which should essentially regulate an imitative art. For instance, if the human form is the object of imitation, it requires but little argument to show that the aim of the true artist should be to choose such conditions as will most correctly display that form; or, at any rate, that there should not be a studied effort to put it into distorted and impossible action. Portions or parts of the figure, that is, should not be made to perform functions for which they are unfitted, and of which, indeed, they are incapable in nature; nor should the most perfect work of creation be represented truncated or in pieces, and, so mutilated, fulfilling, often, with the most complacent expression, ignoble and even repulsive and degrading offices. Yet, in true Gothic all this occurs, and is imitated, in our time, as characteristic of the style. Figures represented in violent action, or as standing, kneeling, or sitting, are squeezed, one over the other, into the hollow mouldings of arched doorways, though in the apex of the arch the upper figures, intended to be upright, are frequently, by this arrangement, in a position nearly, if not quite, horizontal. Again, the most distorted attitudes are given to others, in order to make them fit into angles or spandrels; figures, also, are made to project suddenly at right angles from the walls, to support roof-timbers, or to act as brackets, while their ample draperies show no natural movement, but, instead of hanging or floating, cling horizontally in folds parallel to the figure. In like manner, heads of angels, saints, kings, bishops, and even females, nuns and others, are made to bear heavy weights, to act as corbels, or as terminations to dripstones over windows and doorways, for the undignified function of draining off the rain-water. Now, in Gothic, these anomalies, and the grotesques and even indecency that are seen in gurgoyles or draining-pipes on roofs, in stall-seats and other parts of ecclesiastical buildings, are evidently intentional. They are not, like the crude attempts of the archaic sculptors, the consequence of entire ignorance, nor of primitive rudeness of art; for they occasionally are found associated with a very advanced feeling for a certain kind of beauty, both of form and expression. In the heads of dripstone terminations, and occasionally in drapery, there is evidence of unquestionable power in these respects, sufficient, at any rate, to show that this grotesque employment of sculpture was a part of the system of true Gothic design, and belonged to it.

This peculiar feature in the treatment of Gothic sculpture may go far to explain much that, to modern feeling, appears offensive and anomalous in its practice. Ignorant of the true principles of sculpture, and rude and inexperienced in execution, as were the artists or carvers of the age, it would yet be too much to suppose them so primitive, so ignorant, and so blind, as not to know that the human face was not intended to carry the weight of a column or a rafter; and, therefore, it is reasonable to assume that the fantastic, conventional, and inappropriate uses to which the human figure was applied, formed an element in Gothic design, and, therefore, that truth to nature was not the sculptor's aim. There will be enough to arrest attention in expression, pleasing forms, and, especially, in the graceful though peculiar treatment of drapery found in some of their works, to claim for Gothic artists a large amount of admiration; but we may not shut our eyes to the curious proofs that exhibit these, to us, contradictory and inconsistent features of their art-system; showing, beyond dispute, that they were considered as marks of the style, and proper to it. It is this which makes Gothic sculpture false and ultra-conventional, as a phase of art. Notwithstanding certain pleasing qualities it possesses, it never can be classed as a branch of fine or perfect sculpture; and, for this reason, it never has been and never ought to be placed before students, like the remains of the great schools of Greece, as profitable guides for them to follow.

It must be a matter of surprise to many, even making every allowance for the very natural prejudice against using or imitating *heathen* types in the employment of sculpture for Christian purposes and illustration, why, in early times, the imitative arts in connexion with the purer religion should everywhere be found in so rude and barbarous a state. As before observed, sculpture was no newly-invented art. However neglected its practice had been, still monuments and remains of ancient and superior art abounded, especially in Italy. The missionary priests and monks who first spread amongst us the doctrines of Christianity, had all come from these southern countries where such remains were to be seen on all sides; and it must ever seem strange that, when sculpture and painting were required in the service of the Faith, no higher or nobler ideas of the beauty and dignity appropriate to holy subjects and persons should have existed than such gaunt and uncomely productions as many of those that have reached us.

It is equally unintelligible how such poor art should be found associated in England with what has been called, by its admirers, the highest form of ecclesiastical architecture : namely, the Pointed or Early English. The question involved is embarrassing. It is difficult to conceive that architects who showed themselves so utterly insensible to the glaring deficiencies of the arts employed in connexion with their productions, could have achieved, as is assumed, perfection in their own art. It is rather suggestive that all the arts, architecture as well as painting and sculpture, were, at that time, merely in a state of movement, and not practised on any fixed principles. The constant changes taking place in Gothic architecture itself during the short period of its existence — (scarcely three hundred years),—from the Romanesque to Pointed ; from Pointed to Decorated ; and from Decorated to Perpendicular, when, according to all the best judges of Gothic, the style was fatally declining, point to this conclusion.

This supposition, offered with great deference, does not detract from the real merits of Gothic design, nor from its claim to admiration for what it possesses of the noble, the beautiful, and the picturesque : but its incompleteness, as a whole, comparing it, in this respect, with Grecian architecture—the Parthenon, for instance, with its perfect accessorial sculpture—

suggests that the progress of Gothic architecture was arrested before it had attained the full development of which, no doubt, it was capable.

This, however, is a subject not now to be discussed. There is no common ground of argument as between the two branches of art. Sculpture and painting, being strictly imitative, must be judged by an existing and admitted standard—Nature. In architecture there is no such sure guide, nor, indeed, any guide at all, of the kind. Judging by the varieties in Gothic, in the forms and mode of its outward presentation—showing in this the absence of fixed principles, and, in its rapid decline, the want of vitality—the degree of popularity or admiration each has obtained, may not improbably be mainly referred to fancy and fashion. This is not so with the imitative arts. Here there is a foundation, and a standard which is of all time; and this standard is the highest, as well as the safest, that can be offered for our guidance.

Proceeding now to examine the works somewhat in detail, it may be observed that the sculpture in Westminster Abbey must be regarded under various aspects.

First, in its relation to the architecture, simply as decoration.

Secondly, as "subject"-sculpture; that is, when it is employed to illustrate Scripture, or to represent historical or legendary scenes and incidents.

Thirdly, as "memorial"-sculpture; especially in its

application to monuments to the dead, in tombs and similar erections.

The two latter classes only will form the subject of this discourse, as holding a higher rank in art than works of mere accessorial enrichment or ornament.

Though there are works in the Abbey of an earlier date than those to be brought immediately under notice, there are none of greater interest, in their way, than the series of *rilievi* which decorate the screen on the west side of the chapel of Edward the Confessor. The whole length of this sculpture is 38 ft. 6 in., by 3 ft. in height. The principal figures are about 1 ft. high. The relief is very bold, the irregular concave ground being much hollowed out behind. This curious and interesting work comprises a variety of subjects, real and imaginary, in the life of that pious monarch, King Edward, derived from a chronicle written by Ailred, an ecclesiastic of the time of Henry II. This record was presented by its author to that prince in the year 1163, when, after his canonization, the remains of the Confessor were removed into a new shrine. The subjects are fourteen in number, and they are separated from each other by trefoils, rudely formed by a running ribbon. Commencing on the left hand of the spectator, the designs occur in the following order:—

1. The first refers to the difficulty which arose when Ethelred, the "Unready," proposed to nominate a successor to the crown. Various claimants were considered and rejected. It was then decided by the Council to swear fealty to the child of which the queen Emma, "the pearl of Normandy," was then

pregnant. The nobility are here represented as taking the oath, and the Queen is represented standing crowned and robed, in the midst of a crowded assembly, with her left hand placed upon her waist. On her right hand stands a mitred dignitary of the Church. All the figures are greatly dilapidated.

2. The next compartment represents the birth of Edward, which is supposed to have occurred in 1002. The queen is lying on a couch or bed; in the background are two attendants holding the infant, and other figures are ministering.

3. The third subject is the coronation of Edward. He is seated under a canopy of state, and the crown is being placed on his head by the two archbishops of Canterbury and York, who are expressly mentioned in the chronicle as officiating on that occasion. This is a very full composition, showing a large attendance of nobles and courtiers, and expresses the busy character proper to so important a ceremony. Unfortunately it is impossible, owing to the injury the work has received, to make out accurately any of the minor details of this work.

4. The next compartment illustrates one of the curious legends invented in relation to the abolition by Edward of the Danegelt, or black-mail, paid to the Danes to bribe them not to commit their ravages in this kingdom. " The king," according to Ingulphus, " was induced to do so by the great alarm into which he was thrown on seeing the devil sitting and mocking (*Diabolum, super saccum sedentem et ludentem*) on the tribute collected in one of the royal chambers."

The money, according to the sculpture, was contained, not in sacks but, in casks or barrels. If the figure of the devil was, as is probable, represented sitting or dancing on the treasure, it has disappeared.

5. Represents a scene of King Edward's merciful treatment of a young man who entered the chamber where the king was supposed to be sleeping, and, finding a coffer open, took from it, at three several times, a large sum of money. The king, who had witnessed the whole proceeding, hearing some one approaching, said, "Youth, you are too covetous; but take what you have, and fly." The thief, astonished, fled and escaped pursuit. Hugoline, the chamberlain, on coming back, perceived the loss his negligence in leaving the coffer open had occasioned. Edward, seeing his distress, comforted him by saying, "Be at peace; perhaps he that has taken it has more need of it than ourselves." In the sculpture the story is very simply told, but it requires the above explanation to give it interest. The king appears reclining in his bed, a rich and stately piece of furniture, and a figure—the thief —is kneeling before a chest or coffer.

6. Represents the miraculous appearance of our Lord to King Edward, when partaking of the Sacrament. This vision is related in various ways, one account saying that the wafer itself was converted into the figure of a boy, who first gave his benediction to the king, and then to his attendant, Earl Leofric. This compartment is so much damaged that it affords no means of judging of the art exhibited in it. The king kneels before what looks like a lectern. The officiating

priest is headless, and hands and arms also are wanting. In the background, behind a screen, are seen parts of figures looking on.

7. Exhibits another of the wonderful visions with which the Confessor was said to have been favoured on account of his great sanctity. The king was observed to laugh when, during High Mass, the Sacrament was being administered to him. The explanation he gave of this seeming impropriety, according to his biographer, was that, at the very moment, he saw in a vision the King of Denmark preparing to embark with his army on an expedition to invade England; and that just as he had got into a boat to go on board his ship, he fell over into the sea and perished. "These," said the king, "are the circumstances with which, by Divine revelation, I was made acquainted, and which gave occasion to that hilarity of countenance you remarked." It was subsequently found, on due inquiry, says the historian, that all these events had really happened on the day, and at the hour, and in the manner in which they had been so miraculously revealed to the king. In the foreground of the sculpture a knight in armour is represented as fallen out of a boat into the water. Behind is a vessel filled with armed men. On the right is a castle or some towers, and these also appear to be falling.

8. The eighth compartment represents five persons at a table, and is said to refer to the prophecy of King Edward of the troubles which would arise in consequence of the feuds between Tosti and Harold, the sons of Earl Godwin, and of the death of both these

princes. The king, Earl Godwin, and another figure, probably the queen, are on one side of the table, and two figures, much mutilated, supposed to be Tosti and Harold, are sitting opposite in the foreground. The prediction was said to be fulfilled in both instances:— first, by the discomfiture and death of Tosti, near Stamford, in Yorkshire, in 1066; and, secondly, by the defeat of Harold, who was slain at the battle of Hastings, in Sussex, in the same year.

9. The ninth compartment illustrates a portion of another marvellous vision of King Edward, in which he declared he had seen the Seven Sleepers resting in a cave; and that while he was contemplating them they simultaneously turned on their sides, from the right, on which they were all reposing, to the left. Earl Harold, who was present when the king related the circumstance, proposed that three messengers or ambassadors should immediately be sent to the East, to inquire into the truth of the vision. A soldier, probably a knight or noble, a bishop, and an abbot were dispatched with the king's letters to the Emperor of Constantinople. They were received honourably, and by the emperor's command were conducted to Ephesus, where they were met by the bishop, his clergy, and others, who introduced them into the cave, where they saw the Seven Sleepers lying on their left sides, precisely as the king had described them. The sculpture represents three figures, no doubt the ambassadors, one of which has on what looks like a coronet; they are mounted on horseback, and appear to have arrived at what may be the cave. The Seven Sleepers are

here seen lying side by side, or rather closely packed one over the other, on their left sides, precisely as the king had described them in his vision.

10. This compartment represents, according to the chronicler, the appearance of St. John, in the garb of a pilgrim, to King Edward, and requesting alms. On receiving a ring from the king, the supposed saint disappeared. The figures in this design are much injured. The king occupies the centre of the composition, and a pilgrim or beggar is before him, on the spectator's right hand. Behind the king is a figure which appears to hold a pastoral staff—probably an ecclesiastic, and in front of whom, between the king and himself, is an object not easily defined. It looks like a basket. This design is interesting, from the background being entirely filled in by a large and handsome church. This refers to the fact, mentioned by Ailred, of the king being engaged in the consecration of a church, in honour of St. John, when the pilgrim appeared and requested alms of him for St. John's sake.

11. The next compartment exhibits the king, with figures in attendance, washing his hands in a large salver. It illustrates a miracle effected by the restoration to sight of certain blind men, who are said to have received their cure from washing their faces in the water which had been used by the king. This is one of the most injured works in the series.

12, 13. These two designs refer to parts of the history of St. John's miraculous appearance to Edward, as described in No. 10.

14. The fourteenth, and last compartment, represents a church, with two draped figures standing before it. It has been called the Dedication of Edward the Confessor's Church; but there are not sufficient details to allow of any safe interpretation of its meaning.

There is no evidence to assist in settling the disputed question of the date of this curious work, and it is from circumstances only, connected with other erections in this part of the Abbey, that any probable conclusion can be arrived at. It is now generally attributed to some time in the reign of Henry VI., in the fifteenth century. It was not later than this, and reasons might be adduced for giving it a somewhat earlier date. This, however, is not a matter of any great importance, for the few years only, of less or greater antiquity, would not materially affect the interest that attaches to the work; and this consists rather in its being "subject," or illustrative, sculpture than in any merit it possesses as a work of art. The stories or incidents are told in the most primitive and clumsy manner, and are only intelligible through the aid of the curious legend that, fortunately, has been preserved.

Of the expression in the heads, or of any of the details, it is impossible to form any judgment, as the surface is everywhere greatly injured, and moreover the execution is extremely rude. The figures are ill-proportioned, short and thick, and utterly deficient in anatomical correctness.

This frieze, which, in its time, must have been considered a production of no slight pretension, both from the position it occupies, and the subject treated, shows the very low condition of art in England at fourteen hundred years after Christ. So far from exhibiting anything like progress or development, it literally is suggestive of retrogression; for, as will be seen presently, it is in every respect inferior in art-qualities to sculpture near it of a much earlier date. A proof of the want of education in the artists of the time is the utter disregard shown to consistency in what is called *keeping*. In two of the subjects churches are introduced, one of which, according to Ailred's chronicle, the Confessor is himself consecrating. In both instances the building represented is in a style of very advanced Gothic, unknown till at least three centuries after the Confessor's death.

Although it is clear these works can take no rank as good art, they have an interest of another kind. They claim attention as exhibiting the tone of feeling of the time, and the right application of art to illustrate serious and religious subjects. The traditions of the holy life and experiences of the Confessor were thoroughly believed in; and here art is exercising its true mission in giving expression to ideas that were familiar to popular feeling. Without inquiring into the measure of truth attaching to Abbot Ailred's chronicle, sculpture is here employed in one of its most legitimate functions, especially, as in this case, in association with a sacred edifice. Modern practice may here learn a useful lesson. Rude and incomplete as it is, this work may justly be referred to as a mode in which art might be effectively and advantageously employed in the decoration of Christian churches; substituting, of course, scripture subjects and teaching for the fanciful legends of mediæval chroniclers.

In another part of the Abbey, between this (Henry VII.'s) chapel, and the Chapel of the Kings, as it is called, is another work of a somewhat similar character, though the subjects in it are fewer. This is the screen of the shrine of Henry V. The decoration consists chiefly of statues of various sizes in niches, but there are also groups of figures in two compartments, which come legitimately within the category of subjects. One, the best, is a coronation, comprising several figures, with the king seated in the centre. The work is very rude, and appears to have come from the hands of mere mechanical carvers. Some of the larger single figures exhibit a trifling superiority, and may have been executed by a better class of workmen.

In other parts of the church—for instance, in some spandrels in the chapel of St. John—there also are examples of what may be classed as subject-sculpture, which fully bear out the above remarks as to the rudeness of the art of the time. The more important one may, probably, represent our Lord giving judgment at the Resurrection. The centre figure of the Saviour, if this interpretation be allowed, is seated, and is of larger proportions than those near him. The left hand appears to be raised; the right is broken off. The figures behind are variously employed. One seems to hold a pastoral staff; another, as far as it can be distinguished, is supplicating: there are three on each side. Another corresponding spandrel exhibits a draped female standing on a dragon: the hands are placed together on the breast, as if in prayer. Behind her there appears to be a cross. She is surrounded by foliage, and on one side is a second dragon. This design may be intended to represent the Virgin treading the dragon under her feet.*

From what remains of the figures, draperies, and composition of these designs, the art exhibited is of a very rude quality. The figures want proportion, and they are rather packed than arranged in the spaces they are made to occupy. Two of them in the larger composition are falling on their backs; evidently to accommodate them, in the usual Gothic mode of treatment, to the curve of the arched moulding against which they are placed. Of the details it is impossible to give any opinion, owing to the injury done to the surface of the work; but beyond their use in filling-in and enriching the space occupied by them, which such compositions often do with great effect, they evidently have but little claim to attention.

It will be observed here that the arches of the spandrels spring from human heads—a barbarous misappropriation of the human figure, which has before been adverted to as essentially Gothic.

The recent examination of the Chapter House has restored to light some few examples of early Gothic sculpture. One of these is a life-size, draped, statue,

* It has been suggested that it may more probably be St. Margaret, whom legends represent as slaying a terrific dragon by virtue of the holy symbol.

ill-proportioned and much defaced. All exhibit an extremely rude condition of art.

There is a class of subject-sculpture, especially associated with what may be called ecclesiastical decoration, which, though it must be touched upon with great delicacy, may not be entirely overlooked in this survey. Strange to say, it is only found in religious buildings; and yet it is usually of a character that renders it especially unfitted for such application. This is in the incidents chosen for the ornaments of stall-seats and brackets, and in gurgoyles and drip-stones ; where the jealousy that existed between the regular and the secular clergy was displayed in the grotesque and often highly indelicate carvings in which one body satirized the other. It is difficult to understand how the representation of such coarse buffoonery, and even of the most scandalous subjects, could be permitted by those, usually ecclesiastics of high position, who controlled church decoration; and it is more surprising that it should be found at a time when the most ardent admirers of mediævalism, in all its forms, insist that the most exemplary religious and pious impulse influenced and directed all art. It is thus briefly referred to in this place, because Westminster Abbey is not without examples of this strange and lamentable offence against propriety and good taste. It may be added, however, that, with few exceptions, the instances found here are rather of the broadly humorous than of the indecent type.

Our attention may now be directed to the very remarkable series of statues that are found in the chapel of Henry VII. Here, indeed, may be seen works that, in certain qualities, may challenge comparison with the productions of any school. It is true they are of unequal merit; but the best of them are fine examples of the success of the later mediæval artists in treating drapery, and in the impressive simplicity of *pose*, in single figures.

The works referred to constitute a portion of the decoration of this exquisite architectural triumph of the sixteenth century. The nave of the chapel is divided from the aisles by four arches on each side, and similar arches divide it from five small chapels at the east end. Immediately under the arches, and extending entirely round the chapel, is a range of demi-angels, the upper part of each figure only being shown, projecting from the wall, in high relief. They are rather grotesquely treated: some are draped: some are represented with their bodies thickly feathered, like birds; and, generally, they have rich, curly hair. Their function is to support, on shields, the royal devices of Henry VII.—the rose, portcullis, *fleur-de-lis*, &c. Over these angels are rows of octangular pedestals and niches, enriched with tracery and foliage, containing statues, about 3 ft. high, of saints, martyrs, and other venerable persons. There is here great variety of simple action and a fine feeling for art. The draperies, especially, are largely and grandly arranged. In the heads, also, there will be observed a remarkable attention to proper expression, as well as to appropriate character and form. When the naked figure is introduced, as in the St. Sebastian, it is very conventional, and, as usual, shows no intimate acquaintance with the study of nature; but, in other respects, these works possess merits of a very high class, and have justly been noticed by all the best judges of sculpture as examples, of their kind, thoroughly deserving careful study and imitation. It may be noticed, that though the statues in the nave average about 3 ft. in height, those in the chapels are nearly life-size. They are arranged in threes, over five demi-angels. It is to be lamented that some of these interesting works have been injured, and many removed, and the niches and pannelling destroyed, to make way for comparatively modern monuments—as, for instance, those of Villiers and of Sheffield, Dukes of Buckingham. The statues, of all sizes, employed in the enrichment of this chapel and in the decoration of the "closure," or screen, of the monument of Henry VII., are said to have amounted, originally, to nearly three thousand. Many of the smaller ones, especially those of gilt metal, have, no doubt, been stolen.

In closing this part of our subject, it is to be remarked how very limited was the range of incident or story exhibited in the accessorial sculpture of the Gothic period. Notwithstanding the almost inexhaustible interest and subjects for art to be found in the Holy Scriptures, and the additional opportunities offered by the belief in the countless legends and traditions of the Mediæval Church, there is a marvellous poverty and want of variety of illustration and invention in this respect.

The Monuments.

The earliest examples of sculpture in the Abbey Church of Westminster—and they are believed to be the oldest monuments in England—are seen on some tomb or grave-stones in the east cloister. They are of abbots of the church. One of these is said to be of Vitalis, who died about 1082. Two others are of Crispinus, about 1114, and of Laurentius, who died towards the end of that century. The effigies of these dignitaries are represented in their official robes. That of Vitalis has a mitre on his head, and in one hand are the remains of a pastoral staff. The execution of these works is extremely rude, and the relief very flat. Apart from their antiquarian interest, they possess no peculiarities to arrest the attention of the lover or the historian of art.

It may be observed here that all the earlier monuments with effigies are of ecclesiastics. This may, at first, appear strange, when it would seem to be so much more natural and fitting that crowned heads, kings and queens, princes, or great nobles and knights, warriors and statesmen should be so honoured, and not that such distinction should have been exclusively conferred on the clergy. But here is seen one of the great uses of monumental art, when it is exercised under a real and true impulse. It shows the character of its age. The earliest Christian art, resembling in this all the early monumental sculpture that exists, was employed exclusively in illustrating subjects of religious interest; and when applied as decoration on the tombs of holy persons or martyrs—prior to the representation of the deceased in an effigy—the subjects of the designs, whether in painting or sculpture, were always taken from Scripture or from some sacred tradition. The character of the contemporary art was very rude; but sometimes works of a better character were enlisted into the service, and examples often occur of the pagan subjects of the debased Roman schools being adapted to Christian illustration—a new meaning being given them to fit them for this appropriation. The *motive*, however expressed, was undoubtedly religious, and such decoration was felt to be the only proper accessory on the tombs of departed Christians. At this time no personal or secular element was prominently put forth in such works.

The cause of a change in this treatment or principle, as applied to monuments, is not difficult of explanation.

In the eleventh century, when the effigy of the deceased was first introduced on the gravestone or monument, the Church—meaning by this the clergy—exercised very great power, not only spiritual, but political. Its dignitaries held many of the highest offices of State, and ecclesiastics generally occupied the influential position to which their character, their education and attainments—great, indeed, compared with the universal ignorance of the laity of all ranks—justly entitled them. It is not, therefore, to be wondered at, that the most eminent of its members should, on their decease, receive distinct marks of honour at the hands of their brethren—especially, too, when these could be conferred upon them in the very edifices in which they had held the highest offices. There was, also, a great *esprit de corps* in the members of each foundation. Such memorials testified not only to the merits of the deceased abbot or bishop, in the first place, but, by reflection, to the importance of the religious house to which he belonged; while the tomb itself attracted attention, invited the devotion of the pious, and procured for the church itself many substantial advantages in the way of privileges and offerings from all classes of persons who frequented it, according to their position and means. It must also be borne in mind that all religious edifices were entirely and exclusively under the guardianship of the clergy. Ecclesiastics alone controlled everything connected with the arrangements within the building. In some societies, as is well known, their own members were competent to act as architects, painters, and carvers, and often were employed in the design and the decoration of the church, or monastery, or whatever the building might be. It follows from this that, in erecting memorial monuments of especial honour, the members or chapter of a religious house would, naturally, desire to pay every possible distinction to one of their own body; and thus the bishop or abbot, or other dignitary connected with the particular church would, when the practice of personal representation came into fashion, have his effigy placed over his grave.

This character, or appropriation, rather, of the tomb-monument seems to have prevailed for a century or more. There is not an instance of even a royal effigy during this period; the first regal monument which is found in England so treated, being that of King John, in Worcester Cathedral. Its date is probably early in the thirteenth century, as John died in 1216.

Though the previous strictly religious character of monumental sculpture, admitting only Scripture or sacred subjects in the accessories, was, as has been shown, invaded when the effigy of the deceased was represented, there still was a conventional solemnity and repose in the design of these later works, peculiarly appropriate to their place in a church, and to the intention of the memorial. The figure was represented recumbent, as though extended on his death-bed. Habited usually in the full costume of his rank, with his crozier or pastoral staff by his side, the chalice in his hand, or sometimes with the hands in the action of prayer, the bishop or abbot, or whatever his title, appeared simply as the dead or dying Christian priest. It was a record, a memorial of the individual—no more. There was no ostentatious display of worldly distinction and titles; no vain, boasting epitaph. The name only—and sometimes not even that—with a date, was inscribed round the margin of the stone; and this was followed, occasionally, by a simple petition for divine mercy, or asking the prayers of the passers by.

The principle which is so conspicuously exhibited in these works continued to influence monumental design when, subsequently, such memorials ceased to be confined to the clergy, and were extended to the noble and distinguished among the laity. The recumbent effigy of the deceased surmounted the tomb, within or under which the body was supposed to be deposited. The attitude was still extremely simple, and in perfect repose, excepting when the slight action of the hands, raised on the breast in prayer, showed how the departing spirit was occupied in its last earthly moments. Whether the figure was that of a prince, knight, or lady, it was dressed in the costume of the day; and it gives great antiquarian interest to these monuments to have the assurance that the effigies on them really represent the individuals whom they record in the dresses worn at their respective dates. In a number of instances in which tombs have been opened, the costume in which the deceased was buried—making allowance, of course, for the effect of time—has been found closely to correspond with that given to the sculptured figure. The monument, before alluded to, of King John, at Worcester, was examined late in the last century. Allowing for the changes consequent upon its great age, the dress in which the body was entombed was clearly identical in its forms with that sculptured in the effigy.

The first regal monument in Westminster Abbey, in point of date, having an effigy on it, is that of the founder of the present edifice, Henry III., who died in 1272-3. It stands on the north side of the Chapel of the Kings, and was erected a few years after his death by his son and successor, King Edward I. Henry is represented recumbent, crowned, habited in royal costume, with a mantle reaching to the feet. The head, with its crown of *fleur-de-lis*, rests on two small pillows. Two long curls of hair fall from under this coronet; and the face, which appears small and delicate, and is, no doubt, a portrait, has a beard and moustaches. The action of the hands suggests that the figure may originally have held some object, probably sceptres, no longer remaining. The feet have shoes on them, enriched with a running pattern of diaper gilt. As late as 1681 there was a lion against which the feet rested. This has disappeared, as well as some architectural decoration over the tomb. The material of this extremely interesting statue is bronze; and it is said, by Walpole, who does not, however, mention his authority, that it was considered the first example of metal casting in England. Both the statue and the bed or table beneath are gilt; but the hard coating of dirt that has been suffered to accumulate over it entirely conceals this enrichment. The latter, the table, on which the effigy lies, is diapered with lozenges inclosing a lion *guardant*: of which some indications may still be traced near the pillows.

There is great dignity in the simple *pose* of this statue, and the drapery is very gracefully composed. The workmanship and materials throughout are remarkable. The panels at the sides of the tomb are of polished porphyry, surrounded by a border or framework of mosaic, with gilding and coloured stones. At each corner there are twisted columns, similarly enriched with variously coloured marbles. The lower portion, or base of the monument, still exhibits the signs of its former lavish enrichment, in its lozenges of green jasper, and the remains of elaborate ornamental carving. It is said that King Edward had the precious stones employed in its decoration brought from France in 1281.

There is a peculiarity in the base of this tomb, which is worthy of remark. On the south side—that within the chapel—there are three sunk compartments. The centre one has a pediment supported by pilasters, with an architrave. The side recesses have trefoil heads. It is supposed that these recesses were used as "ambries" or lockers, in which sacred vestments or other objects, and possibly relics, were kept. At the back of each is a cross in mosaic.

It will be observed that the style of architecture exhibited in this work is of a very mixed character, and is highly suggestive of a foreign origin. It is known that Pietro Cavalini was employed by Edward I. in the execution of this tomb, as well as that of Queen Eleanor, and this may fully account for the non-Gothic treatment of the architectural portions of the design.

The monument immediately adjoining that of Henry III. merits attention for the extraordinary elegance and beauty displayed in some of its details. It is that of Eleanor, the wife of Edward I. She died in 1291. The figure, of bronze gilt, is recumbent, habited in the royal costume. There is a calm, gentle expression in the face, which is extremely touching, and the hands especially are designed with the utmost grace.

There has been a question as to the authorship of this very beautiful work, as well as the monument and statue of Henry III., and a patriotic desire has been shown by some writers to attribute them to native artists. Competent judges, and Flaxman among the number, have however inclined to the opinion that foreign sculptors were employed on this and many of the more important works in this country; and Flaxman even thought that the name of Torell, goldsmith, which occurs in a document of the time, should be written Torelli. It may be so; but the expression "goldsmith" may possibly refer only to the gilding of the bronze figure, and this may easily have been done by an Englishman. The best argument for believing that foreign artists were employed in the more important portions of these designs, especially in the figures, is in the general inferiority of those minor decorations which would necessarily be executed by such workmen as could be found in the country; and the mention of a certain Pietro Cavalini, who was, no doubt, employed in a contemporary work, gives strength to this opinion. This is a subject of great interest, but it is not possible at this time to give it the consideration due to it. The occurrence of unquestionably English names in the documents connected with public works proves the existence of native artists or artisans; and it is natural that art-historians should endeavour to show that some of the most interesting works were produced by native sculptors. In some of these, as at Wells, there certainly is no appearance of foreign interference. The gaunt and ill-proportioned figures on the exterior of that building, whatever interest they may have on other grounds, are of the rudest character; and the history and date of the erection of the edifice would justify the belief that ordinary English craftsmen may have executed every part of the work. The sculptures at Lincoln are amongst the best Gothic sculpture existing; and they show a very different and improved feeling, both in design and practice, compared with any work of the kind existing in this country.

The sculpture in the shrine of Henry V. has already been referred to. At the east end of the Chapel of the Kings is the tomb of Henry, with his effigy, or rather what remains of it. It is of oak, much mutilated and headless. It is said originally to have been plated with silver gilt, and that the head itself was of solid silver. Nothing is now left of this work but the rude wooden form upon which the "fine embroydered and gilded plates" were fastened; and it is only here alluded to with reference to the practice, of which there is another example in Westminster Abbey, of plating metal on a *nucleus* or form of wood.

The next monuments especially worthy of remark are in memory of King Edward III., his Queen Philippa, both in the Chapel of the Kings, and of two of their children. This king died in 1377. The royal effigy, of bronze, lies on a table of the same metal, and the whole has been richly gilt. In this statue there is evidence of great care in the portraiture of the deceased monarch. The face is long, and there is a remarkable fall in the lower lip. The hair is also, doubtless, represented as worn by the king. It is long and slightly curling, and the beard is ample and flowing. Altogether it is an interesting example of attention to nature, in transmitting to posterity the likeness of one of England's greatest sovereigns. There are at the same time those conventionalisms of treatment which, while they give its character to Gothic art, remove the work out of the category of really good sculpture. The long drapery in which the king is habited, though extending to the feet, shows a want of truthfulness in the disposition or fall of the folds. They are composed, in straight parallel lines, as if the figure were standing. Among the careful details, it will be observed the shoes are what are now termed "rights and lefts;" erroneously believed to be a very modern fashion of shoemaking. This tomb, like all others in the Abbey, has suffered greatly from neglect, and, there can be no doubt, intentional ill-usage. Much of its enrichment has disappeared, and many of the numerous small statues that decorated it have been stolen. Some of these representing the sons and daughters of Edward were in solid brass gilt.

The tomb of Queen Philippa, the consort of Edward III., still shows proofs of its former magnificence, though it is one of the most injured of the monuments in the Abbey. No fewer than thirty small statues are said to have stood in niches surrounding the tomb, not one of which remains. The effigy of this princess, though injured, happily is in a condition to afford a good idea of her person, as well as of the art of the day. The portrait is evidently carefully studied, and the sculptor who was able to give so much natural character in the treatment of the details was no mean practitioner. Such a work affords additional evidence that there were artists of widely different schools employed in these productions; though it will be seen they were still under the influence of the peculiar mode or style which characterises all, even the best, Gothic sculpture. The costume of this effigy, and especially the cushioned head-dress, gives great antiquarian value to this monument of Queen Philippa.

Leaving for a moment the Chapel of the Kings, in order to include in this notice the monuments of the family of Edward III. existing in the Abbey, attention may be directed first to a small tomb of Petworth marble in the chapel of St. Edmund, on which repose two very small alabaster figures of children of the above king and queen. They represent William of Windsor and Blanche. This interesting memorial of these young persons stands near the fine monument of John of Eltham. It has been much damaged, and the feet not broken but cleanly cut off. The costume of both is characteristic. The prince has flowing hair, with a fillet; the princess, who died in 1340, is represented in a studded bodice, petticoat and mantle, and a raised or horn head-dress, now much broken.

The next monument in the Chapel of the Kings, and the last to be noticed in this part of the Abbey, is that of Richard II. and Anne, his queen. The tomb is of grey Petworth marble, and on each side are canopied niches, with other rich architectural details. The statues are recumbent, and of bronze. It is recorded that the moulds were made and the images cast by certain coppersmiths, Nicholas Broker, Godfrey Prest, of Wood Street, and others, and that the gilding cost above

400 marks. Of this enrichment scarcely any trace remains. The king is habited not in a royal, but in what appears a religious costume. The statue is evidently a portrait, and the hair is most carefully treated. The short beard terminates in two pointed drops. The queen is arrayed in a bodice and long petticoat, showing just the points of the shoes, and a cloak or mantle. The countenance has a pleasing expression ; and the artist has noticed the double chin, which strengthens the probability of the statue being a careful portrait. In the original design the hand of the queen was clasped in that of her husband. The arms of both, which showed this action, have been removed : in all probability stolen.

In these personal monuments, if they may be so called, from having the figure of the deceased upon the tomb, the effigy constitutes the chief interest of the sculpture. But it has been shown that numerous small accessorial figures were also introduced, either as attendant angels, or statues of the apostles, saints, or other persons connected with the family history of the deceased, to enrich the sides of the tomb or the architecture connected with it. The angels appear ministering, sometimes at the head of the figure, on each side of the pillow, sometimes at the feet. They usually are represented kneeling, and holding the chalice, or as *thuriferi*, throwing incense from censers. They are less frequently seen at the feet, where either a lion, or a dog, or other animals, are made to support the feet of the effigy.

The figures in the niches usually are standing in an

attitude of prayer, or with scrolls or books, reading. With respect to technical treatment, considerable improvement will here be observed in the graceful manner in which certain details in these small accessories are represented. The hands of the figures are frequently of great beauty, and the draperies are also most carefully studied. They are large and broad in their masses, varied in design, yet remarkable for simplicity; and where action or movement is to be shown, as in flying or floating angels, the proper character is well expressed; and this often occurs where the dress of the chief figure on the tomb exhibits the stiffness of the earliest art. Of course there is no display of the nude figure; and where any indication of it appears, there is evidence of the usual absence of knowledge of the human form.

Amongst the older monuments to be especially noticed are three in the choir—namely, those of Edmund Crouchback, Earl of Lancaster, son of Edward II.; of Aveline, his wife (1275); and that of Aymer de Valence, Earl of Pembroke (1323). They are admirable illustrations of the elegant and yet rich style of monument of their time. The precise date of their erection is not known; but from the general treatment, the costume, and the architectural details, they may probably all be placed at between the middle of the reign of Edward II. and the beginning of that of Edward III. There is also so much similarity in the general design, that it might fairly be imagined that the same artists were employed on all the three works.

Crouchback died in 1296. His effigy lies on an altar-tomb. He is clad in chain-mail, and wears a close round helmet. The figure is slightly turned to the right,—a movement that may have been intended to convey the idea of looking towards the altar. This monument exhibits the peculiar sculptured enrichment that began at this period to characterise these designs. The sides of the tomb are filled with small figures in niches, under canopies; and the different portions of the lofty canopy which surmounts the whole work abound with decorative details. In the large trefoils, in the apex or pediment are figures of the earl on horseback, armed in mail. The whole was gorgeously coloured and gilt, and remains of this may still be discovered in some parts of the monument.

The monument of Aveline, his wife, the daughter and heiress of William de Fortibus, Earl of Albemarle, consists of an altar-tomb, upon which, under an elevated canopy, reposes a recumbent figure of this lady. The head rests on two cushions, supported by angels. The dress and drapery of this monument are remarkable for the elegant taste displayed in their composition and execution. She is represented in a hood and coif, which fall over her arms, her hands being raised in the act of prayer. The other part of her costume consists of a loose robe and long flowing mantle, reaching to the feet; and in the graceful arrangement of these the sculptor has shown himself a consummate artist.

The third monument referred to, that of Aymer, or Andomar, of Valence, resembles in its general features that of the Countess Aveline, but its dimensions are greater: it is more lofty, and the enrichments appear to have been more elaborate. As in the other examples, the figure is recumbent on an altar-tomb. The earl is habited in chain armour, with a surcoat of his arms. The hands, which no longer exist, were evidently raised on the breast, as if in prayer. There is an interesting and novel passage in the introduction of two small half-kneeling angels at the head of the earl, supporting on their hands a third figure draped. This is too much injured and broken to afford any details, but it has been thought, with great probability, to represent the soul of the deceased being thus supported by angels on its ascent to heaven. No mere description would do entire justice to this very remarkable work. In its details it exhibits the peculiarities of the Gothic style, in its fanciful and elaborate accumulation of crockets, foliated cusps, varied trefoils, and similar fantastic enrichment; but if the purpose of the artist was to produce a striking effect, and to impress the spectator with a solemn yet pleasing train of thought while contemplating this noble and beautiful memorial of the great earl, there can be no question that this monument deserves to be considered, of its class, a most valuable work of art. The sides of the tomb are filled with statues, now, alas! much mutilated, and in a large trefoil panel in the pediment of the canopy appears a knight fully armed, on horseback. The whole of the monument has been richly gilt and painted, and, like the works previously described, was studded, in every part that would allow of it, with shields with heraldic bearings tinted or emblazoned. These tombs are surmounted by lofty enriched canopies, tapering upwards with every variety of accessorial decoration. Crockets run along the exterior lines; while foliage, diapered grounds, trefoils, quatrefoils, enriched cusps, gilding, enamelling, and colour, formed the costly details of these memorials of rank and greatness. The splendour of such works, when the gilding and emblazoning were fresh, may easily be imagined; but it may be a question whether they do not make a stronger appeal to the sentiment in their more sombre and subdued colour, than they would if they were in the freshness of their original decoration. Some restored specimens of old monuments, in which the true colour and gilding have been imitated and repaired, convey an impression far from satisfactory, in an æsthetic sense.

An altar-tomb monument, in the Chapel of St. Edmund, having on it a recumbent effigy of William de Valence, Earl of Pembroke, whose death occurred in France in 1296, deserves especial notice here. The body of the earl is believed, from an expression in the old inscription, now no longer existing, to be deposited in the stone tomb which forms the lower part of the monument, but the effigy is placed above this, on a long wooden chest. The figure is in chain armour, with a surcoat extending to the knees. An enamelled emblazoned shield, suspended by a richly-decorated belt, is on the left side. The head, dressed in a close skull-cap, surrounded by a flowered fillet in which are sockets which formerly held precious stones, rests on an enamelled pillow, and a lion, much mutilated, supports the feet. The hands are raised as in prayer, and the portions of the dress that can be examined closely are diapered. There is also much gilding and enamelling still perceptible in the enrichment of this interesting work. But the circumstance that calls more particularly for notice is, that the statue itself is made of wood (oak), covered with plates of metal (copper), gilt, while the effect of the chain mail is given by engraving on the metal. It is said this monument was erected by Aymer de Valence to his father's memory.

The much-injured monument of John of Eltham, Earl of Cornwall (son of Edward II.), who died in 1334, merits attention as a good specimen of the treatment of such works. The effigy is made of alabaster; and the details, of plate-armour, surcoat, gorget, coroneted helmet, with other accessories, give great antiquarian interest to this work. The coronet is of the ducal form, having alternately small and large trefoil leaves, and it is thought that this is the earliest authority for its being so represented. There is nothing unusual in the style of art exhibited in the sculpture; but with the small attendant angels at the head, and the figures in niches on the side of the tomb, it affords another of the numerous valuable examples of the monumental style of the fourteenth century. There was formerly a very beautiful canopy over this tomb, but there are now no remains of it. The accessorial statues are much broken, and many portions of the monument have doubtless been stolen.

The introduction of knights fully armed and mounted, representing, no doubt, the noble persons whose larger effigies are placed on the tombs, in the decoration of the canopies of the monuments to the two Earls of Pembroke, is the only instance in this church of a reference, in the monuments themselves, to the worldly deeds or occupation of the subjects of the memorial. There are examples in equally early works, in other places, of a deviation from the rule of confining the accessories to religious objects only, as angels, and sometimes relations, and more frequently ecclesiastics, but none occur here except in the instances referred to. Nor is there any example of the double representation of the subject, as in York Minster, and at Lincoln, and elsewhere; first, in the figure of the tomb, habited in the usual costume, and then showing the corruption and decay of the same body in death; either with the skin shrivelled on the bones, or the bare skeleton laid out.

The above examples, selected from the large number of interesting monuments of the Gothic or Mediæval school, are sufficient to convey a notion of the best monumental sculpture of the time. Judged as productions of *fine art*, it need scarcely be said that they fall far short of the excellence that the remains of sculpture of a much older date show the art was capable of attaining. They have, however, their own peculiar merit, arising out of the sentiment which pervades them, as expressive of certain feelings, and for its appropriateness, both to place and object. There is a serious and religious character in the *motive* of these works, which subdues and tranquillises the feelings of those who contemplate them, carrying the reflections of the thoughtful to objects beyond the present. In this respect, however deficient they may be in technical qualities, they fulfil a great purpose, and they stamp the monumental design of the fourteenth and fifteenth centuries with a principle which must be admitted to be one of high value, and well worthy of imitation. It will not be desirable here to multiply the specimens of the immediately following dates after those already particularised; but it may be observed, in support of remarks already made, that the subsequent monuments were not always proofs of progress in this class of sculpture. The technical deficiencies of the works of the two centuries just surveyed were not compensated for by any valuable development of style, though, no doubt, a wider practice induced greater readiness and facility of mere execution. The monumental form, of recumbent dead or dying and praying figures was, however, still preserved. Either by habit, or feeling, this style of treating the subject was happily maintained; but it will be seen that a new feature was, also, admitted into these designs, which interfered disadvantageously with the spirit of the old types.

The tomb of the royal founder of this chapel, upon which are placed the effigies in bronze gilt of Henry VII. and his Queen Elizabeth, is so well known, that it would unnecessarily encroach upon our limited time to describe it in detail. It will be enough generally to state that the statues, as well as the accessories, were designed by a celebrated sculptor of Italy, Pietro Torregiano, the contemporary and rival of Michel Angelo. The figures of the king and queen, of bronze gilt, and dressed in royal costume, are placed on an elaborate tomb of black marble; at the corners of which, somewhat uneasily balanced or sitting, are four nude cherubs or angels. The monument is inclosed within an enriched screen or "closure," also of bronze gilt, but now, like the statues, blackened by the rust of ages. In all parts, where such decoration could be introduced, the work was filled with accessories in the form of small statues, shields, and armorial devices.

This reference to the tomb of Henry VII. might properly conclude our necessarily brief notice of the work in this exquisitely beautiful chapel; but as the name of Torregiano has been mentioned, it will be right to direct attention to one other work, said to be by him, in connection with this building. In the south aisle is the effigy, in bronze gilt, of Margaret, countess of Richmond, the mother of Henry VII. The aged and noble lady is represented in what looks like the dress of a nun or recluse, with a mantle thrown or worn over all. The details of this figure deserve careful examination. The hands, in the act of prayer, are very true in character and form, and, indeed, they give the idea of having been cast from moulds taken from nature.

It need scarcely be said that the accessories of Torregiano's works exhibit much of the bastard style of the Italian school as opposed to true Gothic; and there can be little doubt that the mixture of the classical orders with certain Gothic traditions, is to be traced to the habit or fashion of employing foreign artists on the more important monuments erected in the churches of this country. The recumbent effigy was still insisted on, but the accessories, as is evident in this work, were not required strictly to harmonise with any particular style of architecture; and thus, especially in the designs of the period, during and succeeding the Perpendicular phase of Gothic, are found the most capricious introductions of Corinthian and other architecture of the classical orders,—precisely as they occur in continental design of the time. As this corrupt style was introduced in this country about the time of the Reformation, it has been said, without any reason, that the Reformation was the cause of the change and of the degradation of religious or ecclesiastical art; when the fact is, the same bad and even worse taste is found in Italy, from whence it reached England. The monument itself of Henry VII., confutes the assertion referred to. It was executed by the especial order and direction of the king himself, and by an artist of Italy, long before the great event which is thus assumed to have lowered the tone of religious art. The sixteenth century gives a date to this false style of design, but the corruption of taste is to be sought for, as numerous monuments show, in the productions of those countries which, at that time, were much more advanced in art than England.

The period of true Gothic sculpture may be considered to be completed at this date; that is, about the middle of the sixteenth century. Already sculptured monuments of a more mixed style were executed, and it will be seen that this, in a very short time, entirely superseded the old simple character of

Mediæval and ecclesiastical design, as applied to this class of art.

It has already been seen that lofty highly-enriched canopies formed a striking feature in the early monuments of the Gothic period. The same protecting roof or shrine is found in the monumental design of the post-Mediæval time, and equally exhibiting a great quantity and variety of decoration. Colour, gilding, inlaid marbles, armorial emblazonment, scrolls, were as profusely employed as in the same class of design in the fourteenth and fifteenth centuries; but though there is quite as much meaning in the introduction of lozenges, twisted columns, urns, and other similar ornaments in these cumbrous monuments as in crockets, finials, cusps, trefoils, and the other fanciful devices of the Gothic canopies, the latter were part of, and in harmony with, the architecture with which they were associated, which the ponderous vagaries of the sixteenth and seventeenth centuries were not. This, independently of other circumstances, constitutes the great difference between the two; and it must be admitted that, in an art point of view, the latter offer no compensating qualities.

Two monuments in Westminster Abbey, of great historical interest, at once offer themselves in illustration of these remarks. They are the tombs of Elizabeth Queen of England, and of Mary Queen of Scots. The former stands in the centre of the north aisle of Henry VII.'s Chapel, that of the Scottish queen in the south aisle. As in the monuments of the earlier style, the effigies of these princesses form the main subject of the design. The inferior character of the sculpture of the figures is at once evident, and in both the architecture is overladen with profuse and cumbrous ornamentation, totally void of taste. In the monument of Elizabeth the effigy surmounts an elevated table tomb. The queen is represented in royal costume, with a small crown on her head. In her left hand she holds a globe; in the right a sceptre. The drapery is in large quantity, ill designed, and stands up stiffly, showing a thick mass of irregular edges at the termination of the dress, from which the feet protrude, instead of falling over, as it would in nature, to the ground. The order, if it can be so called, of the architecture of these two monuments is Corinthian; and therefore entirely out of harmony with this beautiful chapel of a most enriched character of Perpendicular Gothic. Queen Mary also is represented recumbent, in full dress, with her hands raised and pressed together, as if in prayer. The dress is elaborately worked, but, like that of Elizabeth, is wanting in true artistic treatment; the folds not falling gracefully, but composed in heavy and straight lines, as in a standing figure, and then gathered in unseemly confusion at the feet. The hands have suffered injury, some of the fingers being broken off; but they are small and elegant in form; and the face has a gentle and pleasing expression. The architectural portions are heavy, and every species of decoration that could be crowded into the design is lavishly introduced.

The remark that has been made on the want of consistency or harmony in the architectural portions of these designs, in relation to the design of the chapel, applies now very universally to productions of the kind. It must ever be a difficulty with regard to all works of later date that are to be placed in older erections. Unless the style of the surrounding architecture be imitated, the more modern works must always appear anomalous. Yet the mere copying of an older style, deprives works of anything like a character consistent with their own date. They lose all contemporary distinction. A modern statue represented recumbent and in prayer is as fitting a type of a Christian in the present day as it was five centuries ago; but placing such a figure under a Gothic canopy, with all the accessories that belong to the peculiar art of a particular and past age of architecture, though it may be very like the older work and very pretty, is, after all, incongruous and an anomaly. The statue expresses a sentiment, and a beautiful because a true one; but copying the architecture of another age is an anachronism. This applies equally, of course, to the adoption of classical as well as Gothic forms. Every work of art should be truthful; and one of its most valuable recommendations is its power to illustrate its own age. If the age has no distinctive expression in its architecture, the difficulty is only increased; for then there can be no real or original design. It must be borrowed and factitious; and such incongruity of parts, unfortunately, is found in all monumental works of the last two centuries. Where there is no original design in architecture to mark the age, it is hopeless to expect improvement in this respect. The artist is driven to adopt such forms, of any age and school, as he may find ready at hand; in his choice being guided only by fashion or by his own preference for a particular style.

Two of the most interesting monuments in the Abbey, have been here selected to illustrate the unfortunate taste that was now introduced. So long as the recumbent figure of the deceased was made the first object, a principle was preserved which gave character and interest to the design; but, soon after this, an entirely new feature was introduced in monumental design. Allegory was resorted to; and the later monuments not only exhibit the effigy of the principal subject of the monument and, occasionally, the figures of descendants, as sons and daughters of all ages, but semi-classical figures of the virtues,—as Temperance, Prudence, and the personification of warlike or learned attainments, in statues of Mars, Minerva, and other heathen images,—overload the design, disturb the religious sentiment of the work, and deprive it of all character of repose.

The Gothic monuments exhibit attendant angels at the head and foot of the effigies, ministering in various ways; and small figures of holy persons, and even of relations, introduced as mere accessories, are seen arranged in niches in the lower part of the tomb. In the later monuments these accompaniments still are found, but they assume a much more pronounced character. Big, naked, chubby boys, winged and fluttering about, or sitting or standing in different parts of the monument, take the place of the small, draped, kneeling figures that support the pillow of the deceased in the Gothic monuments; while lines of sons and daughters, sometimes life-size, are placed in the base, or in the background of the design, kneeling and praying before a lectern. The males usually are arranged on one side, the females on the other. Another peculiarity is often seen in these family tombs; and that is the introduction of deceased children, wrapped in swaddling or grave clothes, lying horizontally, on the side of the sex to which they belong. The monuments of this style,—like the older works, again, in this respect,—are usually richly gilt and painted; and a variety of materials is used in their composition, as coloured marbles, alabaster, and brass, which, at least, produce a gorgeous effect, if they cannot be reconciled with good taste.

The abbey possesses many examples of these designs, in which, notwithstanding the indifferent art exhibited in the sculpture, we still recognise the fond respect for the old religious traditions. The recumbent effigies, with uplifted hands and serious expression, arrest attention and are aids to reflection. But the time came when the more personal honour or glorification of the subject of the monument was to be illustrated, and the quiet tomb character of the design was superseded by the endeavour to give greater prominence to the worldly dignity of the deceased. The figures are now found turned on their sides, and, leaning on their elbow, look out from their resting-place, as if inviting the notice and admiration of the passers by. There are some remarkable examples of designs of the kind, of various degrees of artistic merit, in the Chapel of St. Nicholas. Many of these are in memory of persons eminent in history, and have great interest apart from the illustration they afford of the monumental art of the period. The neighbouring Chapel of St. Edmund also contains some examples worthy of notice.

Three examples of this mixed character may be noticed in this (Henry VII.'s) chapel. They are the monuments of Villiers, Duke of Buckingham, and his family; of Sheffield, Duke of Buckingham; and of the Duke and Duchess of Richmond and Lenox. They occupy three of the chapels at the east end of the nave. These works fully illustrate all the peculiarities referred to, and they are, also, very good specimens of the state of art of the time.

The monument of Villiers,—the "Steenie" and favourite of James I., and the companion of Charles I., —fills almost an entire chapel. The duke and his duchess, dressed in the costume of the time, are represented recumbent, side by side, on a table tomb, over a sarcophagus. At the four angles are figures, above life-size, of Mars, Neptune, Minerva, and another, called Benevolence. At the feet of the effigies is a smaller statue of Fame. The architecture at the back of the tomb is carried up to the vaulting. It is filled with every variety of design, in arms, crests, mottos, scrolls, etc. Three statues of children of the duke and duchess, as well as two female figures, in a reclining posture, holding a shield of arms, are also introduced in this part of the design. To make room for this extensive composition the original architecture, and the statues and demi-angels which formed its enrichment, have been destroyed. The body of the duke was buried in the vault beneath, in September, 1628; one month after his assassination at Portsmouth by Felton. The duchess died in 1643.

The next monument, in the adjoining chapel, is of a somewhat different, but still more objectionable character, from the entire absence of religious or monumental sentiment. It is in memory of John Sheffield, Duke of Buckinghamshire and Normandy; the last of his house. Placed on a raised sarcophagus the figure of the duke, dressed in Roman armour, reclines on a mattress and cushion, in a contemplative position. Near him, in an attitude of grief, the duchess is seated, dressed in the costume of the reign of George I. In the background are military trophies, surmounted by a statue of Time, who is carrying away medallion portraits of the deceased children of the duke. Near this figure are two other statues, of a, then, surviving son, and an angel weeping. At the top of all this are the family arms and ducal coronet. As in the case of the Villiers monument, the original architecture of the chapel and its decoration have been destroyed to make room for this cumbrous design.

The remaining monument referred to, as occupying another of the chapels (the south), is that of Lodowick Stuart, the Duke, and Frances, Duchess of Richmond and Lenox. On a raised sarcophagus lie the coroneted effigies of the duke and duchess. The former is in a suit of highly ornamented plate armour and mantle. His lady is represented in her robes of state. The right hand of the duchess is extended across her body to meet that of the duke, in which it is clasped. On the steps that support the sarcophagus are full-sized mourning statues, of Faith, Hope, Charity, with two children, and Prudence. These figures help to support a fancifully designed, open canopy, and this is surmounted by a statue of Fame, in rapid motion, and most ingeniously poised on one foot. The monument is enriched with various other devices. On each side of the sarcophagus is an inscribed tablet, with two genii or angels removing drapery from a skull. The changed feeling in monumental design, contrasted with the simple, even if tame, uniformity of the earlier works, is strongly exhibited in these examples. It will be observed, however, that one striking feature of the older type is preserved in the first and last of the two monuments referred to. The principal figures are recumbent, and in repose. In that of Sheffield this sentiment is entirely lost sight of. The quality of the sculpture varies in all, but one fact is obvious, and that is the evident progress of technical art and the attention given to composition. Gothic sculpture, notwithstanding its recommendation of simplicity, was wanting, essentially, in practical art and in variety. There is much in the Stuart monument especially that deserves attention for the superior art exhibited in many of the figures, and the draperies are arranged and treated with much skill. The taste shown in the flying figure of Fame may be questionable, especially in a monument in a church; but there is considerable power displayed in its light and expressive action, and the

P

proportions and form of the nude, wherever it occurs, indicate advanced artistic knowledge.

There is a class of monumental design, of which there are many examples in the Abbey, in which it is difficult to perceive any motive or sentiment, beyond that of personal ostentation. An instance of this application of art,—if, indeed it can come into the category of art at all,—is the huge monument in the Chapel of St. Paul, in memory of Lord and Lady Hunsdon. This composition, measuring between 30 and 40 ft. in height, and entirely occupying one end of the chapel, consists of various stages of merely architectural details over and around a sarcophagus; while obelisks, columns with capitals, architraves, and a variety of details, crowd the work from the pavement upwards; the most striking object being a large shield with the emblazoned coat-of-arms of the family. The whole has been profusely decorated and enriched with colour; now, in the course of time, sobered down to a most sombre blackness. The date of this monument is about 1600.

Before noticing a few other works of the sixteenth and seventeenth centuries, it will be proper to make particular reference to two striking monuments in the united Chapels of St. John Evangelist, St. Michael, and St. Andrew. The first is that in memory of Lord and Lady Norris, early in 1600. The effigies of both, in alabaster, lie recumbent on a raised tomb. A canopy is above them; on each side of the composition, at the base, are three kneeling figures, life-size, dressed in the armour of the day, representing the six sons of the above. This monument is very striking, not merely on account of its great size, but for the sentiment expressed in it. Although the sculpture is not fine, *quoad* style and technical value, the motive of the design is good and appropriate. The effigies of the heads of the family reposing in death, with their sons kneeling and praying around them, is a touching and beautiful subject, well fitted for a mortuary chapel.

The next monument in this chapel, to which attention may be called in a few words, is that of Sir Francis Vere, one of the eminent worthies and warriors of the Elizabethan era. Sir Francis, habited in a loose gown, is recumbent on a low bed or table tomb. At each corner is a knight, in full armour, kneeling. They support on their shoulders a large table, which forms a canopy over the principal figure. On this are placed various pieces of armour, supposed to be that of the great soldier lying beneath. The treatment of this design, in which the accessorial figures are made to contribute so prominently to the expression, is as rare as it is effective. They evidently are secondary to the main object, and though the figures are life-size, they take their proper place simply as attendants of honour on the great general who reposes in the centre of the composition.

In the same chapel is a large monument of later date, by Roubiliac, which claims more than a mere passing notice. It is in memory of Mrs. Nightingale. In the lower part of the pyramidal composition, a skeleton, partially draped, issues from the gates of a dark tomb, in the act of hurling a dart at a female above, who, fainting, is supported by her husband. He endeavours to ward off the fatal stroke, leaning forward, with the energy of despair, and extending his hand as a shield or guard between the sinking lady and the weapon of death. This is admirably rendered, and the expression of the dying figure, and the action and graceful form of the falling hand, likewise deserve the highest praise. The poetry of the conception is undeniable. It is full of pathos and touching sentiment. But here is seen the danger of not observing the proper limits between the ideal and the real, the conception and its expression in art. A mere skeleton, a figure of bones, which could not by any means be held together, is here represented with life, power, and strongly-marked expression, grasping an ordinary spear, with which he intends to slay his victim. The dying wife and her protector are supposed to see all this, and the husband endeavours, naturally, to ward off the threatened evil. But a skeleton is not that awful, mysterious visitation called Death; it is simply a painful and repulsive result of dissolution. With all its excellence in point of intention, and especially in its marvellous execution as a piece of marble-carving, this monument offends against propriety and good taste.

Roubiliac is the author of another remarkable and, in many respects, superior work, in the monument to the Duke of Argyll, who died in 1743. The duke is represented falling at the base of a pyramid. Around him are statues of Minerva, History, and Eloquence. The latter, the best figure in the group, is full of action and expression; and, with extended arm, appears to be addressing the spectator. It is a characteristic work of the time, and shows the great powers of Roubiliac in invention and execution; but, like almost all his works,—and it is the common failing,—it is utterly deficient in the repose so essential to give the proper effect to monumental works designed for a place of worship. The same criticism applies to a composition by the same artist, near the Argyll monument, in the south transept, in memory of Handel, the eminent composer. The expression of wrapt attention with which the great master appears to be listening to celestial music is admirably rendered, and the execution of the work is, as usual, wonderful; but the whole design is too theatrical for its destination. It is a composition more adapted to a music-hall than a church.

Scarcely any of the works after this time, however remarkable for other qualities, preserve any of the characteristics appropriate to church monuments. It is rare that allusion is made to death, the hope of a future state, or to the prayerful last moments of the Christian. The statues have a mere portrait character. The action of the figures have reference only to their worldly business and occupation, and the inscriptions record personal virtues, abilities, and prowess. The compositions are crowded with allegorical figures more or less good, as they are founded on or copied from the *antique;* and the recondite classical allusions can only be understood by the few. Such scenic designs as those representing Mr. Thynne attacked and murdered in his carriage; of the shipwrecked Admiral Tyrrell ascending out of the sea to heaven, amidst masses of clouds, while on all sides are the most preposterous accessories, including several life-size allegorical figures, prove the low character of monumental design, though they may, and do, undoubtedly, show considerable artistic power or ingenuity. Truthfulness and individuality were, as has been shown, first sacrificed to the absurd fancy of introducing classical details in the monuments. From ornamental the artist proceeded to personal *pseudo*-classical decoration; and we find the deceased English nobleman, statesman, or soldier, dressed in a Roman cuirass, or toga, or paludamentum, mixed up with modern costume. Sheffield, Duke of Buckingham, in the costume of a Roman emperor, attended by his duchess, in a court dress of the time of George I., has already been noticed; and the English admiral, Sir Cloudesley Shovel, in a Roman cuirass, sandals, and a full-bottomed wig, in his monument in the south aisle of the nave, and many others, equally inconsistent in time and place, show the extent to which this absurd fancy was carried.

It scarcely is necessary to multiply examples of the art that now characterised monumental sculpture. Prominent illustrations have been pointed out, by which the intelligent visitor will be able to realise for himself the leading peculiarities of the styles of the different ages. Hitherto, the motive or purpose of the generality of such works, however strangely expressed in some cases, had reference to the repose of death;

with suggestions of prayer and resignation; and with such accessories as are fitting in memorials placed in a Christian church. Less simple, indeed, than the early Mediæval monuments, still, the later monuments continued to show the religious impulse, and thus to invite serious reflection. In the eighteenth century, though there was better art, technically, this principle began to be lost sight of, and, in the end, it was utterly disregarded.

Having now rapidly reviewed the style and character of the monuments preserved in Westminster Abbey from the earliest regal monument,—that of Henry III., of the thirteenth century,—down to the end of the eighteenth century, it is not expedient to make particular remarks upon the monumental productions of the present age. It may merely be observed, generally, that while they often exhibit considerable knowledge and technical power in sculpture, creditable to their authors, they are, for the most part, simply personal memorials, and have no sentiment, or serious ecclesiastical character or treatment, to make them fitting objects to occupy places in a church. With few exceptions, portraiture has been the favourite and fashionable exercise of sculpture, and this has not been favourable to the exercise of invention, or to the expression of deep sentiment. Where portrait has not been the exclusive practice, the more ambitious designs are made up of classically draped or even of nude statues, in imitation of the antique. Others, expressing the views of the realistic or naturalistic school, represent the individual subjects dressed in the ordinary coats, waistcoats, and breeches of their day. As regards sentiment, some are in the full vigour of life, making speeches, brandishing swords, or calling up their troops; some are standing, in attitudes more or less graceful, doing nothing; while some are sitting comfortably in their armchairs, unoccupied, or, it may be, thinking. In none of these is there the slightest idea of fitness or propriety, with reference to place. Indeed, there are instances in which the extreme want of harmony with surrounding monuments and associations makes such productions not merely inappropriate, but positively offensive to good taste and feeling. They ought never to have been placed in the positions they occupy; and it is even now much to be desired that the more prominent of these statues, especially the single ones,—the most easily dealt with,—should be removed to other sites, where, while the deserts of their originals may be honourably recognised, and the statues raised to their memory be seen by their admiring countrymen, they should no longer be permitted to crowd the floor of a place of worship, where the mind should be occupied with other thoughts than those likely to be suggested by such incongruous associations.

It is not intended, nor is it desirable, that works once admitted into the Abbey should be removed with anything like contumely and disrespect, simply because they do not harmonise with religious sentiment, or are out of *keeping* with the architecture of the church. Honourable sites might still be found for them within the sanctuary, as it were. A cloister, for example, might easily be arranged, or a new one erected, to receive them, or they might be admitted within the restored Chapter-house. Many of the detached statues, especially, might so be placed with great propriety and with good effect. Many of the larger compositions, which interfere fatally with the architecture of the church, cannot, it may be feared, be safely removed; but the floor or pavement of the church itself would thus be freed, in a great measure, from the inconvenient accumulation of works in all respects inappropriate both in character and in place.

III.

WESTMINSTER HALL.

BY EDWARD FOSS, F.S.A.

READ ON JULY 23, 1866.

As this will probably be the last occasion on which the Archæological Institute, as a body, will have an opportunity of visiting Westminster Hall while it continues the theatre in which our civil judicature is administered, a few short notices of the legal uses to which it has been hitherto applied may not be uninteresting to the members.

The original edifice (upon the architectural peculiarities of which I do not pretend to touch) can boast of an antiquity of between seven hundred and eight hundred years, having been erected in the reign of William II., as an appendage to the palace of Westminster. Besides the royal ceremonies and festivities, to which it was at first applied, we may naturally suppose, from its size and convenience, that it was also used as the place for discussing and deciding those great questions in which the Crown was concerned, and also the minor differences always arising between subject and subject. At that time, and for a long period afterwards, such questions were tried before the "king himself," and the barons and prelates of the realm, in what was called the "Aula Regia," or "Curia Regis," a court which accompanied the king wherever he went, but which had its principal seat in the palace of Westminster. Henry II., a hundred years after, is said to have attended personally in his court, and to have made frequent progresses to discover the abuses in the rural jurisdictions.* In more recent times, also, we have some instances of our kings exercising this prerogative. After the lapse of three hundred years we have evidence that King Edward IV. sat three days together in the King's Bench, and was present at a trial for rape.† James I. is the last instance on record. That conceited monarch was not satisfied with sitting on the Bench to hear how justice was administered, but even claimed to exercise judicial power. On Sir Edward Coke calmly telling him that it was not competent for him to decide questions of law, he said that "he thought the law was founded on reason, and that he had reason as well as the judges." Whereupon Coke was obliged to represent to him, "that his Majesty was not learned in the law, which was the mete-wand and measure to try the causes of his subjects, and which protected his Majesty in safety and peace." The king on this was greatly irate, and exclaimed, "that then he should be *under* the law, which was treason to affirm." Whereupon Coke closed the amusing discussion by the

---

* Lord Lyttelton's Henry II. ii. 16.
† Stowe (Thoms' Ed.) 174; State Trials, iii. 942.

following quotation from Bracton: "*Quod rex non debit esse sub homine, sed sub Deo et lege.*"*

At the time of the Conquest, and long after, there were three special periods at which the kings held their courts, or, as it was called, "wore their crowns," with extraordinary solemnity, not only for the consideration of national affairs, but also for the transaction of legal business. These were at Christmas, Easter, and Whitsuntide; answering to our present law terms of Hilary, Easter, and Trinity;—Michaelmas Term having been added at a subsequent period. It is a curious illustration of the antiquity of the Terms that at the Court held at Christmas, 1096, a judgment was pronounced against William, Earl of Eu, for a treasonable conspiracy, on the very day on which Hilary Term, according to the Constitutions of Edward the Confessor, confirmed by William the Conqueror, then began.†

There is no positive evidence of any of these trials taking place in Westminster Hall during the reign of its founder, William II., nor in those of his two successors; but in the records of the reigns of Henry II., Richard I., and John, the expressions "my Court at Westminster," and "my barons and justices," are of frequent occurrence.‡

A great change took place under the last-mentioned monarch. King John, when in England, was in the

* 12 Coke's Reports, 65.
† Madox's Exchequer, i. 8.
‡ Manning's Serviens ad Legem, 171; Dugdale's Orig. Jurid. 49, 50, 92.

habit of making frequent progresses through the kingdom, and of holding his Court in a multiplicity of places, to the great inconvenience and expense of the suitors, who were obliged to follow him, in order that their causes might be tried. By a clause in Magna Charta, dated June 15, 1215, this intolerable grievance was abated. That clause declared that "Common Pleas shall not follow the Court, but shall be held in some certain place;" and though no place is mentioned in the Charter for their future holding, there is no doubt that Westminster Hall was the "certain place" intended. It has been the arena where common pleas have ever since been usually decided, though there are some instances in the reign of Edward III. of this Court being held at York. So strict, however, was the interpretation put upon the words "certain place" by one of our judges, that he resisted the removal of the Court from the original place in Westminster Hall to a more convenient part of the same building.

King John's concession was, no doubt, the precursor of other changes by which the Aula Regia was ultimately abolished, and the present arrangement of the Courts of Chancery, King's Bench, and Exchequer, as well as the Common Pleas, established, with separate judges appointed to preside over each Court.

The precise time at which this division of the courts was effected has been the subject of controversy, into which it is not my present purpose to enter. It is enough to say that at the end of the following reign of Henry III. the office of Chief Justiciary no longer existed, and that a Chief Justice and puisne judges were appointed for the Courts of King's Bench and Common Pleas. In the Court of Exchequer, though there were regular barons, the office of Chief Baron was not instituted till the reign of Edward II.

When I entered the profession, about the beginning of this century, there were only twelve judges in the three courts of Common Law. This number was deemed one of peculiar sanctity, and it was considered a sort of sacrilege to suggest any increase, as if that had been the number ever since the institution. And yet that number had only been the regular staff of the Courts from the reign of Edward VI. (1547); and it had been entirely forgotten that in all the previous reigns the number of judges had constantly varied, sometimes extending to nine in one court, eight in another, and six or five in a third; and sometimes being reduced to three, and even to two. James I., indeed, added one judge to the four judges then acting in each of the Courts, but the increase was discontinued before the end of the reign; and from that time till the reign of William IV. (except during the Commonwealth) the number of judges continued to be twelve. But, in 1830, the accumulation of business was at last met by an additional judge in each court, and ever since that date the Common Law Bench has consisted of fifteen judges.

Among other proofs that the courts met in Westminster Hall in the reign of Edward I., we have an order of that king that William de Brewes, a serjeant-at-law, who had publicly insulted a baron of the Exchequer, named Roger de Hegham, should go, with his body ungirt, his head uncovered, and his coif laid aside, from the Court of King's Bench, at Westminster, through the middle of the Hall, when the Court was full, to the Exchequer, and there ask the Baron's pardon.*

The judges were commonly resident in the city of London, and went to Westminster by water, embarking at the Temple, through which there was evidently a right of way.†

I am afraid that the administration of justice was not very pure at this period, for King Edward, on his return from France, in 1289, was inundated with complaints against the judges for extortion and other transgressions. He found such confirmation of the charges that he made a general clearance of the Bench, dismissing with disgrace all the judges of the two Courts of King's Bench and Common Pleas, except one in each, namely, John de Mettingham in the former, and Elias de Beckingham in the latter, who alone were found untainted. Among other punishments fines were imposed upon them, in proportion to their delinquencies, and that of Ralph de Hengham, the Chief Justice of the Court of King's Bench, for even the venial offence of altering a record by diminishing a fine, is said to have been devoted to the erection of a clock-house on the north side of New Palace Yard, furnished with a clock to be heard in Westminster Hall. The tradition has been noticed by some of the judges in subsequent reigns, who, on being

* Abbreviatio Placitorum, 256.
† New Fœdera, ii. 774.

asked to alter a record, refused to do so, saying that they "meant not to build a clock-house."* In 1370, sixpence a day was paid to John Nicole, "for his wages for the custody of the clock."† The tower remained till 1715, when it was taken down, and the spot where it stood was marked by a dial on one of the houses then erected on its site, and lately pulled down, with the allusive motto "*Discite justitiam moniti.*"‡

The Chancery was also held in Westminster Hall, in a part at the upper end, that was called the Magnum Bancum. There Walter Reginald, Bishop of Worcester, when he was appointed Chancellor in 1310, was inaugurated; and the description that it was "*ubi Cancellarii Regis sedere consueverunt,*" leaves us in doubt when the practice commenced.§ Other records of Edward II. show that the writs were sealed there; and in the same reign we first find it called "*Tabulam Marmoriam,*" which Strype describes as twelve feet in length and three feet in breadth. The "Marble Chair" is also frequently mentioned as the place where the Chancellor sat, and Dugdale tells us that it was fixed in the wall over against the middle of the marble table.‖ But neither the marble chair nor the marble table were to be seen in Dugdale's time (1666), both being built over by the Courts of Chancery and King's Bench. I do not find the precise date of their being

* Southcote, *temp.* Elizabeth; The Court, Charles II.; Holt, William III.
† Issue Roll, 44 Edw. III. 102, 334.
‡ Smith's Antiquities of Westminster, 28, 261.
§ Rot. Claus. 4 Edw. II. m. 26.
‖ Dugdale's Orig. Jurid. 37.

so covered, but that it was before the reign of Henry VIII. is apparent from the touching relation of the filial piety of Sir Thomas More, who, every day, before presiding as Chancellor in his own court, on one side of the Hall, knelt for the blessing of his aged father, who was a judge of the King's Bench, which was on the other side.

The office of Chancellor, long before the time of Sir Thomas More, had attained a much higher position in the State than it originally held. In the time of the Conqueror he was little more than the king's chief chaplain,—his father confessor, in fact,—and had the superior care of his chapel. He seems to have acted more as the private secretary to the sovereign, and to have prepared the various instruments to which the royal seal, which was kept under his direction, was to be attached. He was almost always an ecclesiastic, and resided in the palace. His allowance was five-pence a day, a simnel and two seasoned simnels; a sectary of clear wine, and a sectary of household wine; one large candle, and forty pieces of candle.[*] When he had performed his duties for a sufficient period, or when the king was desirous of a change, he was almost invariably rewarded with a bishopric. Thus Arfastus became Bishop of Helmham; Osbert, Bishop of Exeter; Osmund, Bishop of Salisbury; Maurice, Bishop of London, &c., &c.,—all after they had retired from the Chancellorship.

The daily communication which necessarily sub-

---

[*] Madox's Exchequer, i. 195.

sisted between the king and his Chancellor, naturally led the former to refer frequently to the advice of his officer, who would thus, by degrees, become a confidential counsellor in affairs of state: so that when the office of Chief Justiciary was abolished, the Chancellor became the king's chief legal adviser, and, practically, the Prime Minister of the kingdom. This increase of influence and power was early exemplified in the magnificence displayed by Becket on various occasions.

The simple title of Cancellarius Regis, which the Chancellor bore during the first eleven reigns after the Conquest, began to be considered insufficient, and the grander one of Cancellarius Angliæ was gradually adopted, and was commonly used in the reign of Richard II. Soon after the title of Lord Chancellor was introduced; and in the reign of Henry VII. it culminated in the present designation of Lord High Chancellor. The peculiar jurisdiction which now distinguishes his court seems not to have commenced till about the reign of Edward II. In the exercise of it he was assisted by the twelve clerks or Masters in Chancery, of whom the Master of the Rolls was the head. The first person so named was John de Langton, in 1286, 14 Edward I. He soon after became Chancellor, and ultimately Bishop of Chichester. In subsequent times the Masters of the Rolls held a separate and almost an independent court. The duties of the Master in Chancery were gradually reduced to inquiring into the minor details of the causes, and to reporting thereon to the Court; and in 1852 this ancient office was entirely abolished, after an existence of nearly eight hundred years. The business of the Chancery accumulated to such an extent that it became necessary greatly to enlarge the number of its judges. In 1813 one Vice-Chancellor was added; in 1841, two others; and in 1851 the Equity staff was increased by the appointment of two Lords Justices of Appeal; so that now full work is found for seven judges, to the performance of which, fifty years ago, two were deemed sufficient.

During the Terms the Chancellor sat in Westminster Hall, but during the vacations he heard causes in Lincoln's Inn Hall and other places, and often at his own house, of which instances are mentioned in the times of Sir Thomas More and Lord Chancellor Audley.

In recounting the legal incidents of Westminster Hall, it must not be forgotten that, besides the four Courts of Chancery, King's Bench, Common Pleas, and Exchequer, which were held within its precincts, the Hall itself was occasionally used as a high court of criminal justice for the solemn trial before the Peers of great delinquents, impeached by the House of Commons. One of the earliest, of which there is a particular account, is that against Michael de la Pole, Earl of Suffolk, Chief Justice Tresilian, and others, in the reign of Richard II., which king himself was deposed by the Parliament in this same hall. In subsequent times these trials often took place before commissioners appointed from among the Peers, assisted by some of the judges and other commoners.

Sir Thomas More and Bishop Fisher were tried in this manner; but it is doubtful whether the great hall was used on these occasions, or only the Court of King's Bench. Queen Anne Boleyn's trial took place in the Hall, on a "scaffold" there erected. In every subsequent reign, until that of George IV., many state offenders have there met their fate, whose names it is useless here to enumerate.

There is a print of Westminster Hall as it was prepared for the trial of the Earl of Strafford, in 1640, in which the queen is portrayed as looking out of her cupboard upon a scene in which her royal consort was, a few years after, to appear as a condemned prisoner. Some impeachments were tried before the Lords in their own house; but, during the long reign of George III. the Hall was fitted up four times, for the trials of Lord Byron for the murder of Mr. Chaworth, in 1765; of the Duchess of Kingston, for bigamy, in 1776; of Warren Hastings, which lasted above seven years—from February, 1788, to April, 1795; and of Lord Melville, in 1806; both the latter being for high crimes and misdemeanors. These were the last occasions when the great Hall was converted to such a solemn use, and as sixty years have since elapsed without giving a necessity for a similar display, we may fairly attribute the absence of the occasion to the improvement of society and the general amelioration of the age.

By a curious conjunction, one and the same person in the early reigns held the two offices of Warden of the Palace of Westminster and Warden of the Fleet

Prison. Two records, of the 12th and 24th Edward III., show that there were then stalls for merchandise in, and stables under, Westminster Hall, and that the holder of those offices was allowed to take for his profit eightpence per annum for each stall and stable, and four-pence for each stall only.*

The Hall was also ornamented with "images," and various payments on account of them are recorded in the earlier part of the reign of Richard II. ;† but in the latter part, the ruinous effects of time, and perhaps of a fire, that destroyed one of the adjoining houses, in 1386,‡ had become so visible that about two hundred years after its construction it was considered necessary to undertake substantial repairs. The opportunity was taken to introduce various alterations, and greatly to enlarge the edifice. The contract for part of the works is preserved in Rymer,§ and the restoration was completed in 1399, the last year of Richard's reign, whose deposition was the first public act for which it was used in the Parliament there assembled.

It is not improbable that at this time the old marble chair and table were covered over, and the two Courts of Chancery and King's Bench erected above them. Shops and hawkers were still allowed in the new hall, as in the old, but with higher prices. By a "rental" of 38 Henry VI., the rents of shops varied from two shillings to three shillings and fourpence a Term; and

---

* Topog. et Geneal. i. 520, 523.
† Devon's Issues of the Exch. 227, 230.
‡ Rymer's Fœdera, vii. 548.
§ Rymer's Fœdera, 794.

the " Goers in the Halle," as they were called, were charged from fourpence to twelvepence for the same period, the larger sum being paid by "Robynet Frenshwoman."*

Sir Henry Blunt, in his " Voyage into the Levant," published in 1669, mentions (p. 20) that he rewarded a Turkish boy who gave him a cup of sherbet " with a pocket looking-glass, in a little ivory case, with a comb, such as are sold at Westminster Hall for four or five shillings a-piece." Pepys also in his entertaining Diary, three months before the restoration of Charles II., speaks of a young bookseller in the Hall, and Mrs. Lane and the rest of the maids there, wearing their white scarfs, all having been at his burial. That the booksellers and stationers in the Hall were at that time a privileged class appears from their being exempted from the pains and penalties in the statutes then enacted for appointing licensers and regulating the press.†

In the reign of Henry VI., we are informed by Fortescue, in his work " De laudibus Legum Angliæ," that the sittings of the judges did not exceed three hours, from eight to eleven ; and it appears from the Year Book of 2 Henry VII. fo. 4, that they were not then more severely taxed, rising " because it was past eleven o'clock."

About this time there were certain places in Westminster Hall designated Hell, Purgatory, and Paradise, —names that seem to indicate that they were appro-

* Gent. Mag. Dec., 1853, p. 603.
† Pepys' Diary, Jan. 30, 1659-60 ; and Mr. Bruce's note.

priated, as two of them certainly were, to the confinement of delinquents, according to the varied degrees of punishment for their respective offences. We see from the Illuminations of the Courts, lately published in the thirty-ninth volume of the "Archæologia," which are attributed to the reign of Henry VI., that at the bars of the three Courts of King's Bench, Common Pleas, and Exchequer, certain prisoners are represented; and their place of incarceration might probably be in one or the other of these cells. Some have thought that these extraordinary names were suggested by the titles of the three parts of Dante's "Divina Commedia;" and if it could be shown that Dante's work was familiar to the English world before those names were given to these three repositories, it might fairly be contended, from their succession and order, that Dante was their god-father.

The occurrence, however, of at least one of the names in the reign of Edward III., before Dante was born, tends to destroy the ingenious conceit. In the list of rooms and buildings in the Palace of Westminster, extracted from the original accounts of the expenses of erecting St. Stephen's Chapel in that reign, the following entry occurs:—

"Door of Hell in the Exchequer."

This is followed by another, to which the former probably applies:—

"House called Holle, under the Exchequer."

A third place named in the list may perhaps be the same which afterwards went by the name of Paradise or Heaven:—

"Le Godeshouse in the receipt of the Exchequer."*

Whatever were the uses to which these places were originally applied, it plainly appears that the custody of them was made a source of emolument, and was granted to the "squires of the king's body," and other favourites. Thus, in the Act of Resumption, passed in the first year of Henry VII., the grant of these places (when I find them for the first time so named) to Pierce Carvanell, "Gentleman Usher of our Chamber," is specially excepted. The same document mentions two other places in Westminster Hall of which this usher had a grant—the house under the Exchequer, called Le Puttans, or Potan's House, and the tower and house called Le Grene Lates.† These houses were, in the reign of Edward VI., appropriated to the records and rolls of the Exchequer, and an annuity of £12 13s. 4d. was paid to Sir Andrew Dudley (to whom they had been previously granted) as a compensation for his loss.‡ Hell, Purgatory, and Paradise, and another building called "Heaven," were subsequently converted from cells of confinement to places of recreation and refreshment, still preserving their graceless names, and were frequented by lawyers and others attending the courts; and many are the allusions made to them in that character by dramatic and other authors so early as the reign of James I. In that of George II. great alterations were made in the approaches to Westminster Hall and the Houses of

* Smith's Antiquities of Westminster, 71.
† Rymer's Fœdera, xii. 275, xiii. 34; Rot. Parl. vi. 372.
‡ Rymer's Fœdera, xv. 233.

Parliament, among which Heaven and Purgatory (in the latter of which was preserved the ducking-stool, for the punishment of scolds) were pulled down. Hell and Paradise suffered the same fate in the next reign, about 1793.*

In addition to the trades which were carried on within its precincts, the Hall was made the receptacle of the military banners, taken in battle. We have no record of these triumphant ornaments to its walls before the reign of Charles I., when those taken at the battle of Naseby, in 1645, were displayed there, and were still hanging over the king's head when he was condemned in the same hall, as if to remind him of his disastrous defeat. These banners were supplemented by those taken at Dunbar and Preston in 1650, and afterwards at the battle of Worcester in 1651, "the crowning mercy" of Cromwell; the result of which was the expatriation of Charles II. for nine years. On the restoration of that prince all these memorials of disaster were, it is to be presumed, removed; and we have no notice of their successors till nearly a century afterwards, when the victories of Marlborough supplied a goodly show.

By the effects of natural decay, or of political causes, or perhaps by the influence of better taste, all of them have been since removed; but that they remained there in the reign of George II. we have the testimony of a picture by Gravelot, painted during his thirteen years' residence in this country, representing the interior of the Hall as it then appeared. Ranged along the

* Smith's Westminster, 262, 268.

left side, as you enter, are shops of booksellers, mathematical instrument makers, haberdashers, and sempstresses. At the further end of the Hall are the two courts of King's Bench on the left, and of the Chancery on the right, divided by a flight of steps which led to the entrances of both. In the print these courts are enclosed to a certain height, but not covered; so that the noise in the Hall, and the flirtations of the barristers and attorneys with the sempstresses, must have occasionally disturbed the arguments of the counsel, and disarranged the gravity of the judges. On the right side is the same array of shops, except where it is interrupted by the Court of Common Pleas, which projects into the hall, and is similarly enclosed and uncovered. On both sides of the Hall, above the shops and the Court of Common Pleas, was a continuous display of banners, which, at the date of the picture, were probably those taken at the battle of Blenheim, and the other victories of Marlborough. The Court of Common Pleas was subsequently removed to the outside of the Hall; and the enclosure of the two other courts was completed and carried up to the roof, and thus divided from the exterior noise and racket.

I am not certain at what date the shopkeepers were ousted from the Hall, but in my own recollection, which extends beyond the beginning of the present century, they did not exist. The Courts of Chancery and King's Bench have since disappeared, and are removed, with the other courts, to more convenient sites on the western exterior of the Hall, with entrances into it. Thus the edifice is now little more than a magnificent vestibule to them and to the two houses of parliament, and a place of congregation for lawyers and their clients when attending the courts during Term time. It may possibly be again called into requisition for coronation banquets, and for the trial of State delinquents, though none of the former have been celebrated there for between forty and fifty years; while no less than sixty years have elapsed since any of the latter have taken place.

For the preparation of the coronation banquets the courts, when within the Hall, were obliged to be removed, and the shops and stalls to be boarded over. A petition of the shopkeepers in the reign of George I prays that, as their shops are boarded up for the ceremony of the coronation, the leads and the outsides of the windows of the west side of the Hall may be granted for their use and advantage.*

Besides the coronation banquets, we have record of many others from the earliest time. On New Year's day, 1236, King Henry III. feasted 6000 poor men, women, and children. In 1241, the same king sumptuously entertained there the Pope's legate, and his nobility; and again, in 1243, he celebrated there the nuptials of his brother, Richard Earl of Cornwall, with a banquet, at which it is said there were no less than 30,000 dishes; though where room was found for them it is difficult to imagine. When the repairs of the Hall were completed in 1399, King Richard II. is recorded to have plentifully entertained 10,000 in it, and, it is cautiously noted, "in other rooms of the

* Gent. Mag., Nov., 1853, p. 480.

palace"; for it is clear that the guests would not otherwise have had elbow-room.* Fabyan relates in his Chronicle that Henry VII. in the ninth year of his reign kept a royal feast there;† and the same king used the Hall for certain entertainments, under the name of "disguisyngs," which were exhibited to the people at Christmas. We have the following proof that they were provided or assisted by the Government: an entry occurs in the Issue Roll of a payment of 28*l*. 3*s*. 5¾*d*. (a large sum in those days) to Richard Daland, "for providing certain spectacles or theatres, commonly called scaffolds," for these performances.‡

The royal ceremonies and entertainments, however, nor the legal solemnities to which Westminster Hall was devoted, did not exempt it or its occupiers from the calamities to which inferior buildings and ordinary mortals are liable. Many were the occasions when pestilence, or plague, or sweating sickness, necessitated the adjournment of the Terms, and even the entire desertion of the Hall. Instances of adjournment on that account occur in 1434 in Henry VI.'s reign, and again in 1482 in that of Edward IV. On this account the courts were held at St. Albans in the 26th year of Henry VIII., and at Walden in the 35th year of the same king. In the reign of Elizabeth there were frequent recurrences of similar visitations, the courts being sometimes held at Hertford, and sometimes at St. Albans. Beaumont and Fletcher allude to the

* Stow's London (Thoms' ed.) 173.
† Fabyan's Chronicle, 685.
‡ Devon's Issue Roll, 516.

latter fact when, in their play of "Wit without Money," they make Lance speak of

"Taverns wither'd
As though the Term lay at St. Albans."

During the Great Plague of 1665 the Term was held at Oxford and at Windsor.

The Hall also was visited by the calamity of fire. Archbishop Laud in his Diary records that on Sunday, February 20, 1630-1, the hall was found on fire "by the burning of the little shops or stalls kept therein." It was soon extinguished, and the damage quickly repaired.

Inundations of the Thames also occasionally flooded the Hall. Holinshed mentions two in the reign of Henry III., in 1237, when he says boats might have been rowed up and down, and in 1242, when no one could get into the Hall, except they were set on horseback. He records another, 300 years after, in the reign of Queen Mary, when the Hall was flooded "unto the stair-foot, going to the Chancerie and King's Bench, so that when the Lord Maior of London should come to present the sheriffs to the Barons of the Exchequer, all Westminster Hall was full of water."[*] These visitations were repeated in the last century, in 1735 and 1791; and even so lately as 1841. The rising of the tide on those occasions gave abundant opportunity for the utterance of legal witticisms. In reference to one of these, Henry Fielding, in his dramatic satire of "Pasquin" makes Law say,—

[*] Holinshed, ii. 380, 399; iv. 80.

"We have our omens too. The other day,
A mighty deluge swam into our Hall,
As if it meant to wash away the Law:
Lawyers were forc'd to ride on porters' shoulders;
One, O prodigious omen! tumbled down,
And he and all his briefs were sous'd together."

The jocular poet, no doubt, did not seriously think that his watery "omen" really portended the "washing away of the law" from Westminster Hall; and we can fancy how his indignant verse would flow were he to witness the great clearance to which his favourite fane is doomed—by neither pestilence, fire, nor inundation. In a few short years the lawyers will be expelled from their ancient haunts,—the *religio loci* must be abjured,—and the worshippers must resort to another temple. However magnificent the new structure may be in its exterior, or however convenient in its internal arrangements, it will strike the present ministrants of the law with far less admiration than the venerable sanctuary in which they paid their earliest adorations; and it will afford them a perpetual subject of invidious comparison in their intercourse with the novices of the profession. Such feelings are natural, for who can look back to a period of nearly 800 years, during which Westminster Hall has been devoted to its present objects, without acknowledging a degree of veneration towards the eminent judges who have presided there, and an affectionate reminiscence of the eloquent advocates who have pleaded before them.

But we need not fear that the connection between Westminster Hall and the law will ever be forgotten.

Memory will call to mind the sages who have adorned it, and tradition will still remain. Let us hope that when the new Palace of Justice, so long demanded by the necessities of the times, shall be erected, a succession of able judges will emulate their venerable predecessors, and, with the learning, intelligence, and integrity of future aspirants at the bar, will secure for the new fane as much respect and reverence in times to come, as in times past was attained by Westminster Hall.

IV.
PUBLIC RECORD OFFICE.
By JOSEPH BURTT,
ASSISTANT KEEPER OF THE PUBLIC RECORDS.

DURING the last few years I have given some notices of the Records of the places in which the Institute has held its meetings.

When, however, it was decided that this year's meeting should be held in the metropolis, which owns the most extensive and valuable collection of municipal documents in the kingdom, and which is the depository of the archives of the realm, I felt that my very slight acquaintance with the one collection would remove it from any attempt on my part to present any comments upon it to the consideration of the meeting. It was the hope of those who take the most interest and some trouble in preparing material for these assemblies, that the many illustrations of our history and domestic manners, of the progress of municipal institutions, and the vicissitudes of City life as shown by City records, would have been brought before us by the aid of one who has already done such good service to the subject in his able editorship of that remarkable volume, the " Liber Albus." That hope, however, was disappointed. There still remained the public collection of the National Archives.

I may, perhaps, be permitted to say that the general interest of Englishmen in their noble collection of public records has never been equal to that of the present time. So much has been done of late years to afford opportunities for turning that collection to good practical account,—so much has been culled out of that collection for the illustration of matters of archæological interest, for the elucidation of public and private history, and for the development of our knowledge of early domestic life and manners,—that the crowd of inquirers and searchers has been too considerable for the narrow and inconvenient space allotted to their accommodation in the first Public Record Office of the kingdom, and has induced H.M. Government to supply an addition to the building, which is as conspicuous for its convenience and comfort as the old offices were for the entire absence of those qualities. I need scarce affirm that a good and complete knowledge of the great collection of documents contained in the Public Record Office cannot be attained without long and laborious study and attention. A meeting like this in the metropolis would, it seemed to me, naturally look for some general account of our public records and their history. My long connection with the establishment entrusted with the preservation and administration of a collection of such extent and unrivalled interest appeared to me to make it a duty to attempt to supply this want.

An Archæological Congress in the metropolis would

(it seemed to me) naturally look for some general account of the Public Records, the formation and condition of the collection. And to give some idea of the accidents to which they have been subjected, and a general view of the present contents of the Office, appeared to me the main points proper to be presented to such a meeting. To do more would perhaps be wearisome.

With regard to the history of the different branches of the establishment, the first place is, of course, due to that of the Chancery, as being more intimately connected with the personalty of the Sovereign and the administration of justice and equity. I intend to do my best to avoid technical details and abstruse discussions, so I shall pass by the various etymologies of the word "chancery." While there is no doubt that the office existed in Saxon times, no "Chancery" documents of anything like that antiquity have descended to the present. The rolls called "Cartæ Antiquæ"— the rolls of charters by sovereigns and others conferring gifts and grants upon religious houses and others, which are certainly not earlier than the reign of Richard I.—are the most ancient records of the Court, while the general series of Chancery documents begins in the reign of King John. I must here venture to express the doubt in my own mind as to the previous existence of earlier documents, and I must own that I am not satisfied with the argument that would show that such earlier documents were never made. It appears to me an exceedingly difficult position to maintain, that any of the known series of documents had their origin somewhere about the time, or slightly anterior to the time, of their present commencement.

The rolls of the "Cartæ Antiquæ" are the connecting link between the Courts of Chancery and Exchequer in their earliest stages. The enrolment of these charters, and their confirmation by that act, was from the earliest times considered to be one of the most legitimate sources of revenue, as it certainly was one of the most profitable.

The Court of Exchequer is the section of our administrative arrangements which relates more especially to the fiscal condition of the country, and which affords the earliest existing accounts of the royal and public expenditure.

One of the finest MSS., one of the noblest monuments of a nation's condition existing in any country, is our earliest record of the Court of Exchequer—the Domesday Book of William the Conqueror. It is well known to be a compilation from returns sent in to the Royal Exchequer at Winchester, in consequence of commissions directing inquiries of the minutest character as to the nature, extent, and value of the landed property of the country.* In making those inquiries, and in stating their result, the simple and concise language of the time gives numerous incidental notices illustrating both public and private history, manners and customs, often introduced (it seems) by the merest

* A twelfth-century copy of one of these returns—that for Cambridgeshire—is in the British Museum, and is about to be published by the Royal Society of Literature, under the editorship of Mr. N. E. S. A. Hamilton.

chance or accident. Thus, in describing a holding in Buckinghamshire, it tells us how a damsel, Alunid by name, held land "which Earl Godric granted her as long as he remained Earl, on condition of her teaching his daughter to work embroidery." And many other such notices of the life and manners of the period are either as distinctly referred to among those relating to dues and rights, or may be gathered from them.

The next records of the Exchequer in point of date are the Great Rolls of the Pipe, so called from their shape.* With them our collection of national records begins. The earliest existing roll, that of the 31st year of Henry I., has been published entire; and in the valuable preface to that volume it is clearly shown that the series of such rolls certainly at one time extended through the whole reign of Henry I. Those rolls contain the accounts of the payments into the Exchequer from all the sources of revenue then existing, many of which would have a strange and grating sound upon modern ears. They are chiefly valuable to the historian and the archæologist for the payments entered upon them as claims for allowance by the sheriffs of counties, for sums expended by royal command; thus giving particulars of royal journeyings and requirements, and also of some royal tastes and habits. Among these payments will be found the material for so much existing knowledge of the works

* Another explanation, more fanciful, it seems to me, has been given of this term. It is said that the great rolls of the Exchequer were called "the Pipe Rolls," as being the great "pipe," or conduit, through which the revenue mainly flowed.

executed at royal castles and palaces, which have been used so extensively by our late and lamented friends and contributors, the Rev. Mr. Hartshorne and Mr. Hudson Turner; and to which those who have just favoured us with their valuable discourses upon Windsor Castle and the Abbey of Westminster have been much indebted.

I must again advert to the suggestion, that it seems exceedingly probable the general series of records began shortly after the Conquest, and that Domesday Book could not have stood entirely alone till the reign of Henry I. The original returns from which it was compiled were doubtless long preserved in the Exchequer for reference, for they were the *real* evidence which, for the convenience of the officers, were abstracted—so to speak—into the volumes we now possess. The very work which it was intended to serve—the collection of the incidents of the royal income—must have necessitated other documents and accounts, and it appears to me most probable that Domesday was turned to practical use from the moment of its compilation, and that officers throughout the country answered to the Exchequer for those dues and profits which it enabled them to collect. It is known that the Exchequer was established by William the Conqueror, and there is no good reason why the Pipe Rolls—the great rolls of that court—should have suddenly been called into existence by Henry I., rather than that they are the result of the system of which the Domesday Book is the great and only existing evidence. It appears to me that the construction usually given to the passage in the Red Book of the Exchequer relating to the early Pipe Rolls is not the only one it might bear, and that it is capable of a meaning consistent with the theory I have ventured to advance.

I do *not* intend to go so far as our great dramatist, and argue that at one time our public collection contained the actual accounts of the commencement of the building of the White Tower by Julius Cæsar, but the passage in which allusion is made to them is a very remarkable one.*

In the earliest times of the known history of our public records, they were considered among the treasures of the sovereign, and kept in the storehouses of his plate, jewels, vestments, and relics, the treasuries at Westminster and the Tower of London. Some of the royal title-deeds were, however, placed for a time in royal castles and other places of security. Such of the records as were required for the performance of public business, and for the transaction of any affairs dependent upon the presence of the sovereign, were carried about by the officers having the direction of

* Richard III. Act iii. scene 1. The Prince of Wales (Ed. V.) being conducted to the Tower by Buckingham, says:—

"Did Julius Cæsar build that place, my lord?
"BUCK. He did, my gracious lord, begin that place;
Which since succeeding ages have re-edified.
"PRINCE. Is it upon record? or else reported
Successively from age to age, he built it?
"BUCK. Upon record, my gracious lord.
"PRINCE. But say, my lord, it were not registered;
Methinks the truth should live from age to age."

the royal household. Entries appear upon the rolls of the expenses of packing into casks and hampers, the ready cash required for military expenditure, and also for carefully covering up certain rolls and documents required for use, or that were suddenly called for and required transmission. I may specially mention that transaction in the year 1291, when Edward I., being in Scotland, required certain rolls which had been temporarily lodged in a chest in the New Temple, and which the Treasurer was directed to break open, and take out the rolls specified and send them to the king.

There are many existing references to other dealings with the records of the Chancery and Exchequer in the fourteenth century, orders for their transfer and arrangement, and for their reception into the royal treasuries. As regards the records of the Chancery, there are, however, no existing remains of their old receptacles and modes of deposit of any great interest, and no special references showing that they were other than ordinary bags or chests.

At this present time it is to a section of the Court of Exchequer, the Department of the Treasury of the Receipt, that we must turn, if we have any desire of seeing examples of the most ancient modes of depositing documents. In the portion of the Public Record Office assigned to that department are still preserved a few of the boxes and cases used in the times of the first three Edwards.

The Treasury of the Receipt of the Exchequer was one of the treasuries of the nation and of the sovereign—all, or almost all, in one, for they were very closely united then—which contained the objects acquired by the strong hand of the conqueror, or which had been presented to the sovereign; the regalia, vestments and articles for coronations and state ceremonies, records, and sacred things. And Walter de Stapleton, Bishop of Exeter, the King's Treasurer, who must have had more than an official love for the documents pertaining to his office, arranged them all in good order under their subject-matter or upon some principle of sortation, and put them into chests, cases, and boxes of wood, leather, and wicker, many of which must have been of the quaintest and queerest kind. There are still a few, and but very few, of these articles remaining. They consist of an oblong box, measuring on the outside 16 in. by 14, formed of oak an inch thick, which has been covered with a "gesso" ground, and decorated with light rods of iron having spear-shaped heads of elegant form; a case of "cuir bouilli," the "forcerium correum ferro ligato" of Stapleton's calendar, having the surface covered with *fleur de lis* impressed in a small diamond-shaped panel; and various boxes of wood. One of these, popularly known as "Robert Bruce's coffin," is that in which the documents relating to the ransom of Robert's son David, the noble prisoner of the battle of Neville's Cross, were transmitted to the Royal Treasury. On the lid the inscription of its contents is still quite clear. Besides these, there is a fine massive and still substantial chest, with a ponderous lid studded with large rough nail-heads, and having six strong and independent locks.

It was to this *secretum secretorum* within the Treasury itself that the safety of the Domesday Book and other precious valuables was committed in early times. But, besides arranging the collection, Walter de Stapleton gave facilities for the most illiterate churl about the Exchequer to find any set of such documents that might be wanted if only the subject-matter was known. This he effected by adopting a system of picture-writing on the outside of the case appropriate to its contents. One instance or two must suffice in this place. The coffer containing treaties of marriage was distinguished by a hand-in-hand; three united herrings signified Yarmouth, and a man with a Lochaber axe was the type of Scotland, painted or carved upon a "forcer" or "coffin" containing documents relating to those places. To describe all these, and to refer at all *seriatim* to the miscellaneous collection once in the Royal Treasury, is beyond my present purpose.

Neither shall I attempt anything of a list or catalogue of the records of the Chancery and Exchequer, or give an account of the "Press" room which they occupy. They are of the most miscellaneous description, embracing almost every conceivable subject of interest, not only to the historian and archæologist, but to all who wish to have accurate information respecting the lives, the deeds, and habits of our ancestors, and upon the condition and progress of the country. Upon many such subjects they are the only existing evidence, and there are among them many special and highly interesting documents. As peculiarly worthy of examination and study, may be specified the royal letters, and other early state documents among the records of the Chancery, of which so valuable a specimen has lately been edited in the series of Chronicles published under his Honour's directions, the miscellaneous documents of the Queen's Remembrancer, and of the Treasury of the Exchequer, which abound with rolls of works and buildings, household rolls, inventories, and agreements of various kinds. These documents, referring as they do to the disposal and outlay of the royal revenue, are the vouchers or supplementary materials necessary for the proper auditing of the accounts by the officers of the Exchequer, and which were brought in for that purpose. The system has always been a strict one, and is so at the present day.

The judicial documents, also, of the various courts into which the general jurisdiction exercised by the Curia Regis became divided are full of matters of curious and minute detail, and are not overburdened with the dry and technical particulars of later times. And some most curious particulars of the state of things existing in the city of London in the twelfth century may be gleaned from the proceedings against William-with-the-Long-Beard, set out in the rolls of the Curia Regis. I have also a note before me of a bill for murder at North Ashby, Northampton, in the second year of Edward I., in which the deed is said to have been committed "en un soler qest ultre la porte de mesme le manoir pres de la fenetre de mesme le soler que est vers le South a

4 pees de home vers le North la quele porte est assiz vers le North en joinant a la haute estree nostre seigneur le roy vers le North e joinant al estable del manoir avantdit;" and the deed done by a barbed arrow, "dont la teste fust de feer et dasser la longure de treis pouz de homme et la laure (largeur) deux pouz de homme," the arrow itself three quarters of an ell long, about two inches wide, and fledged with the feathers of the peacock bound on with vermilion silk. To the legal reader, this language will recall that of the early Year Books. Upon the coroners' rolls the causes of death are very illustrative of existing things. Such are the instances of a fall from an apple-tree in a garden overhanging Paternoster Row, down a well of which the sides were formed of so many barrels each three feet high; and other accidents of domestic life. Among that considerable series of documents, the value of which is so well known to all archæologists, the inquisitions, is a small section that has almost failed to attract attention, and which yet fully deserves it. These are the "Proofs of Age." They are the evidence brought forward by parties to establish the age of the heir, and they give the depositions of neighbours and friends upon the subject, and these show that the domestic system of chronology, which is not to be found in the "L'Art de vérifier les Dates," and which would establish the date of the battles of Waterloo or Königrätz by their knowledge of the date of the birth of a favourite child, and the king's advent to the throne by that of the purchase of a gay dress or hat, or the entering upon a new residence, is simply the

continuation of a habit of thought indulged in by English men and women of the thirteenth and fourteenth centuries.

Our collection of national monuments continued to grow and increase—increasing vastly in bulk as they diminished in interest—during the eight centuries which have passed since the Domesday Book was compiled. Many of the great steps in the progress of the country, of its increase in wealth and means, its changes in habits and customs, have produced great additions to different classes of records, or changes in them, with many variations, and subject to many accidents, and especially to that of the neglect of those into whose official charge they often fell as an incident of office, productive of far more trouble than profit or advantage.

Among Public Records are many objects of great curiosity and interest—letters of our sovereigns and great nobles, documents relating to matters of great public importance, golden and other seals, finely executed charters and other instruments. Special mention should be made of those fine volumes, elaborately bound in rich Genoa velvet and decorated with enamelled bosses and clasps, which contain the indentures of services for the soul of Henry VII., for the performance of which the beautiful chapel called after that sovereign was substituted for the "Lady Chapel" of Westminster Abbey.

It must be borne in mind, however, that such special instruments have come into the public collection in the ordinary course of its formation. Collectors have despoiled, not enriched it; and no authorities have been on the watch to fill up gaps by timely purchases. What it should have contained, had its integrity been preserved, we may see by the riches existing elsewhere.

At the latter part of the fifteenth century, when the country was beginning to recover from the effects of the terrible Wars of the Roses, our national muniments received an addition which tells the condition to which society at that time had been reduced. While the king's authority was acknowledged after many a struggle, the ordinary fountains of justice were tainted, and acts of cruelty, hardship, and oppression were committed almost with impunity. House was divided against house, family against family, and no redress for many a hard and savage wrong committed by the powerful over the weak remained, but that appeal to the highest court of the realm which must ever form a distinguishing and most valuable feature in the administration of a monarchy. At this time the equitable jurisdiction of the Chancery had its rise, and the almost analogous action of the King in Council was appealed to most extensively. Committees of that Council, sitting in certain chambers of the king's palace of Westminster—the one with a gay ceiling, decorated with stars, the other in a chamber where all the "requests" of petitioners of any rank or station were received—gave rise to "courts" known by those two names. It is a mistake to suppose that, in its original constitution or action, the Court of Star Chamber deserved the obloquy which its subsequent distortion undoubtedly merited. But then that distortion was in the minds of those who constituted that court. In its first operation, it aimed simply to correct the failure of justice which prevailed generally throughout the country. It is, however, certain that no good spirit existed in the courts of law, as regards this "equitable" jurisdiction. Making allowances for the language in which trained "solicitors" of suits (for it was in getting up such cases that the well-known profession had its rise) stated the cases of their clients, there can be no doubt that the social condition of the country was at the time of the accession of Henry VIII. reduced to a very miserable plight. The proceedings of the Court of Star Chamber for that reign are very numerous, and they generally refer to acts of personal cruelty and oppression; those of the Court of Requests chiefly refer to cases of disputed right, in which the complainants urge that they cannot obtain redress by the ordinary process of law. There can be little doubt that the action of the Courts of Star Chamber and Requests was soon abused; and in the reign of Elizabeth the Attorney-General was a frequent plaintiff. In that reign the Court attained its full maturity, and it administered justice wisely and discreetly; the *morale* of the community at large being certainly unsound, and there being ample cause for its operation. The political persecutions of the time were performed in another Committee of the Council, which had no distinctive name. The actual bulk of the records of these two Courts is very considerable for the period over which they extend, and they have not been examined or used to any great extent.

Besides these two Courts, there sprang up, in the reign of Henry VIII., another, which in its first operation was more oppressive than either, because it brought home to every man of family and property in the country the most rigid and extortionate exactions, and contributed greatly to that decay of regard for the royal authority which culminated in the succeeding century. Established by statute of the twenty-fourth of Henry VIII., the Court of Wards and Liveries had the duty assigned to it of "better serving" the King as regards all the incidents of feudality, which were so considerable a source of the royal revenue. Every device was put into action to prove that the property of any deceased was held of the King "in chief," and with that verdict followed fines and payments upon every imaginable dealing with that property, or the right to do so. Jurors hesitating to return a verdict for the Crown were subjected to all kinds of pressure; and the officers of the Court were particularly enjoined to be careful in the selection of such persons. Jurors then had to give their evidence upon the facts, and were selected for their supposed knowledge of them.

The proceedings of these three Courts still exist in very considerable bulk, and among them are large numbers of private deeds sent in as "exhibits" in cases in progress. That they are full of interest to the biographer and archæologist no one can doubt; but they are not at present capable of being carefully searched, as the greater portion of them are without any means of reference whatever. They relate to a period when so many of the families of rank and mark in later and in present times were obtaining or struggling to make a position for themselves—to a period which comprises the origin of a large portion of our present peerage. It may be mentioned that among the Star Chamber proceedings of the reign of James I. is a remarkable case, in which the family of Cavendish attempted to bring the action of the Court to bear upon a person of inferior position,—one Margaret Chatterton, who had inveigled a scion of their house into a marriage with her. The oppressive action of the Court of Wards and Liveries soon became notorious. An auditor of the Court, John Audley—the name of whose estate near London is preserved in that of the "Audley" streets, near Hyde Park—is taken as a type of oppression and avarice by the elder D'Israeli; and we read of an ancestor of Baron Poltimore having been taken " to ward" by some great person, who carried him into a distant country, bred him up in the drudgery of the family, concealing from him his quality and property, which he only discovered by some accident.

Another extraordinary addition to the collection of public documents was caused by the dissolution of the monasteries and the seizure of their property. With this property came very many of their title-deeds and records; but, alas! a very small portion indeed. There is no doubt that the greater part of them were scattered far and wide; and no collectors of such curious and now valued stores arose till very many of them had perished, by accident or design. Still the "Court of the Augmentation of the Revenues of the Crown," which was specially constituted to deal with the religious houses, and with the great wealth which flowed into the Exchequer by their dissolution, took possession of, and has preserved, a large number of their muniments. It is in this collection that so much of the most curious and valuable information relating to those establishments is to be found. Many of their charters and rolls of accounts of various kinds are still preserved; together with a few cartularies. By some accident, perhaps, many of these documents got into the section of the Treasury of the Exchequer, into which was transmitted the large mass of official and officious papers relating to the dissolution itself, the causes from which it sprang, and the means by which it was designed and carried out.

To the period of the dissolution of the monasteries we may assign the commencement of that later and large series of documents which is the staple of the "State Paper Office" collection, and which is known by the title "Domestic." Any attempt to describe so vast and miscellaneous a collection, extending from the first year of Henry VIII. almost to the present time, must not be here expected: it must be sought for in the valuable and comprehensive Calendars of that series, and of its branches, "Foreign," "Colonial," and "Irish," which are now in the course of formation under the superintendence of the Deputy-Keeper. And in the able prefaces to those Calendars will be seen the best epitome of the general bearing of the documents upon the history of the country, and their value to archæological science. A large addition to the general collection of documents has been made, by the transfer of the old books and papers of various departments of the State to the custody of the Master of the Rolls. Perhaps the most important and interesting of these are those which relate to the business of the Treasury, and which consist chiefly of the minutes of the board upon the various and important matters submitted to its consideration, or otherwise dealt with by it.

It is only within a comparatively recent period that any systematic attention has been bestowed upon the general collection of public records. Those which were required for legal purposes have always been well tended, while their value continued; but those which are most valuable in the consideration of the archæologist have suffered lamentably. It would be a long and unpleasant tale to tell the adventures of many of these most valued documents—how they had lain huddled up in the most unfitting places, covered with dirt, and with no possible facilities for being examined or read—of their being shifted from place to place, and crammed into any cellar or garret that happened to be empty and unfitted for any other purpose—how they have been lost and purloined—how many of the Welsh documents have been actually cast into the sea—and how a large mass of papers, among which were many most curious bills, warrants, and accounts, was sold for waste paper.

Let us be thankful that those times are passed;

now all receive the consideration they deserve. It may be advisable even to reduce the bulk of the Public Records by some careful system of selection. The task of their arrangement and calendaring is no light one. In the year 1833, the estimate for the calendaring of the contents of a single office was £366,800.

As it is, the bulk of the Public Records is enormous. In the main building itself—a building of the most substantial character—are nearly eighty rooms, chiefly cubes of seventeen feet, fitted up in the most economical manner as to space, and entirely filled, or to be filled, with documents. Temporary accommodation is still required outside for a considerable number.

Of the advantages which have accrued to archæological pursuits by the improved condition of the Public Records much need not be said. To deal with them thoroughly would be to review the whole progress of historical writing and antiquarian research since the commencement of the century. The new edition of Dugdale's "Monasticon," edited by the Secretary of the British Museum, the Secretary of the Bodleian Library, and the Keeper of the Records in the Chapter House and the Augmentation Office, was one of the first works upon which documentary evidence was brought to bear on a comprehensive scale; and in the work still in progress, under the hands of Mr. Froude, may be seen how extensively such materials may be used for the general history of the country.

V.

LONDON AND HER ELECTION OF STEPHEN.

BY THE REV. J. R. GREEN, ST. PHILIP'S, STEPNEY.

READ AT THE ARCHÆOLOGICAL MEETING IN LONDON.

FEW periods of English history are more wearisome to the historian, none more carefully avoided by the general reader, than the period which separates the death of Henry I. from the accession of Henry II. The reign of Stephen seems at first sight a mere series of dynastic struggles, purposeless revolutions, battles of kites and crows waged over a nation's agony. But it is in fact to uninteresting periods, such as this, that we have to look for the birth of those great intellectual movements and political principles that leaven all after-history. Behind the veil of blood and fire that hides these stormy years from us a little patience may discern a great religious revival going on, which was to affect in a marked degree the very balance of the Constitution itself. The final defeat of feudalism in the exhaustion of the great houses left England free for the judicial and administrative reforms that throw a lustre over the reign of Henry II. Above all, it was in the Revolution which seated Stephen on the throne that London first assumed that constitutional position which it has retained for so many centuries since. The struggles of the great city against Cnut, her capitulation with William, the charters she wrested from the Conqueror and his son, are enough to prove her importance at an earlier date than this; but with her part in this Revolution begins that peculiar individual influence which she was to exercise on our national history. The London of the great Charter, of the great Remonstrance, of the Bill of Rights, appears first in the London of Stephen.

The last of the Norman kings died as the first December night of 1135 began to darken: "On midwinter day," says the Chronicle, four-and-twenty days after, that is, Stephen received the Crown from the Archbishop's hands. Short, however, as the interval was, it was long enough for an outburst of anarchy, which proved but too true an omen of the days to come. The very rigour of the dead king's rule intensified the outburst; common-law, forest-law, alike broke down: the exile, the disinherited, re-entered their possessions: old feuds, crushed beneath the stern justice of "the Peace-loving King," broke out anew. In the midst of the turmoil, Earl Stephen, Henry's nephew, crossed with a fair wind from Wissant, and landed at early dawn amid terrible thunder and lightning, strange in such winter weather. Repulsed at Dover, shut out from Canterbury, he rode with what speed he might over the frost-bitten fields straight to London. Scant as his train was, his aim was the Crown. The design had not sprung, as his partisans afterwards affirmed, from the news of his uncle's death: ever since the great storm of popular anger which had followed the announcement of the marriage of King Henry's daughter Matilda, the heiress of England, if oaths went for anything, with the Count of Anjou,* the thought of Stephen's accession had been familiar to English minds. Nor had he neglected to back this popular expectation by the formation of a Blesine party pledged to support his claim; among the nobles of England many had already sworn friendship to him or to his brothers.† His claim as nearest male heir of the Conqueror's blood, strengthened now by the marriage of his only rival to the most hated of foreigners, was supported by his personal popularity. He had been the darling of his uncle Henry; and, mere swordsman as he was, his good humour, his generosity, his very prodigality, made him a favourite with all. Nor were more solemn sanctions wanting to the popular enthusiasm; hermits were the truest expression of the religious life of the twelfth century, and the most famous of living English hermits had already saluted him as king. Against the walls of the little Dorsetshire village-church of Haselberg leant the miserable shanty, where, vexed by fevers and macerations, a gaunt solitary waged his battle against the enemy of souls. Originally a hunting parson, Ulric had all at once flung aside his hounds and his vicarage, and, without waiting for episcopal sanction or priestly benediction, had immured himself in this

* Sax. Chronicle ad annum 1127.
† Gesta Stephani, p. 6 (Histor. Society's edition).

jealously closed cell. The fame of his sanctity spread far and wide. Men told how, within the narrow walls, Ulric was being buffeted, scourged, dragged about by infuriate demons; how unearthly lights, flitting from church to cell, told of the visits of angelic comforters. The monks of Montacute furnished him with bread from their cellar; merchants of Bristol tossed uneasily beneath their furs as they thought of the hermit's night-long vigil in the icy waters of his brook, and sent him their costly coverlet on the morrow. Soon he was known as England's one miracle-worker and prophet: bold invectives against the wrong-doer, gentle exhortations to better things came through the closed shutter of the hermit's cell to the ears of courtier and king, for even Henry had turned out of his way to visit him. It was the shrill cry of this solitary that arrested Stephen as he rode with his brother Henry past the hermitage. "Hail, King," shouted Ulric from his pent-house; and Stephen, imagining the hermit had mistaken him for his royal uncle, drew bridle to explain. "It is no error," persisted the hermit, "it is you, Stephen, that I mean; for the Lord hath delivered the realm into your hand;" and then he prayed him, when that day should come, to protect the Church and defend the poor.*

In spite, however, of expectation, intrigue, and prophecy, Stephen's enterprise was still a failure when he appeared before the gates of the capital. No noble had joined the scanty train of Flammands and Nor-

---

* Acta Sanctorum Bolland, iii. 226.

mans that followed him; no town had opened its gates. All hung on the decision of London; nor was it long uncertain what that decision would be. No sooner was the little troop in sight, than London poured out to meet it with uproarious welcome. By the side of the earl's charger, as they led him into the city, men leaped for joy in shouting how they had gotten "another Henry in Stephen."*

Somewhat of the warmth of this reception sprang, doubtless, from the need of a ruler, which London, more than all England, experienced. For the great mourning with which the city had received the news of Henry's death had been roughly interrupted by an event which recalled its own immediate peril. Just without the walls, a knight, who had occupied an inferior position in Henry's court, had availed himself of the interruption of the king's peace to gather a troop of marauders at his back, and to levy blackmail on the country round. The traders could see the pillage of their wains as they wound along the banks of the Thames, or struck eastward along the great white road over good Queen Maud's bridge at Stratford; they could see the smoke and flame rising from their pleasant country houses along the valley of the Fleet. With pillage at her gates, London wanted no far-off Lady, but a present King. "Every realm," the burghers urged in their folk-mote, "was open to mishap where the presence of all rule and head of justice was lacking. Delay was impossible in the election of a king, who was needed at once to restore justice and

* Gesta Steph. p. 3.

the law."* But the present danger only quickened feelings which had their root in the very history of London under the Conquest.

The Conquest had left London as free as it found it: its franchises remained as great under William as they had been under Edward. But it had planted in the very heart of the city, or, if not planted, had raised into far higher importance a wholly new element of civic life. London presents a strong contrast to most other great mercantile cities in the readiness she has ever shown, not only to admit, but to admit to full citizenship, the foreign elements which different ages have introduced. Englishman, Dane, Norman, Gascon, the stream of Flemish immigration flowing steadily from the Conquest on to the accession of the Stuarts, Germans of the Palatinate, Huguenots of Southern France, have clustered century after century round the old Roman Municipium. Long before the landing of William, the Normans had had mercantile establishments in London. In the Institutes drawn up under Ethelred the men of Rouen occupy a special position, inferior only to that of the men of the Emperor. But for the Conquest, however, their settlement would have remained a mere trading colony, such as the Hanse merchants for centuries after maintained in their London Steel-yard. Up to the Conquest, indeed, the position of the "Emperor's men" was even higher than that of the "men of Rouen," and had Henry V. annexed England, as at one time seemed possible, in right of his wife, the mer-

* Gest. Steph. pp. 3, 4.

chants of Köln or Bruges would have started into a civic importance such as the victory of Hastings gave to the Norman traders.

For the immediate effect of the Conquest was to increase the number of the settlers. It is a side of Norman history which has hardly received the notice it deserves, this peaceful invasion of the Norman industrial and trading classes which followed quick on the conquests of the Norman soldiery. Every Norman noble as he quartered himself on English lands, every Norman abbot as he entered his English cloister, gathered French artists or French domestics round him for his new castle or his new church. Around Battle, for instance, French dependents—"Gilbert the Foreigner, Gilbert the Weaver, Mauger the Smith, Benet the Steward, Hugh the Secretary, Baldwin the Tailor"—mixed with the English tenantry.* More especially was this the case with the capital. No sooner had London submitted to Duke William, than "many of the citizens of Rouen and Caen passed over thither, preferring to be dwellers in that city, inasmuch as it was fitter for their trading, and better stored with the merchandise in which they were wont to traffic."† A yet more important result of the Conquest lay in its giving the rapidly-increasing colony a civic existence. It was impossible that the countrymen of the Conqueror should remain strangers in the Conqueror's capital. A curious monument of London's history tells us how quickly

* Chron. de Bello, pp. 14—16.
† Anon. Lambeth, Giles' Beket, ii. 73.

the change took place. In the archives of Guildhall is still preserved a little slip of parchment, in length and breadth hardly bigger than a man's thumb, scored with a few lines in the Old English tongue. It would be difficult to exaggerate the interest or the real importance of this relic—William's Charter to the Burgesses of London—when we remember that the liberties thus preserved became the model and precedent of the great bulk of English municipal charters, or how much of the future of England itself lay hid in the liberties of London. But the simple words of its opening indicate that, while possessing the full rights of citizenship and occupying in William's eyes a position even superior to the older English burgesses, the new colony still preserved its separate existence:—
"William, King, greets Bishop William and Godfrey the Portgrave, and all the burgesses in London, Frenchmen and Englishmen, friendly."*

With one of these Norman burghers the life of St. Thomas brings us in contact, and, scanty as are the details of the story, they agree in a very striking way with the indications afforded us by the charter of the king. The story of the early years of Thomas Beket has very naturally been passed over with little attention by his modern biographers in their haste to fight the battle of his after-career. But long before he became St. Thomas, Archbishop Thomas, or Thomas of Canterbury, he was known as Thomas of London, son (to use his own boast) of "a citizen, living without

---

* Liber Custumarum, i. 25.

blame among his fellow-citizens." So completely was the family adopted into the city, that the monks of Canterbury could beg loans from the burgesses on the plea that the great martyr was a Londoner born; and on the city seal of the fourteenth century, London addressed him as at once her patron and her son, "Me, quæ te peperi, ne cesses, Thoma, tueri." The name of his father, Gilbert Beket, is one of the few that remain to us of the Portreves, the predecessors of the Mayors, under Stephen; he held a large property in houses within the walls; and a proof of his civic importance was long preserved in the annual visit of each newly-elected chief magistrate to his tomb in the little chapel which he had founded in the churchyard of Pauls.* Yet Gilbert was one of the Norman strangers who followed in the wake of the Conqueror. He was by birth a burgher of Rouen, as his wife was of a burgher family of Caen; he claimed kinship with the Norman, Theobald, and received the Norman Baron de l'Aigle as a guest.

But the story of the Bekets does more than illustrate the outer position of the Norman colony: it gives us a glimpse, the more precious because it is unique, [of its inner life. Students of hagiology learn to be cautious about the stories of precocious holiness, the apocryphal gospels of the infancy, which meet him at the outset of most saints' lives; but it is remarkable that in the life of St. Thomas there is no pretension of the kind In the stead of juvenile miracles, we are presented with the vivid little picture

* Liber Albus, p. 26.

of a London home, which sets the Norman colony
fairly before us. We see the very aspect of the house
(the Mercers' Chapel, in Cheapside, still preserves its
site for us), the tiny bed-room, the larger hall opening
directly on the bustle of the narrow Cheap. We gain
a hint from the costly coverlet of purple, sumptuously
wrought, which Mother Rohese flings over her child's
cradle, of the new luxury and taste which the Conquest had introduced into the home of the trader as
into the castle of the noble. A glance at the guests
and relatives of the family shows how the new colony
served as a medium between the city and the court :
the young Baron Richer of Aquila is often there,
hunting and hawking with the boy, as he grows up;
Archdeacon Baldwin and Clerk Eustace look in from
Canterbury, to chat over young Thomas and his
chances of promotion in the curia of Archbishop
Theobald; there is a kinsman, too, of Gilbert's, a
citizen of his own stamp, Osbern Huit-deniers, "of
great name and repute, not only among his fellow-burghers, but also with those of the court."* Without
the home, the Norman influence makes itself felt in a
new refinement of manners and breeding; the young
citizen grows up free and genial enough, but with a
Norman horror of coarseness in his geniality.† London shares in the great impulse which the Conquest
has given to education; the children of her citizens
are sent to the new Priory of Merton; the burghers
flock to the boys' exercises at the schools attached to

* Roger, apud Giles, S. T. C. i. 98.
† "Rusticitatis notam cavens." Anon. Lamb. S. T. C. ii. 74.

the three principal churches of the town. The chief care of Rohese was for her son's education; in his case it is finished at Paris, before the young Londoner passes to the merchant's desk.

The little picture reflects for us very faithfully the double aspect of the new colony,—fully accepting their position among their fellow-citizens, but preserving jealously their Norman connection and Norman feeling; and able, from the lead which they necessarily took among the burghers, to give their Norman tone to civic policy. And in this great crisis of London history it was the Norman antipathy to the Angevin that told strongest for Stephen. For a whole century, the bitterest of provincial feuds had severed Normandy from Anjou; and the marriage of policy by which Henry endeavoured to propitiate his most restless enemy only deepened the hatred of the Normans by the fear of an Angevin master. Their awe of the king-duke hushed, but could not check, the stern resolve to reject his successor. No pages in Orderic's story of the time are more vivid than those in which he tells how Normandy rose as one man when Count Geoffry Plantagenet crossed the border on tidings of Henry's death, to claim the duchy in right of his wife; how the tocsin pealed from every steeple—how farmer and labourer poured out from cottage and grange—how the Angevin marauders, the hated "Guirribecs," were knocked on the head like sheep, and the proud count fled homeward through wood and ford, with loss of baggage and arms. It was hatred and dread of the Angevin that made Normandy offer herself and her dukedom to Theobald of Blois. May it not have been Norman hatred and dread of the Angevin that flung open the gates of London to Theobald's brother, Earl Stephen?

But the reception of Stephen was not merely the result of this hereditary hatred, this national aversion, —it was the effect also of the great religious impulse which England was now sharing with the whole of the Western world. The Angevin counts stood almost alone in bidding it defiance. To the stories, indeed, of Giraldus in his old age we are bound to give no greater credence than to a Royalist lampoon upon the Puritans, or a Jacobite libel on the House of Hanover. But the tenor of their history is everywhere the same. A lurid grandeur of evil, a cynical defiance of religious opinion, hung alike round Fulc Nerra, or Fulc Rechin, or Geoffry Plantagenet. The priest-murder of Henry-Fitz-Empress, the brutal sarcasms of Richard, the embassy of John to the Moslems of Spain, were but the continuance of a series of outrages on the religious feelings of the age which had begun long ere the lords of Anjou had become kings of England. One foul sacrilege of Geoffry Plantagenet, his brutal outrage on the Bishop of Le Mans, was still fresh in the memories of all. From outrages such as these Stephen was free. Rough soldier as he was, he was devout as devotion was understood then, a benefactor of churches, a founder of religious houses. In a word, he partook of the very spirit to which Geoffry and the Angevins stood so darkly opposed; he shared the great revival of religion which was nowhere more conspicuous, nowhere more important than in England.

Pious, learned, and energetic as the bishops and abbots of William's appointment had been, they were not Englishmen. Till Beket's time, no Englishman occupied the throne of Canterbury; till Jocelyn, no Englishman occupied the see of Wells. In language, in manner, in sympathy, the higher clergy were completely severed from the lower priesthood and the people, and the whole influence of the Church, constitutional as well as religious, was for the moment paralysed. Lanfranc, indeed, exercised a great personal power over William, but Anselm stood alone against Rufus, and no voice of ecclesiastical freedom broke the simoniac silence of the thirty years of Henry I. But in the latter days of Henry, and throughout the reign of Stephen, the people left thus without shepherds were stirred by the first of those great religious movements which England was destined afterwards to experience in the Preaching of the Friars, the Lollardism of Wycliffe, the Reformation, the Great Rebellion, and the mission-work of the Wesleys. Everywhere in town and country men banded themselves together for prayer, hermits flocked to the woods, noble and churl welcomed the austere Cistercians as they spread over the moors and forests of the North. A new spirit of enthusiastic devotion woke the slumber of the older orders, and penetrated alike to the home of the noble Walter d'Espec at Rievaulx, or of the trader Gilbert Beket in Cheapside. It is easy to be blinded in revolutionary times, such as those of Stephen, by

T

the superficial aspects of the day ; but, amidst the wars of the Succession, and the clash of arms, the real thought of England was busy with deeper things. We see the force of the movement in the new class of ecclesiastics that it forces on the stage. The worldliness that had been no scandal in Roger of Salisbury becomes a scandal in Henry of Winchester. The new men, Thurstan, and Ailred, and Theobald, and John of Salisbury — even Thomas himself — derive whatever weight they possess from sheer holiness of life or aim. Nor did the Revival affect merely the immediate course of affairs ; it left its stamp on the very fabric of the English Constitution. The paralysis of the Church ceased as the new impulse bound together the prelacy and the people; and its action, as it started into a power strong enough to save England from anarchy, has been felt in our history ever since. The compact between king and people had become a part of constitutional law in the charters of William and Henry, but its legitimate consequence, in the responsibility of the Crown for the execution of the pact, was first drawn out by the ecclesiastical councils of Stephen's reign. From their depositions of Stephen and Matilda flowed the depositions of Edward, of Richard, and of James. Incoherent as their expression of it may at first sight appear, they did express the right of a nation to good government, till the dim, confused feeling took shape in the resolute efforts by which Theobald became at last the restorer of peace and freedom. To the Church—Beket had a plain right to say it afterwards with whatever proud consciousness of having been Theobald's right hand—to the Church Henry owed his crown, and England her deliverance.

London took even more than its share in the great Revival. The city was proud of its religion, of its thirteen greater conventual, and more than a hundred lesser parochial, churches. "I don't think," says the Londoner, Fitz-Stephen, "there is a city in the world that has more praiseworthy customs in the frequenting church, respecting services, keeping feast-days, giving alms, betrothing, marrying, burying religiously." The new impulse was, in fact, changing the very aspect of the city. In its midst Bishop Richard was busy with the vast cathedral which Bishop Maurice had begun; barges came up the river with stone from Caen for the great arches that moved the popular wonder, while street and lane were being levelled to make space for the famous churchyard of St. Paul's. Rahere, the king's minstrel, was raising St. Bartholomew's, beside Smithfield. Alfune had just built St. Giles's at Cripplegate. The old English Crichtenguild had surrendered their soke of Aldgate as a site for the new Priory of the Holy Trinity. The tale of this last house paints better than a thousand disquisitions the temper of the citizens at this time. Prior Norman, its founder, had built cloister and church, had bought books and vestments in so liberal a fashion that at last no money remained to buy bread. The canons were at their last gasp, when many of the city folk looking into the refectory as they paced round the cloister in their usual Sunday procession, saw the tables laid out, but not a single loaf on them. "Here is a fine set out," they exclaimed, "but where is the bread to come from?—'hic est pulcher apparatus sed panis unde veniet.'" The women present vowed at once to bring each a loaf every Sunday, and soon there was bread enough and to spare for the priory and its guests. Thenceforth the house grew, unvexed by mishaps, though a fire once swept eastward to its very walls—it was the fire which, starting from the house of Gilbert Beket, involved London in ruin and himself in poverty.*

Among the women that brought bread to the canons may very possibly have been the mother of Beket. In religion, as in other matters, the little home reflects faithfully the tone of the colony of which it formed a part. However dimly Gilbert Beket passes before us—a civic dignitary, well to do till the great fire—his wife, Rohese, stands out distinctly as the type of the devout woman of her day, prayerful, not unaccustomed to visions, a pilgrim now and then to that Canterbury whose sanctity was so soon to be quickened into new life by the blood of her son; above all, diligent in almsgiving. The prettiest story in all that stormy life of St. Thomas is that birthday scene at home, where year by year the mother weighs her boy against money, clothes, provisions, and gives them to the poor.

This religious enthusiasm, and the dread (well-

* Hearne has given the chronicle of this house in an Appendix to his William of Newborough.

grounded, as it afterwards proved) that in the Angevins would be found the bitterest foes of religion and the Church, may have had some part in the uproarious reception of Stephen by the multitude of London. But the formal recognition which followed was based on far deeper grounds, and has a very different constitutional importance. Neither noble nor prelate, save Henry of Winchester, were there to constitute a National Council; indeed, a week after, when all had gone well for Stephen, but a few nobles, three bishops, and not a single abbot could be mustered to make a show at the coronation. In this great crisis, the Commune of London did not hesitate to take their place. In the election of a king, indeed, London had for some time taken a great constitutional part. When Ethelred's miserable life passed away "all the witan that were in London, and the burgesses, chose Eadmund to be their king."—(Chronicle, ad 1016). On the death of Cnut, the citizens joined with the Danes in raising Harold Harefoot to the throne, in opposition to Harthacnut. The burgesses and butsecarls had united with Archbishop Aldred in the vain attempt to make a king of the Etheling after the fatal defeat of Hastings. By the time of the Conquest, London had become the definite place of the royal election, and the voice of her citizens was accepted as the representative of the popular assent. But the position which the citizens now took was a far greater one than this. In the absence of noble and bishop, they claimed of themselves the right of election. Undismayed by the want of the hereditary counsellors of the Crown, their "aldermen and wiser-folk gathered together the folk-mote, and these providing at their own will for the good of the realm, unanimously agreed to choose a king."*

The very arguments of the citizens are preserved to us as they stood massed, doubtless, in the usual place for the folk-mote at the east end of Paul's, while the bell of the commune swung out its iron summons from the detached campanile beside. "Every kingdom," urged alderman and prudhomme, "was open to mishap, where the presence of all rule and head of justice was lacking. It was no time for waiting; delay was in fact impossible in the election of a king, needed as he was at once to restore justice and the law." But quick on these general considerations followed the bolder assertion of a constitutional right of pre-election, possessed by London alone. "*Their* right and special privilege it was, that on their king's death his successor should be provided by *them;*" and if any, then Stephen, brought as it were by Providence into the midst of them, already on the spot.†

Bold as the claim was, none contradicted it; the solemn deliberation ended in the choice of Stephen, and amidst the applause of all, the aldermen appointed

---

* "Majores itaque natu, consultum quique rectiores consilium coegere, deque regni statu pro arbitrio suo utilia in commune providentes, ad regem eligendum unanimiter conspiravere."—Gesta Stephani, p. 3.

† "Id quoque sui esse juris, suique specialiter privilegii, ut si rex ipsorum quoquo modo obiret, alius suo provisu in regno substituendus succederet."—Gesta Stephani, p. 4.

him king.* Ample securities were taken for the safety of the realm; oath was exchanged against oath; the citizens swore to defend Stephen with money and blood; Stephen swore to apply himself with his whole strength to the pacification of the kingdom.†

From that hour Stephen was king: supporters flocked in fast, and it was at the head of a large body of knights that he marched upon Winchester. But we need not follow the story further. London was true to *her* oath, if Stephen was false to his. But whatever might be the immediate result, with the solemn independent election of a king, the great part which London was to play in England's history had definitely begun. The London of the Normans, of Gilbert Beket, of St. Thomas, had taken its constitutional place in the realm.

* "Regemque, omnium concordanti favore, constituere."—Gesta Stephani, p. 4.
† "Ad omnium eorundem suffragium."—Gesta Stephani, p. 4.

VI.
ROYAL PICTURE GALLERIES.

By GEORGE SCHARF, F.S.A.
SECRETARY AND KEEPER TO THE NATIONAL PORTRAIT GALLERY.

NOTWITHSTANDING the many removals, concealments, and occasional dispersions that have befallen the royal pictures, we find that those still remaining to us, of British historical interest, are much more numerous, and in a far better state of preservation, than might have been expected after the lapse of so long a time, and such frequent dangers; to say nothing of occasional neglect.

As belonging to the earlier periods, we look in vain for the existence of movable pictures painted on a large scale. During the Saxon or Anglo-Norman period of our history, the portraits of reigning monarchs were principally to be found associated with the representation of personages of ecclesiastical or legendary history. They might chiefly be met with under the semblance of such characters as Pharaoh, David, Solomon, Hezekiah, and Herod. Most of these paintings were large mural decorations, executed in fresco or tempera colours upon the walls themselves. The same figures and compositions, on a reduced scale, are constantly to be met with on the pages of the more costly illuminated manuscripts. Perhaps the

Earliest Royal portraits.

Durham Cathedral. A.D. 1190. earliest and most characteristic example of genuine and abstract portraiture in fresco painting is the life-sized, although much damaged, portrait of Richard I. standing on the side wall of a niche, facing the figure of Bishop Pudsey, in the Galilee of Durham Cathedral.

Henry III. 1216-72. Henry III., that liberal patron of art, employed both foreign and native artists in the decoration of his palaces with scriptural histories; and in the year 1245 we read of a London artist, Edward de Westminster, son of Odo the goldsmith, being commissioned to paint in St. Stephen's Chapel a beautiful figure of the Blessed Virgin on one side, and the king and queen on the wall opposite.

Westminster paintings. 1256. William, a monk of Westminster, who served also as chief of the painters at Windsor Castle, executed an allegorical picture under the king's direction at Westminster, in 1256, in the royal lavatory, which represented the king being rescued by his dogs from the seditions and mischiefs plotted against him by his subjects.

Portrait at Windsor. 1270. Only one fragmentary example in colours now remains of the regal portraiture of this period. It is to be seen on the south wall of the deanery cloisters at Windsor. Little, however, now exists, beyond the crowned head, with blue-shaded waving hair and staring eyes. But the drawing is bold, and the general appearance of the face coincides with the beautiful bronze effigy of the monarch, so well preserved in Westminster Abbey, and still more closely corresponds with certain regal figures in some of the manuscripts in the British Museum of the same period.

But it is not my intention to dwell here upon the history of art in this country. I have only ventured to adduce these examples for the purpose of showing what kind of employment our figure-painters met with in those days, and to observe that abstract portraiture, of historic personages, was scarcely ever thought of for its own sake—excepting on coins, seals, and monumental effigies—before the fifteenth century.

I must not, however, omit to mention one very remarkable instance which existed till recently, in St. Stephen's Chapel at Westminster, of a series of royal portraits, displaying the entire family of King Edward III., painted on the east wall. They were represented kneeling, in two distinct groups, one on each side of the high altar. The King and his sons on the north side, and the Queen with her daughters on the south. And there is every reason to suppose that they were done from the life. They were probably the work of the best painter belonging to the royal establishment, and were certainly executed with the richest colours, an exquisite finish, and heightened with a profusion of the finest leaf-gold and silver. After the time when the chapel had been transferred to the service of Parliament, and the walls were concealed by woodwork, plaster, and tapestry, the very existence of these paintings seems to have been forgotten; and it was only on the occasion of enlarging the House of Commons for the accommodation of the Irish Members in 1800 that these valuable relics were discovered.

St. Stephen's Chapel. 1364.

On the 12th of August, 1800, these ancient paintings were once more exposed to the light.* But the haste with which the carpenters' work had to be carried on, in order to secure completion for the opening of Parliament, prevented a satisfactory examination or even removal of any of the more important portions; and they were speedily covered over and closed up again. A few careful tracings and elaborate copies in water-colours had been taken from them; but only in part, and unfortunately very hurriedly. The calamitous fire which broke out and consumed the Houses of Parliament in 1834 entirely destroyed these valuable works of art. It is, however, a fortunate circumstance that carefully-studied transcripts were secured from the paintings at the east end of the chapel at this juncture. Elaborate copies of them, in colours, with complete facsimiles of the original gilding and silvering upon the armour and metal ornaments, were commenced by Mr. Smirke for the Society of Antiquaries, which, together with his original tracings, are still preserved in the Society's apartments at Somerset House. Mr. J. T. Smith also, in his "Antiquities of Westminster," * published many valuable sketches and records of these same paintings. His observations also, made on the spot, at the same time, afford valuable corrections, and a supplement to Mr. Smirke's laborious undertaking.

Advancing to the next reign, we recognise two

* See Smith's "Antiquities of Westminster," pages vi. and viii. of the Preface. Outlines from Mr. Smirke's drawings were published in a folio volume by the Society of Antiquaries, with illustrative text by Sir Henry Englefield. The engravings were published in 1805.

specially interesting examples of regal portraiture. Both represent King Richard II., in royal robes and in full state. The one, a small highly-finished miniature, in profile, hereafter to be described,* and now preserved at Wilton House; the other, an almost colossal figure of the king on his throne, which has in recent years been deposited in the Jerusalem Chamber, Westminster.† Its original position was in the choir of the Abbey; and we may now hope that, since the pure and genuine picture has been recovered from beneath repeated coatings, not merely of dirt, but of dense layers of false painting, the portrait may once more be restored to the place for which it appears to have been intended. *[margin: Richard II. 1377-99.]* *[margin: A.D. 1390.]*

The earliest documentary record we possess of the royal pictures, as a collection, belongs to the period of Henry VIII., and is to be met with in a catalogue or inventory of *"painted tables"* or pictures, occupying several folio pages of a ponderous volume containing *"An account of the king's money, jewels, plate, utensils, apparel, wardrobe stuffs, goods, and chattels, consigned to the care of Sir Anthony Denny at Westminster."* This volume is now deposited in the Record Office. Many other pages are devoted to a very interesting list of King Henry's books. The date of this inventory is April 24th, "the 34th year of our reign" (1542). The account of the pictures in it extends from pages 53 to *[margin: Hen. VIII. 1509-47.]*

---

* See page 346. See also "The Fine Arts Quarterly Review," New Series, for January, 1867, page 32.

† This picture was No. 7 of the National Portrait Exhibition at South Kensington, and has since that time become the subject of a most remarkable restoration. See Appendix.

60; and from these Records, notwithstanding that the descriptions are barren in the extreme and entirely deficient in measurements, a considerable amount of curious and valuable information may be derived.

The pictures may be broadly classed under three heads; namely, 1. Portraits; 2. Religious subjects; and 3. "Historical Descriptions," including maps of particular localities. The second division contains principally various representations of the Virgin Mary and Infant Jesus, Holy Families attended by saints, who, in the absence of any specification of the emblems pertaining to them, or any incidental allusion to their names, are removed beyond all possibility of recognition.

In the British Museum is preserved a similar inventory, made after the King's death, of the "late King's" property, taken "by vertue of a Commission under the greate Scale of England, bearing date at Westminster the viij. day of September, in the first year of our Sovereyne Lord Edwarde the Sixte" (1547). As this volume, being five years later, contains some two or three additional pictures, probably painted expressly for the King during the interval, I prefer to make my extracts from that volume. Here, again, no measurements are given; but some few are distinguished from the rest by being designated as "great Tables," "whole stature," "Little Tables," and "Tables like a book with folding leaves." A superior value is also to be inferred in those cases where curtains to protect them are mentioned. Thus, many of the pictures have, in addition to the brief record of their subject, the following almost unvarying form:—" *With*

ROYAL PICTURES AT WESTMINSTER, A.D. 1542. 287

a curteyne of yellow and white sarconette paned together." * Hen. VIII. 1509-47.

The following are the principal portraits. For the convenience of more ready reference, I have arranged them in alphabetical order. The strange spelling of proper names has been preserved, but the words of each entry are not absolutely given in exact succession.

WESTMINSTER INVENTORY. A.D. 1542-7.

1. "Prince Arthurre, wearing like a redde cappe with a brooche oppon it and a collor of redde and white rooses." *No mention of a curtain.*

This picture is one that I have succeeded in identifying at Windsor Castle, and of which, until my attention was attracted to it, the name had been lost. (See Archæologia, vol. 39, page 245.) It was No. 49 of the recent Portrait Exhibition at South Kensington. (98.)†

2. "Prynce Arthure." *No curtain.* (32.)

3. "Barsele the Countesse of Corne." *With a curtain.* (83.)

4. "The Duke of Burbonne." *A curtain.* (86.)

5. "The Quene of Castile, a little table." *No curtain.* (75.)

6. "The Kynge of Castile's chilberne; a foldinge table." (53.)

7. "The French Kynge, Charles theight." *A curtain.* (84.)

---

* In pictures of the 16th century we sometimes observe representations of framed paintings, hanging on a wall in the background, as if partially covered by curtains attached to rings running on a rod.

† These numbers in brackets refer to the order in which the pictures appear in the original inventory.

Westminster Palace, 1542-7.

8. "**Charles Duke of Burgonde, a little table.**" *With a curtain.* (102.)

9. "**Charles the Great Emperour.**" *With a curtain.*

This Portrait of Charlemagne occurs again in the catalogue of Charles I.'s pictures, and is not at present to be identified among the royal paintings; but an apparently similar picture belongs to the Society of Antiquaries at Somerset House. (114.)

10. "**Charles themprouer, a 'stayned cloth'.**"

This term "stained" appears to have been used for pictures painted in transparent colours upon linen. Many instances of this kind of painting may be met with at this period. (154.)

11. "**Themperouer, his doublet beinge cutte and a Rose-mary braunche in his hande.**" *No curtain.*

This picture is at present at Windsor Castle. (See Archæologia, vol. 39, page 263.) (99.)

12. "**Tholde Emperouer, themprouer that nowe is, and Ferdynando.**" *With a curtain.*

Apparently Maximilian, Charles V., and his brother Ferdinand, as seen in a beautiful little wood-carving at Vienna, where their names are inscribed. This group appears again, but under false names, in the catalogue of Charles I. See *post*, page 335. (16.)

13. "**Thre childerne of the Kynge of Denmarke.**" (Christian II.) *With a curtain.*

Still in the royal collection at Hampton Court. Engraved by G. Vertue, and by him incorrectly named "the children of Henry VII." (See Archæologia, vol. 39, p. 256.) It was No. 58 of the Kensington Portrait Exhibition, and, notwithstanding repeated remonstrances, retained an unqualified designation in the official catalogue of the Exhibition, as "*Prince Arthur, Prince Henry, and Princess Margaret.*" (10.)

14. "**Kynge Edwarde the iiij.**" *With a curtain.*

Of this monarch two portraits on panel still remain at Windsor

Castle. One, rather large, which is extremely well wrought, and surrounded by a peculiar, gilt inner framework, which corresponds with some borderings on other royal portraits of the same period. He is putting a ring on the first finger of his left hand. We shall again meet with this picture in the collection of Charles I. The smaller, but very inferior portrait, also of life-size, but showing little more than the head, was No. 24 of the Kensington Exhibition. (52.) *Inventories of Hen. VIII. 1542-47.*

15. "𝕿𝖍𝖊 𝕶𝖞𝖓𝖌𝖊'𝖘 𝕸𝖆𝖏𝖊𝖘𝖙𝖎𝖊." *With a curtain.* Edw. VI.

This designation of the "King's Majesty" applies to Edward VI., and is, therefore, only to be found in the Inventory of 1547. Before his accession he was merely styled "Prince Edward," and the "Lord Prince his Grace," as will be seen in the earlier catalogue preserved in the Record Office. (46.)

16. "𝕿𝖍𝖊 𝕶𝖞𝖓𝖌𝖊'𝖘 𝕸𝖆𝖏𝖊𝖘𝖙𝖎𝖊, 𝖙𝖍𝖊 𝖜𝖍𝖔𝖑𝖊 𝖘𝖙𝖆𝖙𝖚𝖗𝖊, 𝖎𝖓 𝖆 𝖌𝖔𝖜𝖓𝖊 𝖑𝖎𝖐𝖊 𝖈𝖗𝖞𝖒𝖘𝖊𝖓 𝖘𝖆𝖙𝖙𝖊𝖓 𝖋𝖚𝖗𝖗𝖊𝖉 𝖜𝖎𝖙𝖍 𝖑𝖚𝖘𝖊𝖗𝖓𝖊𝖘." *Protected by a curtain.* (150.)

17. "𝕿𝖍𝖊 𝕶𝖞𝖓𝖌𝖊'𝖘 𝕸𝖆𝖏𝖊𝖘𝖙𝖞, 𝖙𝖍𝖊 𝖜𝖍𝖔𝖑𝖊 𝖘𝖙𝖆𝖙𝖚𝖗𝖊, 𝖘𝖙𝖆𝖞𝖓𝖊𝖉 𝖚𝖕𝖔𝖓 𝖈𝖑𝖔𝖙𝖍𝖊." *Protected by a curtain of green sarcenet.* (47.)

18. "𝕼𝖚𝖊𝖊𝖓 𝕰𝖑𝖎𝖟𝖆𝖇𝖊𝖙𝖍𝖊, 𝕶𝖎𝖓𝖌 𝕰𝖉𝖜𝖆𝖗𝖉'𝖘 𝖂𝖎𝖋𝖋𝖊." *With a curtain.* Elizabeth Woodville.

This picture still exists at Windsor Castle, and it was No. 30 of the Kensington Exhibition. An inferior picture, although in many respects very similar, was contributed to the Exhibition, No. 29, from Hampton Court. (51.)

19. "𝕼𝖚𝖊𝖓𝖊 𝕰𝖑𝖎𝖟𝖆𝖇𝖊𝖙𝖍𝖊." *With a curtain.*

Evidently Elizabeth of York, Consort of King Henry VII. This picture still remains at Windsor Castle, and also belonged to King Charles I. (43.)

20. "𝕿𝖍𝖊 𝕷𝖆𝖉𝖞𝖊 𝕰𝖑𝖎𝖟𝖆𝖇𝖊𝖙𝖍, 𝖍𝖊𝖗 𝕲𝖗𝖆𝖈𝖊, 𝖜𝖎𝖙𝖍 𝖆 𝖇𝖔𝖔𝖐𝖊 𝖎𝖓 𝖍𝖊𝖗 𝖍𝖆𝖓𝖉𝖊, 𝖍𝖊𝖗 𝖌𝖔𝖜𝖓𝖊 𝖑𝖎𝖐𝖊 𝖈𝖗𝖞𝖒𝖊𝖘𝖔𝖓 𝖈𝖑𝖔𝖙𝖍𝖊 𝖔𝖋 𝖌𝖔𝖑𝖉𝖊, 𝖜𝖎𝖙𝖍𝖊 𝖜𝖔𝖗𝖐𝖊𝖘." (Patterned.) *No curtain.* Princess Elizabeth.

U

> Princess Elizabeth, A.D. 1546.

The remains of an early inscription on the upper part of the picture clearly show that it was intended for Queen Elizabeth, when Princess. The dress is richly embroidered with patterns (works). It occurs again in King Charles's catalogue. This very interesting picture has recently been removed from Hampton Court to St. James's Palace. It was No. 247 of the Kensington Portrait Exhibition. (151.)

21. "𝕰𝖑𝖎𝖟𝖆𝖇𝖊𝖙𝖍𝖊 𝖔𝖋 𝕬𝖚𝖘𝖙𝖗𝖞, 𝕼𝖚𝖊𝖓𝖊 𝖔𝖋 𝕯𝖊𝖓𝖒𝖆𝖗𝖐." *With a curtain.*

Most probably Isabella (Elizabeth), wife of Christian II., and sister to the Emperor Charles V. She would consequently be the mother of the three children already specified in No. 13 of this inventory. (29.)

> Eleonora, Queen of France.

22. "𝕰𝖑𝖔𝖓𝖔𝖗𝖆 𝖙𝖍𝖊 𝕱𝖗𝖊𝖓𝖈𝖍𝖊 𝕼𝖚𝖊𝖓𝖊 𝖎𝖓 𝖙𝖍𝖊 𝕾𝖕𝖆𝖓𝖎𝖘𝖍𝖊 𝖆𝖗𝖗𝖆𝖞𝖊 𝖆𝖓𝖉 𝖆 𝖈𝖆𝖕𝖕𝖊 𝖔𝖓 𝖍𝖊𝖗 𝖍𝖊𝖆𝖉𝖉𝖊 𝖜𝖎𝖙𝖍 𝖆𝖓 𝕺𝖗𝖗𝖊𝖓𝖌𝖊 𝖎𝖓 𝖍𝖊𝖗 𝖍𝖆𝖓𝖉𝖊."

Several portraits of this sister of the Emperor Charles V. are still extant; but in the majority of them she is represented holding a letter instead of an orange. A picture, answering to the description given above, was recently in the possession of Mr. H. Graves, the print-seller. A fine portrait of this princess, holding the letter, is still preserved at Hampton Court Palace, No. 319, of the catalogue; and another, on a much smaller scale, belongs to H.R.H. the Duke d'Aumale, at Orleans House. (9.)

23. "𝕱𝖊𝖗𝖉𝖎𝖓𝖆𝖓𝖉𝖔 𝕶𝖞𝖓𝖌𝖊 𝖔𝖋 𝕬𝖗𝖆𝖌𝖔𝖓." *Without a curtain.*

This picture is still preserved at Windsor Castle. It is inscribed: "Le Roy Dun Fernando Dorragon." A similar picture of Ferdinand the Catholic is in the collection of the Society of Antiquaries. This royal picture reappears in the catalogue of Charles I. (135.)

> Francis I.

24. "𝕿𝖍𝖊 𝕱𝖗𝖊𝖓𝖈𝖍𝖊 𝕶𝖞𝖓𝖌𝖊 𝖜𝖍𝖊𝖓 𝖍𝖊 𝖜𝖆𝖘 𝖞𝖔𝖓𝖌𝖊, 𝖆 𝖑𝖎𝖙𝖙𝖑𝖊 𝖗𝖔𝖚𝖓𝖉𝖊 𝖙𝖆𝖇𝖑𝖊." *With a curtain at the time of the earlier Inventory.* (77.)

25. "𝕿𝖍𝖊 𝕱𝖗𝖊𝖓𝖈𝖍𝖊 𝕶𝖞𝖓𝖌𝖊, 𝖍𝖆𝖇𝖎𝖓𝖌 𝖆 𝖉𝖚𝖇𝖑𝖊𝖙 𝖔𝖋 𝖈𝖗𝖞𝖒𝖊𝖘𝖔𝖓 𝖈𝖔𝖑𝖔𝖚𝖗𝖊 𝖆𝖓𝖉 𝖆 𝖌𝖔𝖜𝖓𝖊 𝖌𝖆𝖗𝖓𝖞𝖘𝖍𝖊𝖉 𝖜𝖎𝖙𝖍 𝖐𝖓𝖔𝖙𝖙𝖊𝖘 𝖒𝖆𝖉𝖊 𝖑𝖎𝖐𝖊 𝖕𝖊𝖊𝖗𝖑𝖘."

A small picture of Francis I., corresponding in many respects Inven-
with this, remains at Hampton Court. The Earl of Dudley has a tories of
similar portrait, the size of life. Compare King Charles's cata- Hen. VI
logue, page 111, No. 21. (8.) 1542-47.

26. "𝔗𝔥𝔢 𝔉𝔯𝔢𝔫𝔠𝔥𝔢 𝔎𝔶𝔫𝔤𝔢, 𝔱𝔥𝔢 ℭ𝔲𝔢𝔫𝔢 𝔥𝔦𝔰 𝔴𝔦𝔣𝔣𝔢 𝔞𝔫𝔡 𝔱𝔥𝔢 𝔉𝔬𝔬𝔩𝔢 𝔰𝔱𝔞𝔫𝔡𝔦𝔫𝔤𝔢 𝔟𝔢𝔥𝔶𝔫𝔡𝔢 𝔥𝔦𝔪." *Protected by a curtain.*

This curious, but much injured picture, is still preserved at Hampton Court. A similar painting is at Longleat, the seat of the Marquis of Bath. (71.)

27. "𝔉𝔯𝔢𝔡𝔢𝔯𝔦𝔠𝔨𝔢 𝔱𝔥𝔢 𝔗𝔥𝔦𝔯𝔡𝔢, 𝔈𝔪𝔭𝔢𝔯𝔬𝔲𝔯𝔢, 𝔴𝔦𝔱𝔥 𝔞 𝔠𝔬𝔶𝔣𝔣𝔢 𝔬𝔫 𝔥𝔦𝔰 𝔥𝔢𝔞𝔡𝔢." *Protected by a curtain.* (117.)   Emperor of Germany.

28. "𝔉𝔯𝔢𝔡𝔢𝔯𝔶𝔨 𝔇𝔲𝔨𝔢 𝔬𝔣 𝔖𝔞𝔵𝔬𝔫." *With a curtain.*

Probably Frederick III., called the Wise, who took Lucas Cranach the painter with him to the Holy Land. (27.)

29. "𝔗𝔥𝔢 𝔚𝔦𝔣𝔣𝔢 𝔬𝔣 𝔱𝔥𝔢 𝔩𝔬𝔯𝔡 𝔉𝔶𝔢𝔫𝔫𝔢𝔰; 𝔞 𝔩𝔦𝔱𝔱𝔩𝔢 𝔱𝔞𝔟𝔩𝔢." *With a curtain.* (140.)

30. "𝔥𝔢𝔫𝔯𝔶 𝔱𝔥𝔢 𝔙𝔱𝔥." *Protected by a curtain.*

This interesting profile portrait still remains in the royal collection at Windsor. It also belonged to Charles I., and was subsequently removed to Kensington Palace. It was not included in the Kensington Portrait Exhibition. There are naturally many repetitions of this picture, on account of his universal popularity. (49.)

31. "𝔥𝔢𝔫𝔯𝔶 𝔱𝔥𝔢 𝔙𝔍." *With a curtain.*   English Monarchs

The well-known picture, with the hands clasped. It is in a gilt frame, with the royal arms of France and England in the spandrils to correspond with similar borderings to the portraits of Edward IV. and Richard III. This picture is still at Windsor Castle. There are repetitions of it belonging to the Society of Antiquaries and the British Museum. It appears in the catalogue of pictures belonging to Charles I. (50.)

32. "𝔎𝔦𝔫𝔤𝔢 𝔥𝔢𝔫𝔯𝔶𝔢 𝔱𝔥𝔢 𝔖𝔢𝔳𝔢𝔫𝔱𝔥." *Protected by a curtain.*

English Monarchs.

This picture is more difficult to recognise among the still existing portraits of the monarch. In King Charles's catalogue only one portrait of Henry VII. occurs in the series of "Old heads," and it is distinguished as having "two hands." * (42.)

33. "𝔐𝔢𝔫𝔯𝔶 𝔱𝔥𝔢𝔦𝔤𝔥𝔱, 𝔟𝔢𝔦𝔫𝔤 𝔶𝔬𝔫𝔤𝔢, 𝔴𝔢𝔞𝔯𝔦𝔫𝔤𝔢 𝔥𝔦𝔰 𝔥𝔢𝔞𝔯𝔢, 𝔴𝔦𝔱𝔥 𝔞 𝔣𝔩𝔬𝔴𝔯𝔢 𝔬𝔣 𝔰𝔦𝔩𝔳𝔢𝔯 𝔬𝔭𝔭𝔬𝔫 𝔱𝔥𝔢 𝔩𝔬𝔠𝔨𝔢. 𝔄 𝔱𝔞𝔟𝔩𝔢 𝔴𝔦𝔱𝔥 𝔱𝔴𝔬𝔢 𝔩𝔢𝔞𝔳𝔢𝔰."

Probably leaves or doors to close over it, like a triptych, with a silver ornament, such as adorn the clasps and hinges of books, to fasten it externally. In this the King appears to be bareheaded, but I cannot at present identify it with any known picture. (44.)

34. "𝔎𝔶𝔫𝔤𝔢 𝔐𝔢𝔫𝔯𝔶 𝔳𝔦𝔦𝔦., 𝔱𝔥𝔢𝔫 𝔟𝔢𝔦𝔫𝔤𝔢 𝔶𝔬𝔫𝔤𝔢."

This may possibly be the picture which we shall find more fully specified in the collection of Charles I., where he holds a scroll of parchment in his hand. It was, however, acquired by King Charles I. from Lord Arundel in 1624.† (97.)

35. "𝔎𝔶𝔫𝔤𝔢 𝔐𝔢𝔫𝔯𝔶 𝔱𝔥𝔢𝔦𝔤𝔥𝔱 𝔞𝔫𝔡 𝔍𝔞𝔫𝔢 ℭ𝔲𝔢𝔫𝔢; 𝔞 𝔗𝔞𝔟𝔩𝔢 𝔩𝔦𝔨𝔢 𝔞 𝔟𝔬𝔬𝔨𝔢."

One-half of this folding picture or diptych (containing the figure of the King) may still be traced at Althorp, in Lord Spencer's beautiful little Holbein portrait of Henry VIII. The corresponding figure of the Queen is not so satisfactorily to be identified.‡ (45.)

---

* See page 114, No. 33, of Bathoe's edition.

† See page 119, No. 57, of Bathoe's edition. The picture is now at Hampton Court Palace, and was No. 124 of the Kensington Exhibition.

‡ The Duke of Northumberland's little picture of Jane Seymour at Sion, and Lady De la Warr's portrait at Knole, exhibit the type which accords with the picture formerly painted by Holbein on the wall of the Privy Chamber, at Whitehall. (See Van Leemput's copy at Hampton Court, and Holbein's cartoon belonging to the Duke of Devonshire.) It is remarkable that this is the only consort of Henry VIII., whose name as *Queen* is specified in this inventory. Portraits of Catherine of Arragon and Anne Boleyn are still preserved at Windsor Castle;

36. "⭐ynge ⭐enry theight standing oppon a ⭐pter with three crownes, having a Sarpent withe seven heades com= mynge oute of it, and havinge a swoorde in his hande wherein is writen Verbum Dei." Inventories of Hen. V 1542—

It would be curious to recover this picture of King Henry trampling on the Papal tiara. (64.)

37. "Isabell quene of Castell." *With a curtain.*

This picture still exists at Windsor Castle. Her hair is quite plain, and parted in the middle; she holds a book in her right hand. Inscribed "Le Vaymne Ysabean ne Eastille." It also belonged to King Charles I. See *post*, page 334. (103.)

38. "Jacobbe Kynge of Skottes, with a hawke on his fiste." *Protected by a curtain.* James IV. of Scotland.

A curious copy of this, by Daniel Mytens, in water-colours, was No. 61 of the Kensington Portrait Exhibition. It formerly belonged to King Charles I., and is now the property of Sir William Stirling Maxwell, Bart., M.P. (See Pinkerton's Scottish Iconography.) (134.)

39. "Johanna Archduke of Austrie." *With a curtain.* (108.) Jeanne la Folle?

In the earlier inventory the words are "JOAN ARCHDUCHES OF AUSTRYE."*

but they do not appear in these records. The best portraits of Jane Seymour, by Holbein, are now at Vienna, and at Woburn Abbey, in Bedfordshire.

* Apparently Johanna, wife of the Archduke Philip of Austria, and mother of the Emperor Charles V. As her parents, her husband, and so many members of their family are conspicuous in this inventory, it is scarcely to be supposed that the Emperor's own mother, Jeanne la Folle, would be wanting to the series. In the extracts from King Charles's catalogue, subsequently given, will be found the mention of a portrait of "The Queen of Castile," which occurs almost immediately after one specified as "Queen Isabella of Castilia." See *post*, pages 304 and 334 (51). Johanna, the daughter of Charles V., would, at the date of the first inventory, have been only twelve years old.

40. "𝔇𝔲𝔨𝔢 𝔍𝔬𝔥𝔫." *With a curtain.*

This appears to be the same as a picture bearing the same title, and described in King Charles's catalogue as "looking downwards, in a black habit and cap." This seems to represent John "Sans Peur," Duke of Burgundy, and father of Philip the Good. (131.)

41. "𝔍𝔬𝔥𝔫 𝔉𝔯𝔢𝔡𝔢𝔯𝔦𝔨𝔢 𝔇𝔲𝔨𝔢 𝔬𝔣 𝔖𝔞𝔵𝔬𝔫, 𝔰𝔱𝔞𝔶𝔫𝔢𝔡 𝔬𝔭𝔭𝔬𝔫 𝔏𝔶𝔫𝔫𝔬𝔫 ℭ𝔩𝔬𝔱𝔥𝔢, 𝔟𝔢𝔦𝔫𝔤 𝔥𝔦𝔰 𝔴𝔥𝔬𝔩𝔢 𝔰𝔱𝔞𝔱𝔲𝔯𝔢." (147.)

42. "𝔍𝔲𝔩𝔦𝔲𝔰 ℭ𝔢𝔰𝔞𝔯." *With a curtain.*

Described in King Charles's catalogue as "bald, side faced, in a golden dress like a priest." See *post*, p. 335. (112.)

43. "𝔏𝔢𝔴𝔦𝔰𝔢 𝔱𝔥𝔢 𝔉𝔯𝔢𝔫𝔠𝔥𝔢 𝔎𝔶𝔫𝔤𝔢." *With a curtain.*

Louis XII. (76.) Now at Windsor Castle.

44. "𝔗𝔥𝔢 𝔏𝔞𝔡𝔶 𝔐𝔞𝔯𝔤𝔞𝔯𝔢𝔱 𝔱𝔥𝔢 𝔇𝔲𝔠𝔥𝔢𝔰 𝔬𝔣 𝔖𝔞𝔟𝔬𝔶𝔢." *With a curtain.*

This lady was the sister of Philip le Bel, aunt to Charles V., and Governess of the Netherlands. She had been married in 1501 to Philibert, Duke of Savoy; she became a widow in 1504. The portrait is now in Hampton Court Palace. No. 298 of the catalogue. (18.) See *post*, page 333.

45. "𝔄 𝔴𝔬𝔪𝔞𝔫 𝔥𝔞𝔳𝔦𝔫𝔤𝔢 𝔞 𝔐𝔬𝔫𝔨𝔢𝔶 𝔬𝔫 𝔥𝔢𝔯 𝔥𝔞𝔫𝔡𝔰." *With a curtain.*

Probably Margaret of Scotland. A portrait of similar character is at Queen's College, Oxford. A full length, enlarged by Mytens, from an earlier picture, is still at Hampton Court. (26.)

46. "𝔗𝔥𝔢 ℭ𝔲𝔢𝔫𝔢 𝔬𝔣 ℌ𝔲𝔫𝔤𝔢𝔯𝔶𝔢, 𝔟𝔢𝔦𝔫𝔤𝔢 ℜ𝔢𝔤𝔢𝔫𝔱 𝔬𝔣 𝔉𝔩𝔞𝔲𝔫𝔡𝔢𝔯𝔰."

Of this lady, Mary of Austria, sister of the Emperor, there is in the possession of the Society of Antiquaries a curious portrait, wearing a very broad-brimmed hat, painted on vellum, and richly gilded.*

---

* I believe that this portrait may be identified among the existing Crown pictures (30) at Windsor Castle. The picture is at present called "The Mother of Mary Queen of Scots. See *post*, p. 305, No. 20. See No. 26 of Catalogue of Pictures belonging to the Society,

47. "A woman called Michaell wth a redde rose in thone hande, and layinge thother hande oppon a dogge's back." No curtain. (145.) Inventories of Hen. VIII. 1542-47.

48. "The Duchyes of Myllayne. A greate table, beinge her whole stature."

This very important picture of Christina, niece of the Emperor Charles V., one of the finest of Holbein's works in England, now belongs to the Duke of Norfolk, at Arundel Castle. (See Archæologia, vol. xl., p. 110.) (12.)

49. "The Duchesse of Myllayne."

A smaller picture of the same lady, still preserved at Windsor Castle.* (138.)   Duchess of Milan, A.D. 1538.

50. "The Prince of Orrenge; a stayned cloth." (155.)

51. "Phillipp Archduke of Auster." *With a curtain.*

This appears to be Philip le Bel, father of the Emperor Charles V., and husband of Johanna of Castile. The picture is still preserved at Windsor Castle. (28.)

52. "Philipp Duke of Burgoyne." *With a curtain.*

This portrait of Philip the Good still exists in the royal collection at Windsor Castle. (110.)

53. "Duke Philipp the Hardye." *With a curtain.*

This, although not at present traceable in the royal collections, appears to correspond with an entry in King Charles's catalogue, "Philip, Duke of Burgone, in a black cap, with a golden medal." † (113.)

54. "Kynge Richarde the Thirde." *With a curtain.*

This impressive picture, which is in a frame similar to those of English Sovereign contributed to the Fine Arts Quarterly Review, May, 1864, vol. ii., page 327.

* It was No. 104 of the Kensington Portrait Exhibition. (See also Archæologia, vol. xl., p. 106). This was apparently the first sketch made by Holbein, at Brussels, in 1538

† See page 117, No. 45, of Bathoe's edition.

English portraits. the portraits of Edward IV. and Henry VI., already described, is a very genuine work of art, and very possibly the original of the numerous repetitions or copies that are known to exist. The best are in the National Portrait Gallery (presented by Mr. Gibson-Craig); at Knowsley (the Earl of Derby's), Arundel Castle, Hatfield, and Longleat.* (82.)

This picture occurs again in the collection belonging to King Charles I. See *post*, page 333.

55. "𝕿𝖍𝖊 𝕮𝖔𝖚𝖓𝖙𝖊𝖘 𝖔𝖋 𝕽𝖎𝖈𝖍𝖊𝖒𝖔𝖓𝖉𝖊, 𝕶𝖞𝖓𝖌𝖊 𝕳𝖊𝖓𝖗𝖞𝖊 𝖙𝖍𝖊 𝖘𝖊𝖇𝖊𝖓𝖙𝖍'𝖘 𝖒𝖔𝖙𝖍𝖊𝖗." *Protected by a curtain.*

Now in the royal collection at Windsor Castle, painted on panel. This picture also belonged to King Charles I. There is a similar portrait, on panel, in St. John's College, Cambridge, and a more modern version of it, on canvas, belonging to the Earl of Derby, at Knowsley. These pictures were respectively Nos. 47 and 48 of the Kensington Portrait Exhibition. (48.)

Duke of Savoy. 56. "𝕿𝖍𝖊 𝕯𝖚𝖐𝖊 𝖔𝖋 𝕾𝖆𝖇𝖆𝖚𝖉𝖎𝖊." *With a curtain.* (130.)

57. "𝕾𝖔𝖑𝖞𝖒𝖆𝖓𝖆𝖒𝖊 𝖙𝖍𝖊 𝖙𝖚𝖗𝖖𝖚𝖊, 𝖇𝖊𝖎𝖓𝖌 𝖍𝖎𝖘 𝖜𝖍𝖔𝖔𝖑𝖊 𝖘𝖙𝖆𝖙𝖚𝖗𝖊, 𝖆 𝖘𝖙𝖆𝖞𝖓𝖊𝖉 𝖈𝖑𝖔𝖙𝖍." (160.)

The following pictures are unknown; but the descriptions given with them are nevertheless deserving of consideration:—

58. "𝕬 𝖕𝖎𝖈𝖙𝖚𝖗𝖊 𝖍𝖆𝖇𝖎𝖓𝖌 𝖆 𝕭𝖑𝖆𝖈𝖐𝖊 𝕮𝖆𝖕𝖕𝖊 𝖜𝖎𝖙𝖍𝖊 𝖆 𝖇𝖗𝖔𝖔𝖈𝖍𝖊 𝖆𝖓𝖉 𝖆 𝖈𝖔𝖑𝖔𝖗 𝖔𝖋 𝕾𝖈𝖆𝖑𝖑𝖔𝖕𝖕 𝖘𝖍𝖊𝖑𝖑𝖊𝖘." *With a curtain.*

---

* The rich brown tone, and a certain severity of form in this picture, are quite consistent with the style of, and indeed may have some associations with, the Italian schools of Botticelli or Castagno. During the reign of Richard III., Pietro Perugino, Sandro Botticelli, Andrea del Castagno, and Luca Signorelli, were painting in Italy; whilst, beyond the Alps, Memling, Martin Schoen, and the youthful Albert Durer, were exercising their pencil.

Whilst speaking of contemporaneous art in different countries, it may not be uninteresting to observe that both Raphael and Martin Luther were born in 1483, the year of the accession of our Richard III.

This picture corresponds with the Marquis of Queensberry's fine profile portrait of a young man wearing a black cap and a large golden ensign on the side of it. The collar of the order of St. Michel, composed of scallop shells, is conspicuous on his shoulders. The countenance is very like Louis XII. of France. The picture may be traced again in the royal collections of Charles I. and James II. See *post*, pages 332 and 357.

Inventories of Hen. VIII. 1542-47.

59. "One habinge a longe heare beinge crowned and habinge a roobe like clothe of golde and the furre beinge white." *With a curtain.*

Uncertain portraits.

The picture may possibly be the portrait of Richard II., still in the royal series at Windsor, where he appears crowned, wearing long hair, and has a large white fur cape or tippet, similar to his costume in the Westminster picture and the engraving in the Basiliologia. (78.)

60. "A yonge man habing like thre broches and a rowe of perles oppon his cappe and like a chayne of stone and perles abowte his necke with a bawdrike abowte his shoulders to hange his sworde bye." *Protected by a curtain.* (80.)

61. "One beinge in blacke with this scripture, 'Glorificamus te sancta dei genetrix,' &c." *No curtain.* (101.)

62. "A woman habinge a tier oppon her headde like myter." *With a curtain.* (111.)

63. "A woman in a frenche hoode with a gowne like clothe of gold and blue for sleves." *With a curtain.*

Uncertain female portraits.

Apparently still in the royal collection, No. 303 of the catalogue at Hampton Court.* (104.)

64. "A woman in a frenche hoode in a gowne like clothe of golde the sleves turned up with white and powdered with blacke." *With a curtain.*

* See page 115, No. 36, of Bathoe's edition of King Charles's catalogue. The tighter "blue fore-sleeves" and crimson broad outer sleeves are both observable in the Hampton Court picture.

Uncertain female portraits.

Apparently now at Hampton Court. No. 304 of the catalogue.* (133.)

65. "A woman naked, holdinge a table withe a skripture in it in thone hande and a bracelet oppon thother arme at the opper parte thereof."

This recalls the composition of some of the pictures of Diane de Poictiers. (3.)

66. "A woman, her headde and her necke bare, her garment cutte and pulled out with white." *With a curtain.* (107.)

67. "A woman having lyke a bracelette on her arme and like twooe perles hanging at her eares." *No curtain.* (73.)

68. "A naked woman sitting opon a rocke of stoone wᵗʰ a scripture ober her headde." *No curtain.* (14.)

These are all the portraits contained in the inventory of 1547.

Scriptural subjects.

The Scriptural subjects include "Adam and Eve," "St. Anne," "King Asa," "Asceuerus," "David and Goliathe" (2 pictures), "The fyve wondes," "St. George" (4 pictures),† "St. Jerome" (2 pictures), "Beheading of St. John the Baptist," "Judithe" (2 pictures), "Marye Magdalene" (4 pictures), "The Parable of Mathewe, chapter xviij, a table of russet and blacke, raised with liquide golde and silver" (probably representing the Unjust Steward), "St. Mychaell and St. George." (7.)

"The Historye of Christiana Patiencia." (36.)

* See page 114, No. 35, of Bathoe's edition of King Charles's catalogue.

† One of these four pictures must have been Raphael's well-known picture of St. George on horseback, now at St. Petersburg. See *post*, page 323.

"Prodigus Filius." (19.)   Inventories of Hen. VIII. 1542-47.

"The Birthe of Christe," a table wth twooe foldinge leaues. Hauing in the middes the three Kynges of Colaygne, in the one leaf the Birth of Christ, and thother folding leaf our Lady giving our Lorde sucke." (100.)

"The Salutation of oure Lady in thone leaf. The Three Kyngs of Coloine saluting our lord in the middes, Our Ladye gyvinge our lorde sucke in thother leaffe. A table with two foldinge leaues." (139.)   Sacred subjects.

"Our Lady, Our Lorde sleeping on her breste, and a tree at our ladies backe." *With a curtain.* (58.)   A Triptych.

"Our Lady holding our lorde in her armes with cherries in his hande. A table with two foldinge leaues." (72.)

"Our Ladye with a booke in her one hande and our lord in her other arme and Joseph standinge bye. A great table." *With a curtain.* (85.)

"Our Ladye holdinge our lorde in her lappe and a pomegranette in her hande with an Aungell playing oppon a lute and Josephe standinge bye." *With a curtain.* (105.)

"Our Ladye and Christ sucking and Josephe looking on a booke. A table." *With a curtain.* (31.)

"Our Lady and oure lorde sittinge on her lappe and playinge with her booke, a table with twooe foldinge leaues." (142.)

"Our Lorde crowned with thorne, his arms bownde. Stayned oppon clothe. A little square table." (121.)

"Christe taken down from the Crosse. A table with twooe foldinge leaues." (149.)   A Deposition.

"Our Lady holding our Lorde taken downe from the Crosse in her armes. A table." *With a curtain.* (17.)   A Pietà.

The En-tombment. "𝔅urpall of our 𝔏orde. 𝔄 table of all sondrye woodes joyned togithers."

This appears to have been executed in *tarsia*, a method of operation still practised in Italy. (61.)

"𝔒ur 𝔖abioure blessinge with his one hande and holdinge thother hande oppon the worlde." (127.)

Classic subjects. Among the classic subjects we find "Lucretia Romana" (three pictures): "King Mydas and Myserie; a table of walnuttree raised withe liquide gold and silver." (62.) "A woman holdinge an Onycorne in her lappe." (34.) "Orpheus with sondrye strange beastes and monsters. Stayned oppon clothe." (148.) "Phebus ridinge in his carte in the ayre, with thistorye of him. A stayned cloth." (158.)

In the following pictures the Landscape element appears to preponderate :—

Landscapes. "𝔄 great huntinge aboute a howse of the 𝔇uke of 𝔖arons painted oppon a borde." *A Description.*

"𝔉oure 𝔗ables of parchment sette in frames of woode, and eberye of theym a manor place," viz.:—

"ℌampton 𝔈ourte," "𝔄mboyce," "𝔈ognacke," "𝔊andit." (79.)

Descriptions. Numerous pictures also occur under the heading of "*Description*," which seems to have been a combination of the perspective and figure drawing, with the laying down of a map. The well-known pictures at Hampton Court representing the "Embarkation of Henry VIII. at Dover," and the "Interview at the Field of the Cloth of Gold," would probably have been placed under this denomination. Of this class we find in this inventory:— *Inventories of Hen. VIII. 1542-47.*

Descriptions.

"Discription of the siege and wynnynge of Bolloigne."
"A longe mappe of Constantynenople, Venice, and Naoples."
"Dover and Calice, a large mappe." "All Europe, a mappe of paper." "A description of Florence, with sondrye townes joynynge theronto." "Discription of the citie of Jherusalem, of stayned clothe."

"A Discription of the Castell of Millayne, painted oppon clothe." "A discription of Naoples being biseged with Mounsieur de Londraith, a stayned clothe."

"The Siege of Pavie. *Protected by a curtain.*"

"The Discription of the Siege of Pavie when ye Frenche Kynge was taken. Being of Lynnen clothe stayned."

"The Discription of Rome and the Sacke therof. Of stayned clothe."

"A Discription of the Siege of a towne. Painted oppon clothe."

"A Discription of the Siege of Vienna. Stayned clothe sette oppon borde."

COLOURED SCULPTURES.

There were also several framed pieces of sculpture executed in terra cotta, and coloured to look like life. They were called "pictures made of earthe."

Painted Terra-cottas.

The following subjects were among them:—

"A Discription of Dover, made of earthe. Sette in a boxe of woode."

"A Morian boye with a garment of white and blewe. A picture made of earthe."

Painted Terra-cottas.

"**Moises.** A picture made of earthe, sette in a boxe of woode."

69. "A woman in a purple garment with a garland of green leaves abowte her headde. A picture made of earthe."

70. "A woman with a carnation roobe knitte with a knotte on the lefte sholder and bareheaded, with her heare rouled opp with a white lace. A picture made of earthe."

71. "A woman with a carnation garment after the englishe attier and bareheadded, with her heare rolled op with a white lace. A picture made of earthe, set in a boxe of woode."

72. "A woman her garment beinge Crymeson, her headde tyred after Flanders fasshon. A picture made of earthe."

73. A woman in a roobe of ash coloure, and her heare trussed behynde her ears. A picture made of earthe."

74. "A woman with a coiffe of orrenge coloure oppon her headde. A picture made of earthe, set in a boxe of woode."

Among miscellaneous subjects the following tables deserve to be specified :—

Paintings. "A woman playing opon a lute with a booke before her and a little potte with lillies springinge out thereof." (6.)

"A woman playing oppon a lute and an old Manne holding a glasse in thone hande and a deadde mannes headde in thother hande." (5.)

"Men and women sittinge at a banquet and deathe commynge in makinge them all afraide and one standinge with a sworde to kepe him oute at the dore. A stayned clothe." (156.)

"Sondrye men and women syttinge at a banquette in a woode and a crymeson clothe hange betwexte the croches of

PICTURES AT WESTMINSTER PALACE, A.D. 1542.

twooe trees to shadowe them and a woman on horsebacke with footemen rungnge by her. A stayned clothe." (157.) *Inventories of Hen. VIII. 1542-47.*

"A large table painted with sondrye Images of white and blacke, oppon tike nailed oppon borde." (153.)

"Thoole Worlde. A mappe or a cardemaryne of parchment set in a frame of white woode, with the Kynge's Armes crowned supported by his grace's beastes." *Mappemonde.*

The following extract from the index to the Inventory of 1547, relating to Westminster, will afford some idea of the principal apartments in the old palace as it then existed. The numbers relate to the pages in the volume. *Index to Inventory, 1547.*

" Westminster." . . . . folio 37 *Apartments in Westminster Palace.*
" The Guarderobe." 63
" The Secreate Guarderobe." . . . 91
" The King's own Jewell house in the old gallory." 111
" The study at the hither end of the Long gallory." 113
" The Chairhouse." 115
" The chardge of Sir Anthony Denny." . . 119
Tables with pictures.
" The glass house." 143
" The study next th'old Bedchamber." . . 151
" The old Jewel house." 159
" The New Library." 186

Many works of art were also deposited in St. James's Palace; as appears by the following list taken in 1548.

St. James's Palace. Edw. VI. 1549.

Several among them seem to correspond with those already noted at Whitehall, and had probably been moved away soon after the other inventory was taken.

St. James's House nigh Westminster.

"An inventory of the King's stuff remaining there in the charge and custody of Richard Coke, one of the grooms of the King's Privy Chamber, and keeper of the said house of St. James. Anno secundo regis Edwardi Sexti."

The list of pictures begins at page 446 of the second volume of the Inventory in the British Museum.—Harleian MS. 1419. B.

Foreign Potentates.

1. "Item a table with the picture of Themperor Frederick."

2. "Item a table with the picture of Madam Jahane."*

3. "Item a table with the picture of Christianus Rex Danie." Christian, 2nd King of Denmark, who took refuge for a time in England.

4. "Item a table with the picture of Christ with the scourge in his hand."

5. "Item a table with the picture of Queen Elizabeth."

6. "Item a table with the picture of Carolus Rex Francie."

7. "Item a table with the picture of Duke Phillippe th' Wardy." See *ante*, page 295, No. 53.

8. "Item a table with the picture of Duke Carolus."

9. "Item a table with the picture of Duke John."

10. "Item a table with the picture of David killing Gollias."

* This picture appears to be Johanna of Arragon, wife of Philip le Bel of Austria. See *ante*, p. 293, No. 39.

11. "Item a table with the picture of the Salutation of our Lady in it." _{Edw. VI. Inventory of Pictures at St. James's Palace, 1549.}

12. "Item a folding table with the picture of Christ and iiii pictures more in the same."

13. "Item a table wherein is set a stained cloth being partly the Declaration of th'Appocalipses."

14. "Item a table with the picture of Arthurus Rex Anglie." _{King Arthur.}

15. "Item a table with the picture of the Duke of Savoy." _{Foreign Potentates.}

16. "Item a table with the picture of Julius papa secundus."
Compare post, page 330, No. 8.

17. "Item a table with the picture of Duke Charolus."

18. "Item a table with the picture of Ierome Despaine." *

19. "Item a table with the picture of Argus with this worde—Moderat Durant."

20. "Item a table with the picture of the Quene of Hungrie now regent of Flanders, her head tired in white."
This picture appears to be the one now at Windsor Castle, called "The Mother of Mary Queen of Scots." See ante, page 294, No. 46.

21. "Item a table with the picture of Carolus the fifth Emperor."

22. "Item a table with the picture of th'emperor Maximilian."

23. "Item a table with the picture of roy Don Ferdinand d'Arragon."

24. "Item a table with the picture of John hispanie princeps."

* So the letters clearly read, but the meaning is hard to make out. The same observation applies to the motto in the picture following.

x

25. "Item a table with the picture of Marie Magdalen."

26. "Item a table with the picture of a woman holding an apple in her one hand and the cover of a cup in th'other hand."

<small>"Tables wth pictures in theym."</small>

27. "Item a table with the picture of a naked woman and cupid between her hands."

28. "Item a table with a picture of the Duches of Milan."

29. "Item a table with the picture of Julius Cæsar."

30. "Item a table with the picture of a woman holding a beast in her one hand with this scripture 'fem^{rum} natura hic depicta est.'"

<small>Margaret of Burgundy.</small>

31. "Item a table with the picture of a woman named Domina Margareta dus Burgunds."

32. "Item a table with the picture of King Henry the vii."

33. "Item a table with the picture of the Countess of Richmond and Darbie."

34. "Item a table with the picture of the Assention of Christ."

<small>English Monarchs.</small>

35. "Item a table with the picture of King Edward the iiiith."

36. "Item a table with the picture of King Richard the iii^{dt}."

37. "Item a table with the picture of Queen Elizabeth."

38. "Item a table with the picture of King Henry the vith."

39. "Item a table with the picture of Prince Arthur."

40. "Item a table with the picture of King Henry theight."

41. "Item a table with the picture of Caiphas sitting in Judgment uppon Christ."

42. "Item a table wherein is a man holding a Sword in his one hand and a Sceptre in his other hand, of needle-work partlie garnished with seed pearl." Edw. VI. Inventory of Pictures at St. James's Palace.

43. "Item a table with the picture of the Duches of Richmounte and Darbie sitting upon her knees."

44. "Item a table with the picture of Rex de Castell."

45. "Item a table with the picture of the Assention of Christ upon stained cloth."

46. "Item a table with the picture of Ferdinandus Archiedux Austrie."

47. "Item a table with the picture of Jacobus quartus Rex Scotorum." James, King of Scotland.

48. "Item a table with the picture of Alexander Magnus."

49. "Item a table with pictures wherein is contained this Scripture 'Repleta sum. &c.' with other sayings."

50. "Item a table wherein is contained the Seging of Tournay and Troye."

51. "Item a table with the picture of francis the french King." Francis the First.

52. "Item a table with the picture of Quene Elenor of France."

53. "Item a table with the picture of the Duke of Saxon with a garland of Roses upon his head."

54. "Item a folding table with the V. Doctors, Luther being in the middes of them."

55. "Item a folding table with pictures of frederick Duke of Saxon and John Duke of Saxon."

56. "Item another folding table containing Thre pictures, one named frederick Duke of Saxon, another named John Frederick Duke of Saxon, and the third John Duke of Saxon."

Fall of the Protector Somerset. 1556.

The same volume contains, at page 448, the following remarkable note relating to the custody of the royal property at a critical period in the reign of Edward VI. :—

> "A particular book of all such parcels of stuff, &c., in various places at Westm^r on the xii day of November, in the third year of our Sovereign Lord King Edward the Sixth. The keys of which were in the only keeping of the Duke of Somerset until the time of his apprehension, being in October the said third year, at which time the same keys were delivered to the King's Maties most honorable Council, and by their commandment the doors sealed until the said xiith day of November, at which time, by their appointment, Sr William Herbert, knight of the order, and master of the King's horses, Sir Edward North, knight, one of the King's most honor^{ble} Council, and Sr Walter Mildmay, knight, entered into the same houses, and there took a perfect survey and view of all such things as they found there remaining, and the same stuff, by like order of the Council, they delivered to the hands of James Rufforth to the King's Majesty, for the particulars whereof hereafter ensue."

Wardrobes.

The catalogue itself, of which this is the preamble, contains many curious particulars illustrative of royal costume.

Pictures, however, were not much employed as a means of decorating the ordinary living rooms of a palace. In these times "Hangynges of Arras," with gay patterns, landscapes called "forest-work," and "storied" tapestries covered the walls.

Tapestries.

The "Guardrobe" at the honor of Hampton Court contained, among other "Hanginges," "Tenne peces of wove Arras of the Historie of Abraham." These are still in use, and now line the sides of the Great Hall, where they appear to great advantage.*

---

* John Evelyn observed these tapestries in the same palace during his visit there in 1662. See *post*, page 352.

They afford the best illustration of the scale and effect of the tapestries wrought for the Sistine Chapel from Raphael's celebrated cartoons, which have recently been removed from Hampton Court to London. *[Hampton Court Tapestries.]*

Being of the same period, and executed also in the same rich materials, it is easy to imagine from them the grandeur and brilliancy which Raphael's designs must have exhibited when they came fresh from the looms of Arras. Not only were the silk and woollen threads of the brightest possible hues, but the high lights on the garments of the figures and all the ornamental accessories were wrought in tissues of the finest gold and silver. Many of the colours of the Tapestries at Hampton Court are now faded, and much of the gold of the threads has tarnished; but the chief allowance must be made for those blackened patches, which usurp the place where the shining masses of silver originally stood. On comparing these tapestries with the Sistine series from the "Lives of the Apostles," still preserved in the Vatican, it will be seen that the materials are perfectly alike, and that the ones at Hampton Court have certainly suffered in a less degree. The design of these tapestries is attributed to Bernard Van Orley, a very excellent Flemish artist, who worked in the school of Raphael, and who was entrusted by that great painter with the execution of his (Raphael's) series of designs for tapestry, which are known in the History of Art as the "Arazzi della Scuola nuova." *[Brilliancy of their original condition.]* *[Designed by Bernard Van Orley.]*

At this period, it may be incidentally mentioned, that England was in possession of a *duplicate* set of the original Sistine set of hangings. Pope Leo X, *[Raphael Tapestries.]*

had ordered replicas to be executed for the King of England, and presented them in recognition of his published treatise against the principles of Luther; conferring on him, at the same time (1521), the title of Defender of the Faith. Meanwhile, treasured and admired as these gorgeous productions must have been both at Rome and in London, the original drawings by the artist, the very cartoons themselves, were lying uncared for at Arras, in some of the lumber rooms belonging to the Flemish manufacturers. They were considered to have served their purpose.

Duplicate set of the Vatican Tapestries made for Henry VIII., A.D. 1519.

It was only about the year 1630, that Charles I., at the suggestion of Rubens, became possessed, for a comparatively small sum, of these priceless designs, and to the credit of our rulers they have remained in this country ever since.

The original designs obtained by Charles I.

Notwithstanding Wolsey's care and extravagance in the decoration of his palace at Hampton Court with historical subjects in tapestry (see Harleian MSS., No. 599), we do not find any record of his having collected pictures by great Italian masters at that residence.

It appears, however, from an incidental mention in the travels of the Grand Duke of Tuscany, Cosmo III. (1669), in England,* that the Gallery at Whitehall was originally enriched by Cardinal Wolsey with choice paintings. The Cardinal, however, does not seem to have any claims as a patron of art, and it is remarkable that, among the various portraits still existing of him, there is not one by any artist of repute—although

Paintings at Whitehall Palace.

---

* Travels of Cosmo, &c. 4to. London: 1821. Page 368.

the best Italian painters were assembled in Rome when he resided there—nor is there a single picture of Wolsey that can be said to rank in any way above mediocrity.

[margin: Queen Elizabeth. 1558-1603.]

The next record of the royal pictures as a collection belongs to the reign of Queen Elizabeth, and for this we are indebted to the curious volume of travels by Paul Hentzner, who visited England in the year 1598. The book was published in Latin, and has been translated by Horace Walpole.

At Whitehall Palace,* Hentzner was shown the following portraits:—

[margin: Hentzner's Travels. A.D. 1598.]

"Queen Elizabeth at 16 years old." This is evidently the same as the one already quoted from Henry VIII.'s Inventory of Whitehall.†

[margin: Portrait of Queen Elizabeth when a girl.]

"Henry, Richard, and Edward, Kings of England." The three pictures in remarkable borders already noted in King Henry's Inventory.

"Rosamond." "Lucrece." "Chas. V. Emperor." "Charles Emanuel Duke of Savoy and Catherine of Spain his wife."

"Ferdinand Duke of Florence with his daughters." "Philip King of Spain when he came into England." "Henry 7th, Henry 8th and his mother." This last group very probably the same as the fine picture painted by Holbein on the wall of the Privy Council Chamber at Whitehall that was destroyed in the fire of 1691.

* Page 22 of the 1797 edition, and page 189 of the Latin edition, printed at Nuremberg, 12$^{mo.}$ 1629.
† See page 289, No. 20; and also *post*, page 336.

Windsor Castle. 1558-1603.

Windsor Castle, at this period, does not appear to have been the depository of any very remarkable paintings, as Hentzner, who minutely records everything which he saw there, is entirely silent upon them.

Hentzner speaks of the numerous rooms at Hampton Court palace being adorned with tapestry of gold, silver and velvet, in some of which were woven history pieces, in others Turkish and American dresses "all extremely natural." Here he observed a portrait of Edward VI., a true portrait of Lucretia, a picture of the battle of Pavia (probably the "Description" "stayned on Lynnen Clothe" already quoted), the portraits of Mary Queen of Scots, Ferdinand of Spain, Philip of Spain, and of Henry VIII.

Portrait of Richard II.

William Lambarde the antiquary records an interview which he had with Queen Elizabeth, at Greenwich, August 4th, 1601, when the Queen spoke to him of a portrait of Richard II., which Lord Lumley had given to her. It was then at Whitehall, in the custody of Sir Thomas Knevet.*

James I.

The accession of James I. to the throne of England seems incidentally to have been the means of adding various pictures to our royal collection. Until this period only one portrait of a Scottish king was recorded in the Crown Inventory. James probably introduced portraits of his mother and of his ancestors, and seems to have indulged in collecting and multiplying the likenesses of distinguished persons, since he frequently employed the Dutch painters, Van Somer and Marc Gheeraedts, to whom posterity is under considerable

* Bibliotheca Topographica Britannica, 1780, vol. i. page 525.

obligations. Although their works are to a great degree both stiff and formal, they possessed much individuality of character; and the general appearance of the person was, in almost every instance, fearlessly represented.

James I. 1603-25.

A curious document, setting forth some of the principal acquisitions and inheritances belonging to the king towards the close of his reign, has recently been found among the State Paper Office records. It is entitled "A Note of all such pictures as your highnes (hath) at this present, done by severall famous masters owne handes by the life." The date assigned to this memorandum is October, 1624.

The pictures are twenty-one in number, and specified in the following manner.

Catalogue of Portraits.

1. "*Imprimis.* King James the 3rd of Scotland with his Queene donne by Joan Vanak" (John Van Eyck).*

---

* This is evidently the fine diptych altar-piece which remained at Hampton Court Palace till 1857. It was originally designed for the Trinity College Church of Edinburgh. Such Mr. David Laing has conclusively shown to have been the case in his privately printed memoir* describing the altar-piece, and the historical circumstances connected with it. He establishes also the fact that the kneeling ecclesiastic on the reverse of one of the wings is " Sir Edward Bonkil the first provost of the College of the Trinitie, beside the burgh of Edinburgh." The figure of St. Cecilia, wearing a coronet, and seated at the organ, is probably the deceased Queen Mary of Gueldres, by whom the church was founded. These portraits were for a very long period at Kensington Palace, and were subsequently among the most attractive pictures at Hampton Court. The diptych has, with great propriety, and chiefly through the instrumentality of Mr. David

---

* Edinburgh, 1857, p. 9.

314   HISTORY OF OLD LONDON.

James I. A.D. 1624. Catalogue of Portraits.

2. "Item a Venetian Senator donne by Joan Tibulini" (probably Gentile Bellini).

3. "Item a head to the wast, donne by ould Quintin."

4. "Erasmus Roterodamus, donne by Holbyn" (now No. 324 of Hampton Court).

5. "An ould woman of Hempscherch." (By Martin or Egbert Heemskerk).

6. "The Emperor at whole length, by Titian."

7. "A head of a Venetian Senator, by ould Tintorett."

8. "King Phillipp the 2nd, of Anthonio More."

9. "Lazarus Spinola's head, by Caius" (William Key).

10. "The Prince of Orange, by Michael Johnson."

11. "Your highnes owne picture, by Blyemberch."

12. "The late Queenes picture, by Paule Vanzomor" (van Somer), probably the signed picture, No. 780 of Hampton Court, dated 1617. It was No. 418 of the Kensington Portrait Exhibition.

13. "The Marquesse Hamilton, by Mytens." (No. 41 of Hampton Court Palace. It was No. 522 of the Kensington Portrait Gallery.)

14. "Titian and Arentyne, by the yong Quintyn." (There is a very fine Titian picture of this subject at Windsor Castle, and many repetitions elsewhere. One specially worthy of notice at Cobham Hall.)

15. "Peeter Paule Rubens, one picture done by his owne hand."

16. "The Kynge Henry the 4th of Fraunce, don by Bonnell."

17. "His queene mother of Fraunce, done by younge Purbus."

18. "The Duke Charles of Burbon, done by ———."

Miniatures.

"In lymninge, as follows":—

19.-20. "The queene of Scotland, with the Dolphin of Fraunce, of Gennetts doeinge." This miniature portrait of Mary Queen of Scots, by Janet, is still preserved in the royal library at Windsor Castle. It is one of the most authentic and interesting among the reliable portraits of Mary. The companion portrait

Laing, once more been restored to Scotland. After having been seen at the Manchester Exhibition of Art-Treasures in 1857, the panels, instead of being sent back to Hampton Court, were, by her Majesty's command, transferred to Edinburgh. They are now very appropriately deposited in the Palace of Holyrood.

of the Dauphin, afterwards François II., cannot now be recognised. They both appear in the Catalogue of Charles I.

21. "An other gentlewoman's in hangeinge hayre, done by ye old Oliver" (Isaac Olivier).

22. "The earle of Northumberland, done by old Hilliard."

Charles I. 1625-49.

Both sons of James I. evinced an early interest in Art. Prince Henry had formed a noble collection of paintings and statuary, and designed an apartment at Whitehall expressly for their reception. Charles, even before his accession to the throne, had distinguished himself by the possession of paintings of the highest quality. It was under his authority that the finest productions of the greatest Italian masters made their way to this country. The collection of Vincenzo, Duke of Mantua, containing some of the choicest works of Raphael, Correggio, Giulio Romano, and Titian, arrived in England about the close of 1632.*

_{Agents sent abroad for the purchase of pictures.}

Nicholas Lanier conveyed many of the finest pictures from Venice to Brussels in the beginning of May, 1628, having laden five horses. He carried with him two pictures of Correggio, in tempera, and one of Raffaelle, "the finest pictures in the world," as Daniel Nys writes to Endymion Porter, "and well worth the money paid for the whole [collection], both on account of their rarity and exquisite beauty."† The remainder of the pictures were consigned to the ship *Margaret*. "Among them," Nys continues, in his letter dated Venice, May 12, 1629, "is the Madonna of Raffaelle

* See Original Papers of Rubens, by Noel Sainsbury. 1859. Pages 327 and 339.

† Ibid., pages 325-327.

316   HISTORY OF OLD LONDON.

Chef-d'-œuvres of Raphael, Titian, and Correggio. del Canozzo, for which the Duke of Mantua gave a Marquisate worth 50,000 scudi; and the late Duke of Florence would have given the Duke of Mantua for the said Madonna 25,000 *ducatoni* in ready money. The man who negotiated this matter is still alive. Then there are the twelve Emperors of Titian, a large picture of Andrea del Sarto, a picture of Michelangelo di Caravaggio; other pictures of Titian, Correggio, Giulio Romano, Tintoretto, and Guido Reni, all of the greatest beauty."

Arrival of the best works in England. These passages may suffice to afford a general impression of the tone and spirit in which the royal acquisitions were made, and of the manner in which the King's agents worked. It appears, also, that in 1635 the State's Ambassador presented five pictures to the King at St. James's.

All the choicest productions of art above alluded to arrived safely in England, and are to be traced in the catalogue of the collection at Whitehall prepared for Charles I.

Vander Doort. This compilation is by far the most important of all the records that have hitherto been prepared of the various works of art belonging to the Crown. It was drawn up by Vander Doort, who had the charge "of all the King's Pictures, medals, books, and gems." The latest date that occurs in the body of the book is October, 1639. The original MS. of the Catalogue is still preserved at Oxford, bound in two volumes, which are stamped on both sides with the royal arms, surmounted by a crown and encircled by the garter. The letters C. R. take the place of the usual heraldic supporters. Above the crown is the date 1639. The contents consist partly of fair copies, repetitions, rough writings, and hastily-scribbled notes, all bound together. Many of the pages are covered with a close, strange handwriting, probably Vander Doort's own, which presents many gross irregularities of spelling and curiosities in grammatical construction. The lists seem to have been prepared for the king's own revision. These volumes were formerly in the Ashmolean Museum at Oxford, and have only within the last few years (since 1863) been removed to the Bodleian Library. Vander Doort's position and the nature of his artistic qualifications will be seen by the following account of himself entered in his Catalogue.*

<small>Charles I. 1625-49.</small>

<small>Catalogues at Oxford.</small>

<small>Vander Doort.</small>

"No. 21. Item. Imbost in coloured wax, so big as the life, upon a black ebony pedestal, a woman's head laid in with silver and gold, which was made for the Emperor Rodulphus, who did write divers times for it to be brought to him, but Prince Henry would, upon no terms or conditions, let the same and the maker thereof go out of England, but promising he would give so good entertainment as any Emperor should; whereupon he promised him that when the cabinet-room should be done, that he should have the keeping of all his medals, &c., and £50 a year for service done and to be done, which as yet, by reason of his unseasonable death, was never performed."

<small>"Which was done by Abraham Vander Doort, and given to Prince Henry upon conditions. Which piece is too big to be kept in the cupboards at Whitehall."</small>

The Catalogue was, for the first time, printed in a quarto form by Bathoe, in 1757; and taken, as the title runs, "*from an Original Manuscript in the Ash-*

---

* See Walpole's Anecdotes, edited by Dallaway and Wornum, page 269, for an account of Vander Doort, and of the melancholy termination of his career. Bathoe's Edition of King Charles' Catalogue, page 164, No. 21.

molean Museum at Oxford. The whole transcribed and prepared for the press, and a great part of it printed, by the late ingenious Mr. Vertue, and now finished from his papers."

It is, however, much to be regretted that Vertue's life was not spared to complete the supervision of this reproduction, as many of the errors, omissions, and gratuitous insertions which now disfigure the work would scarcely have been tolerated by so vigilant and zealous an antiquary.

I have, during several visits to Oxford, carefully collated the printed copy with these manuscripts, and regret to observe how little the former is to be trusted. In many places words are mis-read and changed; punctuation altered, and both dimensions of pictures and observations upon them, inserted in the text without any shadow of authority from the original, or any means afforded of distinguishing them. The detection of these faults has several times enabled me at once to identify the description of some particular picture which I had been vainly seeking after.

The chief perplexities have been caused by stops gratuitously foisted in, and by a careless and uncalled for employment of capital letters.

At present it may be sufficient for me to offer a few remarks on some of the peculiarities of this catalogue as compared with the valuable Inventory of Henry VIII.

In the first place, the plan of Vander Doort's catalogue is fuller and more methodised; he specifies the apartments which they occupy: in some instances the writer even advances critical opinions; whilst the circumstances under which a particular work of art came into the royal possession are frequently stated upon the margin with much care. Dimensions in feet and inches are occasionally given. *[Charles I. 1625-49.]*

There is an occasional naïveté about many of the expressions used in his descriptions, and most of the painter's names are loosely spelt. The latter feature certainly indicates that the Keeper's acquaintance with foreign names has been derived from hearsay rather than from books.

Vander Doort uses the word *picture*, not only for models painted, as we have already seen in Henry's Inventory; but for bas-relief representations, and this when speaking of the effigies on gold coins and likewise of a model of King Charles on horseback done by Le Seur. He uses the word *harness* for armour, and *whiskers* for moustaches. Portraits represented to the hips or elbows, he occasionally designates as "*to the shoulders.*" He adopts one means of distinguishing portraits that has already proved very serviceable. In describing separate heads, especially miniatures, Vander Doort generally commences with "*Done upon the right light,*"—meaning thereby that the light is admitted on to the subject from the right side; and, on the other hand, when intending to express the opposite, he avoids using the word "left," but invariably says "Done upon the *wrong* light." *[Peculiarities in Vander Doort's Catalogue.]*

On testing these expressions,—by comparing them with recognised and well-ascertained pictures,—I find that he always intends the word "right" to imply that of the person *represented*, and not of the beholder. Thus ; most of the portraits of Henry VIII., more especially those attributed to Holbein, have the light coming in from the spectator's right, a circumstance which may have tended in some degree to establish the tradition that Holbein was left-handed. These are specified by Vander Doort as "Done upon the wrong light."

A large amount of space in the catalogue is occupied by a list of the Miniatures. They are very numerous and valuable, and it is a great satisfaction to find that the majority of them can still be identified in the royal Library at Windsor.

Pennant says,* that in the time of James I., Whitehall was in a most ruinous state. He determined to rebuild it, and began with pulling down the banquetting rooms built by Elizabeth ; but all that he lived to accomplish was the present building retaining that name, begun in 1619, from a design of Inigo Jones, and now known as the Chapel Royal, Whitehall.

At Whitehall Palace, soon after his accession to the throne, Charles I. assembled all the choicest works of art. The whole number of his pictures amounted to 1,387,† of which 216 were reckoned first-class paintings, and 88 chef-d'œuvres. Some of these were kept also at St. James's and at Hampton Court. The Sculptures, amounting to 399, were principally arranged at his palace at Greenwich. The Miniatures, Books, Medals, and Gems were kept in an apartment called the

---

* Page 139, of "London," fifth edition, 1813.
† Mrs. Jameson's Public Galleries, p. 191.

Cabinet-room at Whitehall, built by order of Prince Henry from a design of Inigo Jones.* It stood on the west side of the road towards St. James's Park, on the site of the present Dover House (Lady Clifden's), between the Horse Guards and the Treasury.

The Cabinet room.

It is remarkable that the locality where the choicest works of art belonging to the Crown were then concentrated, is now occupied by our principal government offices. Smith, in his Antiquities of Westminster,† says that the western side of King Street was formerly bounded by that open space which afterwards became enclosed under the name of St. James's Park. When Henry VIII. had acquired possession of Whitehall, he, in 1531, by exchange with the abbot and convent of Westminster, procured to himself this enclosure, part of which he converted into the beforementioned park; and on the rest he erected a tennis-court, a cock-pit, a bowling-alley, a long stone gallery. All these buildings were on the opposite side of the public street to the original residence. He connected them by two gateways across the street. That nearest to Charing Cross was called Holbein's Gate, and, after serving as the State Paper Office, was demolished in 1750. It crossed the street just below the Banqueting House, at the point between Gwyder House and the Chapel Royal.

Whitehall towards St. James's Park.

Some of the largest pictures seem to have been placed in the Tennis-Court Chamber and the Bear Gallery.

The general arrangement of Whitehall Palace during

* Pennant's London, p. 142.
† Page 20.

Y

the first half of the seventeenth century may still be traced by reference to a curious ground plan * that was taken by John Fisher in the reign of Charles II., and engraved by Vertue, who regarded it as belonging to the year 1680. Cunningham, however, in the "Handbook to London,"† records his conviction that a still earlier date, by ten years, might have been assigned to it.

[margin: Whitehall in the reign of Charles II. A.D. 1670.]

After so long an interval, many of the names of the rooms, as well as of the occupants of the apartments, or "lodgings," as they were then termed, had changed entirely. The general appearance of the buildings at Whitehall, at different periods, may be seen in the Illustrated Pennant in the British Museum Printroom.

On a wall in the Privy Chamber still remained Holbein's painting of Henry VII. and Henry VIII., with their Queens.‡

As not only the pictures themselves, but the manner in which they were arranged during the prosperous days of King Charles I., cannot but possess a par-

---

* Smith's Antiquities of Westminster, p. 19.
† Page 550.
‡ This picture was destroyed in the fire which broke out April 10th, 1691;* but it had fortunately been copied for Charles II. by Remé van Leemput, and his performance still exists at Hampton Court Palace. What yet remained of the old palace was consumed in the second fire, which began January 4th, 1698, and lasted seventeen hours. Cunningham's London, p. 550, and Sanderson's Graphice, p. 24.

---

* Cunningham, p. 549.

ticular interest, I will invite a cursory glance at those apartments in the palace which were specially devoted to works of art, and state as briefly as possible the nature and character of the principal pictures that each room contains, following, of course, the arrangement adopted in Vander Doort's Catalogue.

<small>Charles I. 1625–49</small>

The opening portion of the catalogue does not specify what apartment the pictures occupied. The first division comprises eighty-one paintings, which appear to have been of very various sizes and quality. Their dimensions are stated in feet and inches. They consist principally of Italian pictures. The following is a selection of the principal paintings. The numbers in brackets correspond with those introduced in Bathoe's edition of Vander Doort's catalogue :—

<small>Vander Doort's Catalogue. 1639.</small>

CATALOGUE OF THE KING'S PICTURES BY ABRAHAM VANDER DOORT.

(4.) Titian's Lucretia, a small whole length.

(10.) Raphael's Marquis of Mantua (Frederic, afterwards Duke, born 1500).*

Raphael's St. George, a little picture (14).† See Henry VIII.'s pictures, *ante*, page 298.

Bellini's portrait of a young woman (15), and the Infant Christ and St. John embracing, by Parmigiano (26); both of

---

* Now at Charlecote (Mr. Lucy's) in Warwickshire.

† Now at St. Petersburg. To recover this picture Charles I. gave the volume of Holbein's drawings in exchange. See the engraving in the Crozat Gallery and in Landon, " Œuvres de Raphael," vol. 6, pl. 334. Passavant's Rafael, vol. 2, page 57. He describes it as St. George holding a lance. The painter's name is on the breast of the horse, and the picture belongs to the year 1506. The garter, with only the word HONI visible, encircles the plate armour of the left leg.

Whitehall Pictures.

which the King had obtained of Lord Pembroke in exchange for a small Raphael picture of Judith.

A small picture of Mice, by Raphael * (32). Presented by Sir Henry Wooton.

St. John the Baptist, by Da Vinci † (71).

Two small pictures, by Mantegna, of the Death of the Virgin (27), and a "Sacred Conversation" (33); both crowded with incidents.

Silver embossed plates, by Van Vianen (3).

A beautiful little carving in hone-stone, representing Henry VIII.,‡ a whole length, in full relief, about 6 inches high (12).

Holbein's picture of a German and his wife § (22). It bears date 1512.

Holbein's portrait of a Cornish Gentleman|| (30).

Holbein's Frobenius the printer (43). No. 323 of the Hampton Court Catalogue.

Holbein's portrait of a man in long beard, "almost sidefaced" (46).

Holbein's Erasmus ¶ (49), "fellow" to the Frobenius· No. 324 of the Hampton Court Catalogue.

Holbein's Sir Thomas More (48), in black cap, furred gown, and red sleeves, on a very small circular piece of wood.**

A small picture by Paolo

---

* Such a picture was left by the Duchess of Portland to Mrs. Delany, who bequeathed it to Lady Stamford. See Mrs. Delany's Autobiography, vol. 3, Second Series, page 490, and *post*, page 369.

† A present from the French King, in return for which King Charles sent a Profile of Erasmus by Holbein, and a Holy Family of three figures by Titian.

‡ Probably the work of Nicolas da Modena. Purchased by Mr. J. Dent, of Sudeley Castle, at the Strawberry Hill sale in 1842. It had formerly been the property of Lady Elizabeth Germaine.

§ These figures have been called the parents of Holbein. The picture is now at Hampton Court, No. 336 of the Catalogue.

|| Called "Reskemeer," on the original drawing for it, at Windsor. It is now at Hampton Court, No. 325 of the Catalogue. He was High Sheriff for the county of Cornwall in 1557. See Lodge's Biographical illustrations of Chamberlaine's 4to edition of Holbein's drawings. London: 1812.

¶ Charles had already parted with an Erasmus, by Holbein, "sidefaced, and looking downwards," to the King of France, in return for the St. John by Da Vinci, named above on this page (71).

** The frame and picture seem all to have been of one piece.

Veronese, containing some eleven figures, of the Finding of Moses (11), purchased at Venice by Daniel Nys, the French merchant and agent who procured so many of the finest pictures for the King.

Martin Luther (51), painted by Cranach, in a small "eight-square" ebony frame.

Charles I. 1625-49.

THE CABINET ROOM. *Page 21.**

Thirty-six sculptures in stone, bronze, and wood, are enumerated as placed round the room and in the windows. Among them—

"The King's own picture on horseback, done by the Frenchman" (24), apparently a model (one foot one inch high) for the statue at Charing Cross.

"The picture of the King himself in brass, so big as the life, being only a head. Done by the Frenchman" (35).

A little shagged dog, carved in alabaster, scratching his head with his left foot (33), being done in King Henry VIII.'s time.

Cabinet Room.

Sculptures.

Next follow a list of bas-reliefs, medallions, and a series of copies, in miniature, by Peter Olivier, after Raphael, Correggio, and Titian, from pictures already in the King's possession. These were kept within cupboards, in double-shutting cases, with locks and keys, and glasses over them.

The fine collection of Miniatures,† by Holbein,

---

* These numbers following the names of the apartments refer to the pages in Bathoe's edition of the Catalogue.

† These, it is hardly necessary to state, were termed "*Limnings*," a word applied to all *minute* paintings in water-colour (whether opaque or transparent) upon separate cards, or the parchment leaves of an ancient manuscript. The word has been used indiscriminately as a heading throughout Bathoe's edition of this Catalogue. Every page, whether describing oil pictures, miniatures, or sculptures, commences with "The King's Collection of Limnings." The royal appointment of painter to the crown in Scotland, is traditionally made at the present time under the title of "*Limner*."

326   HISTORY OF OLD LONDON.

Limnings in the Cabinet Room at Whitehall. Janet, Hilliard, Isaac Olivier, and Hoskins, were all arranged within square frames. These "Limnings" amounted altogether to seventy-five in number.

LIMNINGS OR MINIATURES. *Page 32.*

The most important among them are :—

Miniatures. Four Miniatures of Queen Henrietta-Maria (11)—(14).
Four Miniatures of Henry VIII. (45—48).
Three Miniatures of Queen Elizabeth (31), (40), (41).
Isaac Olivier's portrait of Prince Henry (17), of considerable size.
Mary Queen of Scots, as Dauphine (33), by Janet. See *ante*, p. 314.
Eight Miniatures in one frame (24)—(31),* including Henry VIII., Catharine of Arragon, Anne Boleyn, Queen Mary, and Elizabeth. The miniature of Queen Mary, painted in oil on metal, is especially beautiful.

Many of the above miniatures had been presented to the King by the Earl of Suffolk, the Earl of Pembroke (Lord Steward), Sir H. Vane, Lord Feilding.

Books, gems, and medals. BOOKS, GEMS, MEDALS, AND DRAWINGS. *Page 56.*

A collection of fifty-four books of prints, drawings, &c., including a volume of crayon portraits of the nobility of France (42), a 4to book of studies by Michel Angelo (47), and a proof impression of Hollar's engraving from the Richard II. diptych.†
Four large engraved antique cameos.
A large collection of golden coins and medals.
Two large pictures, in guazzo or distemper colours, by Correggio (Mantua pieces), which at this period had no place assigned

---

* This frame, with all the contents as specified in this catalogue, has passed into the collection of the Duke of Buccleuch.

† See post, p. 346.

PICTURES AT WHITEHALL PALACE, A.D. 1639. 327

to them,* but were protected in double-door shutting wooden cases. They are now in the Gallery of Drawings at the Louvre.†

After this are specified a large number of wax "pictures," chiefly medallions, some modelled in relief and others impressed from dies, set upon a black ground in coloured velvet cases, black jet oval and circular boxes.

Among them might be observed the King's portrait when he was only eighteen years of age, the royal arms at the back, and the motto " Si vis omnia subjicere, subjice te rationi, 1636 " (page 78).

TENNIS-COURT. *Page* 83.

The second volume commences with the Tennis-court Chamber, which, according to Fisher's Map of the Palace, must have been on the western side of the public street, that is, towards the Cockpit, in the mass of buildings abutting on St. James's Park.

In the Tennis-court Chamber, Sir James Palmer's lodgings, were five pictures, figure subjects.

The chief among them being :—

"The picture of Queen Mary of Scotland, King James's mother, at length, painted upon a board. Brought from Scotland and given to the King." (1.)

Portrait of the King, when Prince (2), full length; by Abraham Blyenburch. (Qy. Abraham Bloemaert). The name of Cornelius Polenburgh has been erroneously substituted for the above in Bathoe's edition.

Charles I. 1625-49.

Tennis Court.

Portraits.

---

* Bathoe's edition of the Catalogue, p. 76.
† See Landon's "Œuvres de Corrège," planches 59 and 60; and Landon's "Annales du Musée," vol. 2, planches 9 and 69.

Bear Gallery.

BEAR GALLERY. *Page* 84.

The Bear Gallery contained twenty-eight portraits, the size of life, by good painters, and with powerful effects of light and shadow; one Holy Family, by Schidone (15), placed over the door; a picture of three Angels (20), by Salviati; one Scriptural subject (1); and two grand compositions by Rubens; making, with two other Italian pictures, (2) and (26,) thirty-five in all.

Pictures by Rubens.

The "Emblem," or Allegory "of Peace and War" * (13), by Rubens.

The second large picture is the grand composition of "Daniel in the Lion's Den" † (14), presented to the King by Sir Dudley Carleton. Size, 7 ft. 4 in. by 10 ft. 8 in.

Twenty-two out of these portraits were whole length, the size of life; niue of them by Daniel Mytens, two by Van Somer, two by Honthorst, five by Van Dyck (three of them half-lengths), one by Janet, and one by Titian.‡

* This is the fine picture now in the National Gallery. Its history is so well known, that it is sufficient merely to allude to the circumstance that the picture was painted by Rubens during his residence in England on diplomatic service, and that he himself gave it as a present to King Charles. The dimensions are stated to be 6 ft. 8 in. by 9 ft. 11 in. In the present official catalogue of the National Gallery they are 6 ft. 6 in. by 9 ft. 9 in.

† It now belongs to the Duke of Hamilton, at his palace in Scotland.

‡ Three of these paintings by Mytens were adaptations or copies from earlier pictures, namely James IV. with a falcon on his wrist (16), Margaret of Scotland (17), and Mary Queen of Scots (18), the last being turned the reverse way of the panel picture, from which it was taken. The first of these now belongs to Sir William Stirling Maxwell of Keir, and the two last remain in the royal possession, at Hampton Court Palace. The Queen Mary, with the rich black robes and finely massed shadows, is a striking picture. The full

ADAM AND EVE STAIRS. *Page 90.* Charles I. 1625-49.

At the head of the Adam and Eve Stairs, outside of the door of the room, an old Whitehall picture of Adam and Eve, nearly the size of life, painted by Mabuse * (1).

ADAM AND EVE STAIRS-ROOM. *Page 91.* Adam and Eve Room.

Over the door,

" Titian and Aretino," a picture copied by H. Goltius (2).

The room contains twenty-four historical paintings, chiefly Italian ; the largest being Titian's St. Sebastian (4), and The Calling of St. Matthew, painted by Mabuse, a present to the King (13). The latter picture is now at Windsor Castle, after having been for some time at Hampton Court. See *post,* page 373.

Titian and Mabuse.

WHITEHALL.

THE FIRST PRIVY LODGING-ROOM. *Page 96.* Privy Lodgings.

Containing twelve choice historical pictures, and all, with the exception of one by Correggio, painted by Titian. The figures are on a large scale. The best known pictures are—

length of Charles V. with an Irish dog (12) is engraved in Madrazzo's Gallery of Madrid. The Duke of Buckingham in white satin (29), and the Earl of Nottingham, the gallant Admiral of the Fleet that repulsed the Spanish Armada (31), are noble specimens of Myten's ability as a portrait painter. The majority of these pictures measure 7 ft. 4 in. by 4 ft. 6 in.

* This is now at Hampton Court, No. 580 of the Catalogue.

Privy Lodging Room.
Titian's masterpieces.

Tarquin and Lucretia (1), Philip II. and the Princess of Eboli as a naked Venus * (5); The Entombment, "a Mantua piece," † (7); The Supper at Emmaus, "a Mantua piece," ‡ (9); The Marquis del Guasto and his Mistress (10); Titian himself, and a Senator § (11); St. John the Baptist, "a tall narrow piece" (6), by Correggio.

Second Privy Lodging.

SECOND AND MIDDLE PRIVY LODGING-ROOM. *Page 99.*

Containing nineteen pictures, principally Italian, by Titian, Polidoro, and Giulio Romano.

Among them,

Titian's masterpieces.

Giulio Romano.

A Concert, by Titian (1), "a Mantua piece," now in the National Gallery. Titian's Magdalen (14), Titian's Venus del Pardo ‖ (16), presented to the King when he went to Spain. Three heads of a Jeweller in one picture, by Titian (18); Giulio Romano's large altarpiece of the Nativity (11), measuring 9 ft. by 6 ft. 1 in. It is now in the Louvre. ¶ The Birth of Hercules (9), and The Education of Jupiter (12), both by the last-named master. Four narrow frieze-like paintings of antique designs, by Polidoro.** Giulio Romano's "Italian Prelate" ††(8); "Charles Audax" (19), now in the Imperial Gallery at Vienna.‡‡

* Now in the Fitzwilliam Museum at Cambridge.
† Now in the Gallery of the Louvre.
‡ Now in the Louvre.
§ Still in the Royal Collection at Windsor Castle. Compare *ante*, page 314, No. 14.
‖ The real subject is Jupiter and Antiope. The picture is now in the Louvre, No. 468 of the present Catalogue.
¶ No. 293 of the Catalogue.
** All the last-named pictures now remain at Hampton Court.
†† In all probability Raphael's Julius II., which passed from the Queen of Sweden's to the Orleans' Collection, and is now in our National Gallery. See *ante*, page 305, No. 16, for a portrait of Julius II. in the Royal Collection at the time of James I.
‡‡ The picture is now attributed to Hemessen. Along the ledge or table in front is inscribed CAROLVS AVDAX BVR. An old copy still remains at Hampton Court.

PICTURES AT WHITEHALL PALACE, A.D. 1639. 331

THIRD PRIVY LODGING-ROOM, CALLED ALSO THE SQUARE-TABLE ROOM. *Page* 104.

Charles I.
1625-49.
Third
Privy
Lodging.

Containing fifteen of the choicest pictures, exclusively Italian. The following among them are the most important :—

Holy Family, by Raphael (11); "a large piece, painted upon board, by Raphael Urbin, being our Lady, Christ, and Joseph, St. John, St. Anne, entire figures less than the life. A Mantua piece." *

Giulio Romano's Triumph of Vespasian and Titus † (1), painted on panel.

A picture attributed to "Permensius" (6).

"An Italian woman's picture, with her arm naked, dressing herself, and a man holding a looking-glass to her; half a figure, so big as the life, painted upon cloth." "Size, 3 ft. 5 in. by 2 ft. 9 in." ‡

Correggio's celebrated "Jupiter and Antiope" § (12), "a Mantua piece." Correggio's "Mercury teaching Cupid to read" ‖ (13), "a Mantua piece."

Italian master-pieces by Raphael, Giulio Romano, and Correggio.

PRIVY GALLERY, WHITEHALL. *Page* 107.

Privy Gallery.

The Privy Gallery contained seventy-three portraits. Only five out of the series were full length, namely (56), (61), (68), (69), (70).

---

* This is the celebrated picture known as "La Perla," and now in Madrid. See Passavant's Rafael, vol. ii. page 306.

† The picture is now in the Louvre, No. 295 of the Catalogue.

‡ This composition accords with Titian's well-known composition, now in the Louvre, No. 471, called "Titian's Mistress," but more probably representing Alfonso I., Duke of Ferrara and Laura de' Dianti. See Landon, "Œuvres de Titien," pl. 13.

§ Now in the Louvre, No. 28 of the Catalogue. See also Landon, "Annales du Musée," vol. iv. pl. 1.

‖ Now in our National Gallery.

Privy Gallery Whitehall.
The majority are half length, life size, and by painters of eminence. No dimensions appear in this portion of the catalogue.

Foreign Portraits.
Isabella de Valois, wife of Philip II.* (5).

Earl Douglas, "also called Black Dudley, in a black cap with a little medal, being side-faced " † (6), a " Whitehall piece," a spirited profile, wearing the collar of St. Michael. See Inventory of Henry VIII., *ante*, page 296, No 58.

Isabella, wife of the Emperor Charles V. (11), painted by Titian; bought by the King. Now in Warwickshire, at Charlecote, the residence of Mr. Lucy.

The two sisters of Charles V; half-length figures, the size of life (9 and 10). The first, Mary of Hungary, was Governess of the Netherlands, and the second, Isabella (Elizabeth), was married to the King of Denmark.‡

Charles V. (12), a " Whitehall piece,"in armour, holding a truncheon.

The Duke of Alva when young (17), presented by the Earl of Arundel. Now at Windsor.

Leonora, wife of Francis I., and sister of Charles V., holding an orange (19), painted by Janet.§ *Purchased by the King.* No dimensions stated. See Henry VIII. Inventory, *ante*, No. 22, page 290.

Marie de' Medici, by Van Dyck (22), wearing black, and holding "a handful of roses." ||

Above the door: A small drawing with a pen, on parchment (23), representing the Prince of Wales's feathers encircled by the Collar of the Garter, here styled "a collar of roses."

* This corresponds with a fine picture, by Coello, recently belonging to Mr. Davenport Bromley, of Wotton, and of which a fine repetition was exhibited by Mr. Joseph Bond at the British Institution in 1866. No. 90 of the Catalogue.

† It now belongs to the Marquis of Queensberry, and was No. 12 of the recent Portrait Exhibition at Kensington.

‡ This picture appears to be the one now at Hampton Court "in a widow's habit." No. 916 of the Catalogue. Mary of Hungary was No. 284 of Hampton Court Catalogue. See *post*, page 374. Note.

§ A similar picture is now at Hampton Court, but holding a letter instead of the orange here mentioned by Vander Doort.

|| This corresponds with a picture now at Blenheim Palace.

THIRTY-TWO SMALL HISTORICAL PORTRAITS, BEING A CONTINUATION OF THE SAME SERIES. *Page* 112.

Charles I. 1625-49.

At the upper end of the same apartment commences a series of small historical portraits, "*placed at the upper end of the Privy Gallery, towards the Queen's side.*" They are all marked as Whitehall pieces, and divided into two classes; the first being called "*Nine old heads upon board,*" and the second being styled "*Twenty-three little heads, most of them painted without hands, upon board, much smaller than the life.*" The latter number probably occupied a different side of the wall of the gallery. Dimensions are noted against the second portion only.

Privy Gallery. Old Portraits.

The greater part of these "*heads*" appear to be identical with the former entries in King Henry's Inventory, as shown by the following list:—

Royal Portraits.

A young King (Qy. Richard II.), (24). Compare King Henry's Inventory, No. 59, *ante*, p. 297.

Richard III. (25). See Inventory, No. 54, page 295.

Edward IV. (26). No. 14, page 288.

Henry V. (27). No. 30, page 291. There is no king's name given in the original manuscript.

Henry VI. (28). No. 31, page 291.

Margaret of Scotland (29). No. 45, page 294.

King Henry VIII. (Prince Arthur), (30), with red cap and collar about his neck, of white and red roses. See Inventory No. 1, *ante*, p. 287.

Margaret of Richmond, mother of King Henry VII. (31). No. 55, page 296.

Elizabeth of York (32). Compare No. 34 below.

King Henry VII., "with two hands, in a furred gown and a black cap" (33). No. 32, *ante*, page 291.

Elizabeth of York (34). No. 19, page 289.

A lady in a red golden cloth habit (35). See No. 304 of Hampton Court Catalogue.

A lady putting a ring on her left-hand finger (36). See No. 296 of Hampton Court Catalogue.

A White Nun (37), Margaret, Aunt to Charles V., Governess

334 HISTORY OF OLD LONDON.

Privy Gallery, Whitehall. of the Netherlands in 1520. See Inventory, No. 14, *ante*, page 294. It is now No. 298 of the Hampton Court Catalogue.

Henry VIII. when young; a glove in his right hand (38).* See Inventory, No. 35, page 292.

The Princess of Castilion, "in a black dressing, with her hands together" (39). Possibly a wrong name for the picture, now at Windsor, which I recently discovered to be the Duchess of Milan. Compare King Henry's Inventory, No. 49, page 295.

Countess of Cobbona (40). Compare the " Barcele Countess of Corne" of King Henry's Inventory, No. 3, *ante*, page 287. This picture afterwards appears in the collection of James II. See page 23, No. 255, of Bathoe's edition, where it is called "Berscele Countess de Corne."

Elizabeth or Isabella Queen of Denmark. "Elizabeth, the Austrian Queen of Bavaria" (41). Compare No. 296 of the Hampton Court Catalogue. This is probably an erroneous substitution of the word Bavaria for Denmark. See *ante*, page 290, No. 21. Isabella or Elizabeth, the wife of Christian II. and sister of the Emperor, would be the subject most likely to occur in this place. Otherwise the portrait might have been Cunegunda, the sister of Maximilian I., and married to Albert, Duke of Bavaria, in 1487.

The Emperor Frederick, side-faced, with a golden cap (42). See King Henry's Inventory, No. 27, *ante*, page 291.

Philip le Bel (43). See No. 51, *ante*, page 295.

Charles VIII. of France†(44). See No. 7, *ante*, page 287.

Philip of Burgundy (45), (probably the Hardy). See No. 52.

Louis XII. of France (46). See No. 43, *ante*, page 294.

Prince Arthur when young (47), " in his minority, in a black cap and golden habit, holding in his right hand a white gilly flower." See King Henry's Inventory, No. 2, *ante*, page 287. This picture is no longer in the royal collections, but old copies, illustrating the type, are occasionally to be met with. See "Archæologia," vol. xxxix., pages 249 and 462.

Elizabeth, Queen of Edward

---

* Now at Althorp, and may have had originally a companion picture of Jane Seymour, of similar treatment, as shown by the Cartoon by Holbein and Van Leemput's copy, now at Hampton Court, *post*, p. 356.

† Bathoe prints " King Charles XII.," but the original manuscript says simply " the King of France."

IV. (48). See No. 18, *ante*, page 289.

Isabella of Castile (49). See No. 37, *ante*, page 293, now at Windsor.

Ferdinand of Arragon (50). See No. 23, *ante*, page 290.

The Queen of Castile (51). See page 293, No. 39.

Charlemagne, "Charles Magnus, in a furred cap, with a glory about his head;" no dimensions are given (52). A similar picture to this now belongs to the Society of Antiquaries.

Philip (Audax) the Bold (53). Compare No. 53, *ante*, page 295.

Julius Cæsar, "side-faced (54). See No. 42, *ante*, page 294.

Duke John (Sans Peur) of Burgundy (55), "looking downwards, in a black habit and cap."* Father of Philip the Good, murdered 1419. See No. 40, *ante*, page 294.

Charles I. 1625-49.

This concludes the thirty-two Old Heads (9 + 23), as distinctly specified. Those that follow are apparently of a larger size; but no dimensions are in the original catalogue, although in Bathoe's edition measurements are given to the following:— *Privy Gallery Portraits.*

Henry VIII., his Queen (Catherine Parr), Edward VI., and the Princesses Mary and Elizabeth † (56).

King Henry when young, holding a scroll (57). Compare No. 34 of the Inventory, *ante*, p. 292.

Upon the door of the "Chair-room."—A small group of three half-figures, Maximilian, Charles V., and Ferdinand, in one frame.‡ (58.)

Henry VIII. Family Picture.

---

* A portrait of this Duke, engraved in Montfaucon's "Monumens de la Monarchie Française," vol. iii. pl. xxx. No. 2, exhibits the above-mentioned peculiarities of the eyes looking down, and a black dress and cap.

† This is the first mention of this picture in any catalogue. Judging by the countenance of the King, and the ages of the children, it appears to have been painted almost at the close of his reign. It is painted on canvas, and now at Hampton Court. No. 510 of the Catalogue.

‡ Apparently a medallion, carved in wood. See King Henry's Inventory, No. 12, *ante*, page 288. This composition corresponds with a beautiful little box-wood carving at Vienna. See "Arneth Monumente

Privy Gallery, Whitehall.

Philip II. when young, in black dress lined with white fur* (59).

"Two men children and one woman child playing at a table." The three children of the King of Denmark † (60). See Inventory, No. 13, *ante*, page 288.

King Edward VI., when Prince, "at length, in a red satin coat, lined with white fur, and in a white suit" (61). "A Whitehall piece." No dimensions given. See Inventory of 1547, No. 16, *ante*, p. 289.

Foreign Portraits.

Archduke Charles of Austria (62). Father of the Emperor Ferdinand II., and of Margaret, wife of Philip III. of Spain. Born 1540; died 1590. "A Whitehall piece."

The old Duke of Savoy (63), "so big as life to the shoulders, with a white cross on *black* armour."

"The aforesaid Duke's son, with a white cross on *white* armour, so big as life to the shoulders" (64). Both pictures brought from Savoy by Sir Hen. Wooton, and presented by him to the King.

Queen Elizabeth, when young, in a red dress, holding a book ‡ (65). No dimensions are given in Van Doort's original MS. See Inventory, No. 20, page 289, and also page 311.

King James, in white, with a hat and feather (66). "A Whitehall piece."

Small picture of the Conversion of St. Paul (67). "A Whitehall piece."

The young Palsgrave, "at length" (68).

in Wien," fol. 1858, pl. 1, No. 128. In Vander Doort's Catalogue the names are wrongly set down as Henry VIII., Emperor Frederick and his son, Maximilian Primo. This last word is wrongly printed by Bathoe as "*Prince.*"

* This picture, printed on panel, is now at Hampton Court, No. 291 of the Catalogue. It was No. 209 of the recent Portrait Exhibition. A similar picture is in the possession of Earl Stanhope, painted on canvas.

† This picture has, as before stated, been falsely engraved by Vertue as the children of King Henry VII. of England. (See "Archæologia," vol. xxxix. p. 256.)

‡ This picture, inscribed with her name in the corner, has recently been removed from Hampton Court to St. James's Palace. It first appears in the Inventory of 1547, and must therefore have been painted between that time and 1542, which contains no mention either of it, or of the full-length of Prince Edward, in red.

PICTURES AT WHITEHALL PALACE, A.D. 1639.   337

The Archduke Matthias, "at length" (69).
The Duke of Savoy, when young, in armour, attended by his page, "so big as the life, at length" (70). "A Whitehall piece."
A daughter of the Duke of Savoy, fair, and adorned with jewels (71).
The three children of the Palsgrave (72). That is of the

King and Queen of Bohemia, two girls and a boy, nephew and nieces of King Charles. They are represented, each in a separate oval compartment, side by side. The punctuation of the description has been sadly blundered in Bathoe's transcript.*
A daughter of the Duke of Savoy (73). Showing two hands, having a dark complexion, with diamonds and chains.

Charles I. 1625-49.

WITHDRAWING ROOM,
OR, THE KING'S BREAKFAST CHAMBER. *Page* 123.

Breakfast Chamber.

contained, above the table,—
Van Dyck's fine picture of the children of Charles I., with great dog, which is now in the Van Dyck gallery at Windsor Castle (1). This picture was painted in 1637, and purchased by King George III. from Lord Portmore. It is one of the very few works of the ancient masters acquired by that monarch.
Over a door was Giulio Romano's "Mermaid, with young Mermaids" † (2). "A Mantua piece."

KING'S BEDCHAMBER. *Page* 123.

The King's Bedchamber contained family portraits, and a few choice pictures of religious and classic subjects.

Bedchamber.

At the bed-side was a small "Holy Family," by Raphael (9), "Our Lady, Christ, and St. John," little entire figures, half as big as the life."

Above the chimney, "The Duke of Buckingham and Family" (8), done by Honthorst, "half figures, so big as the life."

Holy Family by Raphael.

* This picture is now at Buckingham Palace, in the green drawing-room, where it was quite recently entitled "Children of Henry VII." (See Archæologia, vol. xxxix. p. 461.)

† This picture has lately been restored to public view in the rooms at Hampton Court Palace.

z

Portraits by Honthorst.

Bedchamber, Whitehall.

This fine picture is now at Buckingham Palace, over a door in one of the drawing-rooms.

Van Dyck's portrait of "Queen Henrietta Maria," in white satin (1), "to the knees," now at Windsor.

"The King of Bohemia," on board, "to the shoulders, in a cloak, with one hand" (2), by Honthorst.

"The Queen of Bohemia," in yellow and black, with one hand holding a fan, "to the shoulders" (4), by Honthorst.

"Prince Henry," in armour, enlarged, by Mytens, after Olivier, "to the shoulders" (3).

"The Children of the King of Bohemia," by Poelemburgh (7). Numerous small full-length figures in a landscape. Now at Hampton Court Palace. No. 311 of the Catalogue. See *post*, p. 369.

LITTLE ROOM. *Page* 125.

Little Room.

This small apartment, between the Withdrawing-room and the Long Gallery, contained principally Italian pictures, and portraits of painters by themselves. The most distinguished among them was Titian's large picture, on canvas, of "The Entombment" (3), "a Mantua piece," with three crosses in the distance, and the figure of Christ, "painted in shortning." *

Portraits.

Portraits of the Painters by themselves—namely, Rubens(2), Van Dyck (4), Mytens (5), *over the door*, and an old man with a long beard (6), by Michal Johnson Mireveldt.

Raphael.

Portrait, by Raphael, of a man (15) "in a two-peaked black cap, in a black habit, with his right hand holding his garment at his breast."

Portrait of a Gardener (Arborist)† to the Duke of Florence (14), attributed to Andrea del Sarto, but bearing the monogram of Franciabigio on a prun-

---

* The great picture, now in the Louvre, we have already noticed in the First Privy Lodging-room. (See *ante*, p. 330.) Against this picture, in Vander Doort's original MS., is the following note:—

"*This piece was by your Ma^{ts} appointm^t. removed into the Queen's Bedchamb. above the chimney.* 1639. *Octo.*"

† The word in Vander Doort's MS. is "*Harborest,*" which Bathoe explains as the "Harbinger."

ing knife at the back. Now at Windsor Castle.

Portrait of an old shaven man, like a friar, holding his right hand to his breast, and in his left hand a scroll of paper (13), on canvas.

Charles I. 1625-49.

LONG GALLERY. *Page* 130.

The *King's Long Gallery, towards the Orchard*, contains one hundred and three pictures; very varied in character.

Long Gallery.

The chief picture, and probably the one occupying the upper end of the gallery, is Van Dyck's large family piece of King Charles and Queen Henrietta, with their two children; Westminster being seen across the water in the distance (1). Size, 9 ft. 8 in. by 8 ft.

This grand composition is now in the Van Dyck room at Windsor Castle. Repetitions of it are at Chiswick, the Duke of Devonshire's, and at Goodwood, the Duke of Richmond's.

Giulio Romano, painted by himself (21).

Over the door, towards Lord Holland's lodgings, a Spanish Landscape, with St. Peter receiving the Keys, in the foreground (26).

An Angel defending three Churchmen by driving from them naked figures, personifying the Vices (27). Half-length figures. The picture is attributed to Palma Giovane.*

Portrait of a young man with red sleeves (28), signed G. P. 48. By George Penz. Now at Hampton Court. No. 903 of the Catalogue.

Above the door of His Majesty's Robes, a Saint, by Guercino, holding a scroll in his right and leaning on his left hand (30).

Above the chimney, a water-colour picture, by Lucas Van Leyden (33), "containing some fifteen figures, half so big as the life, sitting, playing at chess."

The good thief and the bad thief on their crosses (34 and 36); being two leaves of a triptych, the centre having contained Our Lord on the cross.

Rome set on fire, "where the people flying with pack and sack, containing upon the first ground

Van Dyck.

Lucas Van Leyden.

* The three principal personages are not tonsured, but one wears a richly embroidered cope; apparently a portrait of Cardinal Granvelle, Minister of Philip II. Now at Hampton Court, transferred from panel to canvas. No. 145 of the Catalogue.

some seventeen figures, besides the little ones, in the landskip afar off" (35). "A Mantua piece, said to be of Giulio Romano." Compare the fine cartoon (in powerful colours) now in the Louvre.

Above the Duke of Lenox's door, Half figure of a woman, by Palma Vecchio, with yellow hair, white habit, and white wide sleeves, holding her right hand to the left sleeve (40). Life size.

St. Anthony of Padua, side-faced, looking up and holding a branch of white lilies (46). "A Mantua piece," by Domenico Feti.

Above the Duke of Lenox's door, "A black-complexioned man, with his right hand on a table, in black slashed sleeves, with white under it, in a little falling-peaked band, stitched with silk" (47). "A Mantua piece." Size, 2 ft. 5 in. by 2 ft.

At the lower end of the gallery, beside the Orchard window-door, a piece of "Lantyr (Atalanta), to whom is presented by a young man, a wild boar, and Envy lying on the ground, with some other figures" (59). "A Mantua piece." Painted upon panel by Giulio Romano.

On the other side of the window, Jupiter between two female figures, the one Pallas and the other a woman "holding the flame of Jupiter's thunderbolt" (60). "A Mantua piece, painted on panel by Giulio Romano."

Upon the third window-post, a piece of our Lady, copied at the Escurial, after Raphael, by Mich. de la Croy (66), or Michael Cross. Our Lady in a yellow and blue habit, embracing Christ in both her arms, she looking about her left shoulder (73). Half a figure, almost so big as the life; said to be a copy after Raphael. (See Walpole's Anecdotes, page 264 of Dallaway and Wornum's edition.)

Above my Lord of Monmouth's door, a woman's picture in a black habit and scarf, said to be done by Rubens when he was in Italy (75). Size, 2 ft. 5 in. by 1 ft. 7 in.

The two daughters of Philip II., in their childhood (82).[*] Two whole-length standing figures, a dog on table between them. Presented to the King by Lord Ancram.

Giulio Romano's figure of Temperance (83), half-length, emptying water from one vessel into another; a man in red, with

---

[*] Isabella, afterwards Governess of the Netherlands, and Catherine, married to Charles Emanuel, Duke of Savoy. Now at Buckingham Palace, over a door in the green drawing-room.

both his hands at his breast, standing by. "A Mantua piece."

Above Lord Ancram's door, Rembrandt's own portrait, in a black cap and furred habit, with a little golden chain upon both his shoulders (87). Presented to the King by the Earl of Ancram.*

A large picture of a naked Venus, sitting at a table, with a looking-glass, white vase, and water-glass on it; Cupid at her right shoulder, with a bow in his hand (95). Painted by Palma Giovane.†

"Leda," by Paul Veronese (98); upon a white bed, with a white swan, holding with her right hand under a purple curtain. Exchanged with Lady Buckingham for a Mantua piece.

Between the 16th and last window, "An old woman with a great scarf upon her head, with a peaked falling band"‡ (101). Done by Rembrandt. Presented by the Earl of Ancram. This appears to have been a companion picture to Rembrandt's own portrait, No. 87.

Charles I. 1625-49.

Long Gallery.

Rembrandt's mother, called the Countess of Desmond.

DUCHESS OF SHREWSBURY'S LODGINGS. *Page 151.*

In the *Duchess of Shrewsbury's Lodgings*, above the chimney, placed during the time of her abode there, "Judith cutting off the head of Holofernes" (103). Purchased by Frosley. Size, 2 ft. 5 in. by 2 ft.

Duchess of Shrewsbury's Lodgings.

KING'S CHAIR-ROOM. *Page 151.*

The *King's Chair-room*, in the Privy Gallery, containing thirty-four pictures, placed round about the chair-room by the King.

These pictures are very varied in character; some

Chair-Room or Throne-room.

---

* Rembrandt's portrait of his mother, now called the Countess of Desmond, was in the same gallery, and appears under No. 101 of this Catalogue. It was also presented by Lord Ancram.

† Compare this composition with the engraving of a similar picture by Teniers, which is now in the Imperial Gallery at Vienna, attributed to Correggio. See Landon, "Vie et Œuvre du Corrège," pl. 66.

‡ This has subsequently acquired the false designation of the Countess of Desmond. See Lord Orford's Works, 1798, 4to., vol. i., page 217, for a valuable note on the subject.

of them by Albert Durer, Holbein, Rubens, Isaac Olivier, Janet, Mireveldt, and Italian masters, including several historical portraits.

Chair or Throne-room at Whitehall.

Equestrian portrait by Van Dyck.
Van Dyck's "King Charles," upon a yellow horse, one following him carrying his "head-piece" (helmet), "which was the model whereby the great picture was made" (3); size 3 ft. 2 in. by 2 ft. Now in the picture-gallery at Buckingham Palace. The great picture is now at Blenheim.

"Sotto Cleeve and his Wife" (7 and 8), painted by himself. "Bought by the King." Now at Windsor Castle.

Kings of Scotland.
"James I.," aged six years, in cap and feather, with a falcon on his right fist (10). Given to the King by Mr. Robert Young. A similar, but larger, picture is now in the National Portrait Gallery.

King James V. of Scotland, with the Scottish arms by. "Both his hands one over another" (12). Now at Windsor Castle.

"Erasmus," copied by G. Penz, after Holbein (13). Now at Windsor Castle.

Queen Mary of Scotland, "in her white morning habit" (14). Given by the Marquis of Hamilton. (A defaced picture.)

"Queen Mary of Scotland" (15), similar to the preceding, said to be done by Janet. Given by Lord Denbigh. Both of them measure 1 ft. by 9 in. Now at Hampton Court. It was No. 321 of the South Kensington Portrait Exhibition.

"An Interior," by Steenwyck, with a figure of the King walking in it, painted by Cornelis Janssens (19).

"Albert Durer, when young, in long yellow hair" (25), painted by himself. Presented to the King by the city of Nuremberg. This corresponds with the picture now in the gallery at Florence.

"Albert Durer's Father" (26), in a black Hungarian cap. This picture corresponds with one now belonging to the Duke of Northumberland. Engraved by Hollar.

Holbein's "Portrait of a Merchant opening a letter with a knife" (29). Now at Windsor Castle. One of the Steelyard fraternity.

A holy family, by some unknown Italian painter, under a green curtain, "Christ reaching some Cherries to Joseph" (33). See *ante*, p. 299.

Isaac Olivier's portrait, "a big limning," of Prince Henry. A red curtain by him, and tents pitched in the distant field (34). This valuable miniature is now preserved in the royal library at Windsor Castle.

PICTURES AT WHITEHALL PALACE, A.D. 1639. 343

More pictures in the chair-room :—*Page* 161.   Charles I. 1625-49.

Rubens's "model and first pattern" for the ceiling in the Banquetting House (5), which was sent for the King's approbation, was suspended from the ceiling over the table, painted upon cloth, in a gilded frame. Size, 1 ft. 3½ in. by 1 ft. 10 in.

"The King's Head," looking into the fields (10).

The Queen's picture, stitched in silk (16).

Van Dyck's portrait of Lady Shirley in a Persian dress (18). Now at Petworth House.

The Marquis del Guasto and family as Mars, Venus, and Cupid (20).

Four pictures by Guido, of the "Labours of Hercules" (19), with figures larger than life. They are now in the Louvre, Nos. 335 to 338 in the Catalogue.

Vander Doort's "Head of a Woman," modelled in coloured wax, inlaid with gold and silver (21), intended for the Emperor Rudolph, but detained by Prince Henry, who pressed the artist into his service. See *ante*, p. 317.

French Portrait, supposed to represent Charles IX. of France (24). Bought by the King. Size 1 ft. 2½ inches by 10½ inches.

Chair or Throne-room.

Vander Doort's model.

IN STORE. *Page* 166.

In Store in the Passage-room between the Banquet- Store-*ting House and the Privy Lodgings :—* room.

The great picture of "St. George," by Rubens (1). Bought by the King of Sir Endymion Porter. This dramatic picture is now in the Queen's Gallery at Buckingham Palace. It was brought back to England in 1798 among the Flemish pictures of the Orleans Collection. Purchased of Mr. Morland by George IV. See Mr. Jameson's Private Galleries, page 41.

Raphael's Cartoons * (2) :—

* It is said by Dorigny, on the authority of the Lord Chamberlain, in his dedication to George I., who knighted him, that Charles I. had purchased them, for a large sum, from Flanders, at the suggestion of Rubens. See also Walpole's " Anecdotes," edited by Dallaway and Wornum, p. 272. An interesting series of copies from them by Mytens still exists at Knole, and many repetitions in tapestry are distributed over the country in ancient family residences.

Whitehall Store-rooms. Raphael's Cartoons.

"In a slit deal wooden case, some two cartoons of Raphael Urbin's, for hangings to be made by, and the other five are, by the King's appointment, delivered to Mr. Franciscus Cleane, at Mortlack, to make hangings by." No dimensions given.

"Mary of Guise, the King of Scotland, King James the 5th's wife, mother to Queen Mary of Scotland" (3).*

Honthorst portraits.

Honthorst's large picture of "The family of the King and Queen of Bohemia in the clouds, with the Duke of Buckingham presenting their children to them, as allegorical figures" (4). No dimensions given, but mentioned as "a very large piece." Now on a staircase at Hampton Court Palace.

"Diana and Calisto, a large piece. The figures half so big again as life. Made for a pattern for hangings" (6).

"Mucius Scaevola" (7). "A Whitehall piece."

IN STORE. *Page* 168.

In the little Store-room in the Bear Gallery :—

"The Duke of Brunswick, Bishop of Halberstadt" (2), "to the shoulders," on panel, by Michael Johnson Mireveldt.

Albert Durer's large print of "Maximilian's Triumph" (3).

Broughel's (?) "Blind leading the Blind" (4). "A water-coloured piece. A Mantua piece."

THE QUEEN'S BEDCHAMBER. *Page* 169.

Queen's Bedroom.

A little piece of "A Bacchus Triumph; many little entire figures." Apparently a highly-finished painting in chiaroscuro. "Done at Venice; done in black and white" (8).

THE QUEEN'S LITTLE DRESSING-ROOM. *Page* 169.

Queen's Dressing-room.

"The Queen's own picture," in a shepherd's habit (9). Done by Honthorst.

"The King's Niece," in a shepherd's habit (11). Done by Honthorst.†

---

* Apparently the panel picture with a shield of arms, and date 1611, in the background, now at Hampton Court, No. 315 of the Catalogue.

† Apparently the Princess Sophia, mother of George I. The picture is said to be at Wilton House.

PICTURES AT WHITEHALL PALACE, A.D. 1639.

"The Queen's Sister, the Duchess of Savoy," when she was young (12), in her blue embroidered habit. This lady was Christina, the second daughter of Henri IV. of France, married to Victor Amadeus of Savoy in 1619.

"The Queen herself," before she was married (13).

"The now Prince of Spain" (14). The Infant Don Balthasar, eldest son of Philip IV. He died 1646.

"An engraving of the King and Queen together" (15).*

Charles I. Portraits. 1625-49.

THE QUEEN'S SECOND BEDCHAMBER. *Page* 170.

Contains five pictures, all of them representing the Holy Family.

Queen's Second Bedroom.

"Our Lady and Christ' (16). "New and fresh made, done in France. Removed from Somerset House Gallery."

"Our Lady, Christ, St. John, and Joseph" (17). By Luca Coniagio (Luca Cambiasi or Cangiaci).

"Our Lady, Christ, and Joseph" (18). A copy, by Gentileschi.

"Our Lady and Christ." "Said to be of Raphael. Painted upon a heavy board. She reaching, with her right hand, flowers to Christ, and with her left hand holding a book. *Removed by the King himself out of the Long Gallery into the Queen's Bedchamber*" (19).

Van Dyck's "Our Lady with Christ, where many Angels are a dancing. *Removed by the King himself out of the Little Room by the Long Gallery*" † (20).

Holy Families.

QUEEN'S WITHDRAWING CHAMBER. *Page* 171.

Above the chimney, "A Susanna, with the two Elders" (21).

Withdrawing-room.

* Apparently the engraving by Van Voerst, from Van Dyck's fine picture of King Charles and his Queen holding a wreath between them. The picture is now in Buckingham Palace, over a door in one of the drawing-rooms. A copy in limning, done by Hoskins when the original was at Denmark House, appears in Vander Doort's Catalogue, p. 37, No. 15.

† Now in the Collection at St. Petersburg, to which it passed, with other pictures, belonging to the Houghton Gallery.

IN STORE. *Page* 171.

Whitehall Store-room.
"*The following are kept in several places, and are yet unplaced*":—

Portraits.

Titian's Holy Family. "She sitting on the ground, in a blue garment, with Christ on her lap; with Joseph in a yellow drapery, with three angels in a landscape. A Mantua piece" (22).

"Queen Mary of Scotland" (23); as big as life, to the shoulders, her name being thereby written in great letters. Thought to be done by Frederick Zuccaro. Changed with Lord Holland for the King's picture in brass.*

Richard II. (Diptych.)
The Queen, when she was a child; with gold flowers, made in a head-dressing, upon a red ground (25). Painted upon cloth, "being but meanly done."

An Interior, "wherein the Queen is painted in little, at length, standing by a blue table, in white apparel" (26). By

"John Van Beliame" (Belcamp).

A similar piece, "by Houkgest, with the Queen's picture therein, done by Cornelius Johnson, whereof the dress is unfinished" (27).

"The Procession of the Knights of the Garter"† (27 A). A long narrow piece, "in black and white," by Van Dyck.

Copies, by Greenbury, from portraits of Albert Durer and his father (28). The originals have already been specified in the King's Chair-room; see *ante*, page 342.

"King Richard II., attended by his Patron Saints, kneeling to the Virgin, surrounded by Angels" (30). It is called "an altarpiece, with two shutting all-over gilded doors."‡ "On

---

* Compare the picture of Mary of Guise, with an inscription, now at Hampton Court, No. 315 of the Catalogue.

† Now at Belvoir Castle.

‡ This is the earliest record which I remember of the exquisite and well-preserved diptych now belonging to the Pembroke family at Wilton House. Hollar has engraved this diptych with extreme accuracy, and his engraving dedicated to the King, bears the same date as Vander Doort's Catalogue—namely, 1639.—(See Parthey's "Hollar," No. 229, page 42.) A proof impression of this plate, in the King's Collection, has already been noticed. See *ante*, p. 326.

the outside of the door, the arms of Edward the Confessor, with a red hat and mantle." Obtained by the King, through Sir James Palmer,* from Lord and Lady Jennings, "in the way of exchange for his Majesty's own picture, in oil-colours, by Lemons."

Charles I. 1625-49. Richard II. (Diptych.)

LONG GALLERY. *Page* 174.

Long Gallery.

In the Long Gallery, and in the little room at the upper end of the Long Gallery, are enumerated many statues, and fragments in bronze and marble, most of them antiques, Greek and Roman. They were mounted on wooden pedestals and placed in the windows.

Antique Sculptures.

CHAIR-ROOM. *Page* 180.

In the Chair-room, at this time, were several statues in brass and marble, both ancient and modern. They were twelve in number. The most important of them appears to have been "the King's statue, cast in brass, by the Frenchman, Le Sueur; being a bust upon a black pedestal, with a helmet on his head, whereupon a dragon, after the ancient Roman fashion; being in height, with the pedestal and all together, three feet"(1).

Chair-room.

Sculptures.

This completes the general view of the most remarkable objects among King Charles's extensive collection

* K. C. C. p. 72. Sir James Palmer had already presented some pictures to the King, and seems to have been employed in making designs for tapestry. King Charles gave a picture of a Bacchanalian subject into his hands for the express purpose of being copied in Mortlake tapestry. See King Charles Catalogue, by Bathoe, p. 159. He copied Titian's "Tarquin and Lucrece." Palmer succeeded Sir T. Rowe as Chancellor of the Order of the Garter.

of works of art. The incidental notes and references, introduced on the foregoing pages, may tend to show that although many of the finest productions of the great masters are no longer in this country, the majority of the historical portraits yet remain in the Royal Collection, and that even those portraits which have passed into other hands are fortunately still retained within our shores.

On reviewing the foregoing Catalogue of the King's property, it will be obvious that many of the descriptions had been hastily drawn up from the pictures themselves, and with very little reference to earlier records. Several names had already perished, and we find that, among the foreign portraits specified as "Whitehall pieces," those numbered 35, 36, and 60, are merely called "ladies" and "men and women children." (See *ante*, page 336, No. 60). They might have been ascertained by a reference to King Henry's Inventory of 1542.

The unfortunate valuation, sale, and dispersion of King Charles's magnificent collection after his death, are too generally known to render any special account necessary on the present occasion.

The Commons resolved upon the disposal of the property belonging to the King, Queen, and Prince, March 23, 1649, and ordered everything to be inventoried, appraised, and sold.

Vertue prepared extracts from one of the Parliamentary appraised lists, together with notes of the prices at which the pictures were actually sold, as an introduction to the printed edition of Vander Doort's

Catalogue. They were taken from a MS. then in the possession of John Anstis, Garter King-at-Arms. I have, however, been favoured by Lord Methuen with the use of a still more valuable list of the pictures and their appraisements, which formerly belonged to Sir Paul Methuen. The MS. is signed and sealed on the last page by G. Wither, Jo: v: Belcamp, Memprière, and A. Mildmay. *Appraisement of the King's pictures.*

According to this document, the pictures at Oatlands were viewed and appraised September 13, 1649.

At Windsor, the Wardrobe and "*tapistry-hangings* *were viewed and appraised September 15, 1649. Signed* '*Thomas Greene, Bertie.*'" They were in the custody of Col. Whichcote, Governor of Windsor Castle. *Windsor.*

Next follows, "*A true inventorie of the goods viewed in Wimbleton House, being the remainder of which goods were left by the Queen; the rest being removed thence to Somerset House.*" No date is given. *Wimbledon.*

These are followed by "*A true Inventory of severall Pictures now remaining in Somerset House in the custody of Mr. Henry Browne and appraised the — September, 1649. They came from Whitehall and St. James's.*" *Somerset House.*

The next heading is—

"*In the withdrawing-roome begins the pictures belonging to Somerset House, with some few belonging to Whitehall.*" Afterwards, the headings change successively to "In the Closet," "Pictures in the Gallery," "In the Great Closet," and, finally, "In the Cross Gallery at Somerset House."

Removal of the King's pictures.

All the pictures described in this MS., notwithstanding the extreme brevity of most of the entries, can be identified with the fuller descriptions prepared by Vander Doort; and in some instances, the spelling of the names of artists, and of the persons represented, throws a considerable light upon the difficult passages of the Dutchman's own writing.

It would appear from this Parliamentary Inventory, that the pictures were removed from Whitehall to Somerset House previous to the sale. Raphael's Cartoons having been reserved by Cromwell at the price of 300*l*. We do not, however, find that any use, beyond serving as "patterns" for tapestry, was made of these noble works of art, until the time when William III. built the Gallery at Hampton Court expressly for their reception.

Foreign purchasers A.D. 1649.

Clarendon, in his History,* refers to the melancholy dispersion of the King's property. The chief purchasers were Philip IV. of Spain, Christina of Sweden, the Duke of Alva, Cardinal Mazarin, the Duc de Richelieu, and the Archduke Leopold, Governor of the Netherlands. Through the last-named purchaser, many English pictures passed to the Imperial Gallery at Vienna. Two private and wealthy connoisseurs, Eberhard Jabach, and a Dutch gentleman, Gerard Van Reynst, became possessed of many of the choicest works of art. Jabach afterwards sold his acquisitions to Louis XIV., and they now enrich the Louvre; whilst

* Vol. iv. p. 547 of the 1849 Oxford edition. For many curious and valuable particulars see Walpole's Anecdotes, edited by Dallaway and Wornum, pp. 282-290, and Disraeli's Curiosities of Literature, vol. ii. pp. 326-335 of 1858 edition.

the States-General purchased from the widow of Van Reynst all that he had obtained, and presented them to Charles II., on the occasion of his restoration to the throne of his ancestors. By this means a large number of pictures in the Catalogue of Charles I. was recovered.*

Charles II. 1660-85.

The Grand Duke of Tuscany, Cosmo III., during his travels in England in 1669, visited Whitehall. He has left a curious and elaborate description of the King's palace and the Banquetting-room. He observes in one passage: "In the gallery, formerly enriched by Cardinal Wolsey with choice paintings, which were taken away and sold by Cromwell, there are now fastened up some vile daubings of battles by sea and land, in the time of Henry VIII. The other gallery, alongside the King's Chamber, which is the first in front of the Antichamber, is entirely naked; all its treasures, consisting of a prospect of a beautiful meadow, laid out like a garden, planted with trees and beautiful hedges of roses, and having four rows of statues in the middle, part of which are of bronze and standing, part of white marble, and, for the most part, in a sitting posture. In the centre, which is surrounded by the statues, there rises a certain structure encircled by iron rails, composed of many and different kinds of dials of various shapes."†

Dismantled Galleries.

---

* The pictures thus acquired may still be distinguished by reference to a volume of engravings that was published of Van Reynst's gallery, generally known under the title "Cabinet du Bourgmestre Reynst," consisting of thirty-three plates, principally engraved by Corn, Vischer.

† Translation of Travels of Cosmo through England. 4to. Published at London: 1821. Page 368.

Hampton Court Palace retained its decorations. Evelyn's Diary, A.D. 1662.

The following description of Hampton Court Palace, two years after the Restoration, will be read with interest, from the Diary of the excellent John Evelyn: "Hampton Court is as noble and uniform a pile, and as capacious as any Gothic architecture can have made it. There is an incomparable furniture in it, especially hangings designed by Raphael, very rich with gold; also many rare pictures, especially the Cæsarean Triumphs of Andrea Mantegna, formerly the Duke of Mantua's; of the tapestries, I believe the world can show nothing nobler of the kind than the stories of Abraham and Tobit." *

Both sets of "hangings" and Mantegna's original paintings of the Triumphs of Julius Cæsar still constitute the principal features of Hampton Court Palace.† The mention of gold being woven in with the tapestries designed by Raphael, shows that they could not have been the original cartoons, which are executed in plain "tempera" or watercolours, on paper, and that they were not the splendid series of tapestries, wrought by order of the Pope as a present for Henry VIII., that remained treasured by his descendants till the unfortunate sale of the crown property after the death of Charles I. The latter were purchased by Don Alonzo de Carnas, the Spanish minister resident in London, who

---

* Diary of John Evelyn, 9th June, 1662.

† Tapestries were also wrought from these designs. Three of the series are at Boughton, the seat of the Duke of Buccleuch. See Passavant's Kunstreise durch England. 8vo., London 1833; p. 189. Other sets are mentioned in the Catalogue of James II.'s effects.

transmitted them to Spain, after which they passed into the possession of the Dukes of Alva.* {James II. 1685-88.}

A catalogue of pictures belonging to Charles II. and James II., formerly preserved in the Earl of Oxford's library, affords some very interesting particulars respecting the royal property during the second half of the 17th century. The total number of works of art is 1,383, and the list is signed at the end by "Will. Chiffinch." The catalogue was printed by Bathoe in 1758, to correspond with the one of King Charles already published. {Catalogue signed by W. Chiffinch.}

The first portion contains 683 pictures, of various proportions—some being specified as "to the waste," and others as "at length,"—including miniatures or limnings, and these can for the most part be identified with the ones previously described in the Catalogue of Charles I. A special record is made, at page 60, of the sum of eighty thousand pounds having been paid for the Mantuan collection. The concluding note, on the same page, deserves attention: "Those called the Dutch presents, were several pictures first belonging to King Charles, and sold to a curious man in Holland, Myn Heer Reyntz, who, when he died,

---

* In 1824 they were brought back to England, and publicly exhibited by Mr. Tupper in London. They were subsequently removed to Liverpool, and finally deposited in the Royal Museum of Berlin. See Gunn's "Cartonensia," 1831, pp. 32, et seq. Peachum, in his "Compleat Gentleman," p. 154 of the 1661 edition, thus alludes to them :—" Those stately hangings of arras containing the history of St. Paul out of the Acts (than which eye never beheld more absolute art, and which long since you might have seen in the Banquetting house at White Hall) were wholly of Raphael's invention." {Raphael Tapestries.}

Recovery of a few of the Royal Pictures.

the States purchased them, and sent them as a present back to King Charles the Second, after the Restoration, when the Ambassadors from Holland came to settle a peace in England."

Windsor Castle.

The remaining portion is classified into "Pictures in the Queen Dowager's custody," "Pictures in Windsor Castle," and "at Hampton Court," comprising altogether 1,247 entries.* As the size of the pictures is not in any one instance stated, all hope of conclusive identification is destroyed. After the enumeration of the pictures above stated, follows an exclusive account of King James's pictures; being a list "of his Majesty's pictures, &c. that were not the late King's, in Windsor Castle." And also of "Pictures in Whitehall of his Majesty's that were not the late King's."

Whitehall.

In the first portion—namely, among those pictures which belonged to Charles II. at Whitehall—we again recognise the series of small old heads of English and foreign princes in Nos. 189, 190, 198 to 203, 250 to 264, and 422 to 424, which have already been noticed *ante*, p. 333.

The Emperor Charles V. is recognisable under No. 571, "A man's head with a long chin, in a cut doublet, by Jennett." See *ante*, p. 288, No. 11.

A series of the old "*limnings*" extends from Nos. 575 to 628, and again from 643 to 650.

King Charles II. regained some of the finest portraits of his father, of himself and family, by Van

---

* In the original catalogue, the pictures are not continuously numbered throughout; but divided into separate localities. The highest amount of consecutive numbers is 537.

Dyck; namely, Nos. 742, 745, 749, 753, 771. He kept them at Windsor, where they still remain, in the Van Dyck room. The great family-picture of the King and Queen seated, was then at Whitehall, No. 173.

{James II. 1685–88.}

There are many portraits of eminent artists painted by themselves, extending from No. 107 to No. 135. Rembrandt's mother is recognizable under No. 113, as "an old woman's picture in a veil." See *ante*, p. 341. No. 123, "Raphael's picture in a black habit and black cap, done by himself," appears to be the same as the portrait of a young man, now at Hampton Court, No. 278 of the Catalogue, with the name RAFFAELLO VRBINAS. FEC. inscribed round the clasp in front of his black dress.*

In this catalogue we first meet with several pictures of historical importance, and which, in our time, constitute some of the leading features of the collection at Hampton Court Palace; namely, the series of Mantegna's Triumphs of Julius Cæsar—"nine of Cæsar's triumphs," 986—994. These were at Hampton Court, as previously shown by John Evelyn's notice of them.†

{Andrea Mantegna's Triumphs of Julius Cæsar.}

The great paintings of the Embarkation of Henry VIII. at Dover, and his meeting with Francis I. at the "Field of the Cloth of Gold," are entered among the pictures at Whitehall as the work of "Holbein," and are thus described: "King Henry the 8th going in triumph into Bulloigne," No. 85; "King Henry the 8th going to Bulloigne, a sea piece," No. 86. Also

{Henry VIII. Historical Pictures.}

* See *post*, page 371.   † See *ante*, p. 352.

Historical Portrait Pictures. we find in the same series "A large piece, being the Battle of Spurrs," No. 87, and "King Henry the 8th and Maximilian the Emperor encamped," "by Holbein," No. 90. These were probably the pictures alluded to by the Grand Duke of Tuscany in the passage above quoted, *ante*, p. 351.

"King Henry the 8th when he was prince, at length, in red," "by Holbein," No. 1047, then at Hampton Court Palace, is probably a large picture still there representing the Earl of Surrey.

Queen Elizabeth and the Three Goddesses. The curious picture of Queen Elizabeth and the Three Goddesses, by Lucas de Heere, is thus described: "Venus and Pallas, and Queen Elizabeth coming in," "by De Cheere," No. 934. It was then, and still is, at Hampton Court.

Holbein's painting in the Privy Chamber. The small copy in oil, which Remée van Leemput made from Holbein's painting on the wall of the Privy Chamber—and of which there is no notice in Charles I.'s Catalogue—was at this time preserved at Whitehall. It is thus entered: "King Henry the 8th, being a copy after the piece upon the wall in the Privy Chamber, by Remy." No. 355.

A remarkable picture of King Richard II., but with no painter's name or any dimensions to guide us, recalls the famous Westminster whole-length portrait previously referred to. The picture was at Hampton Court in the time of Charles II., and is thus entered in the Catalogue: "King Richard the 2nd, sitting in a chair with his crown on his head." No. 869. It is apparently no longer in the royal possession.

Diptych. The celebrated diptych, with two early portraits of a King and Queen of Scotland * at their devotions, and attended by their patron saints, recently removed from Hampton Court Palace to Holyrood, were at Hampton Court during the time of Charles II. They are thus entered in the Catalogue: "One of the Kings of Scotland at devotion, crowned by St. Andrew; James IV." No. 955; and "One of the Queens of Scotland at devotion, a saint in armour by her." No. 960.† James II. 1685-88. James III. of Scotland.

Among the early portraits we recognise the fine profile of the Earl of Douglas (see *ante*, p. 332), although the description here given of it, "still at Whitehall," is somewhat erroneous: "Earl Douglas's head, surnamed —— Blackson, by a good Italian hand." No. 393. Douglas.

"Mary Queen of Scots, to the waste," No. 926, at Hampton Court, appears to be Mary of Guise; whilst similar words applied to No. 408, at Whitehall, and "a copy of it," No. 409, in the same place, equally refer to the well known portrait of Mary Stuart wearing the white veil and "barbe" of a widow in mourning. The name of "Jennett" is also given as the painter of No. 408. King Charles I. had, as we have seen, two portraits of this type in his possession.‡ Mary Queen of Scots.

"Mary Queen of Scotland, at length:" "by Mytens," No. 15, at Whitehall, is the picture adapted, and turned

---

* James III. and Margaret, daughter of Christiern I. of Denmark.

† They were seen to great advantage at the Manchester Exhibition of 1857, where the remarkable ecclesiastic paintings on the reverse of each panel attracted the special attention of connoisseurs. They were Nos. 433 and 433A of the Exhibition Catalogue.

‡ See Bathoe's edition of the Catalogue, p. 155, Nos. 14 and 15.

the reverse way, from one painted from the life at Sheffield. (See *ante*, p. 328, No. 18.)

Margaret Douglas is recorded in the following entry: "Lady Margaret, mother to Henry King of Scotland, at length," No. 16. The picture is very large, and now at Hampton Court Palace, No. 513 of the Catalogue.

Various Portraits.

A curious portrait, "by Honthorst," at Whitehall, "The Duke of Monmouth's mother, half length," No. 429, may now be very difficult to trace. A series of beautiful miniatures, both "limnings" and "enamels," commences with No. 1164, on page 96. They are at the present time, for the most part, framed in one of the bedrooms at Windsor Castle, and in excellent preservation; Madam Gwynn (1183) and the Duke of Monmouth's Mother (1170) being among them.

Mother of the Duke of Monmouth.

In this catalogue may be found the origin of a singular error, which has been continued in the catalogues of Hampton Court Palace even to the present time; which is the calling two Austrian princesses, born respectively in the years 1575 and 1577, by the names of our English Queens, Mary and Elizabeth.[*] They were thus regarded at Whitehall Palace after the Restoration:—"Queen Elizabeth's head when she was a child," No. 415, and "Queen Mary's head when she was a child" No. 416. It is scarcely requisite to add that Queen Mary ascended the throne of England in 1553, and was succeeded by her sister Elizabeth in 1558. These

Misnomers at Hampton Court.

[*] They are Nos. 281 and 282 of the Hampton Court Catalogue. (See "Archæologia," vol. xxxix. p. 461.)

little princesses were daughters of the Archduke Charles of Austria. Mary Christierna was born November, 1574, and Elizabeth born in March, 1577. Their sister Margaret became Queen of Philip III. of Spain.*

King Charles II. was never distinguished by his patronage of art. Even the well-known series of the Beauties of his time did not emanate from himself. The first collective appearance of the Beauties of King Charles's Court occurs in the List of King James's own pictures at Windsor Castle. They never belonged to King Charles; they came to be Crown property through James II., whose first wife, the Duchess of York, had commanded Sir Peter Lely to paint them.†

They remained at Windsor till after the accession of William IV., and were always spoken of up to that period as the "*Windsor Beauties.*"‡ By their removal to Hampton Court they produce some confusion, since they have had the effect of eclipsing a set of Beauties already there; painted by Kneller expressly for that palace, and known by the distinctive title of the "*Hampton Court Beauties.*' The Windsor Beauties, as enumerated in King James's Catalogue, were originally

[margin: Spanish Infant Princesses.]

[margin: Anne Hyde, Duchess of York. Married 1659, died 1673.]

---

* These portraits are on canvas, well painted, and probably the work of a Spanish artist.

† The Duchess desired to have the handsomest women of the time painted, and the series was commenced with portraits of her own lovely maids of honour. See Mrs. Jameson's Public Galleries, p. 320.

‡ They were still at Windsor when Mrs. Jameson's "Beauties of the Court of King Charles the 2nd" was published in 1833. In 1835 they appeared among the pictures at Hampton Court, according to a catalogue preserved at the Lord Chamberlain's office.

Windsor Beauties. ten in number, and their names run in the following order (beginning with No. 1111):—1. Duchess of Cleveland; 2. Duchess of Richmond; 3. Mrs. Middleton; 4. Lady Northumberland; 5. Lady Sunderland; 6. Lady Falmouth; 7. Lady Denham; 8. Lady Denham's sister (Lady Whitmore); 9. Lady Rochester; 10. Lady Grammont.

In Bickham's account of Windsor Castle, published in his "Deliciæ Britannicæ," 1742, five additional ladies have been added to the list, namely, Mrs. Knott, Mrs. Lawson, Lady Byrom, the Duchess of Somerset, and Lady Ossory.

Nell Gwynn. The Duchess of Portsmouth and Nell Gwynn do not appear to have at any time formed part of the series before its removal to Hampton Court.

In King James's Catalogue there are three entries of equestrian portraits of Charles I. They are numbered respectively 359, 1076, and 880. Two are distinguished by the words "on a dun horse;" and the third by the mention "Mons. St. Antoine by *Equestrian Portraits of King Charles I.* him." This is the group now in the Van Dyck room at Windsor. The other pictures seem to be the small sketch, and the grand finished picture from it, now at Blenheim. The Duke of Marlborough puchased the latter from the Duke of Bavaria, and after its return to England the picture remained at Marlborough House till the year 1818, when it was removed to Blenheim.*

* See De Piles' Art of Painting, Lond., 8vo., 1706, page 412, for a notice of the picture being then in Bavaria, and Catalogue of Pictures at Blenheim by G. Scharf. London, 8vo., 1862, p. 36.

In the year 1683, the Marchese Luca Casimiro degl' Albizzi visited England, and his travels were recorded in manuscript by Dr. A. Forzoni. At Windsor he observed a full-length portrait of Mary Queen of Scots (probably the picture still there), and, over a chimney-piece, a finely-wrought piece of embroidery, "*un' educazione di fanciulli,*" by the hands of Mary Queen of Scots.*

{Italian Journal.}

{William and Mary 1689-1702.}

The Court does not seem to have been immediately driven from Whitehall Palace by the fire which consumed the long stone gallery, and the lodgings of the Duchess of Portsmouth in April, 1691. Queen Mary is recorded as having in the October following received addresses from both Houses of Parliament in the drawing-room at Whitehall. This must have been the Withdrawing-room adjoining the Banqueting-hall.†

{Fire at the Palace, 1691.}

A melancholy picture is given incidentally in Ward's London of the desolation of Whitehall Palace after the second conflagration :—" We crossed the palace-yard, on the east end of which lay the relics of Westminster clock-house in a confused heap; from thence we passed to the tennis-court, and went forwards to Whitehall, whose ruins we viewed with no little concern, as consumed by flames near so much water, and all that artists, at the cost of our greatest kings, had improved to delight and stateliness, remains dissolved in rubbish ; those spacious rooms where majesty has sat so oft,

{The Palace in ruins.}

---

* See Catalogue of the Temporary Museum of the Archæological Institute at Edinburgh in 1856, by A. Way, p. xxii.

† Lives of the Queens of England, by Agnes Strickland. Vol. vii. p. 339 ; edition 1853.

attended with the glories of the Court,—the just, the wise, the beautiful—now huddled in confusion, as if the misfortunes of princes were visited on their palaces as well as persons. Through several out-courts we came to Scotland Yard, covered with recumbent soldiers who were basking in the sun." *

(margin: Whitehall in ruins.)

KENSINGTON.

When William III. purchased Kensington Palace in 1691, he employed Sir Christopher Wren to make additions to it, and he divided his time between Kensington and Hampton Court. It became the favourite residence of his beloved Queen, and she died there.

(margin: Kensington.)

Immediately after the demise of King William, this Palace was fitted up for the residence of Queen Anne and Prince George of Denmark.

George I. employed Kent to build the cupola room and great staircase. Kent also, under the King's particular instructions, painted the figures and decorations on the walls.

(margin: Decorations by Kent.)

George II. and Queen Caroline passed much of their time at Kensington, and the Queen expended large sums upon the improvement of the palace and gardens. She generally resided here with the royal family, in the absence of the King when on the Continent. Her Majesty held a court at Kensington regularly every Sunday after divine service.†

HAMPTON COURT.

Hampton Court Palace, meanwhile, had undergone

* Lives of the Queens of England by Agnes Strickland, vol. vii. p. 383.
† Faulkner's History of Kensington, p. 481.

extensive alterations, and received many additions, to suit the requirements of a royal residence. Sir Christopher Wren completed the Fountain Court in 1690, and built the beautiful Ionic colonnade leading to the principal entrance. Laguerre painted the "Labours of Hercules" in the external lunettes of Sir Christopher Wren's new building. George II. and Queen Caroline were the last sovereigns that resided with their families at Hampton Court. *[margin: William and Mary. 1689-1702. New Buildings by Wren, 1690.]*

King William had the Cartoons by Raphael properly joined and laid down upon canvas, under the direction of the painter Henry Cooke.* He employed Sir Christopher Wren to build a gallery at Hampton Court expressly for their reception. The "Triumphs of Julius Cæsar," by Mantegna, were also in the same palace. *[margin: Cartoons by Raphael.]*

At Hampton Court, in 1742,† were many whole-length pictures by Van Somer, Mytens, Van Dyck, and Honthorst; but the works of Sir Godfrey Kneller and Verrio occupied the largest amount of space, both on walls and ceilings. Over the chimney-piece in the drawing-room was Van Dyck's standing portrait of Charles I., in royal robes, which is now at Windsor.‡ Andrea Mantegna's cartoons were in the Queen's drawing-room. Full-length portraits of various members of the Brunswick family, Lady Margaret Lenox, *[margin: Historical Portraits.]*

---

* Walpole's Anecdotes, edited by Dallaway and Wornum, p. 603, and Ruland's Notes on the Cartoons, 1866,.p. 7.

† Bickham's Deliciæ Britannicæ, p. 121.

‡ This is the fine standing figure so admirably engraved by Sir Robert Strange.

Hampton Court. and Mary Queen of Scots (Mytens) were in the Queen's state audience room.

The Queen's Gallery or Tapestry Gallery contained, as now, seven fine pieces of tapestry from the designs *French Tapestry.* of Le Brun, representing the History of Alexander the Great. They were set up in their present order about the beginning of the reign of George I. General Cadogan brought them from Flanders, where they had been purchased at a common auction at a very inferior price.*

In the apartments belonging to Frederick Prince of Wales, were several whole-lengths of Spanish ministers and foreign potentates. Raphael's Cartoons were in the *Gallery of Admirals.* "Great council chamber or Cartoon Gallery." The Admiral's Gallery contained fifteen portraits of renowned admirals by Sir Godfrey Kneller and Michael Dahl. The Beauty room held nine portraits of the most distinguished ladies; Queen Mary by Wissing, the rest by Kneller. They are named in the following *Hampton Court Beauties.* order. "1. Lady Peterborough. 2. Lady Ranelagh. 3. Lady Middleton. 4. Miss Pitt. 5. Duchess of St. Albans. 6. Lady Essex. 7. Lady Dorset. 8. Queen Mary. 9. The Duchess of Grafton."

On the Queen's Staircase was the large picture by *Honthorst.* Honthorst, representing the Duke of Buckingham in the character of Mercury introducing the children of the King of Bohemia to King Charles 1st and his Queen.† It still occupies the same position, and has

---

* Bickham, *ut supra*, p. 81.
† See *ante*, p. 344.

been carefully cleaned within the last few years by Mr. H. Merritt.

George II. 1727-60.

WINDSOR.

At Windsor Castle, at the same date (1742), there were not many very remarkable paintings. A large equestrian portrait of Prince George of Denmark, by Dahl, was over the chimney in the Queen's guard-chamber.*

Van Dyck's Lady Venetia Digby was over the chimney in the King's drawing-room. The Beauty-room contained fourteen of Sir Peter Lely's most distinguished female Beauties, already referred to.† The picture of Rembrandt's mother, now called the Countess of Desmond;‡ various portraits of Queen's of England, and portraits of Erasmus and other learned men, were in the Blenheim closet.§ Queen Elizabeth's picture gallery, now the library, included whole-lengths of King James I. and his Queen by Van Somer, Henry VIII. by Holbein, the Two Misers by Quentin Matsys, Titian and Aretino, Bandinello by Correggio, two views of Windsor Castle by Vorsterman, and the Battle of Spurs, with TERVAINE inscribed over it; Giulio Romano's Burning of Rome (see *ante*, p. 339).

Historical Portraits.

Rembrandt's Mother.

Misers by Quentin Matsys.

The extensive works of Sir Godfrey Kneller and Sir James Thornhill, decorating St. George's Hall and the great Staircase have entirely passed away. The ceiling of the Hall was "*embellished with the repre-*

Sir Godfrey Kneller.

---

* Deliciæ Britannicæ, pp. 152, 184.
† *Ante*, p. 359. ‡ See *ante*, p. 341.
§ Pote's Windsor, p. 419.

366   HISTORY OF OLD LONDON.

St. George's Hall at Windsor Castle.

sentation of *William III. surrounded by the Graces;*" and the same monarch was represented in State seated on a throne at the upper end. Over a side door, just by the gallery, was "*a fine portrait of the Lady who lost her garter at an assembly.*" These, together with various allegorical figures and a picture of the Institution of the Order of the Garter, were commenced by Verrio and completed by Kneller. The grand staircase was designed and executed by Sir James Thornhill, who also completed all the paintings under the dome.

Queen Caroline's China-closet now the Blenheim Room.

After 1743, the portrait picture of the so-called Children of Henry VII. by Holbein (see *ante,* pp. 288 and 336), was hung over the chimney in Queen Caroline's china-closet opening out of the Picture Gallery. It had previously been in her Majesty's closet at Kensington.* Van Dyck's "Charles II. in armour when a boy," was in the King's bedchamber; and Kneller's much-talked-of "Converted Chinese," † was in the King's drawing-room. The presence-chamber was adorned with Van Dyck's portrait of the Duke of Gloucester; the Countess of Dorset (his governess), by the same artist, and a picture of Sarpi (Father Paul), by Tintoretto.

ST. JAMES'S.

St. James's in 1766.

A few historical portraits of considerable value were lodged at St. James's Palace in 1766.‡ Among them Van Somer's "Earl of Pembroke, lord chamberlain," a

---

* See "Archæologia," vol. xxxix. p. 256; and Pote's Windsor, 1749, p. 420.

† Now at Buckingham Palace.

‡ Pote's Windsor, p. 418, 1749; Delic. Brit. p. 187; Dodsley's London, vol. vi. p. 336, 1761.

BUCKINGHAM PALACE UNDER GEORGE II. 367

half-length picture; Jeffery Hudson, the dwarf, by George III. Mytens; Adam and Eve, by Mabuse; Mary Queen of Scots, the version of the Sheffield picture, by Mytens;* Darnley and his brother, the size of life, by De Heere.† 1760-1820.

BUCKINGHAM PALACE.

Raphael's Cartoons were removed to the Queen's palace in St. James's Park from Hampton Court about 1764. In the "English Connoisseur," published 1766, vol. ii. page 3, they are spoken of as "*lately removed;*" thence they were taken to Windsor Castle in 1787 or 1788; and in 1814 once more restored to Hampton Court by the Prince Regent.‡ Raphael's Cartoons removed to London.

KENSINGTON.

Kensington Palace during the reign of George II. appears to have contained many, if not most, of the finest pictures.§ We especially note Van Dyck's pictures of King Charles and his Queen; Van Dyck's Cupid and Psyche; Van Dyck's Three Children of Charles I.; The Widow Eliot, by Riley; two heads erroneously named Queen Mary and Queen Elizabeth when children (see *ante*, p. 358); "Queen Elizabeth in a Chinese dress, drawn when she was a prisoner at Woodstock;" Portraits by Van Dyck at Kensington. Queen Elizabeth in a fancy dress.

* See *ante*, pp. 328 and 358.
† English Connoisseur, vol. i. p. 184.
‡ Ruland, p. 7; Dodsley's London, vol. iii. p. 155.
§ Dodsley's London, vol. iii. p. 269; English Connoisseur, vol. i. p. 145.

Kneller's portraits of King William and Queen Mary, in their coronation robes—(he was knighted for painting these pictures); Domenichino's "St. Agnes," whole length; Rubens' large Holy Family, with St. Francis in adoration; Pontormo's "Venus and Cupid," after Michael Angelo; Van Dyck's "Second Duke of Buckingham and his brother"; Guido's pictures of "Venus attired by the Graces," and "Perseus and Andromeda"; and Holbein's "Edward VI."

In the Painted Gallery were many large pictures, especially Van Dyck's "Charles I. on horseback coming through an arch," at one end of the gallery, and Van Dyck's "King and Queen, seated, with their children," at the opposite extremity; Tintoretto's grand pictures of "Esther fainting before Ahasuerus," and "Apollo and the Nine Muses."

Palma's "Adoration of the Shepherds," "The Woman of Samaria," and Giulio Romano's "Birth of Jupiter," were in the same apartment.

Over the chimney a circular Madonna and Child, attributed to Raphael. This picture still remains at Kensington Palace in the same position.

Queen Caroline had before this period, accidentally discovered, in a bureau at Kensington, a volume containing Holbein's original drawings of the most eminent persons belonging to the court of Henry VIII.* These the Queen desired to have arranged on the walls of her closet next to the state bedroom, together with frames containing choice miniatures and medallions,

* See Walpole's Anecdotes edited by Dallaway and Wornum, p. 84.

accompanied by a few oil pictures of special delicacy and historical interest. The miniature portraits and copies by Peter Olivier contained in those frames correspond with those enumerated in Vander Doort's catalogue. Among the oil paintings are "Two Mice,"* by Raphael (see *ante*, p. 324, and No. 654 of King James's Collection); and Queen Elizabeth when princess, in a red dress (see *ante*, pp. 289, 311 and 336).

<small>George II. 1727-1760.</small>

General Monck, by Cooper, unfinished; Holbein and his Wife, in tempera, on linen, two separate pictures, which have been recently removed from Hampton Court to the library at Windsor.

<small>Portraits.</small>

The Children of "Henry VII.," or rather of the King of Denmark. (See *ante*, pp. 288 and 336, and "Archæologia," vol. xxxix. p. 256.)

Children of the King and Queen of Bohemia. (See *ante*, p. 338.)

A catalogue of the entire contents of this room was taken by Mr. G. Vertue in September, 1743, by command of Queen Caroline.

<small>Vertue's Catalogue.</small>

It appears that about the time of the fire at Whitehall, the series of old heads and foreign portraits were transferred to Kensington, as Vertue—on the title to his engravings from them, in Rapin, published 1736—mentions them as being in the latter palace; and Walpole, in the first edition of his "Anecdotes," 1762, especially alludes to the early royal portraits at Kensington. He also (p. 47) speaks of a chamber of very ancient portraits,—among them one of the

<small>Royal Portraits.</small>

---

* Page 19, No. 123 of Bathoe's edition. "In a small square black frame, 2¼ inches by 3½ inches, Two Mice, painted by Raphael."

Duke of Norfolk,—as then existing in the Princess Dowager's house at Kew.

Henry IV. Portrait. It is somewhat remarkable, that in none of the lists above cited, is any mention made of Henry IV. But his portrait, now at Windsor, first appeared by name at Kensington among the royal portraits of the earlier series. It agrees with the type adopted in the "Baziliωlogia," published in 1618, which has been so many times repeated in various sets of English monarchs distributed over the country. The hanging head-dress is clearly of the beginning of the fifteenth century, and seems inseparable from portraits of Chaucer and Philip the Good. This fashion is also conspicuous in some of the foreground figures in Van Eyck's "Adoration of the Lamb."*

Walpole. Walpole, in his "Anecdotes," pronounced the Kensington picture to be a duplicate of the one at Kensington, although the latter is in reality infinitely superior. Walpole was easily persuaded to do this by the notes he had purchased from Vertue.

These old portraits were at Kensington Palace in the year 1820, and they appear in Faulkner's history of that parish, page 554.

The most ancient historical ones were deposited in the "Private Closet."

"Henry IV., to the waist," is No. 630. Portraits

* Vertue engraved his portrait of Henry IV. for Rapin's History of England, in 1732, from a picture belonging to Lord Essex at Hampton Court, in Herefordshire. In the illustrative text which accompanied Vertue's plates, afterwards issued separately in 1736, the engraver refers to the "ancient picture on board in the Palace of Kensington" as being *similar* to it.

of Catherine of Arragon, No. 643, and Anne Boleyn, No. 645, are also specified. A great number of additional portraits seem also to have been added from other residences. A portrait of Raphael, by himself (162), with a brooch on his breast, is said to have been presented by Earl Cowper to King George III.* The large diptych paintings of James III. and his Queen (Nos. 157 and 166) that had previously been at Hampton Court, now made their appearance within these walls.†

A catalogue of these Kensington pictures was taken by Benjamin West, at the King's desire, in 1818.‡ Many of the dimensions were inserted, and dates and inscriptions on the pictures carefully observed.

George IV. 1820-30.

CARLTON HOUSE.

About 1802, the Prince of Wales had begun to form his own private collection, under the guidance and advice of Lord Farnborough; and in 1812 he also obtained the choice collection of Flemish and Dutch pictures that had been formed by Sir Francis Baring.§ These pictures, with many subsequent additions, are now concentrated in the Picture Gallery at Buckingham Palace.

Carlton House.

In the year 1816, two of Raphael's Cartoons—"The Miraculous Draught," No. 1, and "Paul Preaching at Athens," No. 96, were exhibited to the public at the British Institution, and the rest followed in consecutive

Raphael's Cartoons, A.D. 1816.

---

* Compare *ante*, page 355.
† See *ante*, p. 356.
‡ Faulkner's Kensington, p. 499.
　Mrs. Jameson's Private Picture Galleries, p. 4.

years: thus, in 1817, the "Elymas," No. 1, and the "Death of Ananias," No. 133. In 1818, "The Beautiful Gate," No. 1, "Feed my Sheep," No. 124; and in 1819, the series was completed by the display of "The Sacrifice at Lystra," No. 124.

<small>British Institution, Pall Mall.</small>

GREENWICH HOSPITAL.

<small>Donation to Greenwich Hospital.</small>

In 1824, King George IV. transferred the series of portraits of Admirals, painted by Kneller, Lely, and Dahl, from Hampton Court Palace, to the Governors of Greenwich Hospital, where they now decorate the great Hall.

In the following year, his Majesty presented the fine whole-length, by Mytens, of the Admiral Howard, Earl of Nottingham, with the Spanish Armada tossing on the waves in the distance.*

BUCKINGHAM PALACE AND CARLTON HOUSE.

<small>Alterations at Buckingham Palace and destruction of Carlton House.</small>

In May, 1825, in consequence of the alterations about to be made by Nash at Buckingham Palace, the whole of the pictures belonging to that residence were removed to Kensington.

In 1826 and the following year, the Carlton House pictures, acquired by the Prince of Wales under the circumstances above mentioned, were exhibited collectively at the British Institution. They entirely occupied the walls of the gallery during two consecutive years.

HAMPTON COURT PALACE.

<small>Concentration of</small>

King William IV., on his accession, ordered all the

---

* See *ante*, p. 329. See Locker's Admirals, 4to, Lond., 1831.

pictures accumulated at Kensington Palace to be transferred to Hampton Court. His desire was to have them shown to better advantage, and to enable the public to participate in these advantages. The granting a free access to these valuable works of art to the general public, has tended to exercise a far more beneficial effect upon public taste than has hitherto been acknowledged. *[margin: Royal pictures at Hampton Court. William IV. 1830-7.]*

At the time of this extensive removal, which lasted during the years 1833, 1834, 1835, several pictures of historical importance were removed to Windsor Castle, and among them, from Kensington, the series of old portraits which originally belonged to Henry VIII., at Whitehall. They are now arranged with great good taste and judgment, in a small apartment at the foot of the stairs leading to the royal pew of the chapel. Holbein's fine portrait of Sir Henry Guildford, apparently obtained from the Arundel Collection,* was for some time at Hampton Court, and is now at Windsor. The curious picture "of James 1st praying at the tomb of his father, Lord Darnley," was at Hampton Court till 1853, when it was transferred to Windsor Castle. The singular picture of "The Calling of St. Matthew," attributed to Mabuse, was at Buckingham Palace in 1842. It is now at Windsor.† *[margin: Extensive change of localities of Pictures.]*

Several pictures were removed, in 1834, from the green dressing-room, Buckingham Palace, to the royal residence at Kew.

* See Anstis' Register of the Order of the Garter, London, folio, 1724, vol. 2, p. 244, and Mrs. Jameson's Public Galleries, vol. 2, p. 344.

† See *ante*, p. 329, and Mrs. Jameson's Private Picture Galleries, p. 27.

HOLYROOD PALACE.

Removal of Scottish Portraits to Edinburgh.

At the time of the great Manchester Exhibition, in 1857, it was suggested that the celebrated diptych painting of the King and Queen of Scotland (see *ante*, pp. 313 and 356), which had been lent by her Majesty from Hampton Court Palace, would be more appropriately placed in her royal residence at Holyrood, and for which, in all probability, the picture had originally been painted. The suggestion, chiefly promoted by Mr. D. Laing, readily found favour, and was, before the close of the same year, removed to Holyrood Palace. A few more pictures were selected for transfer from Hampton Court to Holyrood, and accordingly the following pictures, taken, with their numbers, from the catalogue of the time, were removed from Hampton Court in 1864 :—

The Mother of Lord Darnley.

The Countess of Lenox,* 284 ; Queen Anne of Den-

* I am under a strong impression that this picture now lies under a false designation. It differs considerably from the authentic portraits of the Countess of Lenox at Hampton Court, No. 513 of the Catalogue, and from the kneeling figure in the picture at Windsor, representing the parents and infant son of Darnley praying before his tomb. In those instances the eyes of the Countess are pale blue grey ; the eyebrows very arched, and of a pale brown colour. In the picture above mentioned the eyes are very dark brown, and the eyebrows of a different character. My expectation is that the picture will prove to be the portrait of Mary of Hungary, sister to the Emperor, and governess of the Netherlands. It is a very fine portrait, signed and dated "*Antonius more pingebat*, 1554," and has the brand of C. R. crowned on the back of the panel ; thereby proving that it really belonged to Charles I. It corresponds with the description already cited from Vander Doort's Catalogue. See *ante*, p. 332, No. 9.

mark, 578; King Charles II., small, whole length, by Russell, 607; King James II., same scale as preceding, 604; King James I., by Van Somer, 334; The Children of Charles I., after Van Dyck, 639; Henry Prince of Wales, 269; The Admirable Crichton, 335; James Stuart, when young, 626; Lord Darnley and his Brother, when boys, 512; King of Bohemia, 312; Queen of Bohemia, 312; and The Pretender, James Stuart, when a boy, 626. *Removal of Scottish Portraits from London to Edinburgh.*

At the same time, a curious picture, called Mary Queen of Scots, was forwarded to the Scottish capital from St. James's Palace.

ST. JAMES'S PALACE.

St. James's Palace has, in the course of last year, received some accessions from Hampton Court. The interesting whole-length of Henry Prince of Wales, in armour, No. 454, is placed there in the Long Gallery. As the suit of armour, decorated with golden thistles and roses, which he wears, is identical with the suit still preserved in the guard-chamber at Windsor, it is much to be hoped that, in the event of any further change, the picture may be destined to a position near it in the Castle. *St. James's Palace.*

The beautiful picture of the Princess Elizabeth, in a red dress, holding a book (see *ante*, pp. 289, 311 and 336), now in the first state-room of St. James's, would also have made an interesting addition to the Henry VIII. pictures at Windsor Castle. This would be the more appropriate, considering that Windsor Castle, in which Queen Elizabeth appears to have so much

No portrait of Queen Elizabeth at Windsor Castle.

delighted, does not at present contain even a single portrait of her.

HAMPTON COURT PALACE. 1867.

At Hampton Court great improvements have recently taken place. Many of the finest pictures have been cleaned, and all are now in the course of a better system of arrangement. These changes are the result of a thoroughly matured scheme laid down by the lamented Prince Consort, and it may indeed be said that all the good now performed in respect to our national collections of art, is but a realization of his wise and benevolent intentions.

APPENDIX.

Since the London Congress of the Archaeological Institute in July last, and after the termination of the Portrait Exhibition, at South Kensington, the Dean and Chapter of Westminster confided the Westminster Portrait of Richard II. (*ante*, page 285) to the care of Mr. Geo. Richmond, R.A., for purposes of cleaning and reparation. This eminent portrait-painter bestowed his personal attention and practical experience, with unremitting zeal, upon the picture during many weeks, and the result, both in an artistic and antiquarian point of view, has far exceeded the most sanguine hopes that could have been entertained of its recovery. The picture, as seen at the Manchester and Kensington Exhibitions, was found to have been an absolute falsification. Not only was the original surface covered with several layers of thick paint, but the figure itself was converted into a totally different personage; whilst clumsy, ignorant art was substituted for portraiture of the most delicate and refined quality. These high qualities were fully recovered by Mr. Richmond, who worked with the assistance of Mr. H. Merritt, the well-known picture restorer. For a longer account and elaborate details, the writer of this paper refers to an article which he contributed to the January number, 1867, of the "Fine Arts Quarterly Review," p. 27.

THE END.

BRADBURY, EVANS, AND CO., PRINTERS, WHITEFRIARS.

ALBEMARLE STREET, LONDON,
October, 1866.

MR. MURRAY'S
GENERAL LIST OF WORKS.

ALBERT'S (THE PRINCE) SPEECHES AND ADDRESSES ON PUBLIC OCCASIONS; with an Introduction giving some Outlines of his Character. Portrait. 8vo. 10s. 6d.; or *Popular Edition.* Portrait. Fcap. 8vo, 1s.

ABBOTT'S (REV. J.) Philip Musgrave; or, Memoirs of a Church of England Missionary in the North American Colonies. Post 8vo. 2s.

ABERCROMBIE'S (JOHN) Enquiries concerning the Intellectual Powers and the Investigation of Truth. *14th Edition.* Fcap. 8vo. 6s. 6d.

———————— Philosophy of the Moral Feelings. *13th Edition.* Fcap. 8vo. 4s.

ACLAND'S (REV. CHARLES) Popular Account of the Manners and Customs of India. Post 8vo. 2s.

ÆSOP'S FABLES. A New Translation. With Historical Preface. By Rev. THOMAS JAMES. With 100 Woodcuts, by TENNIEL and WOLF. *50th Thousand.* Post 8vo. 2s. 6d.

AGRICULTURAL (THE) JOURNAL. Of the Royal Agricultural Society of England. 8vo. *Published half-yearly.*

AIDS TO FAITH: a Series of Theological Essays. By various Writers. Edited by WILLIAM THOMSON, D.D., Archbishop of York. 8vo. 9s.

AMBER-WITCH (THE). The most interesting Trial for Witchcraft ever known. Translated from the German by LADY DUFF GORDON. Post 8vo. 2s.

ARCHITECTURE OF AHMEDABAD, with Historical Sketch and Architectural Notes by T. C. HOPE, and JAMES FERGUSSON, F.R.S. With 2 Maps, 120 Photographs, and 22 Woodcuts. 4to. 5l. 5s.

———————— BEJAPOOR, with Historical Sketch and Architectural Essay by Col. MEADOWS TAYLOR and JAS. FERGUSSON. With 2 Maps, 76 Photographs, and 13 Woodcuts. Folio. 10l. 10s.

———————— DHARWAR and MYSORE. With Historical Sketch and Architectural Essay by Col. MEADOWS TAYLOR and JAS. FERGUSSON. With 2 Maps, 100 Photographs, and numerous Woodcuts Folio. 12l. 12s.

ARMY LIST (THE). *Published Monthly by Authority.* 18mo. 1s. 6d.

ARTHUR'S (LITTLE) History of England. By LADY CALLCOTT. *New Edition, continued to* 1862. Woodcuts. Fcap. 8vo. 2s. 6d.

ATKINSON'S (MRS.) Recollections of Tartar Steppes and their Inhabitants. Illustrations. Post 8vo. 12s.

AUNT IDA'S Walks and Talks; a Story Book for Children. By a LADY. Woodcuts. 16mo. 5s.

B

AUSTIN'S (JOHN) LECTURES ON JURISPRUDENCE; or, the Philosophy of Positive Law. 3 Vols. 8vo. 30s.

——— (SARAH) Fragments from German Prose Writers. With Biographical Notes. Post 8vo. 10s.

ADMIRALTY PUBLICATIONS; Issued by direction of the Lords Commissioners of the Admiralty:—

A MANUAL OF SCIENTIFIC ENQUIRY, for the Use of Travellers. Edited by Sir JOHN F. HERSCHEL, and Rev. ROBERT MAIN. *Third Edition.* Woodcuts. Post 8vo. 9s.

AIRY'S ASTRONOMICAL OBSERVATIONS MADE AT GREENWICH. 1836 to 1847. Royal 4to. 50s. each.

——— ASTRONOMICAL RESULTS. 1848 to 1858. 4to. 8s. each.

——— APPENDICES TO THE ASTRONOMICAL OBSERVATIONS.

1836.—I. Bessel's Refraction Tables.
   II. Tables for converting Errors of R.A. and N.P.D. into Errors of Longitude and Ecliptic P.D. } 8s.
1837.—I. Logarithms of Sines and Cosines to every Ten Seconds of Time.
   II. Table for converting Sidereal into Mean Solar Time. } 8s.
1842.—Catalogue of 1439 Stars. 8s.
1845.—Longitude of Valencia. 8s.
1847.—Twelve Years' Catalogue of Stars. 14s.
1851.—Maskelyne's Ledger of Stars. 6s.
1852.—I. Description of the Transit Circle. 5s.
   II. Regulations of the Royal Observatory. 2s.
1853.—Bessel's Refraction Tables. 3s.
1854.—I. Description of the Zenith Tube. 3s.
   II. Six Years' Catalogue of Stars. 10s.
1856.—Description of the Galvanic Apparatus at Greenwich Observatory. 8s.
1862.—I. Seven Years' Catalogue of Stars. 10s.
   II. Plan of the Building and Ground of the Royal Observatory, Greenwich.
   III. Longitude of Valencia. } 3s.

——— MAGNETICAL AND METEOROLOGICAL OBSERVATIONS. 1840 to 1847. Royal 4to. 50s. each.

——— ASTRONOMICAL, MAGNETICAL, AND METEOROLOGICAL OBSERVATIONS, 1848 to 1864. Royal 4to. 50s. each.

——— ASTRONOMICAL RESULTS. 1848 to 1864. 4to.

——— MAGNETICAL AND METEOROLOGICAL RESULTS. 1848 to 1864. 4to. 8s. each.

——— REDUCTION OF THE OBSERVATIONS OF PLANETS. 1750 to 1830. Royal 4to. 50s.

——————————— LUNAR OBSERVATIONS. 1750 to 1830. 2 Vols. Royal 4to. 50s. each. 1831 to 1851. 4to. 20s.

BERNOULLI'S SEXCENTENARY TABLE. *London*, 1779. 4to.

BESSEL'S AUXILIARY TABLES FOR HIS METHOD OF CLEARING LUNAR DISTANCES. 8vo.

——— FUNDAMENTA ASTRONOMIÆ: *Regiomontii*, 1818. Folio. 60s.

BIRD'S METHOD OF CONSTRUCTING MURAL QUADRANTS. *London*, 1768. 4to. 2s. 6d.

——— METHOD OF DIVIDING ASTRONOMICAL INSTRUMENTS. *London*, 1767. 4to. 2s. 6d.

COOK, KING, AND BAYLY'S ASTRONOMICAL OBSERVATIONS. *London*, 1782. 4to. 21s

ADMIRALTY PUBLICATIONS—*continued.*
ENCKE'S BERLINER JAHRBUCH, for 1830. *Berlin,* 1828. 8vo. 9s.
GROOMBRIDGE'S CATALOGUE OF CIRCUMPOLAR STARS. 4to. 10s.
HANSEN'S TABLES DE LA LUNE. 4to. 20s.
HARRISON'S PRINCIPLES OF HIS TIME-KEEPER. PLATES 1797. 4to. 5s.
HUTTON'S TABLES OF THE PRODUCTS AND POWERS OF NUMBERS. 1781. Folio. 7s. 6d.
LAX'S TABLES FOR FINDING THE LATITUDE AND LONGITUDE. 1821. 8vo. 10s.
LUNAR OBSERVATIONS at GREENWICH. 1783 to 1819. Compared with the Tables, 1821. 4to. 7s. 6d.
MASKELYNE'S ACCOUNT OF THE GOING OF HARRISON'S WATCH. 1767. 4to. 2s. 6d.
MAYER'S DISTANCES of the MOON'S CENTRE from the PLANETS. 1822, 3s.; 1823, 4s. 6d. 1824 to 1835, 8vo. 4s. each.
—— THEORIA LUNÆ JUXTA SYSTEMA NEWTONIANUM. 4to. 2s. 6d.
—— TABULÆ MOTUUM SOLIS ET LUNÆ. 1770. 4to. 5s.
—— ASTRONOMICAL OBSERVATIONS MADE AT GOTTINGEN, from 1756 to 1761. 1826. Folio. 7s. 6d.
NAUTICAL ALMANACS, from 1767 to 1870. 8vo. 2s. 6d. each.
—————— SELECTIONS FROM THE ADDITIONS up to 1812. 8vo. 5s. 1834-54. 8vo. 5s.
—————— SUPPLEMENTS, 1828 to 1833, 1837 and 1838. 8vo. 2s. each.
—————— TABLE requisite to be used with the N.A. 1781. 8vo. 5s.
POND'S ASTRONOMICAL OBSERVATIONS. 1811 to 1835. 4to. 21s. each.
RAMSDEN'S ENGINE for DIVIDING MATHEMATICAL INSTRUMENTS. 4to. 5s.
—————— ENGINE for DIVIDING STRAIGHT LINES. 4to. 5s.
SABINE'S PENDULUM EXPERIMENTS to DETERMINE THE FIGURE OF THE EARTH. 1825. 4to. 40s.
SHEPHERD'S TABLES for CORRECTING LUNAR DISTANCES. 1772. Royal 4to. 21s.
—————— TABLES, GENERAL, of the MOON'S DISTANCE from the SUN, and 10 STARS. 1787. Folio. 5s. 6d.
TAYLOR'S SEXAGESIMAL TABLE. 1780. 4to. 15s.
—————— TABLES OF LOGARITHMS. 4to. 3l.
TIARK'S ASTRONOMICAL OBSERVATIONS for the LONGITUDE of MADEIRA. 1822. 4to. 5s.
—————— CHRONOMETRICAL OBSERVATIONS for DIFFERENCES of LONGITUDE between DOVER, PORTSMOUTH, and FALMOUTH. 1823. 4to. 5s.
VENUS and JUPITER: OBSERVATIONS of, compared with the TABLES. *London,* 1822. 4to. 2s.
WALES' AND BAYLY'S ASTRONOMICAL OBSERVATIONS. 1777. 4to. 21s.
WALES' REDUCTION OF ASTRONOMICAL OBSERVATIONS MADE IN THE SOUTHERN HEMISPHERE. 1764—1771. 1788. 4to. 10s. 6d.

LIST OF WORKS

BARBAULD'S (Mrs.) Hymns in Prose for Children. With 112 Original Designs. Small 4to. 5s. Or *Fine Paper*, 7s. 6d.

BARROW'S (Sir John) Autobiographical Memoir. From Early Life to Advanced Age. Portrait. 8vo. 16s.

———— Life, Exploits, and Voyages of Sir Francis Drake. With numerous Original Letters. Post 8vo. 2s.

BARRY (Sir Charles) Life of an Architect. By Rev. Alfred Barry, D.D. With Portrait and Illustrations. 8vo. (*Nearly Ready.*)

BATES' (H. W.) Records of a Naturalist on the River Amazons during eleven years of Adventure and Travel. *Second Edition*. Illustrations. Post 8vo. 12s.

BEES AND FLOWERS. Two Essays. By Rev. Thomas James. Reprinted from the "Quarterly Review." Fcap. 8vo. 1s. each.

BERTHA'S Journal during a Visit to her Uncle in England. Containing a Variety of Interesting and Instructive Information. *Seventh Edition*. Woodcuts. 12mo. 7s. 6d.

BIRCH'S (Samuel) History of Ancient Pottery and Porcelain: Egyptian, Assyrian, Greek, Roman, and Etruscan. With 200 Illustrations. 2 Vols. Medium 8vo. 42s.

BLUNT'S (Rev. J. J.) Undesigned Coincidences in the Writings of the Old and New Testament, an Argument of their Veracity: containing the Books of Moses, Historical and Prophetical Scriptures, and the Gospels and Acts. *9th Edition*. Post 8vo. 6s.

———— History of the Church in the First Three Centuries. *Third Edition*. Post 8vo. 7s. 6d.

———— Parish Priest; His Duties, Acquirements and Obligations. *Fourth Edition*. Post 8vo. 7s. 6d.

———— Lectures on the Right Use of the Early Fathers. *Second Edition*. 8vo. 15s.

———— Plain Sermons Preached to a Country Congregation. *Second Edition*. 3 Vols. Post 8vo. 7s. 6d. each.

———— Essays on various subjects. 8vo. 12s.

BISSET'S (Andrew) History of England during the Interregnum, from the Death of Charles I. to the Battle of Dunbar, 1648—50. Chiefly from the MSS. in the State Paper Office. 8vo. 15s.

BERTRAM'S (Jas. G.) Harvest of the Sea: a Contribution to the Natural and Economic History of British Food Fishes. With 50 Illustrations. 21s.

BLAKISTON'S (Capt.) Narrative of the Expedition sent to explore the Upper Waters of the Yang-Tsze. Illustrations. 8vo. 18s.

BLOMFIELD'S (Bishop) Memoir, with Selections from his Correspondence. By his Son. *2nd Edition*. Portrait, post 8vo. 12s.

BOOK OF COMMON PRAYER. Illustrated with Coloured Borders, Initial Letters, and Woodcuts. A new edition. 8vo. 18s. cloth; 31s. 6d. calf; 36s. morocco

PUBLISHED BY MR. MURRAY. 5

BORROW'S (GEORGE) Bible in Spain; or the Journeys, Adventures, and Imprisonments of an Englishman in an Attempt to circulate the Scriptures in the Peninsula. 3 Vols. Post 8vo. 27s.; or *Popular Edition*, 16mo, 3s. 6d.

—————— Zincali, or the Gipsies of Spain; their Manners, Customs, Religion, and Language. 2 Vols. Post 8vo. 18s.; or *Popular Edition*, 16mo, 3s. 6d.

—————— Lavengro; The Scholar—The Gipsy—and the Priest. Portrait. 3 Vols. Post 8vo. 30s.

—————— Romany Rye; a Sequel to Lavengro. *Second Edition*. 2 Vols. Post 8vo. 21s.

—————— WILD WALES: its People, Language, and Scenery. *Popular Edition*. Post 8vo., 6s.

BOSWELL'S (JAMES) Life of Samuel Johnson, LL.D. Including the Tour to the Hebrides. Edited by Mr. CROKER. Portraits. Royal 8vo. 10s.

BRACE'S (C. 'L.) History of the Races of the Old World. Post 8vo. 9s.

BRAY'S (MRS.) Life of Thomas Stothard, R.A. With Personal Reminiscences. Illustrated with Portrait and 60 Woodcuts of his chief works. 4to.

BREWSTER'S (SIR DAVID) Martyrs of Science; or, Lives of Galileo, Tycho Brahe, and Kepler. *Fourth Edition*. Fcap. 8vo. 4s. 6d.

—————— More Worlds than One. The Creed of the Philosopher and the Hope of the Christian. *Eighth Edition*. Post 8vo. 6s.

—————— Stereoscope: its History, Theory, Construction, and Application to the Arts and to Education. Woodcuts. 12mo. 5s. 6d.

—————— Kaleidoscope: its History, Theory, and Construction, with its application to the Fine and Useful Arts. *Second Edition*. Woodcuts. Post 8vo. 5s. 6d.

BRITISH ASSOCIATION REPORTS. 8vo.
York and Oxford, 1831-32, 13s. 6d.
Cambridge, 1833, 12s.
Edinburgh, 1834, 15s.
Dublin, 1835, 13s. 6d.
Bristol, 1836, 12s.
Liverpool, 1837, 16s. 6d.
Newcastle, 1838, 15s.
Birmingham, 1839, 13s. 6d
Glasgow, 1840, 15s.
Plymouth, 1841, 13s. 6d.
Manchester, 1842, 10s. 6d.
Cork, 1843, 12s.
York, 1844, 20s.
Cambridge, 1845, 12s.
Southampton, 1846, 15s.
Oxford, 1847, 18s.
Swansea, 1848, 9s.
Birmingham, 1849, 10s.
Edinburgh, 1850, 15s.
Ipswich, 1851, 16s. 6d.
Belfast, 1852, 15s.
Hull, 1853, 10s. 6d.
Liverpool, 1854, 18s.
Glasgow, 1855, 15s.
Cheltenham, 1856, 18s.
Dublin, 1857, 15s.
Leeds, 1858, 20s.
Aberdeen, 1859, 15s.
Oxford, 1860, 25s.
Manchester, 1861, 15s.
Cambridge, 1862, 20s.
Newcastle, 1863, 25s.
Bath, 1864, 18s.
Birmingham, 1865, 25s.

BROUGHTON'S (LORD) Journey through Albania and other Provinces of Turkey in Europe and Asia, to Constantinople, 1809—10. *Third Edition*. Illustrations. 2 Vols. 8vo. 30s.

—————— Visits to Italy. 3rd *Edition*. 2 vols. Post 8vo. 18s.

LIST OF WORKS

BRITISH (MURRAY) CLASSICS. A Series of Standard English Authors, printed from the most correct text, and edited with notes. 8vo.

Already Published.

I. GOLDSMITH'S WORKS. Edited by PETER CUNNINGHAM, F.S.A. Vignettes. 4 Vols. 30s.

II. GIBBON'S DECLINE AND FALL OF THE ROMAN EMPIRE. Edited by WILLIAM SMITH, LL.D. Portrait and Maps. 8 Vols. 60s.

III. JOHNSON'S LIVES OF THE ENGLISH POETS. Edited by PETER CUNNINGHAM, F.S.A. 3 Vols. 22s. 6d.

IV. BYRON'S POETICAL WORKS. Edited, with Notes. 6 vols. 45s.

In Preparation.

LIFE AND WORKS OF POPE. Edited by REV. WHITWELL ELWIN.
HUME'S HISTORY OF ENGLAND. Edited, with Notes.
LIFE AND WORKS OF SWIFT. Edited by JOHN FORSTER.
LIFE AND WORKS OF DRYDEN. Edited, with Notes.

BUBBLES FROM THE BRUNNEN OF NASSAU. By an Old Man. 7th Edition, with Illustrations. Post 8vo. 7s. 6d.

BUNYAN (JOHN) and Oliver Cromwell. Select Biographies. By ROBERT SOUTHEY. Post 8vo. 2s.

BURGON'S (Rev. J. W.) Memoir of Patrick Fraser Tytler. Second Edition. Post 8vo. 9s.

———— Letters from Rome. Illustrations. Post 8vo. 12s.

BURN'S (COL.) Dictionary of Naval and Military Technical Terms, English and French, and French and English. Fourth Edition. Crown 8vo. 15s.

BURR'S (G. D.) Instructions in Practical Surveying, Topographical Plan Drawing, and on sketching ground without Instruments. Fourth Edition. Woodcuts. Post 8vo. 6s.

BUTTMAN'S LEXILOGUS; a Critical Examination of the Meaning of numerous Greek Words, chiefly in Homer and Hesiod. Translated by Rev. J. R. FISHLAKE. Fifth Edition. 8vo. 12s.

———— CATALOGUE OF IRREGULAR GREEK VERBS. With all the Tenses extant—their Formation, Meaning, and Usage, accompanied by an Index. Translated, with Notes, by Rev. J. R. FISHLAKE. Fifth Edition. Revised by Rev. E. VENABLES. Post 8vo.

BUXTON'S (SIR FOWELL) Memoirs. With Selections from his Correspondence. By his Son. Portrait. 8vo. 15s. Abridged Edition. Portrait. Fcap. 8vo. 2s. 6d.

———— (CHARLES, M.P.) IDEAS OF THE DAY ON POLICY. A New and Enlarged Edition. 8vo.

PUBLISHED BY MR. MURRAY. 7

BYRON'S (LORD) Life, Letters, and Journals. By THOMAS MOORE. Plates. 6 Vols. Fcap. 8vo. 18s.

——— Life, Letters, and Journals. By THOMAS MOORE. Portraits. Royal 8vo. 9s.

——— Poetical Works. Portrait. 6 Vols. 8vo. 45s.

——— Poetical Works. Plates. 10 Vols. Fcap. 8vo. 30s.

——— Poetical Works. 8 Vols. 24mo. 20s.

——— Poetical Works. Plates. Royal 8vo. 9s.

——— Poetical Works. Portrait. Crown 8vo. 6s.

——— Childe Harold. With 80 Engravings. Small 4to. 21s.

——— Childe Harold. 16mo. 2s. 6d.

——— Childe Harold. Vignettes. 16mo. 1s.

——— Childe Harold. Portrait. 16mo. 6d.

——— Tales and Poems. 24mo. 2s. 6d.

——— Miscellaneous. 2 Vols. 24mo. 5s.

——— Dramas and Plays. 2 Vols. 24mo. 5s.

——— Don Juan and Beppo. 2 Vols. 24mo. 5s.

——— Beauties. Poetry and Prose. Portrait, Fcap. 8vo. 3s. 6d.

CARNARVON'S (LORD) Portugal, Gallicia, and the Basque Provinces. From Notes made during a Journey to those Countries. *Third Edition.* Post 8vo. 3s. 6d.

——— Recollections of the Druses of Lebanon. With Notes on their Religion. *Third Edition.* Post 8vo. 5s. 6d.

CAMPBELL'S (LORD) Lives of the Lord Chancellors and Keepers of the Great Seal of England. From the Earliest Times to the Death of Lord Eldon in 1838. *Fourth Edition.* 10 Vols. Crown 8vo. 6s. each.

——— Lives of the Chief Justices of England. From the Norman Conquest to the Death of Lord Tenterden. *Second Edition.* 3 Vols. 8vo. 42s.

——— Shakspeare's Legal Acquirements Considered. 8vo. 5s. 6d.

——— Life of Lord Chancellor Bacon. Fcap. 8vo. 2s. 6d.

——— (GEORGE) Modern India. A Sketch of the System of Civil Government. With some Account of the Natives and Native Institutions. *Second Edition.* 8vo. 16s.

——— India as it may be. An Outline of a proposed Government and Policy. 8vo. 12s.

——— (THOS.) Short Lives of the British Poets. With an Essay on English Poetry. Post 8vo. 3s. 6d.

CALLCOTT'S (LADY) Little Arthur's History of England. *New Edition, brought down to the present time.* With Woodcuts. Fcap. 8vo. 2s. 6d.

LIST OF WORKS

CASTLEREAGH (THE) DESPATCHES, from the commencement of the official career of the late Viscount Castlereagh to the close of his life. Edited by the MARQUIS OF LONDONDERRY. 12 Vols. 8vo. 14s. each.

CATHCART'S (SIR GEORGE) Commentaries on the War in Russia and Germany, 1812-13. Plans. 8vo. 14s.

CAVALCASELLE AND CROWE'S History of Painting in Italy, from the Second to the Sixteenth Century, from recent researches, as well as from personal inspection of the Works of Art in that Country. With 100 Illustrations. Vols. I. to III. 8vo. 63s.

——————— Notices of the Lives and Works of the Early Flemish Painters. Woodcuts. Post 8vo. 12s.

CHILD (G. CHAPLIN, M.D.) Benedicite; or, Song of the Three Children; being Illustrations of the Power, Wisdom, and Goodness of the Creator. 2 Vols. Fcap. 8vo.

CHORLEY'S (H. F.) STUDIES OF THE MUSIC OF MANY NATIONS; including the Substance of a Course of Lectures delivered at the Royal Institution. 8vo. (In the Press.)

CHURTON'S (ARCHDEACON) Gongora. An Historical Essay on the Age of Philip III. and IV. of Spain. With Translations. Portrait. 2 Vols. Small 8vo. 15s.

CICERO: HIS LIFE AND TIMES. With his Character viewed as a Statesman, Orator, and Friend. With a Selection from his Correspondence and Orations. By WILLIAM FORSYTH, Q C. New Edition. With Illustrations. 8vo.

CLIVE'S (LORD) Life. By REV. G. R. GLEIG, M.A. Post 8vo. 3s. 6d.

COLCHESTER (LORD). The Diary and Correspondence of Charles Abbott, Lord Colchester, Speaker of the House of Commons, 1802-1817. Edited by his Son. Portrait. 3 Vols. 8vo. 42s.

COLERIDGE (SAMUEL TAYLOR). Specimens of his Table-Talk. New Edition. Portrait. Fcap. 8vo. 6s.

COLONIAL LIBRARY. [See Home and Colonial Library.]

COOK'S (REV. Canon) Sermons Preached at Lincoln's Inn Chapel, and on Special Occasions. 8vo. 9s.

COOKERY (MODERN DOMESTIC). Founded on Principles of Economy and Practical Knowledge, and adapted for Private Families. By a Lady. New Edition. Woodcuts. Fcap. 8vo. 5s.

CORNWALLIS (THE) Papers and Correspondence during the American War,—Administrations in India,—Union with Ireland, and Peace of Amiens. Edited by CHARLES ROSS. Second Edition. 3 Vols. 8vo. 63s.

COWPER'S (MARY, COUNTESS) Diary while Lady of the Bedchamber to Caroline Princess of Wales, 1714—20. Edited by Hon. SPENCER COWPER. Second Edition. Portrait. 8vo. 10s. 6d.

CRABBE'S (REV. GEORGE) Life, Letters, and Journals. By his Son. Portrait. Fcap. 8vo. 3s.

——————— Life and Poetical Works. Plates. 8 Vols. Fcap. 8vo. 24s.

——————— Life and Poetical Works. Plates. Royal 8vo. 7s.

CROKER'S (J. W.) Progressive Geography for Children. *Fifth Edition.* 18mo. 1s. 6d.
────── Stories for Children, Selected from the History of England. *Fifteenth Edition.* Woodcuts. 16mo. 2s. 6d.
────── Boswell's Life of Johnson. Including the Tour to the Hebrides. Portraits. Royal 8vo. 10s.
────── Essays on the Early Period of the French Revolution. 8vo. 15s.
────── Historical Essay on the Guillotine. Fcap. 8vo. 1s.
CROMWELL (OLIVER) and John Bunyan. By ROBERT SOUTHEY. Post 8vo. 2s.
CROWE'S AND CAVALCASELLE'S Notices of the Early Flemish Painters; their Lives and Works. Woodcuts. Post 8vo. 12s.
────── History of Painting in Italy, from 2nd to 16th Century. Derived from Historical Researches as well as inspection of the Works of Art in that Country. With 100 Illustrations. Vols. I. II. and III. 8vo. 21s. each.
CUMMING'S (R. GORDON) Five Years of a Hunter's Life in the Far Interior of South Africa; with Anecdotes of the Chace, and Notices of the Native Tribes. *New Edition.* Woodcuts. Post 8vo. 5s.
CUNNINGHAM'S (ALLAN) Poems and Songs. Now first collected and arranged, with Biographical Notice. 24mo. 2s. 6d.
CURETON (REV. W.) Remains of a very Ancient Recension of the Four Gospels in Syriac, hitherto unknown in Europe. Discovered, Edited, and Translated. 4to. 24s.
CURTIUS' (PROFESSOR) Student's Greek Grammar, for the use of Colleges and the Upper Forms. Translated under the Author's revision. Edited by DR. WM. SMITH. Post 8vo.
────── Smaller Greek Grammar for the use of the Middle and Lower Forms, abridged from the above. 12mo. 3s. 6d.
────── First Greek Course; containing Delectus, Exercise Book, and Vocabularies. 12mo. 3s. 6d.
CURZON'S (HON. ROBERT) ARMENIA AND ERZEROUM. A Year on the Frontiers of Russia, Turkey, and Persia. *Third Edition.* Woodcuts. Post 8vo. 7s. 6d.
────── Visits to the Monasteries of the Levant. *Fifth Edition.* Illustrations. Post 8vo. 7s. 6d.
CUST'S (GENERAL) Annals of the Wars of the 18th & 19th Centuries. 9 Vols. Fcap. 8vo. 5s. each.
────── Lives and Characters of the Warriors of the 17th Century who have Commanded Fleets and Armies before the Enemy. 2 Vols. Post 8vo. 16s.
DARWIN'S (CHARLES) Journal of Researches into the Natural History of the Countries visited during a Voyage round the World. Post 8vo. 9s.
────── Origin of Species by Means of Natural Selection; or, the Preservation of Favoured Races in the Struggle for Life. *Fourth Edition, revised.* Post 8vo. 14s.
────── Fertilization of Orchids through Insect Agency, and as to the good of Intercrossing. Woodcuts. Post 8vo. 9s.
────── Domesticated Animals and Cultivated Plants; or, the Principles of Variation, Inheritance, Re-version, Crossing, Interbreeding, and Selection under Domestication. With Illustrations. Post 8vo. (*In Preparation.*)

DAVIS'S (NATHAN) Visit to the Ruined Cities of Numidia and Carthaginia. Illustrations. 8vo. 16s.

―――― (SIR J. F.) Chinese Miscellanies: a Collection of Essays and Notes. Post 8vo. 6s.

DAVY'S (SIR HUMPHRY) Consolations in Travel; or, Last Days of a Philosopher. *Fifth Edition.* Woodcuts. Fcap. 8vo. 6s.

―――― Salmonia; or, Days of Fly Fishing. *Fourth Edition.* Woodcuts. Fcap. 8vo. 6s.

DELEPIERRE'S (OCTAVE) History of Flemish Literature. From the Twelfth Century. 8vo. 9s.

DENNIS' (GEORGE) Cities and Cemeteries of Etruria. Plates. 2 Vols. 8vo. 42s.

DERBY'S (EDWARD, EARL OF) Translation of the Iliad of Homer into English Blank Verse. *Fifth Edition, Revised.* 2 Vols. 8vo. 24s.

DE ROS'S (LORD) Memorials of the Tower of London. With Illustrations. Crown 8vo. 10s. 6d.

DIXON'S (W. HEPWORTH) Story of the Life of Lord Bacon. Portrait. Fcap. 8vo. 7s. 6d.

DOG-BREAKING; the Most Expeditious, Certain, and Easy Method, whether great excellence or only mediocrity be required. With a Few Hints for those who Love the Dog and the Gun. By LIEUT.- GEN. HUTCHINSON. *Fourth Edition.* With 40 Woodcuts. Crown 8vo. 15s.

DOMESTIC MODERN COOKERY. Founded on Principles of Economy and Practical Knowledge, and adapted for Private Families. *New Edition.* Woodcuts. Fcap. 8vo. 5s.

DOUGLAS'S (GENERAL SIR HOWARD) Life and Adventures; From Notes, Conversations, and Correspondence. By S. W. FULLOM. Portrait. 8vo. 15s.

―――― Theory and Practice of Gunnery. *5th Edition.* Plates. 8vo. 21s.

―――― Military Bridges, and the Passage of Rivers in Military Operations. *Third Edition.* Plates. 8vo. 21s.

―――― Naval Warfare with Steam. *Second Edition.* 8vo. 8s. 6d.

―――― Modern Systems of Fortification. Plans. 8vo. 12s.

DRAKE'S (SIR FRANCIS) Life, Voyages, and Exploits, by Sea and Land. By JOHN BARROW. *Third Edition.* Post 8vo. 2s.

DRINKWATER'S (JOHN) History of the Siege of Gibraltar, 1779-1783. With a Description and Account of that Garrison from the Earliest Periods. Post 8vo. 2s.

DU CHAILLU'S (PAUL B.) EQUATORIAL AFRICA, with Accounts of the Gorilla, the Nest-building Ape, Chimpanzee, Crocodile, &c. Illustrations. 8vo. 21s.

PUBLISHED BY MR. MURRAY. 11

DUFFERIN'S (LORD) Letters from High Latitudes, being some
Account of a Yacht Voyage to Iceland, &c., in 1856. *Fourth Edition.*
Woodcuts. Post 8vo.

——— Lispings from Low Latitudes, or the Journal of
the Hon. Impulsia Gushington. With 24 Plates. 4to. 21s.

DYER'S (THOMAS H.) History of Modern Europe, from the
taking of Constantinople by the Turks to the close of the War in
the Crimea. 4 Vols. 8vo. 60s.

EASTLAKE'S (SIR CHARLES) Italian Schools of Painting. From
the German of KUGLER. Edited, with Notes. *Third Edition.* Illustrated from the Old Masters. 2 Vols. Post 8vo. 30s.

EASTWICK'S (E. B.) Handbook for Bombay and Madras, with
Directions for Travellers, Officers, &c. Map. 2 Vols. Post 8vo. 24s.

EDWARDS' (W. H.) Voyage up the River Amazon, including a
Visit to Para. Post 8vo. 2s.

ELDON'S (LORD) Public and Private Life, with Selections from
his Correspondence and Diaries. By HORACE TWISS. *Third Edition.*
Portrait. 2 Vols. Post 8vo. 21s.

ELLIS (REV. W.) Visits to Madagascar, including a Journey to
the Capital, with notices of Natural History, and Present Civilisation
of the People. *Fifth Thousand.* Map and Woodcuts. 8vo. 16s.

——— (MRS.) Education of Character, with Hints on Moral
Training. Post 8vo. 7s. 6d.

ELLESMERE'S (LORD) Two Sieges of Vienna by the Turks.
Translated from the German. Post 8vo. 2s.

ELPHINSTONE'S (HON. MOUNTSTUART) History of India—the
Hindoo and Mahomedan Periods. *Fifth Edition, Revised.* Map. 8vo. 18s.

ENGEL'S (CARL) Music of the Most Ancient Nations; particularly
of the Assyrians, Egyptians, and Hebrews; with Special Reference to
the Discoveries in Western Asia and in Egypt. With 100 Illustrations.
8vo. 16s.

ENGLAND (HISTORY OF) from the Peace of Utrecht to the Peace
of Versailles, 1713—83. By LORD MAHON (Earl Stanhope). *Library
Edition,* 7 Vols. 8vo. 93s.; or *Popular Edition,* 7 Vols. Post 8vo. 35s.

——— From the First Invasion by the Romans, down to
the Present Year of Queen Victoria's Reign. By MRS. MARKHAM. *New
and Cheaper Edition.* Woodcuts. 12mo. 4s.

——— (THE STUDENT'S HUME). From the Invasion of
Julius Cæsar to the Revolution of 1688. By DAVID HUME. Corrected
and continued to 1858. Edited by WM. SMITH, LL.D. Woodcuts. Post
8vo. 7s. 6d.

——— A Smaller History of England for Young Persons.
By DR. WM. SMITH. Woodcuts. 18mo. 3s. 6d.

——— Little Arthur's History of England. By LADY
CALLCOTT. Woodcuts. 18mo. 2s. 6d.

ENGLISHWOMAN IN AMERICA. Post 8vo. 10s. 6d.

ESKIMAUX and English Vocabulary, for Travellers in the Arctic
Regions. 16mo. 3s. 6d.

ESSAYS FROM "THE TIMES." Being a Selection from the LITERARY PAPERS which have appeared in that Journal. *Seventh Thousand.* 2 vols. Fcap. 8vo. 8s.

ETHNOLOGICAL SOCIETY OF LONDON, TRANSACTIONS. New Series. Vols. I. to IV. 8vo.

EXETER'S (BISHOP OF) Letters to Charles Butler, on his Book of the Roman Catholic Church. *New Edition.* Post 8vo. 6s.

FAMILY RECEIPT-BOOK. A Collection of a Thousand Valuable and Useful Receipts. Fcap. 8vo. 5s. 6d.

FARRAR'S (REV. A. S.) Critical History of Free Thought in reference to the Christian Religion. Being the Bampton Lectures, 1862. 8vo. 16s.

————— (F. W.) Origin of Language, based on Modern Researches. Fcap. 8vo. 5s.

FEATHERSTONHAUGH'S (G. W.) Tour through the Slave States of North America, from the River Potomac to Texas and the Frontiers of Mexico. Plates. 2 Vols. 8vo. 26s.

FERGUSSON'S (JAMES) Palaces of Nineveh and Persepolis Restored. Woodcuts. 8vo. 16s.

————— History of Architecture in all Countries: from the Earliest Times to the Present Day. With 1200 Illustrations. 2 Vols. 8vo. Vol. I. 42s.

————— History of the Modern Styles of Architecture: forming the Third and Concluding Volume of the above work. With 312 Illustrations. 8vo. 31s. 6d.

————— Holy Sepulchre and the Temple at Jerusalem; being the Substance of Two Lectures delivered at the Royal Institution, 1862 and '65. Woodcuts. 8vo. 7s. 6d.

FISHER'S (REV. GEORGE) Elements of Geometry, for the Use of Schools. *Fifth Edition.* 18mo. 1s. 6d.

————— First Principles of Algebra, for the Use of Schools. *Fifth Edition.* 18mo. 1s. 6d.

FLOWER GARDEN (THE). By REV. THOS. JAMES. Fcap. 8vo. 1s.

FONNEREAU'S (T. G.) Diary of a Dutiful Son. Fcap. 8vo. 4s. 6d.

FORBES' (C. S.) Iceland; its Volcanoes, Geysers, and Glaciers. Illustrations. Post 8vo. 14s.

FORSTER'S (JOHN) Arrest of the Five Members by Charles the First. A Chapter of English History re-written. Post 8vo. 12s.

————— Grand Remonstrance, 1641. With an Essay on English freedom under the Plantagenet and Tudor Sovereigns. *Second Edition.* Post 8vo. 12s.

————— Sir John Eliot: a Biography, 1590—1632. With Portraits. 2 Vols. Crown 8vo. 30s.

————— Biographies of Oliver Cromwell, Daniel De Foe, Sir Richard Steele, Charles Churchill, Samuel Foote. *Third Edition.* Post 8vo. 12s.

FORD'S (RICHARD) Handbook for Spain, Andalusia, Ronda, Valencia,
Catalonia, Granada, Gallicia, Arragon, Navarre, &c. *Third Edition.*
2 Vols. Post 8vo. 30s.

———— Gatherings from Spain. Post 8vo. 3s. 6d.

FORSYTH'S (WILLIAM) Life and Times of Cicero. With Selections
from his Correspondence and Orations. *New Edition.* Illustrations.
8vo.

FORTUNE'S (ROBERT) Narrative of Two Visits to the Tea
Countries of China, 1843-52. *Third Edition.* Woodcuts. 2 Vols. Post
8vo. 18s.

———— Third Visit to China. 1853-6. Woodcuts. 8vo. 16s.

———— Yedo and Peking. With Notices of the Agriculture and Trade of China, during a Fourth Visit to that Country. Illustrations. 8vo. 16s.

FOSS' (Edward) Judges of England. With Sketches of their
Lives, and Notices of the Courts at Westminster, from the Conquest to
the Present Time. 9 Vols. 8vo. 114s.

FRANCE (HISTORY OF). From the Conquest by the Gauls to
Recent Times. By Mrs. MARKHAM. *New and Cheaper Edition.* Woodcuts. 12mo. 4s.

———— (THE STUDENT'S HISTORY OF). From the Earliest
Times to the Establishment of the Second Empire, 1852. By W. H.
PEARSON. Edited by WM. SMITH, LL.D. Woodcuts. Post 8vo. 7s. 6d.

FRENCH (THE) in Algiers; The Soldier of the Foreign Legion—
and the Prisoners of Abd-el-Kadir. Translated by Lady DUFF GORDON.
Post 8vo. 2s.

GALTON'S (FRANCIS) Art of Travel; or, Hints on the Shifts and
Contrivances available in Wild Countries. *Third Edition.* Woodcuts. Post 8vo. 7s. 6d.

GEOGRAPHY, ANCIENT (THE STUDENT'S MANUAL OF). By Rev.
W. L. BEVAN. Woodcuts. Post 8vo. 7s. 6d.

———— MODERN (THE STUDENT'S MANUAL). By Rev.
W. L. BEVAN. Woodcuts. Post 8vo. *In the Press.*

———— Journal of the Royal Geographical Society of
London. 8vo.

GERMANY (HISTORY OF). From the Invasion by Marius, to Recent
times. By Mrs. MARKHAM. *New and Cheaper Edition.* Woodcuts.
12mo. 4s.

GIBBON'S (EDWARD) History of the Decline and Fall of the
Roman Empire. Edited, with Notes, by DEAN MILMAN and M. GUIZOT.
A New Edition. Preceded by his Autobiography. And Edited, with
Notes, by Dr. WM. SMITH. Maps. 8 Vols. 8vo. 60s.

———— (The Student's Gibbon); Being an Epitome of the
above work, incorporating the Researches of Recent Commentators. By
Dr. WM. SMITH. Woodcuts. Post 8vo. 7s. 6d.

GIFFARD'S (EDWARD) Deeds of Naval Daring; or, Anecdotes of
the British Navy. New Edition. Fcap. 8vo. 3s. 6d.

GOLDSMITH'S (OLIVER) Works. A New Edition. Printed from
the last editions revised by the Author. Edited by PETER CUNNINGHAM. Vignettes. 4 Vols. 8vo. 30s.

GLADSTONE'S (RIGHT HON. W. E.) Financial Statements of 1853, 60, 63, and 64; with Speeches on Tax-Bills and Charities. *Second Edition.* 8vo. 12s.

———— Farewell Address at the University of Edinburgh. *Fourth Edition.* 8vo. 2s. 6d.

———— Speeches on Parliamentary Reform in 1866. Post 8vo.

GLEIG'S (REV. G. R.) Campaigns of the British Army at Washington and New Orleans. Post 8vo. 2s.

———— Story of the Battle of Waterloo. Post 8vo. 3s. 6d.

———— Narrative of Sale's Brigade in Affghanistan. Post 8vo. 2s.

———— Life of Robert Lord Clive. Post 8vo. 3s. 6d.

———— Life and Letters of Sir Thomas Munro. Post 8vo. 3s. 6d.

GONGORA; An Historical Essay on the Times of Philip III. and IV. of Spain. With Illustrations. By ARCHDEACON CHURTON. Portrait. 2 vols. Post 8vo. 15s.

GORDON'S (SIR ALEX. DUFF) Sketches of German Life, and Scenes from the War of Liberation. From the German. Post 8vo. 3s. 6d.

———— (LADY DUFF) Amber-Witch: A Trial for Witchcraft. From the German. Post 8vo. 2s.

———— French in Algiers. 1. The Soldier of the Foreign Legion. 2. The Prisoners of Abd-el-Kadir. From the French. Post 8vo. 2s.

GOUGER'S (HENRY) Personal Narrative of Two Years' Imprisonment in Burmah. *Second Edition.* Woodcuts. Post 8vo. 12s.

GRAMMARS (LATIN and GREEK). See CURTIUS; SMITH; KING EDWARD VITH., &c. &c.

GREECE (THE STUDENT'S HISTORY OF). From the Earliest Times to the Roman Conquest. By WM. SMITH, LL.D. Woodcuts. Post 8vo. 7s. 6d.

———— (A SMALLER HISTORY OF, FOR YOUNG PERSONS). By DR. WM. SMITH. Woodcuts. 16mo. 3s. 6d.

GRENVILLE (THE) PAPERS. Being the Public and Private Correspondence of George Grenville, including his PRIVATE DIARY. Edited by W. J. SMITH. 4 Vols. 8vo. 16s. each.

GREY (EARL) The Correspondence of the late Earl Grey with King William IVth. and Sir Herbert Taylor, from November, 1830, to the Passing of the Reform Act in 1832. 8vo.

———— On Parliamentary Government and Reform; with Suggestions for the Improvement of our Representative System, and an Examination of the Reform Bills of 1859—61. *Second Edition.* 8vo. 9s.

———— (SIR GEORGE) Polynesian Mythology, and Ancient Traditional History of the New Zealand Race. Woodcuts. Post 8vo. 10s. 6d.

GRUNER'S (LEWIS) Brick and Terra-Cotta Buildings of Lombardy, Fourteenth and Fifteenth Centuries. From careful Drawings and Restorations. Engraved and printed in Colours. Illustrations. Small folio. *Nearly Ready.*

PUBLISHED BY MR. MURRAY.   15

GUIZOT'S (M.) Meditations on the Essence of Christianity, and on the Religious Questions of the Day. Post 8vo. 9s. 6d.
—————— Meditations on the Actual State of the Christian Religion. Post 8vo.
GROTE'S (George) History of Greece. From the Earliest Times to the close of the generation contemporary with the death of Alexander the Great. *Fourth Edition.* Maps. 8 vols. 8vo. 112s.
—————— Plato, and the other Companions of Socrates. *Second Edition.* 3 Vols. 8vo.
—————— (Mrs.) Memoir of Ary Scheffer. Post 8vo. 8s. 6d.
—————— Collected Papers. 8vo. 10s. 6d.
HALLAM'S (Henry) Constitutional History of England, from the Accession of Henry the Seventh to the Death of George the Second. *Seventh Edition.* 3 Vols. 8vo. 30s. Or Popular Edition, 3 Vols., Post 8vo, 18s.
—————— History of Europe during the Middle Ages. *Tenth Edition.* 3 Vols. 8vo. 30s. Or Popular Edition, 3 Vols., Post 8vo, 18s.
—————— Literary History of Europe, during the 15th, 16th and 17th Centuries. *Fourth Edition.* 3 Vols. 8vo. 36s. Or Popular Edition, 4 Vols., Post 8vo., 24s.
—————— Historical Works. Containing History of England,—Middle Ages of Europe,—Literary History of Europe. 10 Vols. Post 8vo. 6s. each.
—————— (Arthur) Remains; in Verse and Prose. With Preface, Memoir, and Portrait. Fcap. 8vo. 7s. 6d.
HAMILTON'S (James) Wanderings in North Africa. With Illustrations. Post 8vo. 12s.
HART'S ARMY LIST. (*Quarterly and Annually.*) 8vo. 10s. 6d. and 21s. each.
HANNAH'S (Rev. Dr.) Bampton Lectures for 1863; the Divine and Human Elements in Holy Scripture. 8vo. 10s. 6d.
HAY'S (J. H. Drummond) Western Barbary, its wild Tribes and savage Animals. Post 8vo. 2s.
HEAD'S (Sir Francis) Horse and his Rider. Woodcuts. Post 8vo. 5s.
—————— Rapid Journeys across the Pampas. Post 8vo. 2s.
—————— Bubbles from the Brunnen of Nassau. Illustrations. Post 8vo.
—————— Emigrant. Fcap. 8vo. 2s. 6d.
—————— Stokers and Pokers; or, N.-Western Railway. Post 8vo. 2s.
—————— (Sir Edmund) Shall and Will; or, Future Auxiliary Verbs. Fcap. 8vo. 4s.
HEBER'S (Bishop) Journey through the Upper Provinces of India, from Calcutta to Bombay, with an Account of a Journey to Madras and the Southern Provinces. *Twelfth Edition.* 2 Vols. Post 8vo. 7s.
—————— Poetical Works, including Palestine, Europe, The Red Sea, Hymns, &c. *Sixth Edition.* Portrait. Fcap. 8vo. 6s.
—————— Hymns adapted to the Weekly Church Service of the Year. 16mo. 1s. 6d.
HERODOTUS. A New English Version. Edited, with Notes and Essays, historical, ethnographical, and geographical, by Rev. G. Rawlinson, assisted by Sir Henry Rawlinson and Sir J. G. Wilkinson. *Second Edition.* Maps and Woodcuts. 4 Vols. 8vo. 48s.

LIST OF WORKS

HAND-BOOK—TRAVEL-TALK. English, French, German, and Italian. 18mo. 3s. 6d.

——————— NORTH GERMANY,—HOLLAND, BELGIUM, and the Rhine to Switzerland. Map. Post 8vo. 10s.

——————— KNAPSACK GUIDE—BELGIUM AND THE RHINE. Post 8vo. (In the Press.)

——————— SOUTH GERMANY, Bavaria, Austria, Styria, Salzberg, the Austrian and Bavarian Alps, the Tyrol, Hungary, and the Danube, from Ulm to the Black Sea. Map. Post 8vo. 10s.

——————— KNAPSACK GUIDE—THE TYROL. Post 8vo. (In the Press.)

——————— PAINTING. German, Flemish, and Dutch Schools. Edited by DR. WAAGEN. Woodcuts. 2 Vols. Post 8vo. 24s.

——————— LIVES OF THE EARLY FLEMISH PAINTERS, with Notices of their Works. By CROWE and CAVALCASELLE. Illustrations. Post 8vo. 12s.

——————— SWITZERLAND, Alps of Savoy, and Piedmont. Maps. Post 8vo. 9s.

——————— KNAPSACK GUIDE — SWITZERLAND. Post 8vo. 5s.

——————— FRANCE, Normandy, Brittany, the French Alps, the Rivers Loire, Seine, Rhone, and Garonne, Danphiné, Provence, and the Pyrenees. Maps. Post 8vo. 10s.

——————— KNAPSACK GUIDE — FRANCE. Post 8vo. (In the Press.)

——————— PARIS AND ITS ENVIRONS. Map. Post 8vo. 5s.

——————— SPAIN, Andalusia, Ronda, Granada, Valencia, Catalonia, Gallicia, Arragon, and Navarre. Maps. 2 Vols. Post 8vo. 30s.

——————— PORTUGAL, LISBON, &c. Map. Post 8vo. 9s.

——————— NORTH ITALY, Piedmont, Liguria, Venetia, Lombardy, Parma, Modena, and Romagna. Map. Post 8vo. 12s.

——————— CENTRAL ITALY, Lucca, Tuscany, Florence, The Marches, Umbria, and the Patrimony of St. Peter's. Map. Post 8vo. 10s.

——————— ROME AND ITS ENVIRONS. Map. Post 8vo. 9s.

——————— SOUTH ITALY, Two Sicilies, Naples, Pompeii, Herculaneum, and Vesuvius. Map. Post 8vo. 10s.

——————— KNAPSACK GUIDE—ITALY. Post 8vo. 6s.

——————— SICILY, Palermo, Messina, Catania, Syracuse, Etna, and the Ruins of the Greek Temples. Map. Post 8vo. 12s.

——————— PAINTING. The Italian Schools. From the German of KUGLER. Edited by Sir CHARLES EASTLAKE, R.A. Woodcuts. 2 Vols. Post 8vo. 30s.

——————— LIVES OF THE EARLY ITALIAN PAINTERS, AND PROGRESS OF PAINTING IN ITALY, from CIMABUE to BASSANO. By Mrs. JAMESON. A New Edition. Woodcuts. Post 8vo. In the Press.

——————— NORWAY, Map. Post 8vo. 5s.

——————— DENMARK, SWEDEN, and NORWAY. Maps. Post 8vo. 15s.

HAND-BOOK—GREECE, the Ionian Islands, Albania, Thessaly, and Macedonia. Maps. Post 8vo. 15s.

———— TURKEY, Malta, Asia Minor, Constantinople, Armenia, Mesopotamia, &c. Maps. Post 8vo.

———— EGYPT, Thebes, the Nile, Alexandria, Cairo, the Pyramids, Mount Sinai, &c. Map. Post 8vo. 15s.

———— SYRIA AND PALESTINE, Peninsula of Sinai, Eldom, and Syrian Desert. Maps. 2 Vols. Post 8vo. 24s.

———— BOMBAY AND MADRAS. Map. 2 Vols. Post 8vo. 24s.

———— RUSSIA, POLAND, and FINLAND. Maps. Post 8vo. 12s.

———— MODERN LONDON. A Complete Guide to all the Sights and Objects of Interest in the Metropolis. Map. 16mo. 3s. 6d.

———— WESTMINSTER ABBEY. Woodcuts. 16mo. 1s.

———— IRELAND — Dublin, Belfast, Donegal, Galway, Wexford, Cork, Limerick, Waterford, the Lakes of Killarney, Coast of Munster, &c. Maps. Post 8vo. 12s.

———— KENT AND SUSSEX, Canterbury, Dover, Ramsgate, Sheerness, Rochester, Chatham, Woolwich, Brighton, Chichester, Worthing, Hastings, Lewes, Arundel, &c. Map. Post 8vo. 10s.

———— SURREY AND HANTS, Kingston, Croydon, Reigate, Guildford, Winchester, Southampton, Portsmouth, and Isle of Wight. Maps. Post 8vo. 10s.

———— BERKS, BUCKS, AND OXON, Windsor, Eton, Reading, Aylesbury, Uxbridge, Wycombe, Henley, the City and University of Oxford, and the Descent of the Thames to Maidenhead and Windsor. Map. Post 8vo. 7s. 6d.

———— WILTS, DORSET, AND SOMERSET, Salisbury, Chippenham, Weymouth, Sherborne, Wells, Bath, Bristol, Taunton, &c. Map. Post 8vo. 7s. 6d.

———— DEVON AND CORNWALL, Exeter, Ilfracombe, Linton, Sidmouth, Dawlish, Teignmouth, Plymouth, Devonport, Torquay, Launceston, Truro, Penzance, Falmouth, &c. Maps. Post 8vo. 10s.

———— NORTH AND SOUTH WALES, Bangor, Carnarvon, Beaumaris, Snowdon, Conway, Menai Straits, Carmarthen, Pembroke, Tenby, Swansea, The Wye, &c. Maps. 2 Vols. Post 8vo. 12s.

———— GLOUCESTER, HEREFORD, AND WORCESTERSHIRE. Map. Post 8vo.

———— STAFFORD, DERBY, AND LEICESTERSHIRE. Map. Post 8vo. (Just Ready.)

———— YORKSHIRE. Map. Post 8vo. (Just Ready.)

———— THE LAKES. WESTMORELAND, CUMBERLAND, &c. Maps. Post 8vo. 6s. 6d.

———— SOUTHERN CATHEDRALS OF ENGLAND— Winchester, Salisbury, Exeter, Wells, Chichester, Rochester, Canterbury. With 110 Illustrations. 2 Vols. Crown 8vo. 24s.

———— EASTERN CATHEDRALS OF ENGLAND — Oxford, Peterborough, Norwich, Ely, and Lincoln. With 90 Illustrations. Crown 8vo. 18s.

———— WESTERN CATHEDRALS OF ENGLAND— Bristol, Gloucester, Hereford, Worcester, and Lichfield. With 50 Illustrations. Crown 8vo. 16s.

LIST OF WORKS

HOME AND COLONIAL LIBRARY. A Series of Works adapted for all circles and classes of Readers, having been selected for their acknowledged interest and ability of the Authors. Post 8vo. Published at 2s. and 3s. 6d. each, and arranged under two distinctive heads as follows:—

CLASS A.
HISTORY, BIOGRAPHY, AND HISTORIC TALES.

1. SIEGE OF GIBRALTAR. By JOHN DRINKWATER. 2s.
2. THE AMBER-WITCH. y LADY DUFF GORDON. 2s.
3. CROMWELL AND BUNYAN. By ROBERT SOUTHEY. 2s.
4. LIFE OF SIR FRANCIS DRAKE. By JOHN BARROW. 2s.
5. CAMPAIGNS AT WASHINGTON. By REV. G. R. GLEIG. 2s.
6. THE FRENCH IN ALGIERS. By LADY DUFF GORDON. 2s.
7. THE FALL OF THE JESUITS. 2s.
8. LIVONIAN TALES. 2s.
9. LIFE OF CONDE. By LORD MAHON. 3s. 6d.
10. SALE'S BRIGADE. By REV. G. R. GLEIG. 2s.
11. THE SIEGES OF VIENNA. By LORD ELLESMERE. 2s.
12. THE WAYSIDE CROSS. By CAPT. MILMAN. 2s.
13. SKETCHES OF GERMAN LIFE. By SIR A. GORDON. 3s. 6d.
14. THE BATTLE OF WATERLOO. By REV. G. R. GLEIG. 3s. 6d.
15. AUTOBIOGRAPHY OF STEFFENS. 2s.
16. THE BRITISH POETS. By THOMAS CAMPBELL. 3s. 6d.
17. HISTORICAL ESSAYS. By LORD MAHON. 3s. 6d.
18. LIFE OF LORD CLIVE. By REV. G. R. GLEIG. 3s. 6d.
19. NORTH - WESTERN RAILWAY. By SIR F. B. HEAD. 2s.
20. LIFE OF MUNRO. By REV. G. R. GLEIG. 3s. 6d.

CLASS B.
VOYAGES, TRAVELS, AND ADVENTURES.

1. BIBLE IN SPAIN. By GEORGE BORROW. 3s. 6d.
2. GIPSIES OF SPAIN. By GEORGE BORROW. 3s. 6d.
3 & 4. JOURNALS IN INDIA. By BISHOP HEBER. 2 Vols. 7s.
5. TRAVELS IN THE HOLY LAND. By IRBY and MANGLES. 2s.
6. MOROCCO AND THE MOORS. By J. DRUMMOND HAY. 2s.
7. LETTERS FROM THE BALTIC. By a LADY. 2s.
8. NEW SOUTH WALES. By MRS. MEREDITH. 2s.
9. THE WEST INDIES. By M. G. LEWIS. 2s.
10. SKETCHES OF PERSIA. By SIR JOHN MALCOLM. 3s. 6d.
11. MEMOIRS OF FATHER RIPA. 2s.
12. 13. TYPEE AND OMOO. By HERMANN MELVILLE. 2 Vols. 7s.
14. MISSIONARY LIFE IN CANADA. By REV. J. ABBOTT. 2s.
15. LETTERS FROM MADRAS. By a LADY. 2s.
16. HIGHLAND SPORTS. By CHARLES ST. JOHN. 3s. 6d.
17. PAMPAS JOURNEYS. By SIR F. B. HEAD. 2s.
18. GATHERINGS FROM SPAIN. By RICHARD FORD. 3s. 6d.
19. THE RIVER AMAZON. By W. H. EDWARDS. 2s.
20. MANNERS & CUSTOMS OF INDIA. By REV. C. ACLAND. 2s.
21. ADVENTURES IN MEXICO. By G. F. RUXTON. 3s. 6d.
22. PORTUGAL AND GALLICIA. By LORD CARNARVON. 3s. 6d.
23. BUSH LIFE IN AUSTRALIA. By Rev. H. W. HAYGARTH. 2s.
24. THE LIBYAN DESERT. By BAYLE ST. JOHN. 2s.
25. SIERRA LEONE. By a LADY. 3s. 6d.

⁎ Each work may be had separately.

HANDBOOK OF FAMILIAR QUOTATIONS. From English Authors. *Third Edition.* Fcap. 8vo. 5s.

HESSEY (Rev. Dr.). Sunday—Its Origin, History, and Present Obligations. Being the Bampton Lectures for 1860. *Second Edition.* 8vo. 16s. Or *Third and Popular Edition.* Post 8vo. 9s.

HICKMAN'S (Wm.) Treatise on the Law and Practice of Naval Courts-Martial. 8vo. 10s. 6d.

HILLARD'S (G. S.) Six Months in Italy. 2 Vols. Post 8vo. 16s.

HOLLWAY'S (J. G.) Month in Norway. Fcap. 8vo. 2s.

HONEY BEE (The). An Essay. By Rev. Thomas James. Reprinted from the "Quarterly Review." Fcap. 8vo. 1s.

HOOK'S (Dean) Church Dictionary. *Ninth Edition.* 8vo. 16s.

────── (Theodore) Life. By J. G. Lockhart. Reprinted from the "Quarterly Review." Fcap. 8vo. 1s.

HOPE'S (A. J. Beresford) English Cathedral of the Nineteenth Century. With Illustrations. 8vo. 12s.

HORACE (Works of). Edited by Dean Milman. With 300 Woodcuts. Crown 8vo. 21s.

────── (Life of). By Dean Milman. Woodcuts, and coloured Borders. 8vo. 9s.

HOUGHTON'S (Lord) Poetical Works. Fcap. 8vo. 6s.

HUME'S (The Student's) History of England, from the Invasion of Julius Cæsar to the Revolution of 1688. Corrected and continued to 1858. Edited by Dr. Wm. Smith. Woodcuts. Post 8vo. 7s. 6d.

HUTCHINSON (Gen.) on the most expeditious, certain, and easy Method of Dog-Breaking. *Fourth Edition.* Enlarged and revised, with 40 Illustrations. Crown 8vo. 15s.

HUTTON'S (H. E.) Principia Græca; an Introduction to the Study of Greek. Comprehending Grammar, Delectus, and Exercise-book, with Vocabularies. *Third Edition.* 12mo. 3s. 6d.

IRBY AND MANGLES' Travels in Egypt, Nubia, Syria, and the Holy Land. Post 8vo. 2s.

JAMES' (Rev. Thomas) Fables of Æsop. A New Translation, with Historical Preface. With 100 Woodcuts by Tenniel and Wolf. *Forty-eighth Thousand.* Post 8vo. 2s. 6d.

JAMESON'S (Mrs.) Lives of the Early Italian Painters, from Cimabue to Bassano, and the Progress of Painting in Italy. *New Edition.* With Woodcuts. Post 8vo.

JESSE'S (Edward) Gleanings in Natural History. *Eighth Edition.* Fcp. 8vo. 6s.

JOHNS' (Rev. B. G.) Blind People; their Works and Ways. With Sketches of the Lives of some famous Blind Men. With Illustrations. Post 8vo.

JOHNSON'S (Dr. Samuel) Life. By James Boswell. Including the Tour to the Hebrides. Edited by Mr. Croker. Portraits. Royal 8vo. 10s.

────── Lives of the most eminent English Poets. Edited by Peter Cunningham. 3 vols. 8vo. 22s. 6d.

KEN'S (BISHOP) Life. By a LAYMAN, Author of "Life of the Messiah." *Second Edition.* Portrait. 2 Vols. 8vo. 18s.

———— Exposition of the Apostles' Creed. Extracted from his "Practice of Divine Love." Fcap. 1s. 6d.

———— Approach to the Holy Altar. Extracted from his "Manual of Prayer" and "Practice of Divine Love." Fcap. 8vo. 1s. 6d.

KENNEDY'S (GENERAL SIR J. SHAW) Notes on the Battle of Waterloo. With a Memoir of his Life and Services, and a Plan for the Defence of Canada. With Map and Plans. 8vo. 7s. 6d.

KING'S (REV. C. W.) Antique Gems; their Origin, Use, and Value, as Interpreters of Ancient History, and as Illustrative of Ancient Art. *Second Edition.* Illustrations. 8vo.

KING EDWARD VITH's Latin Grammar; or, an Introduction to the Latin Tongue, for the Use of Schools. *Seventeenth Edition.* 12mo. 3s. 6d.

———— First Latin Book; or, the Accidence, Syntax, and Prosody, with an English Translation for the Use of Junior Classes. *Fifth Edition.* 12mo. 2s. 6d.

KIRK'S (J. FOSTER) History of Charles the Bold, Duke of Burgundy. Portrait. 2 Vols. 8vo. 30s.

KERR'S (ROBERT) GENTLEMAN'S HOUSE; OR, HOW TO PLAN ENGLISH RESIDENCES, FROM THE PARSONAGE TO THE PALACE. With Tables of Accommodation and Cost, and a Series of Selected Views and Plans. *Second Edition.* 8vo. 24s.

———— Ancient Lights; a Book for Architects, Surveyors, Lawyers, and Landlords. 8vo. 5s. 6d.

KING GEORGE THE THIRD'S CORRESPONDENCE WITH LORD NORTH, 1769-82. Edited, with Notes and Introduction, by W. BODHAM DONNE. 2 vols. 8vo. (*Published by Permission.*)

KUGLER'S Italian Schools of Painting. Edited, with Notes, by SIR CHARLES EASTLAKE. *Third Edition.* Woodcuts. 2 Vols. Post 8vo. 30s.

———— German, Dutch, and Flemish Schools of Painting. Edited, with Notes, by DR. WAAGEN. *Second Edition.* Woodcuts. 2 Vols. Post 8vo. 24s.

LAYARD'S (A. H.) Nineveh and its Remains. Being a Narrative of Researches and Discoveries amidst the Ruins of Assyria. With an Account of the Chaldean Christians of Kurdistan; the Yezedis, or Devil-worshippers; and an Enquiry into the Manners and Arts of the Ancient Assyrians. *Sixth Edition.* Plates and Woodcuts. 2 Vols. 8vo. 36s.

*** A Popular Account of the above Work. With Illustrations. Post 8vo. 5s.

———— Nineveh and Babylon; being the Result of a Second Expedition to Assyria. Plates. 8vo. 21s. On *Fine Paper*, 2 Vols. 8vo. 30s.

*** A Popular Account of the above Work. With Illustrations. Post 8vo. (*In the Press.*)

LESLIE'S (C. R.) Handbook for Young Painters. With Illustrations. Post 8vo. 10s. 6d.

———— Autobiographical Recollections, with Selections from his Correspondence. Edited by TOM TAYLOR. Portrait. 2 Vols. Post 8vo. 18s.

LESLIE'S (C. R.) Life of Sir Joshua Reynolds. With an Account of his Works, and a Sketch of his Cotemporaries. By C. R. LESLIE and TOM TAYLOR. Portraits and Illustrations. 2 Vols. 8vo. 42s.

LETTERS FROM THE BALTIC. By a LADY. Post 8vo. 2s.

——————— MADRAS. By a LADY. Post 8vo. 2s.

——————— SIERRA LEONE By a LADY. Post 8vo. 3s. 6d.

LEWIS' (SIR G. C.) Essay on the Government of Dependencies. 8vo. 12s.

——— Glossary of Provincial Words used in Herefordshire and some of the adjoining Counties. 12mo. 4s. 6d.

——— (M. G.) Journal of a Residence among the Negroes in the West Indies. Post 8vo. 2s.

LIDDELL'S (DEAN) History of Rome. From the Earliest Times to the Establishment of the Empire. With the History of Literature and Art. 2 Vols. 8vo. 28s.

——————— Student's History of Rome, abridged from the above Work. With Woodcuts. Post 8vo. 7s. 6d.

LINDSAY'S (LORD) Lives of the Lindsays; or, a Memoir of the Houses of Crawfurd and Balcarres. With Extracts from Official Papers and Personal Narratives. *Second Edition.* 3 Vols. 8vo. 24s.

LISPINGS from LOW LATITUDES; or, the Journal of the Hon. Impulsia Gushington. Edited by LORD DUFFERIN. With 24 Plates. 4to. 21s.

LITTLE ARTHUR'S HISTORY OF ENGLAND. By LADY CALLCOTT. 150*th Thousand.* With 20 Woodcuts. Fcap. 8vo. 2s. 6d.

LIVINGSTONE'S (DR.) Popular Account of his Missionary Travels in South Africa. Illustrations. Post 8vo. 6s.

——————— Narrative of an Expedition to the Zambezi and its Tributaries; and of the Discovery of Lakes Shirwa and Nyassa. 1858-64. By DAVID and CHARLES LIVINGSTONE. Map and Illustrations. 8vo. 21s.

LIVONIAN TALES. By the Author of "Letters from the Baltic." Post 8vo. 2s.

LOCKHART'S (J. G.) Ancient Spanish Ballads. Historical and Romantic. Translated, with Notes. *New Edition.* Post 8vo. 2s. 6d.

LONDON'S (BISHOP OF) Dangers and Safeguards of Modern Theology. Containing Suggestions to the Theological Student under present difficulties. *Second Edition.* 8vo. 9s.

LOUDON'S (MRS.) Instructions in Gardening. With Directions and Calendar of Operations for Every Month. *Eighth Edition.* Woodcuts. Fcap. 8vo. 5s.

LUCAS' (SAMUEL) Secularia; or, Surveys on the Main Stream of History. 8vo. 12s.

LUCKNOW: a Lady's Diary of the Siege. Fcap. 8vo. 4s. 6d.

LYELL'S (SIR CHARLES) Elements of Geology; or, the Ancient Changes of the Earth and its Inhabitants considered as Illustrative of Geology. *Sixth Edition.* Woodcuts. 8vo. 18s.

——————— Principles of Geology; or, the Recent Changes of the Earth and its Inhabitants considered as Illustrative of Geology. *Tenth Edition.* With Illustrations. Vol. I. 8vo. (*To be completed in Vols.*)

——————— Geological Evidences of the Antiquity of Man. *Third Edition.* Illustrations. 8vo. 14s.

LYTTELTON'S (LORD) Ephemera. Post 8vo. 10s. 6d.

LYTTON'S (LORD) Poems. *New Edition.* Post 8vo. 10s. 6d.

———— Lost Tales of Miletus. *Second Edition.* Post 8vo. 7s. 6d.

MACPHERSON'S (MAJOR S. C.) Memorials of Service in India, while Political Agent at Gwalior during the Mutiny, and formerly employed in the Suppression of Human Sacrifices in Orissa. Edited by his Brother. With Portrait and Illustrations. 8vo. 12s.

MAHON'S (LORD) History of England, from the Peace of Utrecht to the Peace of Versailles, 1713—83. *Library Edition.* 7 Vols. 8vo. 93s. *Popular Edition,* 7 Vols. Post 8vo. 35s.

———— Life of Condé, surnamed the Great. Post 8vo. 3s. 6d.

———— Life of Belisarius. *Second Edition.* Post 8vo. 10s. 6d.

———— Life of William Pitt, with Extracts from his MS. Papers. *Second Edition.* Portraits. 4 Vols. Post 8vo. 42s.

———— Miscellanies. *Second Edition.* Post 8vo. 5s. 6d.

———— "Forty-Five;" a Narrative of the Rebellion in Scotland. Post 8vo. 3s.

———— History of British India from its Origin till the Peace of 1783. Post 8vo. 3s. 6d.

———— Spain under Charles the Second; 1690 to 1700. *Second Edition.* Post 8vo. 6s. 6d.

———— Historical and Critical Essays. Post 8vo. 3s. 6d.

———— Story of Joan of Arc. Fcap. 8vo. 1s.

McCLINTOCK'S (CAPT. SIR F. L.) Narrative of the Discovery of the Fate of Sir John Franklin and his Companions in the Arctic Seas. *Twelfth Thousand.* Illustrations. 8vo. 16s.

McCULLOCH'S (J. R.) Collected Edition of RICARDO's Political Works. With Notes and Memoir. *Second Edition.* 8vo. 16s.

MACDOUGALL'S (COL.) Modern Warfare as Influenced by Modern Artillery. With Plans. Post 8vo. 12s.

MAINE (H. SUMNER) On Ancient Law: its Connection with the Early History of Society, and its Relation to Modern Ideas. *Third Edition.* 8vo. 12s.

MALCOLM'S (SIR JOHN) Sketches of Persia. Post 8vo. 3s. 6d.

MANSEL (REV. H. L.) Limits of Religious Thought Examined. Being the Bampton Lectures for 1858. *Fourth Edition.* Post 8vo. 7s. 6d.

MANSFIELD (SIR WILLIAM) On the Introduction of a Gold Currency into India: a Contribution to the Literature of Political Economy. 8vo. 3s. 6d.

MANTELL'S (GIDEON A.) Thoughts on Animalcules; or, the Invisible World, as revealed by the Microscope. *Second Edition.* Plates. 16mo. 6s.

MANUAL OF SCIENTIFIC ENQUIRY, Prepared for the Use of Officers and Travellers. By various Writers. Edited by Sir J. F. HERSCHEL and Rev. R. MAIN. *Third Edition.* Maps. Post 8vo. 9s. (*Published by order of the Lords of the Admiralty.*)

PUBLISHED BY MR. MURRAY.   23

MARKHAM'S (Mrs.) History of England. From the First Invasion by the Romans, down to Recent Times. *New and Cheaper Edition.* Woodcuts. 12mo. 4s.

────── History of France. From the Conquest by the Gauls, to Recent Times. *New and Cheaper Edition.* Woodcuts. 12mo. 4s.

────── History of Germany. From the Invasion by Marius, to Recent Times. *New and Cheaper Edition.* Woodcuts. 12mo. 4s.

────── (CLEMENTS, R.) Travels in Peru and India, for the purpose of collecting Cinchona Plants, and introducing Bark into India. Maps and Illustrations. 8vo. 16s.

MARKLAND'S (J. H.) Reverence due to Holy Places. *Third Edition.* Fcap. 8vo. 2s.

MARRYAT'S (JOSEPH) History of Modern and Mediæval Pottery and Porcelain. With a Description of the Manufacture. *Second Edition.* Plates and Woodcuts. 8vo. 31s. 6d.

────── (HORACE) Jutland, the Danish Isles, and Copenhagen. Illustrations. 2 Vols. Post 8vo. 24s.

────── Sweden and Isle of Gothland. Illustrations. 2 Vols. Post 8vo. 28s.

MATTHIÆ'S (AUGUSTUS) Greek Grammar for Schools, abridged from the Larger Grammar. By Blomfield. *Ninth Edition.* Revised by EDWARDS. 12mo. 3s.

MAUREL'S (JULES) Essay on the Character, Actions, and Writings of the Duke of Wellington. *Second Edition.* Fcap. 8vo. 1s. 6d.

MAYNE'S (CAPT.) Four Years in British Columbia and Vancouver Island. Its Forests, Rivers, Coasts, and Gold Fields, and Resources for Colonisation. Illustrations. 8vo. 16s.

MELVILLE'S (HERMANN) Typee and Omoo; or, Adventures amongst the Marquesas and South Sea Islands. 2 Vols. Post 8vo. 7s.

MILLS' (REV. JOHN) Three Months' Residence at Nablus, with an Account of the Modern Samaritans. Illustrations. Post 8vo. 10s. 6d.

MILMAN'S (DEAN) Historical Works. 15 Vols. Post 8vo. 6s. each. Containing,
  1. HISTORY OF THE JEWS. 3 Vols.
  2. HISTORY OF EARLY CHRISTIANITY. 3 Vols.
  3. HISTORY OF LATIN CHRISTIANITY. 9 Vols.

────── Character and Conduct of the Apostles considered as an Evidence of Christianity. 8vo. 10s. 6d.

────── Translations from the Agamemnon of Æschylus and Bacchanals of Euripides; with Passages from the Lyric and Later Poets of Greece. With Illustrations, crown 8vo. 12s.

────── Life and Works of Horace. With 300 Woodcuts. Vols. Crown 8vo. 30s.

────── Poetical Works. Plates. 3 Vols. Fcap. 8vo. 18s.

────── Fall of Jerusalem. Fcap. 8vo. 1s.

────── (CAPT. E. A.) Wayside Cross. A Tale of the Carlist War. Post 8vo. 2s.

MEREDITH'S (MRS. CHARLES) Notes and Sketches of New South Wales. Post 8vo. 2s.

MESSIAH (THE): A Narrative of the Life, Travels, Death, Resurrection, and Ascension of our Blessed Lord. By a LAYMAN. Author of the " Life of Bishop Ken." Map. 8vo. 18s.

MICHIE'S (ALEXANDER) Siberian Overland Route from Peking to Petersburg, through the Deserts and Steppes of Mongolia, Tartary, &c. Maps and Illustrations. 8vo. 16s.

MODERN DOMESTIC COOKERY. Founded on Principles of Economy and Practical Knowledge and adapted for Private Families. *New Edition*. Woodcuts. Fcap. 8vo. 5s.

MOORE'S (THOMAS) Life and Letters of Lord Byron. Plates. 6 Vols. Fcap. 8vo. 18s.

——— Life and Letters of Lord Byron. Portraits. Royal 8vo. 9s.

MOTLEY'S (J. L.) History of the United Netherlands : from the Death of William the Silent to the Twelve Years' Truce, 1609. Embracing the English-Dutch struggle against Spain; and a detailed Account of the Spanish Armada. Portraits. 2 Vols. 8vo. 30s.

MOUHOT'S (HENRI) Siam, Cambojia, and Lao; a Narrative of Travels and Discoveries. Illustrations. 2 vols. 8vo. 32s.

MOZLEY'S (REV. J. B.) Treatise on Predestination. 8vo. 14s.

——— Primitive Doctrine of Baptismal Regeneration. 8vo. 7s. 6d.

MUNDY'S (GENERAL) Pen and Pencil Sketches in India. *Third Edition*. Plates. Post 8vo. 7s. 6d.

——— (ADMIRAL) Account of the Italian Revolution, with Notices of Garibaldi, Francis II., and Victor Emmanuel. Post 8vo. 12s.

MUNRO'S (GENERAL SIR THOMAS) Life and Letters. By the REV. G. R. GLEIG. Post 8vo. 8s. 6d.

MURCHISON'S (SIR RODERICK) Russia in Europe and the Ural Mountains. With Coloured Maps, Plates, Sections, &c. 2 Vols. Royal 4to. 5l. 5s.

——— Siluria ; or, a History of the Oldest Rocks containing Organic Remains. *Fourth Edition*. Map and Plates. 8vo.
(*In the Press.*)

MURRAY'S RAILWAY READING. Containing:—

WELLINGTON. By LORD ELLESMERE. 6d.
NIMROD ON THE CHASE. 1s.
ESSAYS FROM "THE TIMES." 2 Vols. 8s.
MUSIC AND DRESS. 1s.
LAYARD'S ACCOUNT OF NINEVEH. 5s.
MILMAN'S FALL OF JERUSALEM. 1s.
MAHON'S "FORTY-FIVE." 3s.
LIFE OF THEODORE HOOK. 1s.
DEEDS OF NAVAL DARING. 3s. 6d.
THE HONEY BEE. 1s.
JAMES' ÆSOP'S FABLES. 2s. 6d.
NIMROD ON THE TURF. 1s. 6d.
ART OF DINING. 1s. 6d.
HALLAM'S LITERARY ESSAYS. 2s.
MAHON'S JOAN OF ARC. 1s.
HEAD'S EMIGRANT. 2s. 6d.
NIMROD ON THE ROAD. 1s.
CROKER ON THE GUILLOTINE. 1s.
HOLLWAY'S NORWAY. 2s.
MAUREL'S WELLINGTON. 1s. 6d.
CAMPBELL'S LIFE OF BACON. 2s. 6d.
THE FLOWER GARDEN. 1s.
LOCKHART'S SPANISH BALLADS. 2s. 6d.
TAYLOR'S NOTES FROM LIFE. 2s.
REJECTED ADDRESSES. 1s.
PENN'S HINTS ON ANGLING. 1s.

MUSIC AND DRESS. By a LADY. Reprinted from the " Quarterly Review." Fcap. 8vo. 1s.

NAPIER'S (SIR CHAS.) Life; chiefly derived from his Journals and Letters. By SIR W. NAPIER. *Second Edition*. Portraits. 4 Vols. Post 8vo. 48s.

——— (SIR WM.) Life and Letters. Edited by H. A. BRUCE, M.P. Portraits. 2 Vols. Crown 8vo. 28s.

——— English Battles and Sieges of the Peninsular War. *Fourth Edition*. Portrait. Post 8vo. 9s.

PUBLISHED BY MR. MURRAY. 25

NAUTICAL ALMANACK. Royal 8vo. 2s. 6d. (*By Authority.*)

NAVY LIST. (*Published Quarterly, by Authority.*) 16mo. 2s. 6d.

NEW TESTAMENT (THE) Illustrated by a Plain Explanatory Commentary, and authentic Views of Sacred Places, from Sketches and Photographs. Edited by ARCHDEACON CHURTON, M.A., and REV. BASIL JONES, M.A. With 110 Illustrations. 2 Vols. Crown 8vo. 30s. cloth; 52s. 6d. calf; 63s. morocco.

NICHOLLS' (SIR GEORGE) History of the English, Irish and Scotch Poor Laws. 4 Vols. 8vo.

———— (Rev. H. G.) Historical Account of the Forest of Dean. Woodcuts, &c. Post 8vo. 10s. 6d.

NICOLAS' (SIR HARRIS) Historic Peerage of England. Exhibiting the Origin, Descent, and Present State of every Title of Peerage which has existed in this Country since the Conquest. By WILLIAM COURTHOPE. 8vo. 30s.

NIMROD On the Chace—The Turf—and The Road. Reprinted from the "Quarterly Review." Woodcuts. Fcap. 8vo. 3s. 6d.

OXENHAM'S (REV. W.) English Notes for Latin Elegiacs; designed for early Proficients in the Art of Latin Versification, with Prefatory Rules of Composition in Elegiac Metre. *Fourth Edition.* 12mo. 3s. 6d.

OXFORD'S (BISHOP OF) Short Life of William Wilberforce. Condensed and Revised from the larger Biography. 8vo. (*In the Press.*)

PARIS' (Dr.) Philosophy in Sport made Science in Earnest; or, the First Principles of Natural Philosophy inculcated by aid of the Toys and Sports of Youth. *Ninth Edition.* Woodcuts. Post 8vo. 7s. 6d.

PEEL'S (SIR ROBERT) Memoirs. Edited by EARL STANHOPE and Right Hon. E. CARDWELL. 2 Vols. Post 8vo. 7s. 6d. each.

PENN'S (RICHARD) Maxims and Hints for an Angler and Chessplayer. *New Edition.* Woodcuts. Fcap. 8vo. 1s.

PENROSE'S (F. C.) Principles of Athenian Architecture, and the Optical Refinements exhibited in the Construction of the Ancient Buildings at Athens, from a Survey. With 40 Plates. Folio. 5l. 5s.

PERCY'S (JOHN, M.D.) Metallurgy of Iron and Steel; or, the Art of Extracting Metals from their Ores and adapting them to various purposes of Manufacture. Illustrations. 8vo. 42s.

———— Metallurgy of Lead, Silver, Gold, Platinum, Tin, Nickel, Cobalt, Antimony, Bismuth, Arsenic, and other Metals. 8vo. (*In the Press.*)

PHILLIPP (C. S. M.) On Jurisprudence. 8vo. 12s.

PHILLIPS' (JOHN) Memoirs of William Smith, the Geologist. Portrait. 8vo. 7s. 6d.

———— Geology of Yorkshire, The Coast, and Limestone District. Plates. 4to. Part I., 20s.—Part II., 30s.

———— Rivers, Mountains, and Sea Coast of Yorkshire. With Essays on the Climate, Scenery, and Ancient Inhabitants. *Second Edition*, Plates. 8vo. 15s.

PHILPOTTS' (BISHOP) Letters to the late Charles Butler, on his "Book of the Roman Catholic Church." *New Edition.* Post 8vo. 6s.

POPE'S (ALEXANDER) Life and Works. *A New Edition.* Containing nearly 500 unpublished Letters. Edited, with a NEW LIFE, Introductions and Notes, by REV. WHITWELL ELWIN. Portraits. 8vo. (*In the Press.*)

PORTER'S (REV. J. L.) Five Years in Damascus. With Travels to Palmyra, Lebanon and other Scripture Sites. Map and Woodcuts. 2 Vols. Post 8vo. 21s.

―――― Handbook for Syria and Palestine: including an Account of the Geography, History, Antiquities, and Inhabitants of these Countries, the Peninsula of Sinai, Edom, and the Syrian Desert. Maps. 2 Vols. Post 8vo. 24s.

PRAYER-BOOK (Illustrated), with 1000 Illustrations of Borders, Initials, Vignettes, &c. Edited, with Notes, by REV. THOS. JAMES. Medium 8vo. 18s. cloth; 31s. 6d. calf; 36s. morocco.

PUSS IN BOOTS. With 12 Illustrations. By OTTO SPECKTER. 16mo. 1s. 6d. or Coloured, 2s. 6d.

QUARTERLY REVIEW (THE). 8vo. 6s.

RAMBLES among the Turkomans and Bedaweens of the Syrian Deserts. *Second Edition.* Post 8vo. 10s. 6d.

RANKE'S Ecclesiastical and Political History of the Popes of Rome during the 16th and 17th Centuries. Translated from the German by SARAH AUSTIN. 3 Vols. 8vo.

RAWLINSON'S (REV. GEORGE) Herodotus. A New English Version. Edited with Notes and Essays. Assisted by SIR HENRY RAWLINSON and SIR J. G. WILKINSON. *Second Edition.* Maps and Woodcut. 4 Vols. 8vo. 48s.

―――― Historical Evidences of the truth of the Scripture Records stated anew. *Second Edition.* 8vo. 14s.

―――― Five Great Monarchies of the Ancient World, Chaldæa, Assyria, Media, Babylonia, and Persia. Illustrations. 4 Vols. 8vo. 16s. each.

REJECTED ADDRESSES (THE). By JAMES AND HORACE SMITH. Fcap. 8vo. 1s.

RENNIE'S (D. F.) British Arms in Peking, 1860; Kagosima, 1862. Post 8vo. 12s.

―――― Peking and the Pekingese: Being a Narrative of the First Year of the British Embassy in China. Illustrations. 2 Vols. Post 8vo. 24s.

―――― Story of Bhotan and the Dooar War; including Sketches of a Residence in the Himalayas and Visit to Bhotan in 1865. Map and Woodcut. Post 8vo. 12s.

REYNOLDS' (SIR JOSHUA) Life and Times. Commenced by C. R. LESLIE, R.A., continued and concluded by TOM TAYLOR. Portraits and Illustrations. 2 Vols. 8vo. 42s.

―――― Descriptive Catalogue of his Works. With Notices of their present owners and localities. By TOM TAYLOR and CHARLES W. FRANKS. With Illustrations. Fcap. 4to. (*In the Press.*)

RICARDO'S (DAVID) Political Works. With a Notice of his Life and Writings. By J. R. M'CULLOCH. *New Edition.* 8vo. 16s.

RIPA'S (FATHER) Memoirs during Thirteen Years' Residence at the Court of Peking. From the Italian. Post 8vo. 2s.

ROBERTSON'S (Canon) History of the Christian Church. from the Apostolic Age to the Death of Boniface VIII., A.D. 1122—1304. 3 Vols. 8vo.

ROBINSON'S (Rev. Dr.) Later Biblical Researches in the Holy Land. Being a Journal of Travels in 1852. Maps. 8vo. 15s.

———— Physical Geography of the Holy Land. Post 8vo. 10s. 6d.

ROME (The Student's History of). From the Earliest Times to the Establishment of the Empire. By Dean Liddell. Woodcuts. Post 8vo. 7s. 6d.

———— (A Smaller History of, for Young Persons). By Wm. Smith, LL.D. Woodcuts. 16mo. 3s. 6d.

ROWLAND'S (David) Manual of the English Constitution; Its Rise, Growth, and Present State. Post 8vo. 10s. 6d.

———— Laws of Nature the Foundation of Morals. Post 8vo. 6s.

RUNDELL'S (Mrs.) Domestic Cookery, adapted for Private Families. *New Edition.* Woodcuts. Fcap. 8vo. 5s.

RUSSELL'S (J. Rutherfurd) History of the Heroes of Medicine. Portraits. 8vo. 14s.

RUXTON'S (George F.) Travels in Mexico; with Adventures among the Wild Tribes and Animals of the Prairies and Rocky Mountains. Post 8vo. 3s. 6d.

SALE'S (Sir Robert) Brigade in Affghanistan. With an Account of the Defence of Jellalabad. By Rev. G. R. Gleig. Post 8vo. 2s.

SALLESBURY'S (Edward) The Children of the Lake. A Poem. Fcap. 8vo.

SANDWITH'S (Humphry) Siege of Kars. Post 8vo. 3s. 6d.

SCOTT'S (G. Gilbert) Secular and Domestic Architecture, Present and Future. *Second Edition.* 8vo. 9s.

———— (Rev. Robert, D.D., Master of Baliol) Sermons, preached before the University of Oxford. Post 8vo. 8s. 6d.

SCROPE'S (G. P.) Geology and Extinct Volcanoes of Central France. *Second Edition.* Illustrations. Medium 8vo. 30s.

SHAW'S (T. B.) Student's Manual of English Literature. Edited, with Notes and Illustrations, by Dr. Wm. Smith. Post 8vo. 7s. 6d.

———— Specimens of English Literature. Selected from the Chief English Writers. Edited by Wm. Smith, LL.D. Post 8vo. 7s. 6d.

SIERRA LEONE; Described in Letters to Friends at Home. By A Lady. Post 8vo. 3s. 6d.

SIMMONS (Capt. T. F.) on the Constitution and Practice of Courts-Martial; with a Summary of the Law of Evidence as connected therewith, and some Notice of the Criminal Law of England, with reference to the Trial of Civil Offences. *5th Edition.* 8vo. 14s.

SOUTH'S (John F.) Household Surgery; or, Hints on Emergencies. *Seventeenth Thousand.* Woodcuts. Fcp. 8vo. 4s. 6d.

SMILES' (SAMUEL) Lives of British Engineers; from the Earliest Period to the Death of Robert Stephenson; with an account of their Principal Works, and a History of Inland Communication in Britain. Portraits and Illustrations. 3 Vols. 8vo. 63s.

—————— Lives of Boulton and Watt. Comprising a History of the Invention and Introduction of the Steam Engine. With Portraits and 70 Illustrations. 8vo. 21s.

—————— Story of George Stephenson's Life, including a Memoir of Robert Stephenson. With Portraits and 70 Woodcuts. Post 8vo. 6s.

—————— James Brindley and the Early Engineers. With Portrait and 50 Woodcuts. Post 8vo. 6s.

—————— Self-Help. With Illustrations of Character and Conduct. Post 8vo. 6s.

—————— Translated into French as a Reading-Book for Schools. Post 8vo. 5s.

—————— Industrial Biography: Iron-Workers and Tool Makers. A companion volume to "Self-Help." Post 8vo. 6s.

—————— Workmen's Earnings—Savings—and Strikes. Fcap. 8vo: 1s. 6d.

SOMERVILLE'S (MARY) Physical Geography. *Fifth Edition.* Portrait. Post 8vo. 9s.

—————— Connexion of the Physical Sciences. *Ninth Edition.* Woodcuts. Post 8vo. 9s.

STANLEY'S (DEAN) Sinai and Palestine, in Connexion with their History. Map. 8vo. 14s.

—————— Bible in the Holy Land. Woodcuts. Fcap. 8vo. 2s. 6d.

—————— St. Paul's Epistles to the Corinthians. 8vo. 18s.

—————— History of the Eastern Church. Plans. 8vo. 12s.

—————— Jewish Church. First and Second Series. 8vo. 16s. each.

—————— Historical Memorials of Canterbury. Woodcuts. Post 8vo. 7s. 6d.

—————— Memorials of Westminster Abbey. 8vo.

—————— Sermons in the East, with Notices of the Places Visited. 8vo. 9s.

—————— Sermons on Evangelical and Apostolical Teaching. Post 8vo. 7s. 6d.

—————— ADDRESSES AND CHARGES OF BISHOP STANLEY. With Memoir. 8vo. 10s. 6d.

SOUTHEY'S (ROBERT) Book of the Church. *Seventh Edition.* Post 8vo. 7s. 6d.

—————— Lives of Bunyan and Cromwell. Post 8vo. 2s.

SPECKTER'S (OTTO) Puss in Boots. With 12 Woodcuts. Square 12mo. 1s. 6d. plain, or 2s. 6d. coloured.

PUBLISHED BY MR. MURRAY.   29

SMITH'S (DR. WM.) Dictionary of the Bible; its Antiquities, Biography, Geography, and Natural History. Illustrations. 3 Vols. 8vo. 105s.
——— Concise Bible Dictionary, for Families and Students. Illustrations. Medium 8vo. 21s.
——— Smaller Bible Dictionary, for Schools and Young Persons. Illustrations. Post 8vo. 7s. 6d.
——— Dictionary of Christian Antiquities: from the Times of the Apostles to the Age of Charlemagne. Illustrations. Medium. 8vo. (In preparation)
——— Biblical and Classical Atlas. Small folio. (In preparation.)
——— Dictionary of Greek and Roman Antiquities. Woodcuts. 8vo. 42s.
——— Smaller Dictionary of Greek and Roman Antiquities, compiled from the above Work. Woodcuts. Crown 8vo. 7s. 6d.
——— Dictionary of Greek and Roman Biography and Mythology. Woodcuts. 3 Vols. 8vo. 5l. 15s. 6d.
——————— Greek and Roman Geography. Woodcuts. 2 Vols. 8vo. 80s.
——— Classical Dictionary for Schools, compiled from the above works. With 750 Woodcuts. 8vo. 18s.
——— Smaller Classical Dictionary, abridged from the above Work. Woodcuts. Crown 8vo. 7s. 6d.
——— Complete Latin-English Dictionary for Schools. With Tables of the Roman Calendar, Measures, Weights, and Money. 8vo. 21s.
——— Smaller Latin-English Dictionary, abridged from the above Work. 12mo. 7s. 6d.
——— Latin-English Vocabulary; for Phædrus, Cornelius Nepos, and Cæsar. 2nd Edition. 12mo. 3s. 6d.
——— Copious English-Latin Dictionary, compiled from original sources. 8vo. and 12mo. (In the Press.)
——— Smaller Classical Mythology for Schools. With Illustrations. 12mo. 8s. 6d.
——— Principia Latina—Part I. A Grammar, Delectus, and Exercise Book, with Vocabularies. 6th Edition. 12mo. 3s. 6d.
————————————— Part II. A Reading-book of Mythology, Geography, Roman Antiquities, and History. With Notes and Dictionary. 3rd Edition. 12mo. 3s. 6d.
————————————— Part III. A Latin Poetry Book. Hexameters and Pentameters; Eclog. Ovidianæ; Latin Prosody &c. 2nd Edition. 12mo. 3s. 6d.
————————————— Part IV. Latin Prose Composition. Rules of Syntax, with Examples, Explanations of Synonyms, and Exercises on the Syntax. Second Edition. 12mo. 3s. 6d.
————————————— Part V. Short Tales and Anecdotes for Translation into Latin. 12mo. 3s.
——— Student's Greek Grammar for the Higher Forms. By Professor CURTIUS. Post 8vo. 7s. 6d.
——— Smaller Greek Grammar, abridged from the above Work. 12mo. 3s. 6d.
——— Student's Latin Grammar for the Higher Forms. Post 8vo. 7s. 6d.
——— Smaller Latin Grammar, abridged from the above Work. 12mo. 3s. 6d.

STANHOPE'S (EARL) History of England, from the Peace of Utrecht to the Peace of Versailles, 1713-83. *Library Edition.* 7 vols. 8vo. 93s. Or *Popular Edition.* 7 vols. Post 8vo. 5s. each.
———— History of British India, from its origin till the Peace of 1783. Post 8vo. 3s. 6d.
———— "Forty-Five;" a Narrative of the Rebellion in Scotland. Post 8vo. 3s.
———— Spain under Charles the Second. Post 8vo. 6s. 6d.
———— Historical and Critical Essays. Post 8vo. 3s. 6d.
———— Life of William Pitt. With Extracts from his MS. Papers. *Second Edition.* Portraits. 4 Vols. Post 8vo. 42s.
———— Miscellanies. *Second Edition.* Post 8vo. 5s. 6d.
———— Life of Belisarius. Post 8vo. 10s. 6d.
———— Life of Condé. Post 8vo. 3s. 6d.

STUDENT'S HUME. A History of England from the Invasion of Julius Cæsar to the Revolution of 1688. By DAVID HUME. Corrected and continued to 1858. Woodcuts. Post 8vo. 7s. 6d. Questions on, 2s.
*** A Smaller History of England. 12mo. 3s. 6d.
———— HISTORY OF FRANCE; from the Earliest Times to the Establishment of the Second Empire, 1852. By W. H. PEARSON, M.A. Woodcuts. Post 8vo. 7s. 6d.
———— HISTORY OF GREECE; from the Earliest Times to the Roman Conquest. With the History of Literature and Art. By WM. SMITH, LL.D. Woodcuts. Crown 8vo. 7s. 6d. (Questions, 2s.)
*** A SMALLER HISTORY OF GREECE. 12mo. 3s. 6d.
———— HISTORY OF ROME; from the Earliest Times to the Establishment of the Empire. With the History of Literature and Art. By Dean LIDDELL. Woodcuts. Crown 8vo. 7s. 6d.
*** A SMALLER HISTORY OF ROME. 12mo. 3s. 6d.
———— GIBBON; an Epitome of the Decline and Fall of the Roman Empire. Incorporating the Researches of Recent Commentators. Woodcuts. Post 8vo. 7s. 6d.
———— MANUAL OF ANCIENT GEOGRAPHY. By Rev. W. L. BEVAN, M.A. Woodcuts. Post 8vo. 7s. 6d.
———— MODERN GEOGRAPHY. By Rev. W. L. BEVAN. Woodcuts. Post 8vo. (*In the Press.*)
———— OLD TESTAMENT HISTORY. Maps and Woodcuts. Post 8vo. 7s. 6d. each.
———— NEW TESTAMENT HISTORY. Maps and Woodcuts. Post 8vo. 7s. 6d.
———— MORAL PHILOSOPHY. By W. FLEMING, D.D. Post 8vo.
———— ENGLISH LANGUAGE. By GEO. P. MARSH. Post 8vo. 7s. 6d.
———— ENGLISH LITERATURE. By T. B. SHAW, M.A. Post 8vo. 7s. 6d.
———— SPECIMENS OF ENGLISH LITERATURE. Selected from the Chief Writers. By THOMAS B. SHAW, M.A. Post 8vo. 7s. 6d.
———— BLACKSTONE: a Systematic Abridgment of the Entire Commentaries. By R. MALCOLM KERR, LL.D. Post, 8vo. 7s. 6d.

ST. JOHN'S (CHARLES) Wild Sports and Natural History of the
Highlands. Post 8vo. 3s. 6d.

——————— (BAYLE) Adventures in the Libyan Desert and the
Oasis of Jupiter Ammon. Woodcuts. Post 8vo. 2s.

STEPHENSON (GEORGE and ROBERT). The Story of their
Lives. By SAMUEL SMILES. With Portraits and 70 Illustrations.
Medium. 8vo. 21s. Or Popular Edition, Post 8vo. 6s.

STOTHARD'S (THOS.) Life. With Personal Reminiscences.
By Mrs. BRAY. With Portrait and 60 Woodcuts. 4to. 21s.

STREET'S (G. E.) Gothic Architecture in Spain. From Personal
Observations during several journeys through that country. Illustrations. Medium 8vo. 50s.

——————— Brick and Marble Architecture of Italy in the
Middle Ages. Plates. 8vo. 21s.

SULLIVAN'S (SIR EDWARD) Conquerors, Warriors, and Statesmen
of India; an Historical Narrative of the most Important Events, from
the Invasion of Mahmoud of Ghizni to that of Nadir Shah. 8vo.

SWIFT'S (JONATHAN) Life, Letters, Journals, and Works. By
JOHN FORSTER. 8vo. (In Preparation.)

SYME'S (PROFESSOR) Principles of Surgery. 5th Edition. 8vo. 12s.

TAIT'S (BISHOP) Dangers and Safeguards of Modern Theology,
containing Suggestions to the Theological Student under Present Difficulties. 8vo. 9s.

TAYLOR'S (HENRY) Notes from Life, in Six Essays on Money,
Humility and Independence, Wisdom, Choice in Marriage, Children,
and Life Poetic. Fcap. 8vo. 2s.

THOMSON'S (ARCHBISHOP) Sermons, Preached in the Chapel of
Lincoln's Inn. 8vo. 10s. 6d.

THREE-LEAVED MANUAL OF FAMILY PRAYER; arranged
so as to save the trouble of turning the Pages backwards and forwards.
Royal 8vo. 2s.

TREMENHEERE'S (H. S.) The Franchise a Privilege and not a
Right, proved by the Political Experience of the Ancients. Fcap. 8vo.
2s. 6d.

TRISTRAM'S (H. B.) Great Sahara. Wanderings South of the
Atlas Mountains. Map and Illustrations. Post 8vo. 15s.

TWISS' (HORACE) Public and Private Life of Lord Chancellor Eldon,
with Selections from his Correspondence. Portrait. Third Edition.
2 Vols. Post 8vo. 21s.

TYLOR'S (E. B.) Researches into the Early History of Mankind,
and the Development of Civilization. Illustrations. 8vo. 12s.

TYNDALL'S (JOHN) Glaciers of the Alps. With an account of
Three Years' Observations and Experiments on their General Phenomena. Woodcuts. Post 8vo. 14s.

TYTLER'S (PATRICK FRASER) Memoirs. By REV. J. W. BURGON
M.A. 8vo. 9s.

32   LIST OF WORKS PUBLISHED BY MR. MURRAY.

VAUGHAN'S (Rev. Dr.) Sermons preached in Harrow School. 8vo. 10s. 6d.

WAAGEN'S (Dr.) Treasures of Art in Great Britain. Being an Account of the Chief Collections of Paintings, Sculpture, Manuscripts, Miniatures, &c. &c., in this Country. Obtained from Personal Inspection during Visits to England. 4 Vols. 8vo.

VAMBERY'S (Arminius) Travels in Central Asia, from Teheran across the Turkoman Desert on the Eastern Shore of the Caspian to Khiva, Bokhara, and Samarcand in 1863. Map and Illustrations. 8vo. 21s.

WELLINGTON'S (The Duke of) Despatches during his various Campaigns. Compiled from Official and other Authentic Documents. By Col. Gurwood, C.B. 8 Vols. 8vo. 21s. each.

———————— Supplementary Despatches, and other Papers. Edited by his Son. Vols. I. to XII. 8vo. 20s. each.

———————— Selections from his Despatches and General Orders. By Colonel Gurwood. 8vo. 18s.

———————— Speeches in Parliament. 2 Vols. 8vo. 42s.

WILKINSON'S (Sir J. G.) Popular Account of the Private Life, Manners, and Customs of the Ancient Egyptians. *New Edition.* Revised and Condensed. With 500 Woodcuts. 2 Vols. Post 8vo. 12s.

———————— Handbook for Egypt.—Thebes, the Nile, Alexandria, Cairo, the Pyramids, Mount Sinai, &c. Map. Post 8vo. 15s.

———————— (G. B.) Working Man's Handbook to South Australia; with Advice to the Farmer, and Detailed Information for the several Classes of Labourers and Artisans. Map. 16mo. 1s. 6d.

WILSON'S (Bishop Daniel) Life, with Extracts from his Letters and Journals. By Rev. Josiah Bateman. *Second Edition.* Illustrations. Post 8vo. 9s.

———————— (Genl. Sir Robert) Secret History of the French Invasion of Russia, and Retreat of the French Army, 1812. *Second Edition.* 8vo. 15s.

———————— Private Diary of Travels, Personal Services, and Public Events, during Missions and Employments in Spain, Sicily, Turkey, Russia, Poland, Germany, &c. 1812-14. 2 Vols. 8vo. 26s.

———————— Autobiographical Memoirs. Containing an Account of his Early Life down to the Peace of Tilsit. Portrait. 2 Vols. 8vo. 26s.

WORDSWORTH'S (Canon) Journal of a Tour in Athens and Attica. *Third Edition.* Plates. Post 8vo. 8s. 6d.

———————— Pictorial, Descriptive, and Historical Account of Greece, with a History of Greek Art, by G. Scharf, F.S.A. *New Edition.* With 600 Woodcuts. Royal 8vo. 28s.

BRADBURY, EVANS, AND CO., PRINTERS, WHITEFRIARS.

www.ingramcontent.com/pod-product-compliance
Lightning Source LLC
Chambersburg PA
CBHW022109290426
44112CB00008B/603